PERFECT WORLD

8 Rie Aruga

(Kensetsu Inc.)

contents

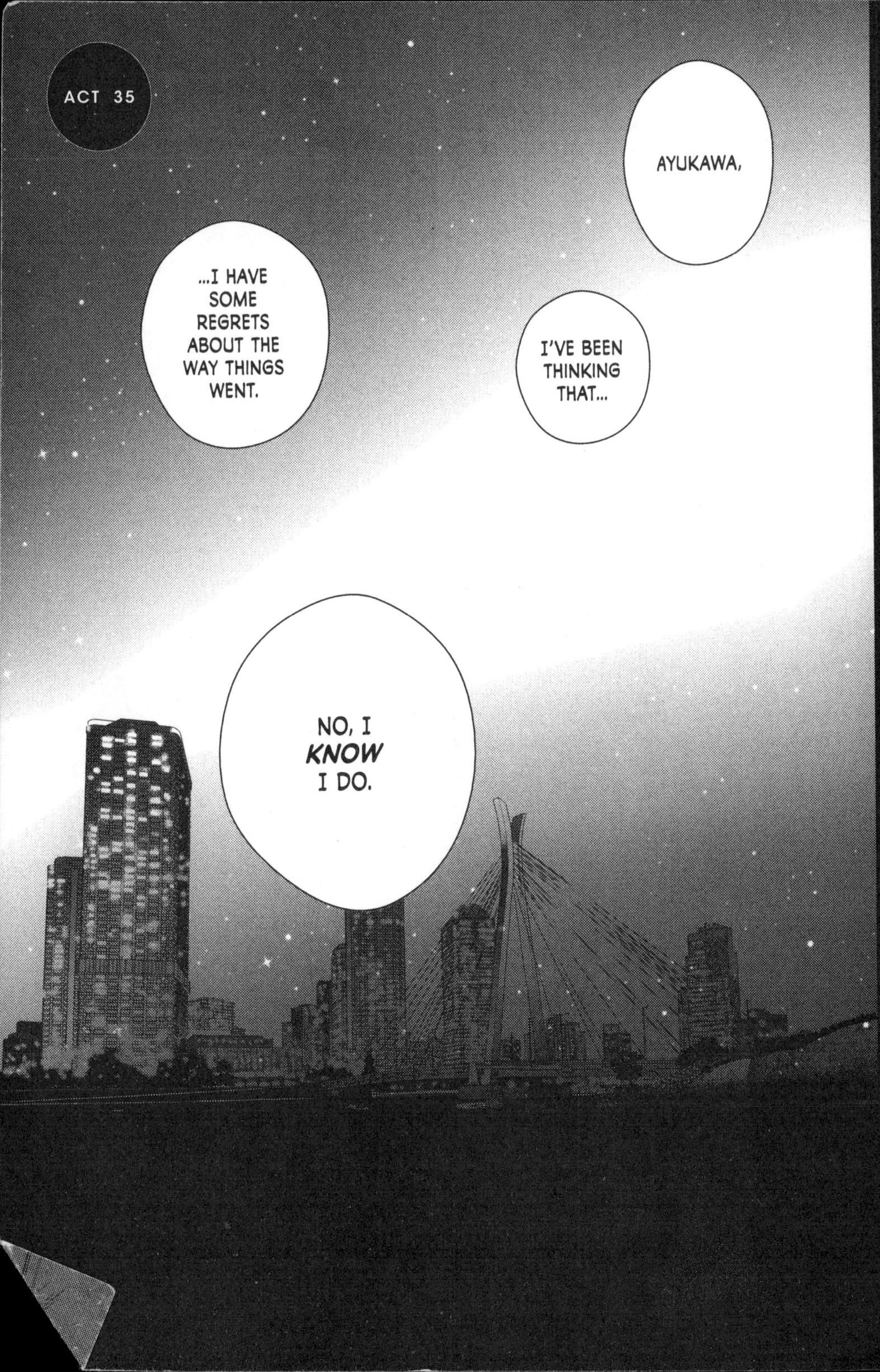
ACT 35
AYUKAWA,
I'VE BEEN THINKING THAT...
...I HAVE SOME REGRETS ABOUT THE WAY THINGS WENT.
NO, I *KNOW* I DO.

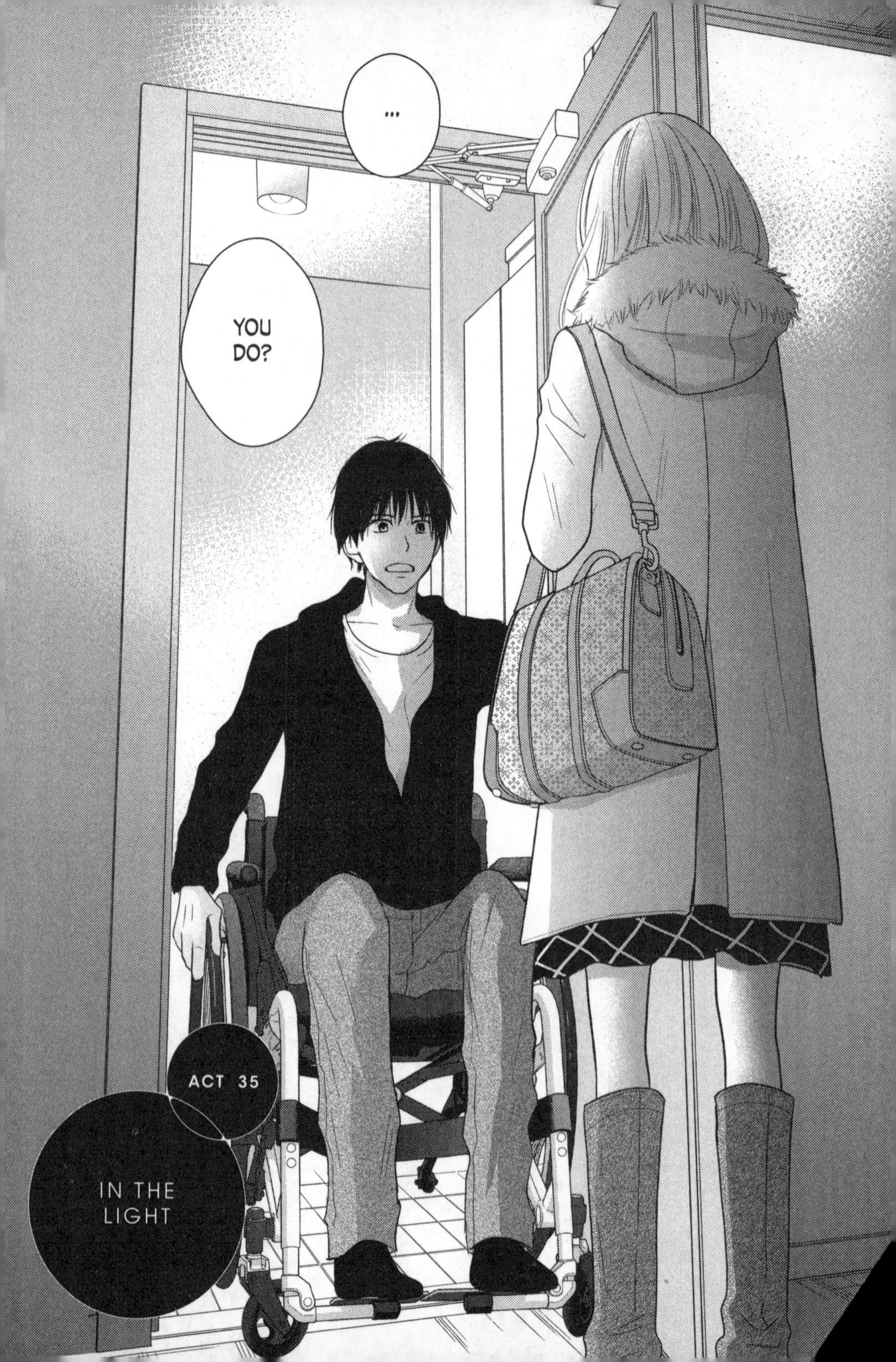
...
YOU DO?
ACT 35
IN THE LIGHT

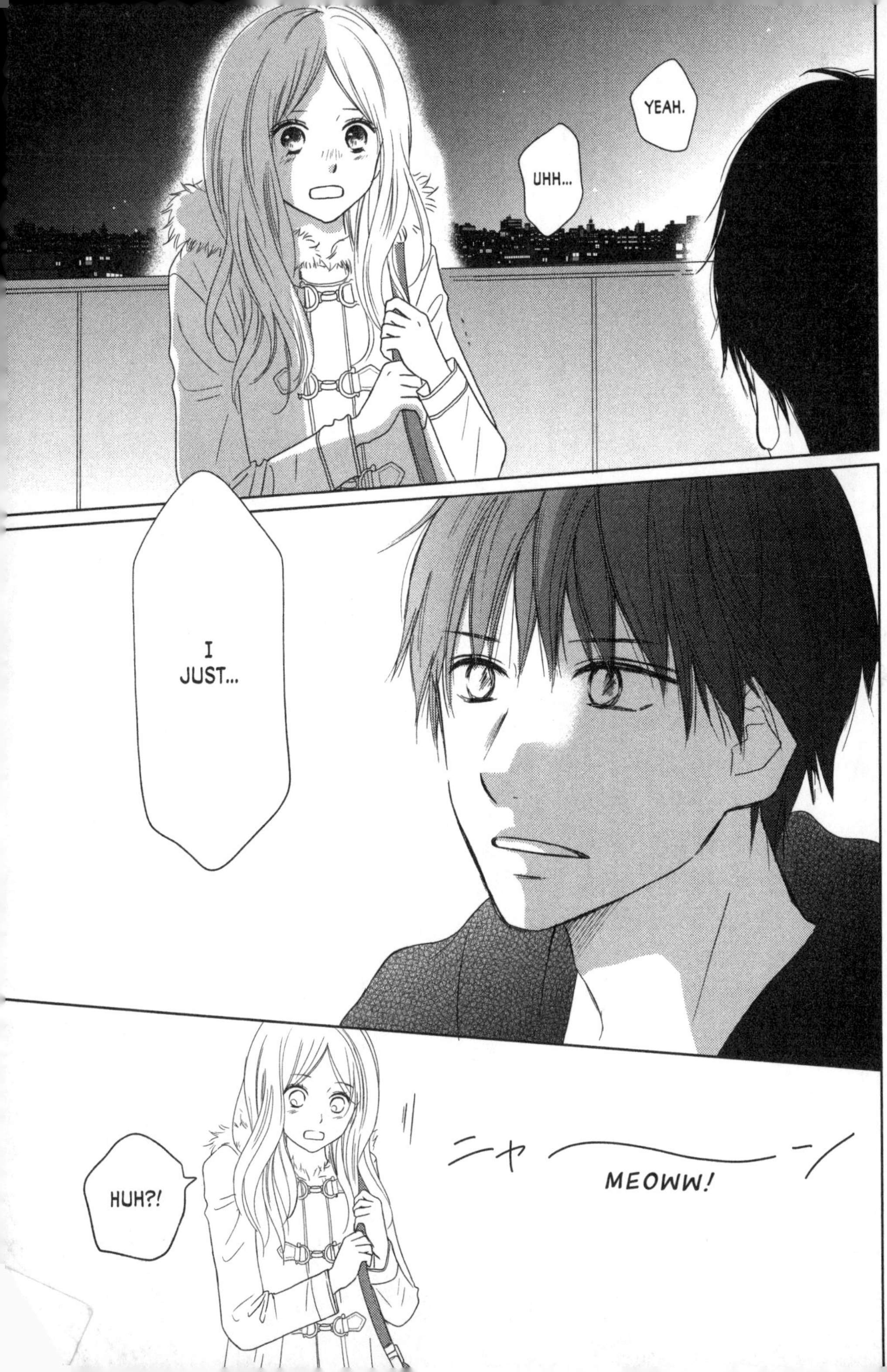
YEAH.
UHH...
I JUST...
ニャーーー
MEOWW!
HUH?!

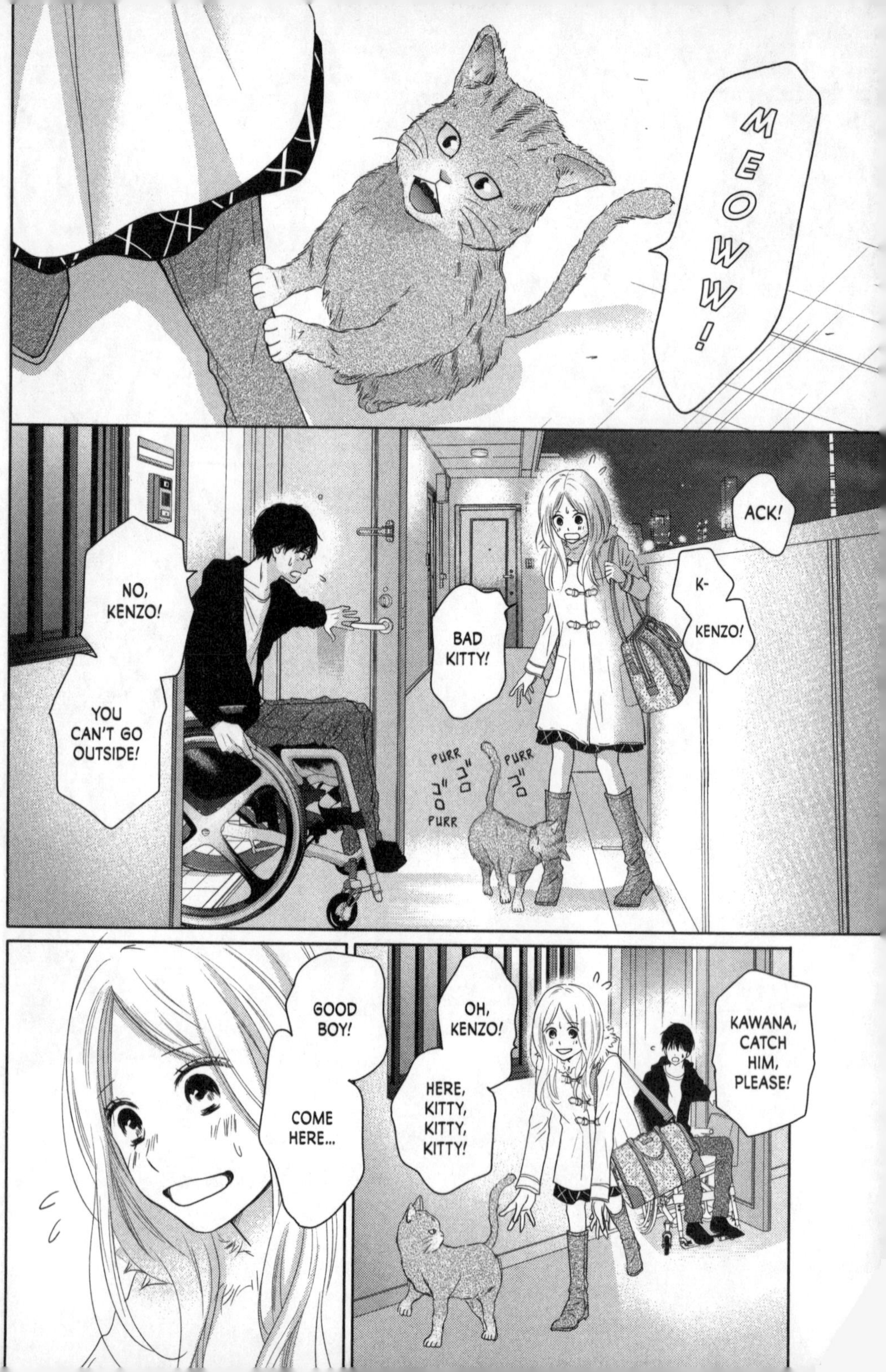
MEOWW!
ACK!
K-
KENZO!
BAD KITTY!
PURR
PURR
PURR
NO, KENZO!
YOU CAN'T GO OUTSIDE!
KAWANA, CATCH HIM, PLEASE!
OH, KENZO!
HERE, KITTY, KITTY, KITTY!
GOOD BOY!
COME HERE...

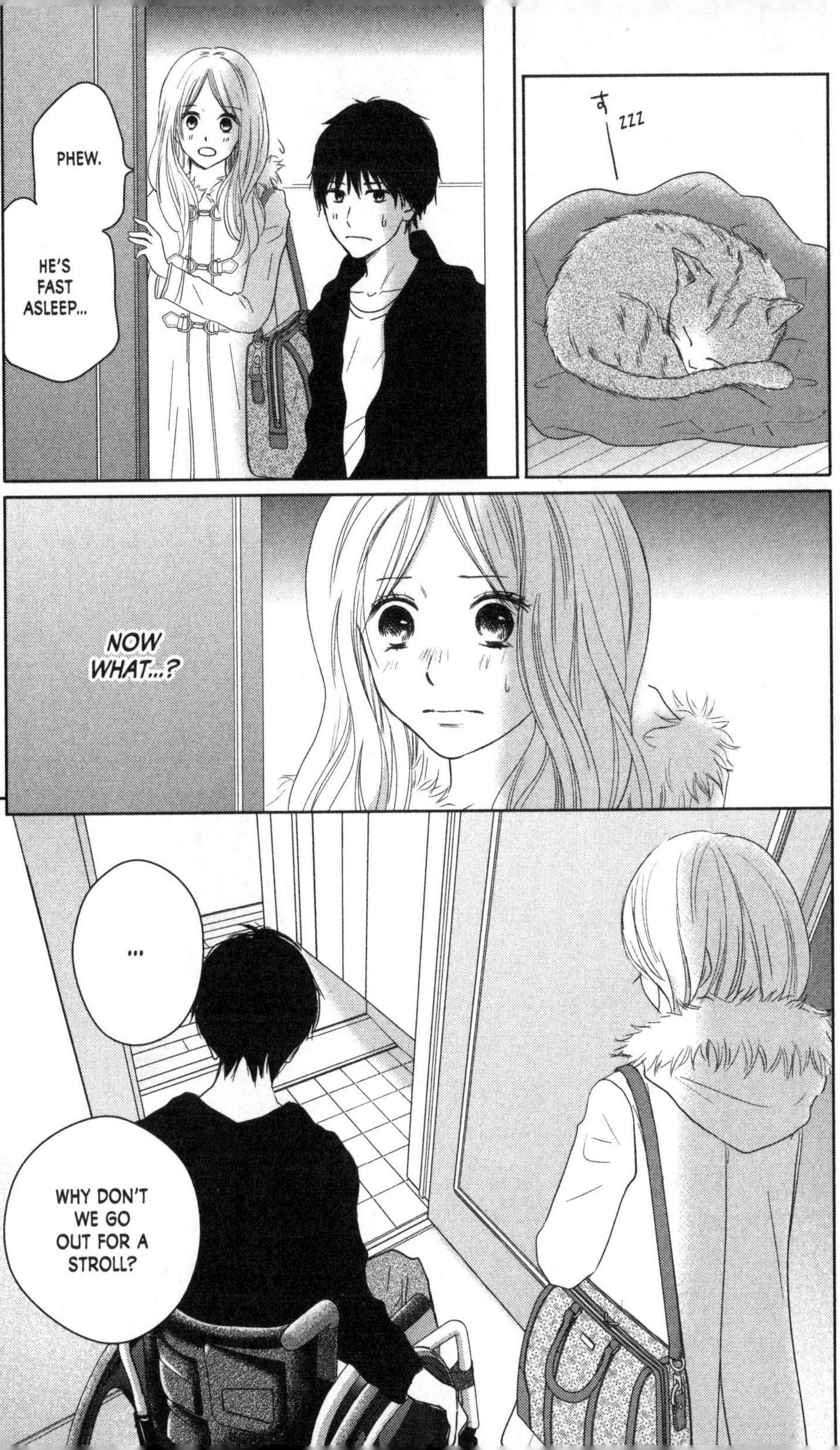
す
zzz
PHEW.
HE'S FAST ASLEEP...
NOW WHAT...?
...
WHY DON'T WE GO OUT FOR A STROLL?

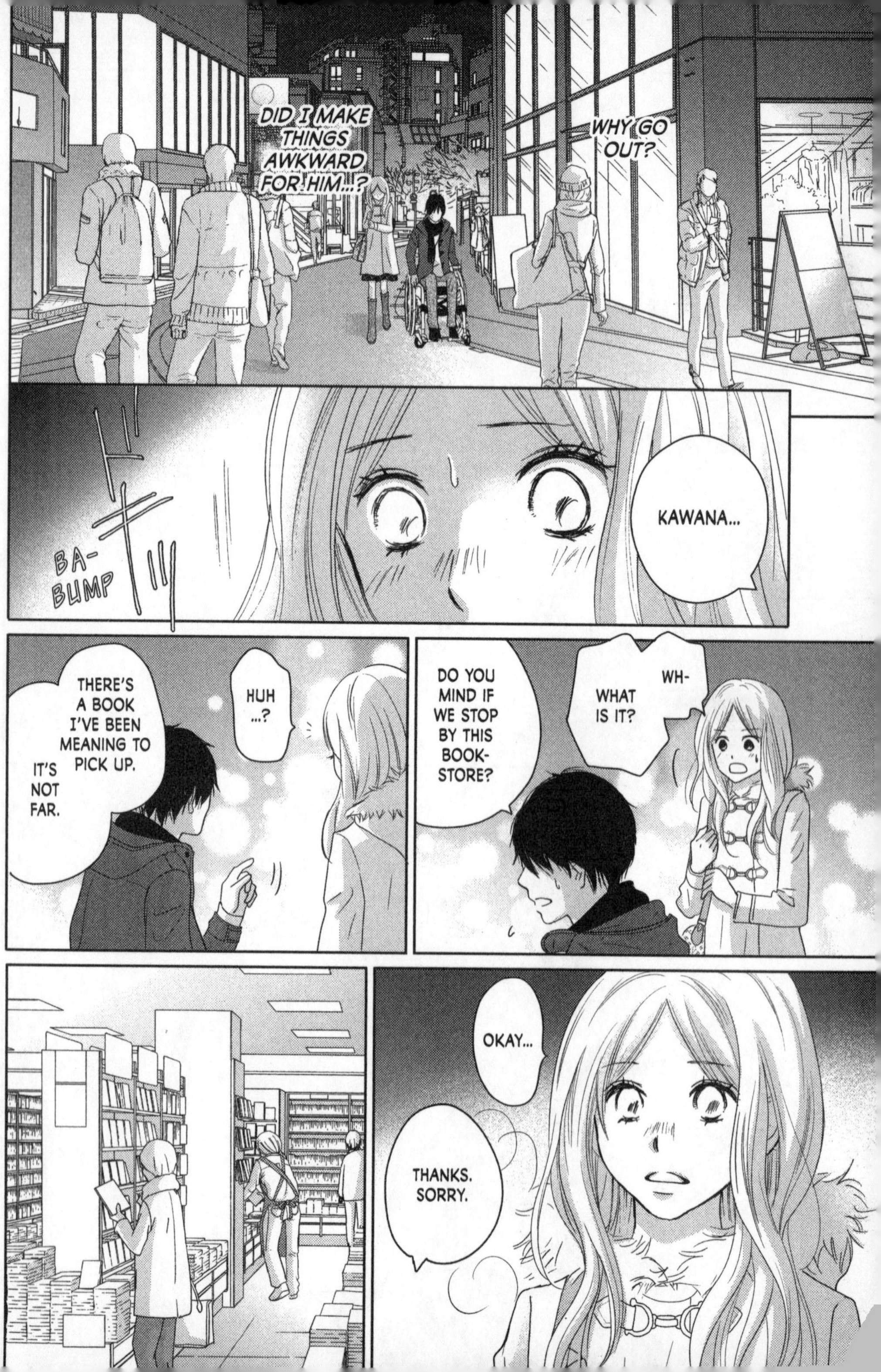
WHY GO OUT?
DID I MAKE THINGS AWKWARD FOR HIM...?
KAWANA...
BA-BUMP
WH- WHAT IS IT?
DO YOU MIND IF WE STOP BY THIS BOOK-STORE?
HUH ...?
THERE'S A BOOK I'VE BEEN MEANING TO PICK UP.
IT'S NOT FAR.
OKAY...
THANKS. SORRY.

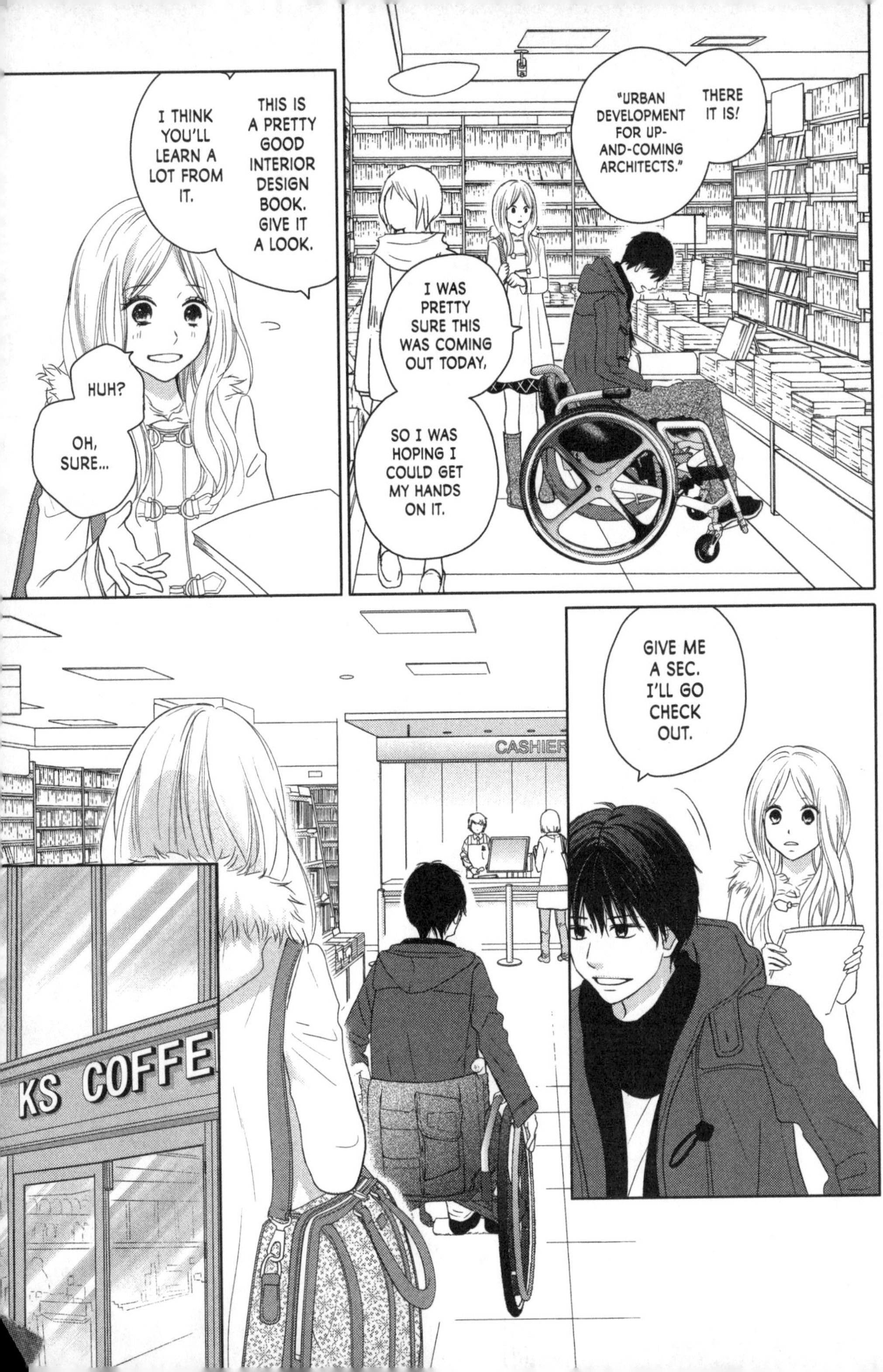
THERE IT IS!
"URBAN DEVELOPMENT FOR UP-AND-COMING ARCHITECTS."
I WAS PRETTY SURE THIS WAS COMING OUT TODAY,
SO I WAS HOPING I COULD GET MY HANDS ON IT.
THIS IS A PRETTY GOOD INTERIOR DESIGN BOOK. GIVE IT A LOOK.
I THINK YOU'LL LEARN A LOT FROM IT.
HUH?
OH, SURE...
GIVE ME A SEC. I'LL GO CHECK OUT.
CASHIER
KS COFFE

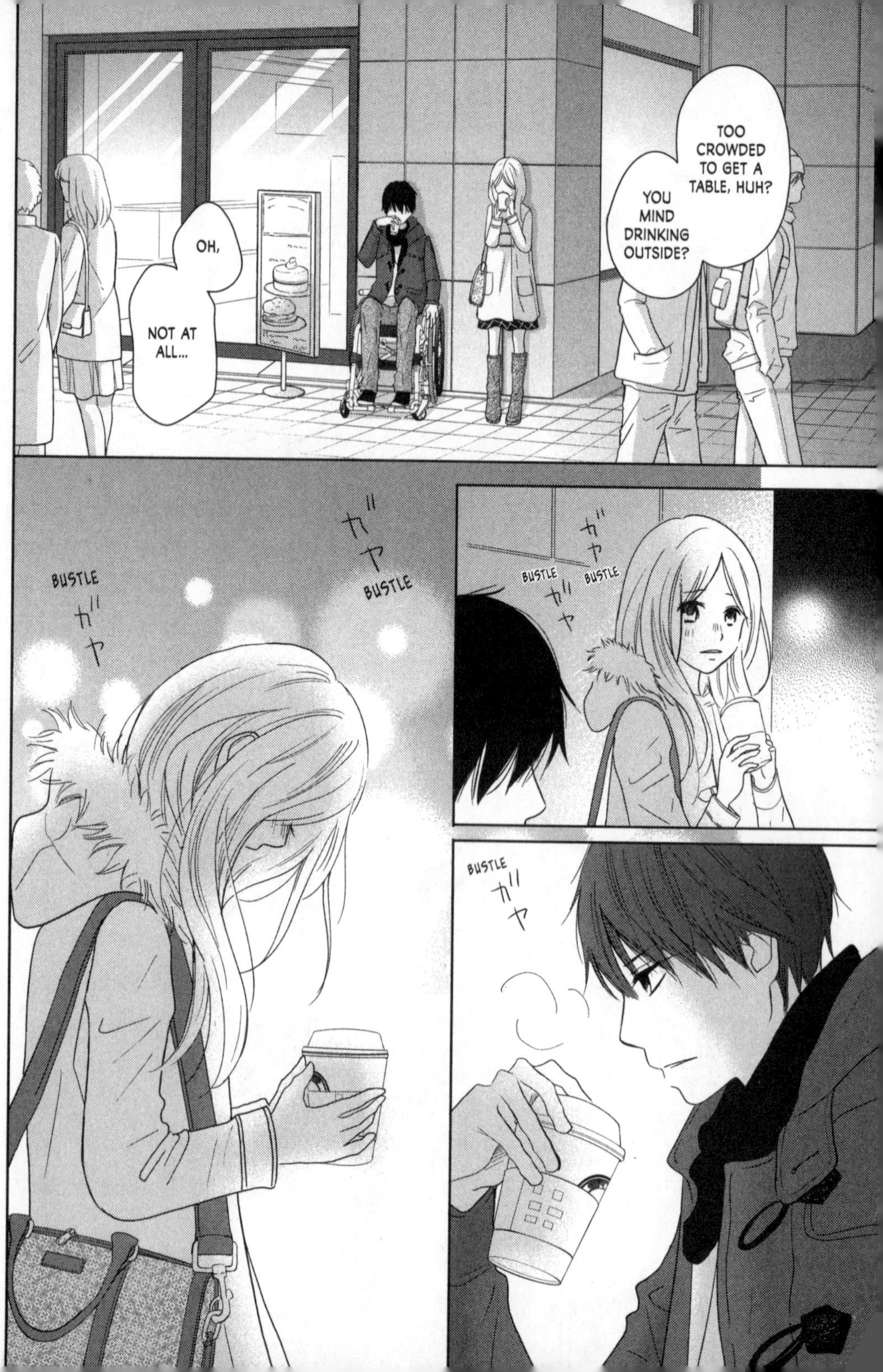
TOO CROWDED TO GET A TABLE, HUH?
YOU MIND DRINKING OUTSIDE?
OH,
NOT AT ALL...
ガヤ
BUSTLE
ガヤ
BUSTLE
BUSTLE
ガヤ
ガヤ
BUSTLE
BUSTLE
ガヤ

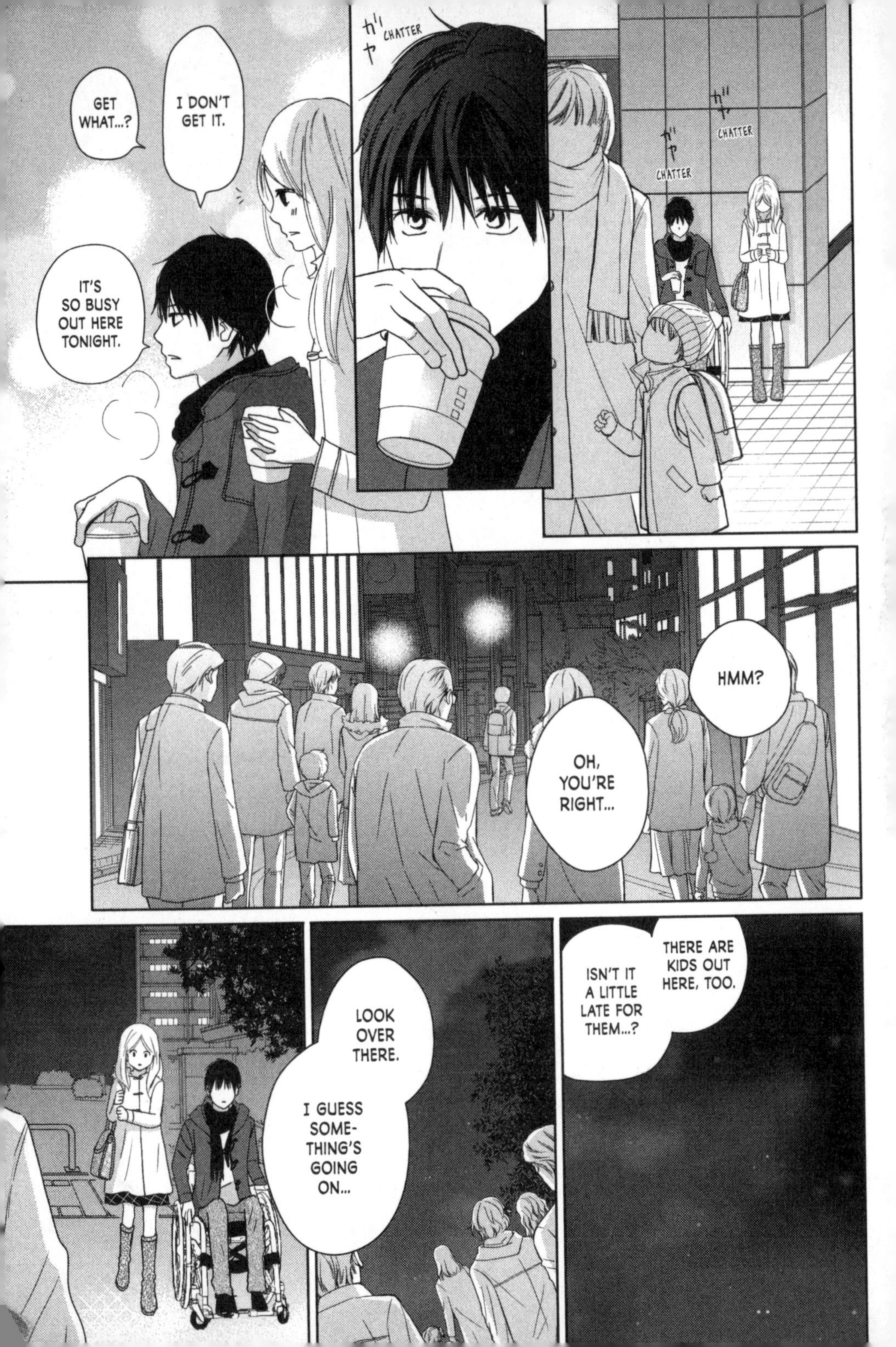
ガヤ CHATTER
ガヤ CHATTER
ガヤ CHATTER
I DON'T GET IT.
GET WHAT...?
IT'S SO BUSY OUT HERE TONIGHT.
HMM?
OH, YOU'RE RIGHT...
THERE ARE KIDS OUT HERE, TOO.
ISN'T IT A LITTLE LATE FOR THEM...?
LOOK OVER THERE.
I GUESS SOME-THING'S GOING ON...

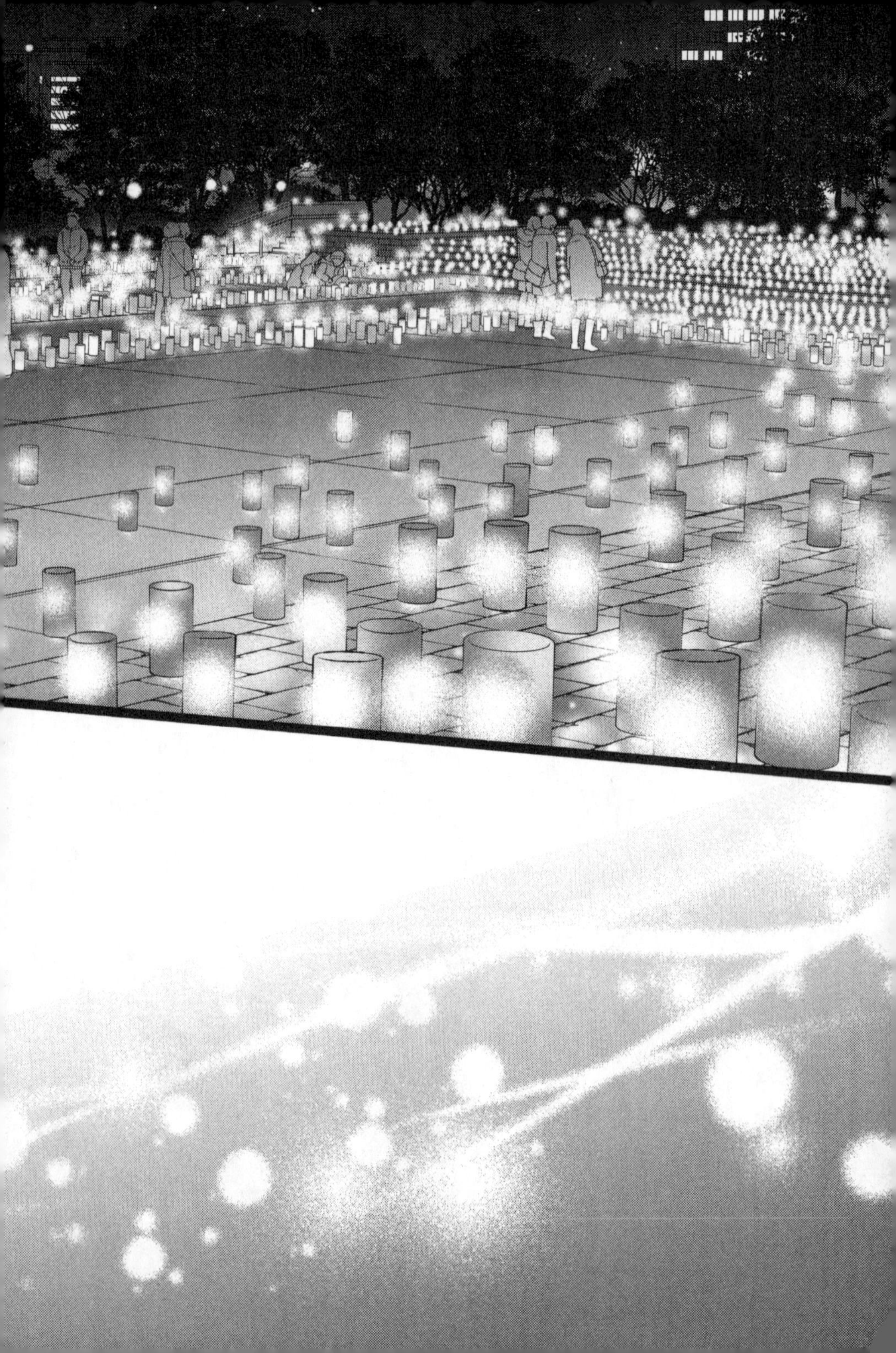

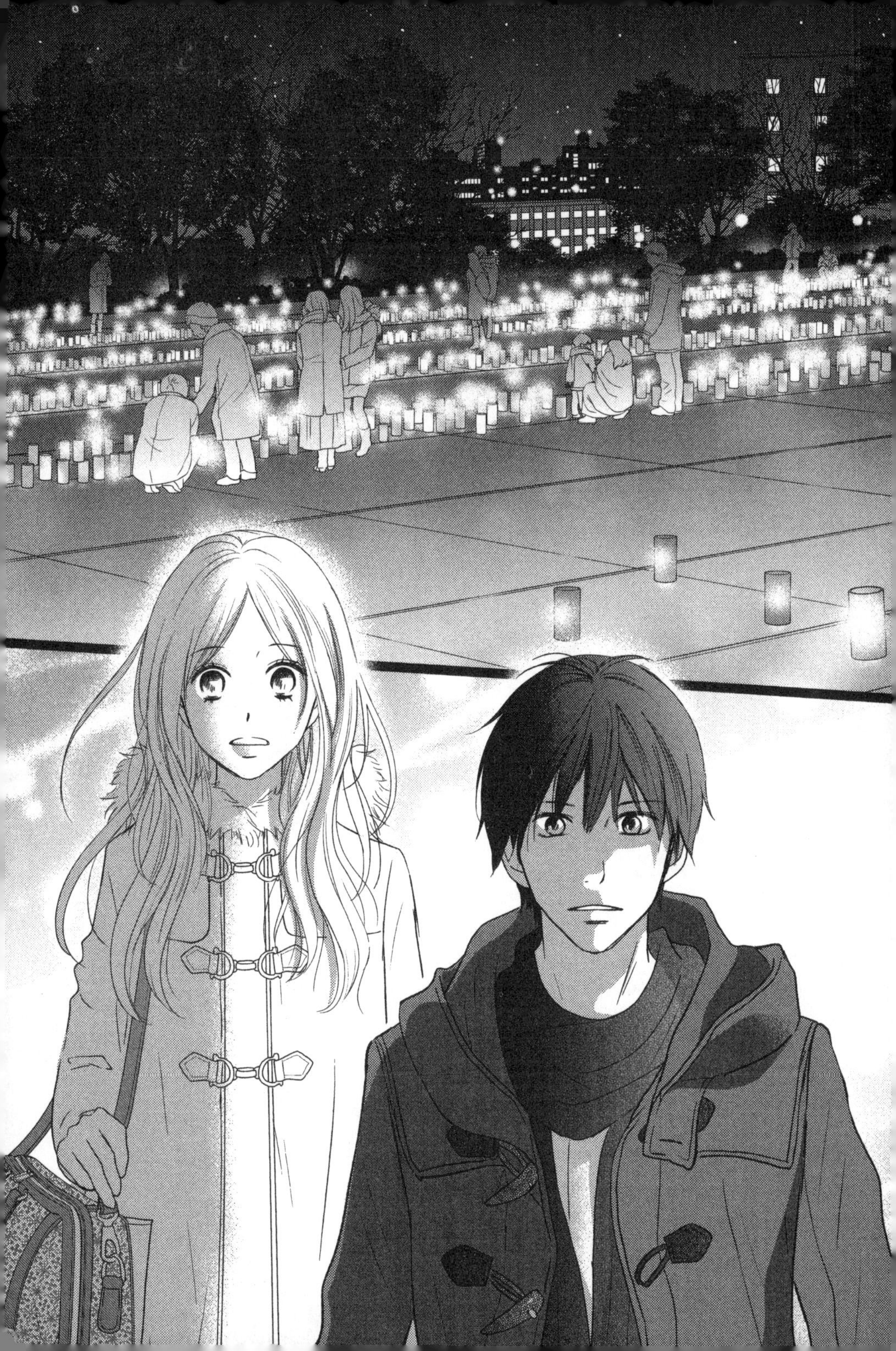

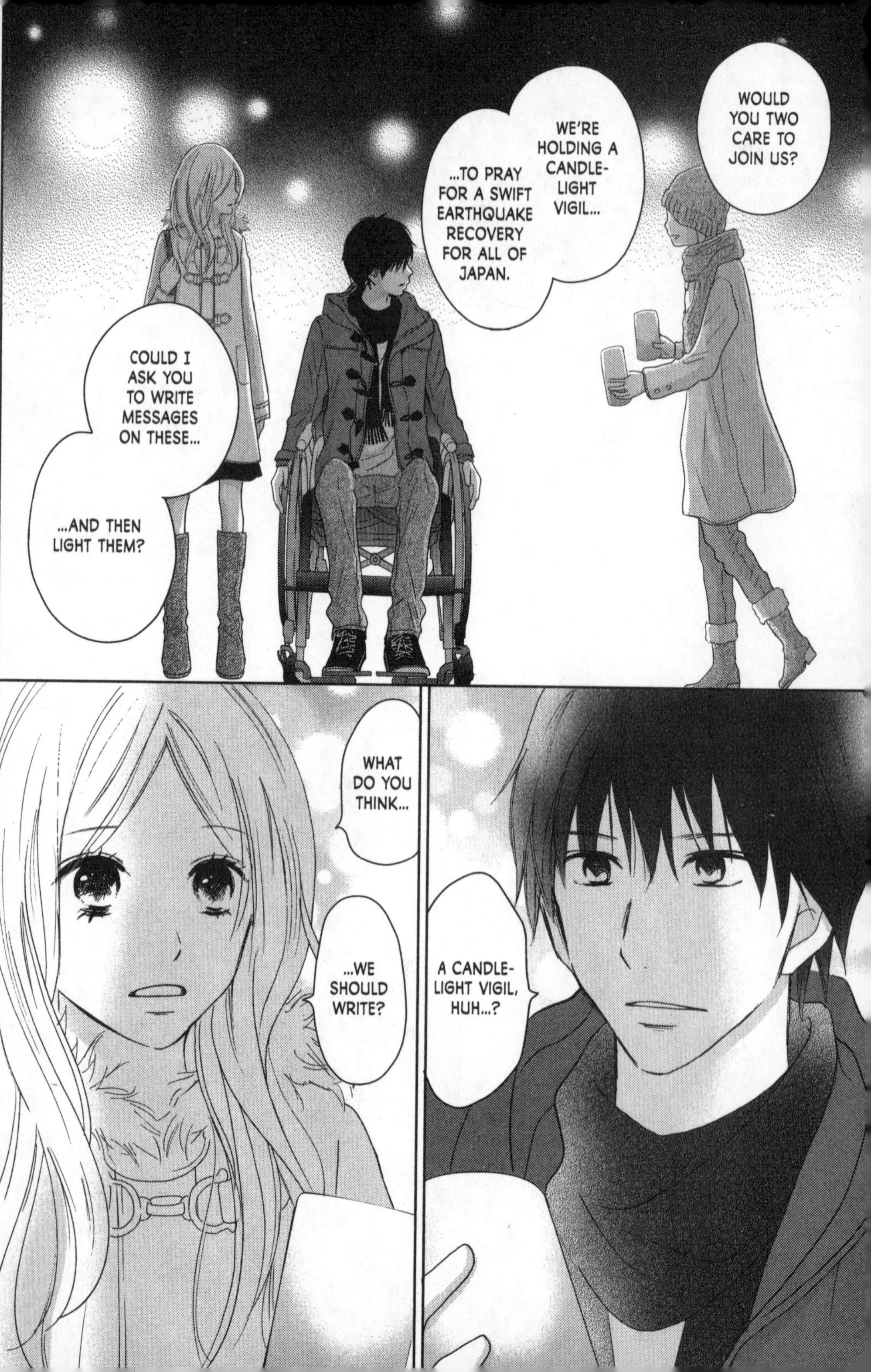
WOULD YOU TWO CARE TO JOIN US?
WE'RE HOLDING A CANDLE-LIGHT VIGIL...
...TO PRAY FOR A SWIFT EARTHQUAKE RECOVERY FOR ALL OF JAPAN.
COULD I ASK YOU TO WRITE MESSAGES ON THESE...
...AND THEN LIGHT THEM?
A CANDLE-LIGHT VIGIL, HUH...?
WHAT DO YOU THINK...
...WE SHOULD WRITE?

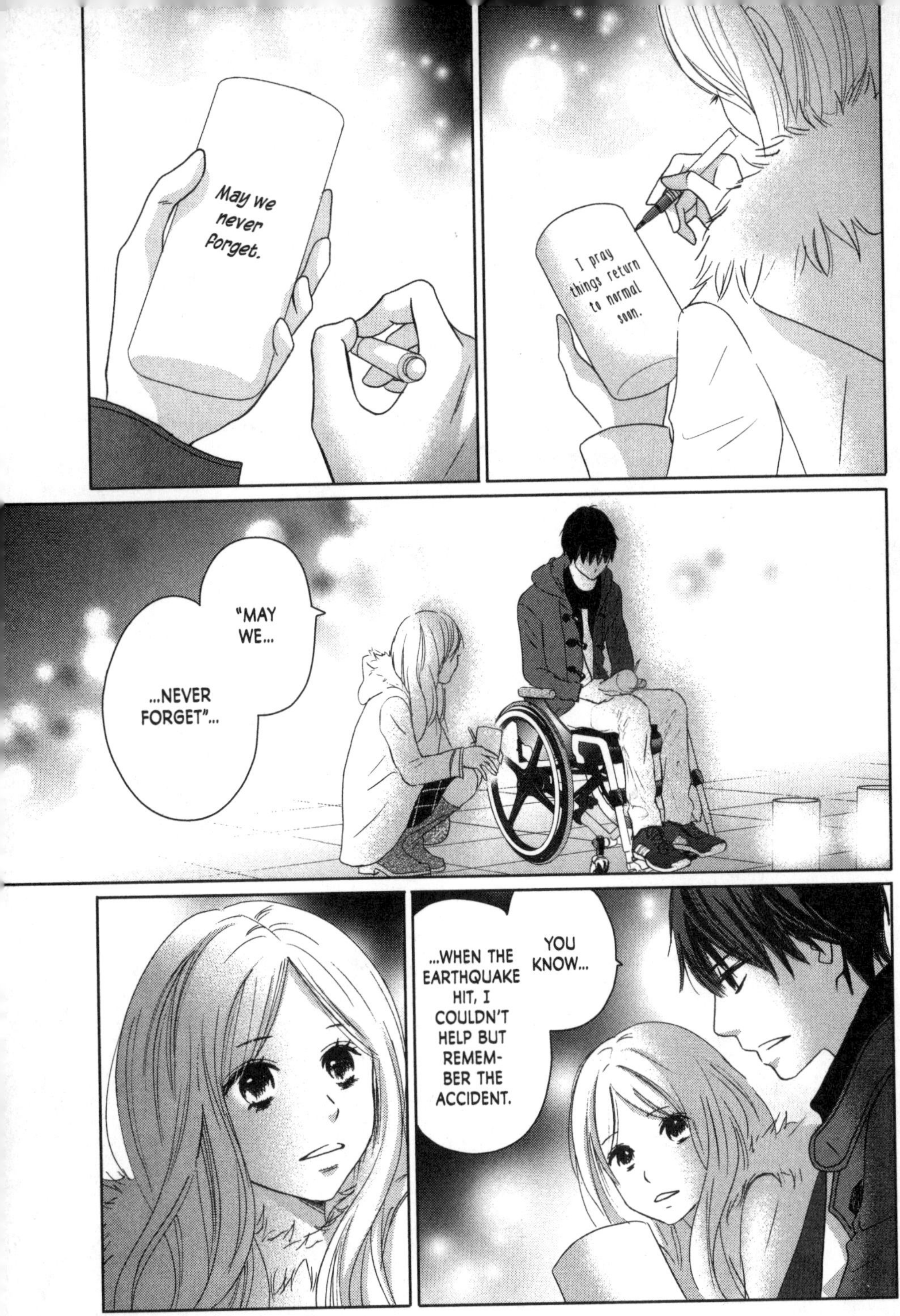
I pray things return to normal soon.
May we never forget.
"MAY WE...
...NEVER FORGET"...
YOU KNOW...
...WHEN THE EARTHQUAKE HIT, I COULDN'T HELP BUT REMEM-BER THE ACCIDENT.

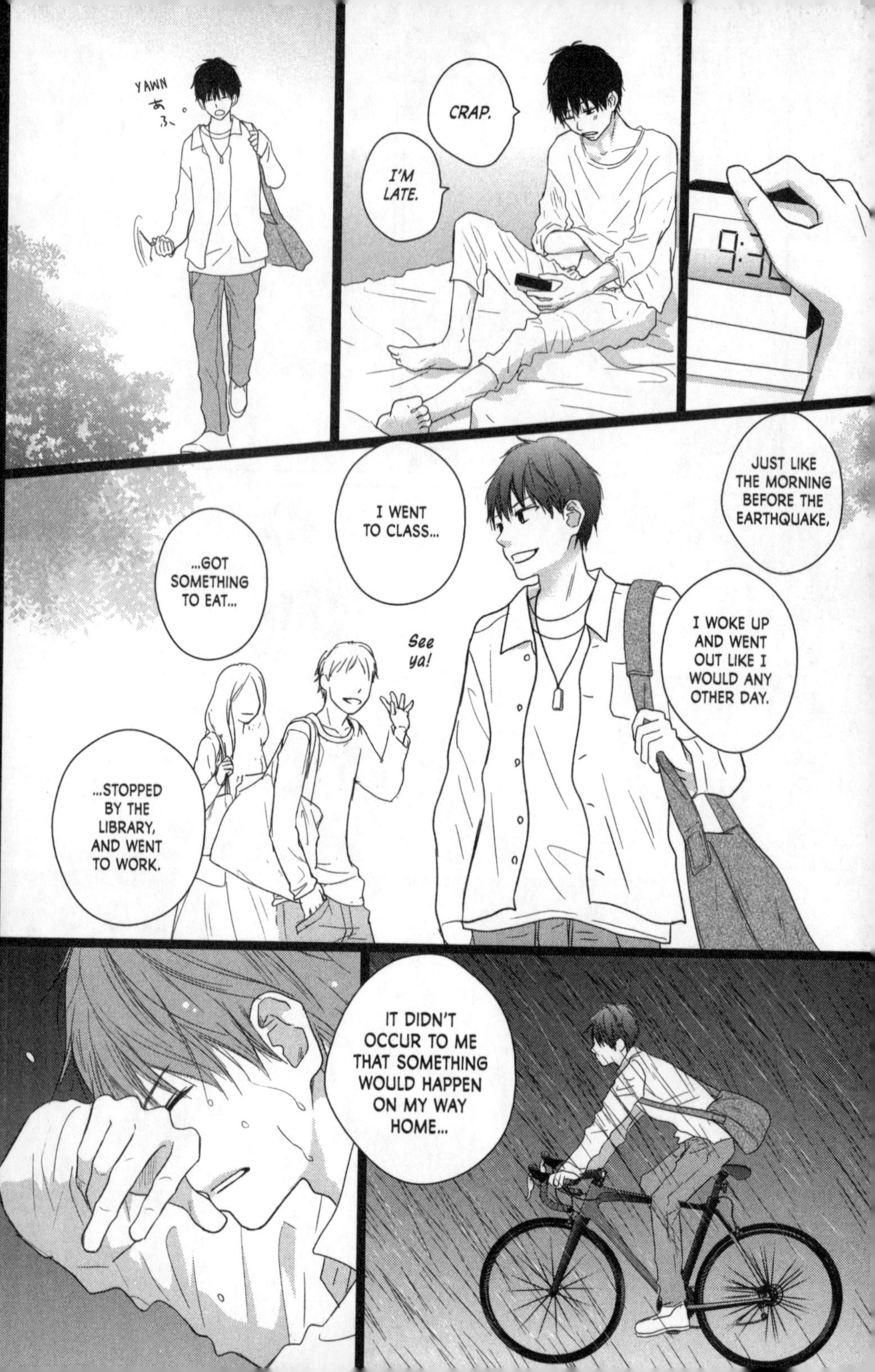
CRAP.
I'M LATE.
YAWN
あふ。
JUST LIKE THE MORNING BEFORE THE EARTHQUAKE,
I WOKE UP AND WENT OUT LIKE I WOULD ANY OTHER DAY.
I WENT TO CLASS...
See ya!
...GOT SOMETHING TO EAT...
...STOPPED BY THE LIBRARY, AND WENT TO WORK.
IT DIDN'T OCCUR TO ME THAT SOMETHING WOULD HAPPEN ON MY WAY HOME...

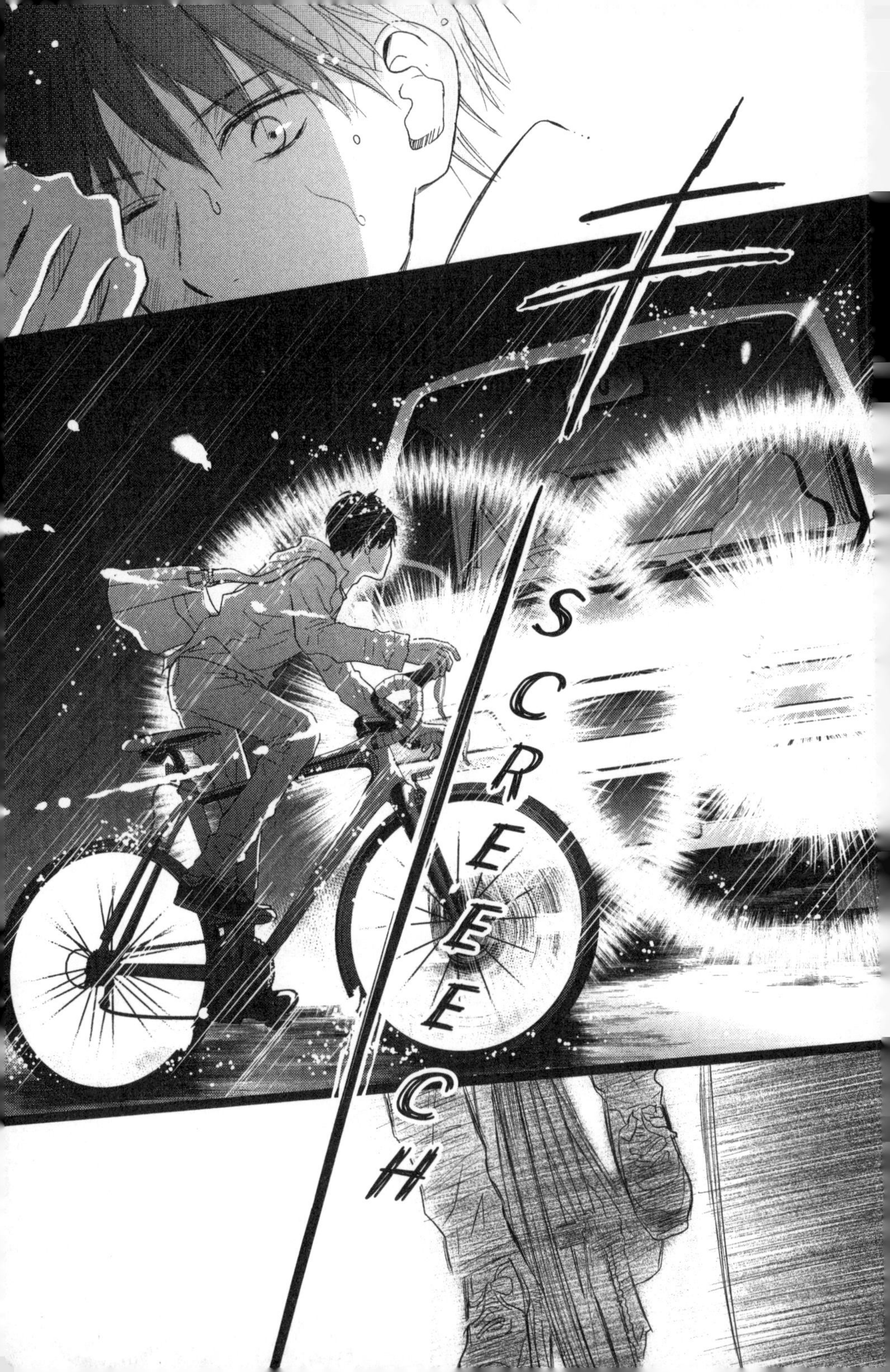
SCREEECH

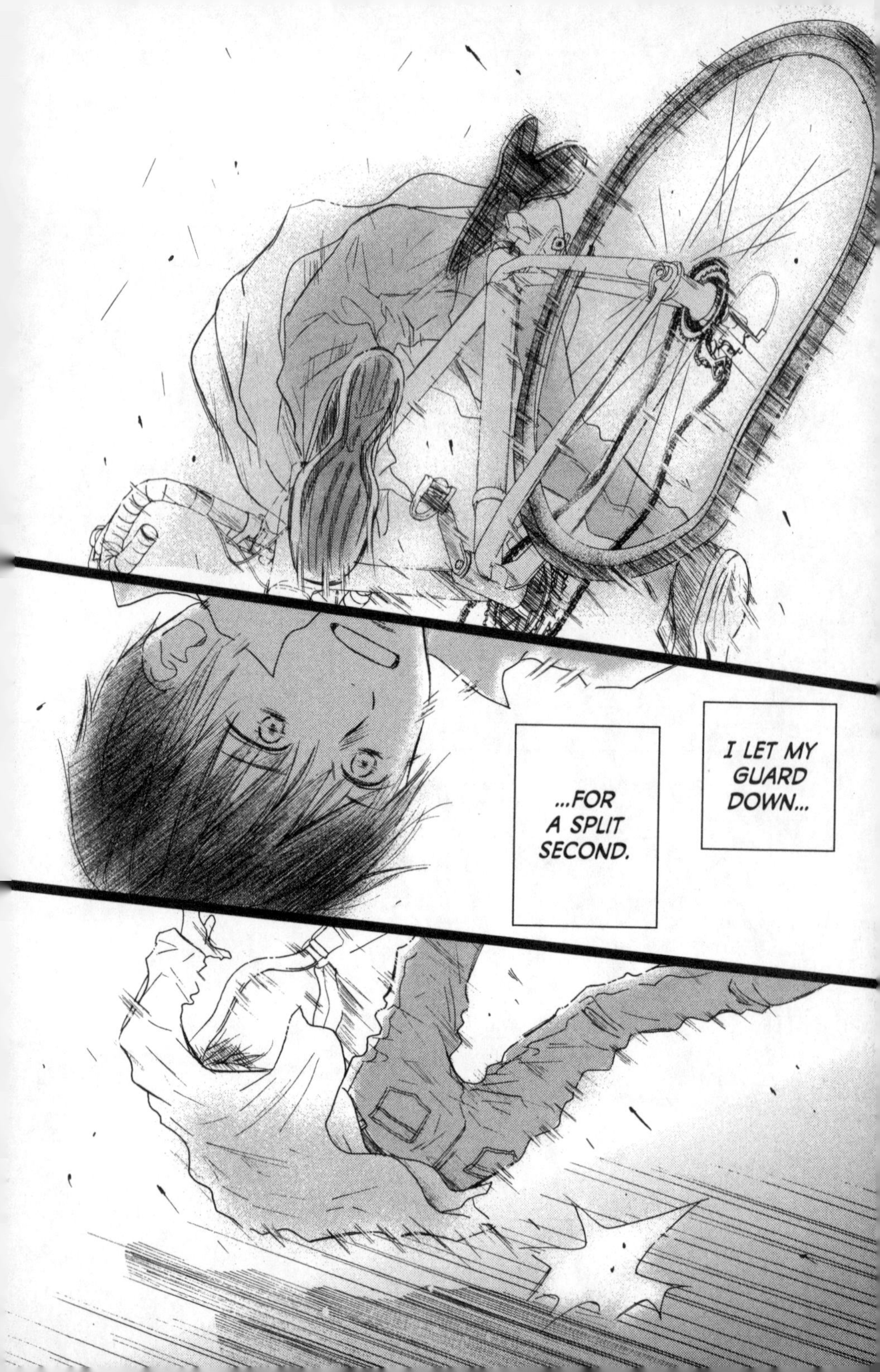
I LET MY GUARD DOWN...
...FOR A SPLIT SECOND.

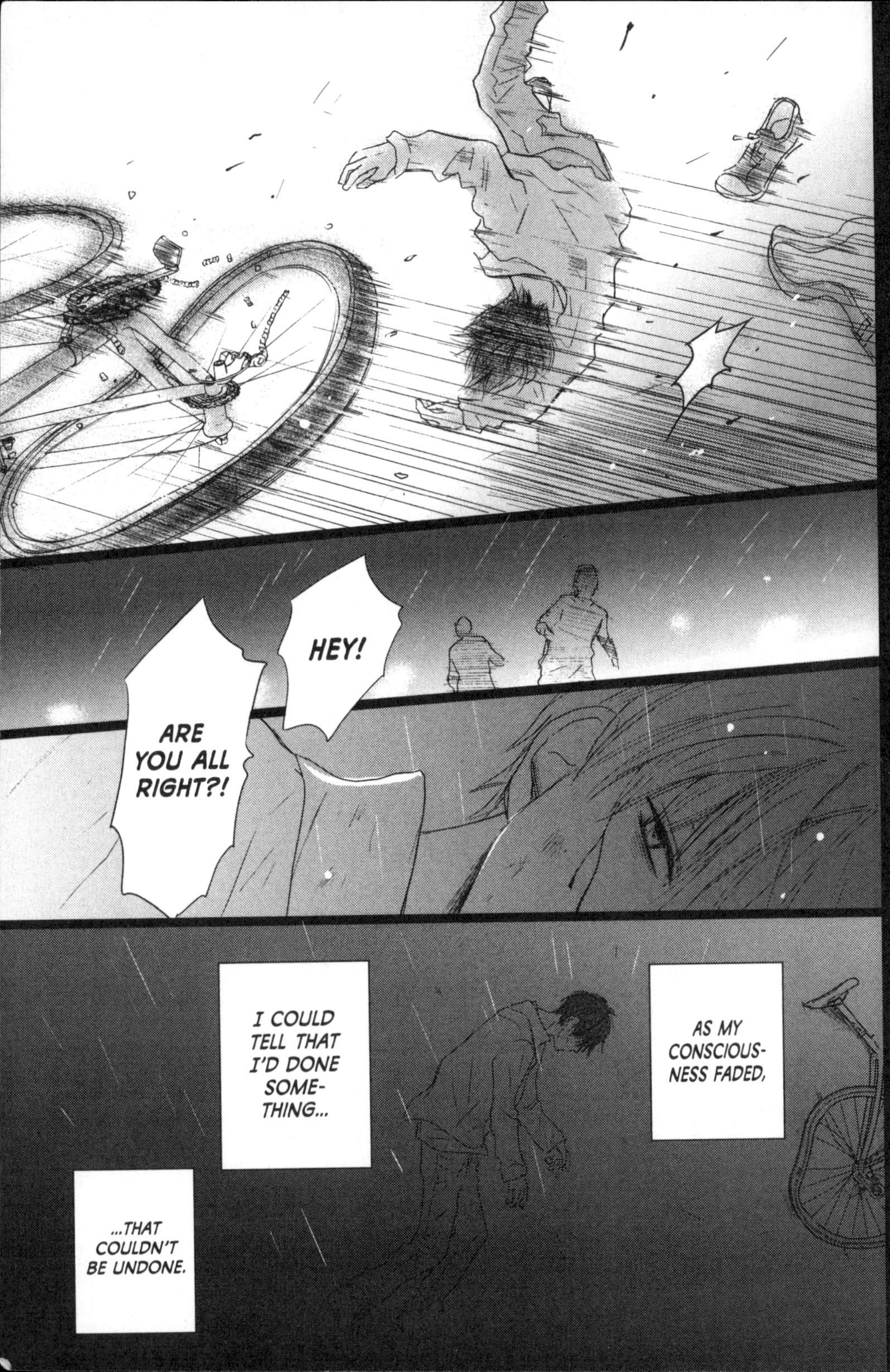
HEY!
ARE YOU ALL RIGHT?!
AS MY CONSCIOUS-NESS FADED,
I COULD TELL THAT I'D DONE SOME-THING...
...THAT COULDN'T BE UNDONE.

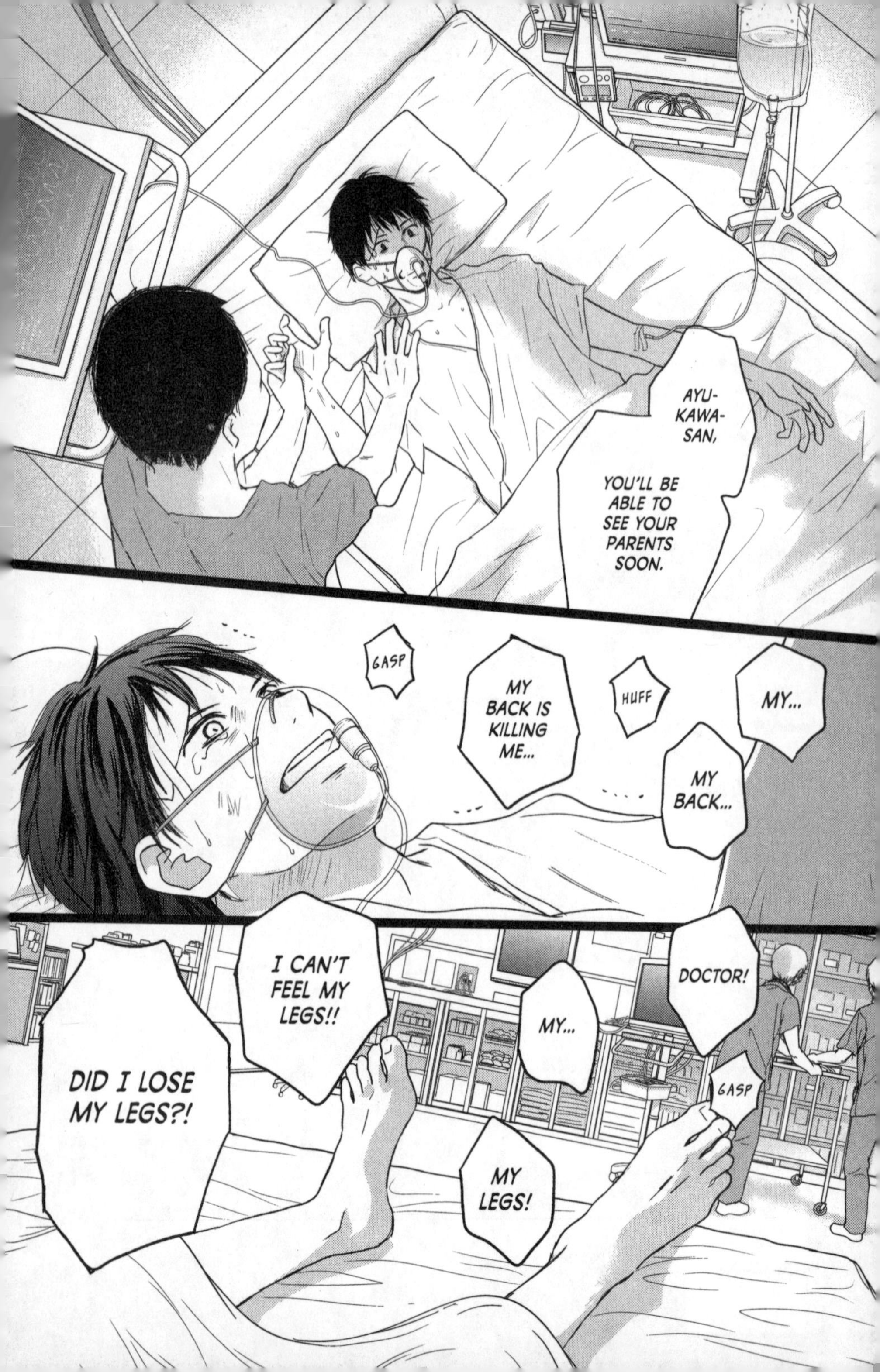
AYU-KAWA-SAN, YOU'LL BE ABLE TO SEE YOUR PARENTS SOON.
MY...
HUFF
MY BACK...
MY BACK IS KILLING ME...
GASP
DOCTOR!
GASP
MY...
MY LEGS!
I CAN'T FEEL MY LEGS!!
DID I LOSE MY LEGS?!

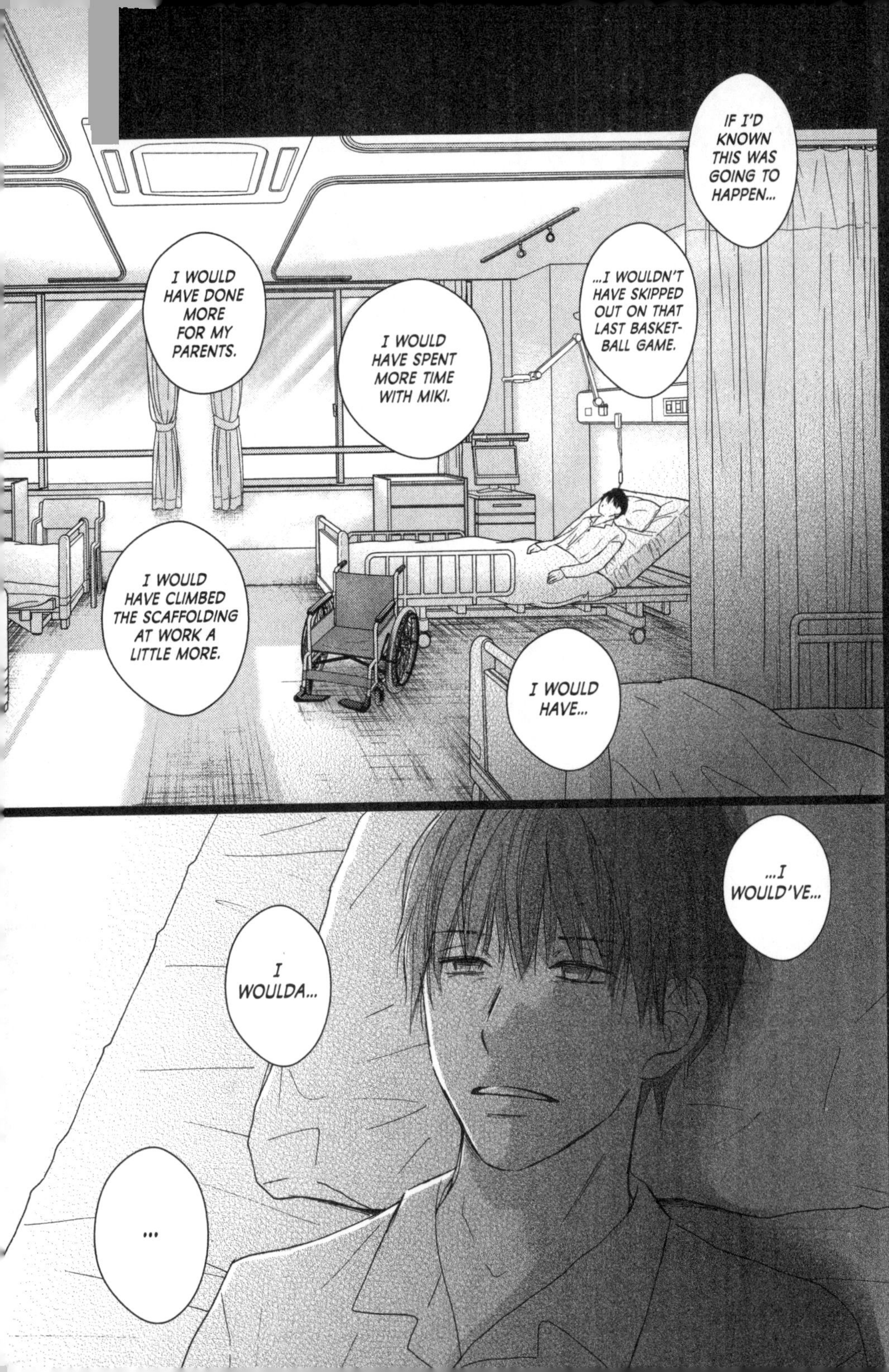
IF I'D KNOWN THIS WAS GOING TO HAPPEN...
...I WOULDN'T HAVE SKIPPED OUT ON THAT LAST BASKET-BALL GAME.
I WOULD HAVE SPENT MORE TIME WITH MIKI.
I WOULD HAVE DONE MORE FOR MY PARENTS.
I WOULD HAVE CLIMBED THE SCAFFOLDING AT WORK A LITTLE MORE.
I WOULD HAVE...
...I WOULD'VE...
I WOULDA...
...

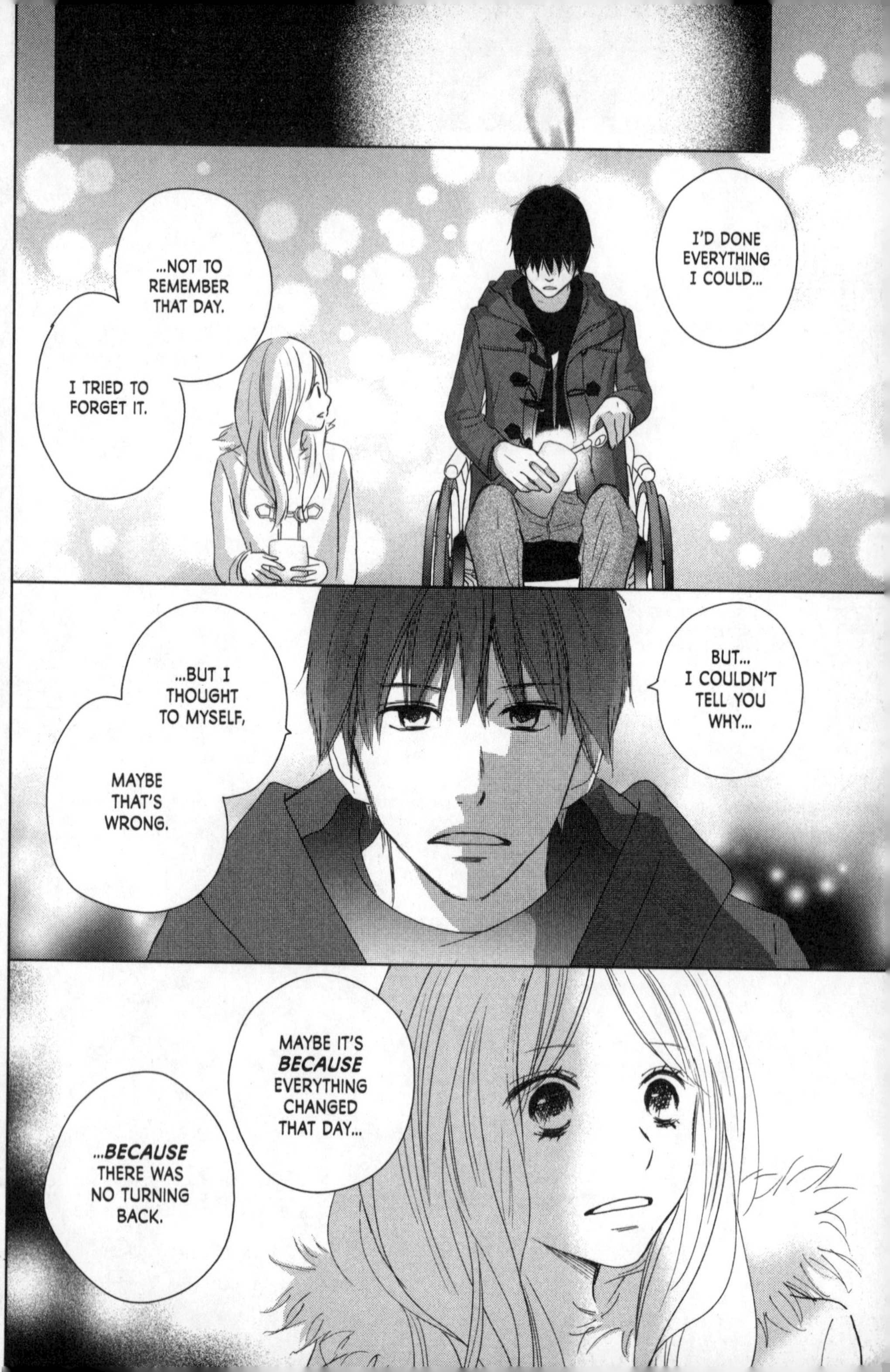
I'D DONE EVERYTHING I COULD...
...NOT TO REMEMBER THAT DAY.
I TRIED TO FORGET IT.
BUT... I COULDN'T TELL YOU WHY...
...BUT I THOUGHT TO MYSELF,
MAYBE THAT'S WRONG.
MAYBE IT'S *BECAUSE* EVERYTHING CHANGED THAT DAY...
...*BECAUSE* THERE WAS NO TURNING BACK.

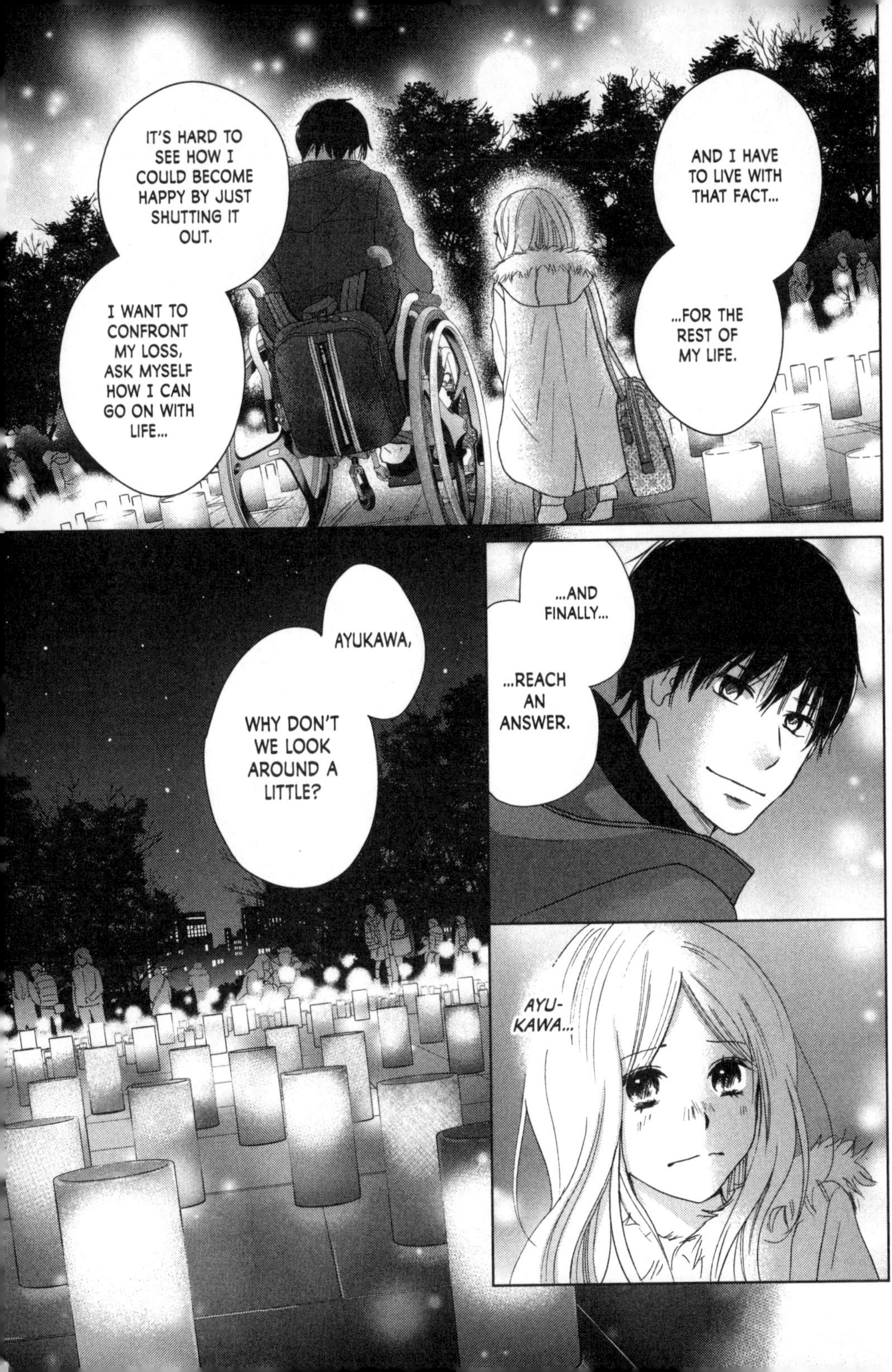
AND I HAVE TO LIVE WITH THAT FACT...
...FOR THE REST OF MY LIFE.
IT'S HARD TO SEE HOW I COULD BECOME HAPPY BY JUST SHUTTING IT OUT.
I WANT TO CONFRONT MY LOSS, ASK MYSELF HOW I CAN GO ON WITH LIFE...
...AND FINALLY...
...REACH AN ANSWER.
AYU-KAWA...
AYUKAWA,
WHY DON'T WE LOOK AROUND A LITTLE?

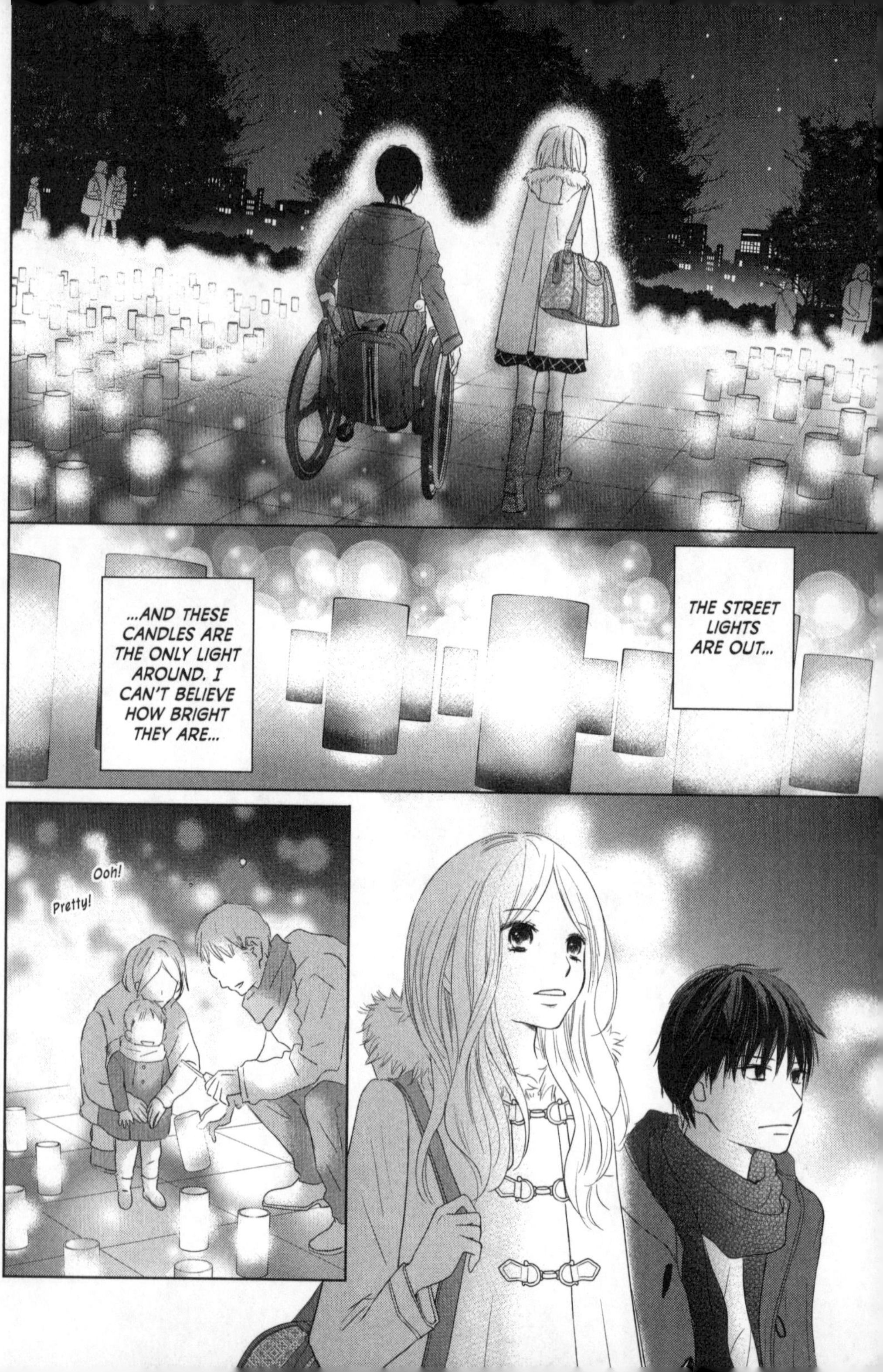
THE STREET LIGHTS ARE OUT...
...AND THESE CANDLES ARE THE ONLY LIGHT AROUND. I CAN'T BELIEVE HOW BRIGHT THEY ARE...
Ooh!
Pretty!

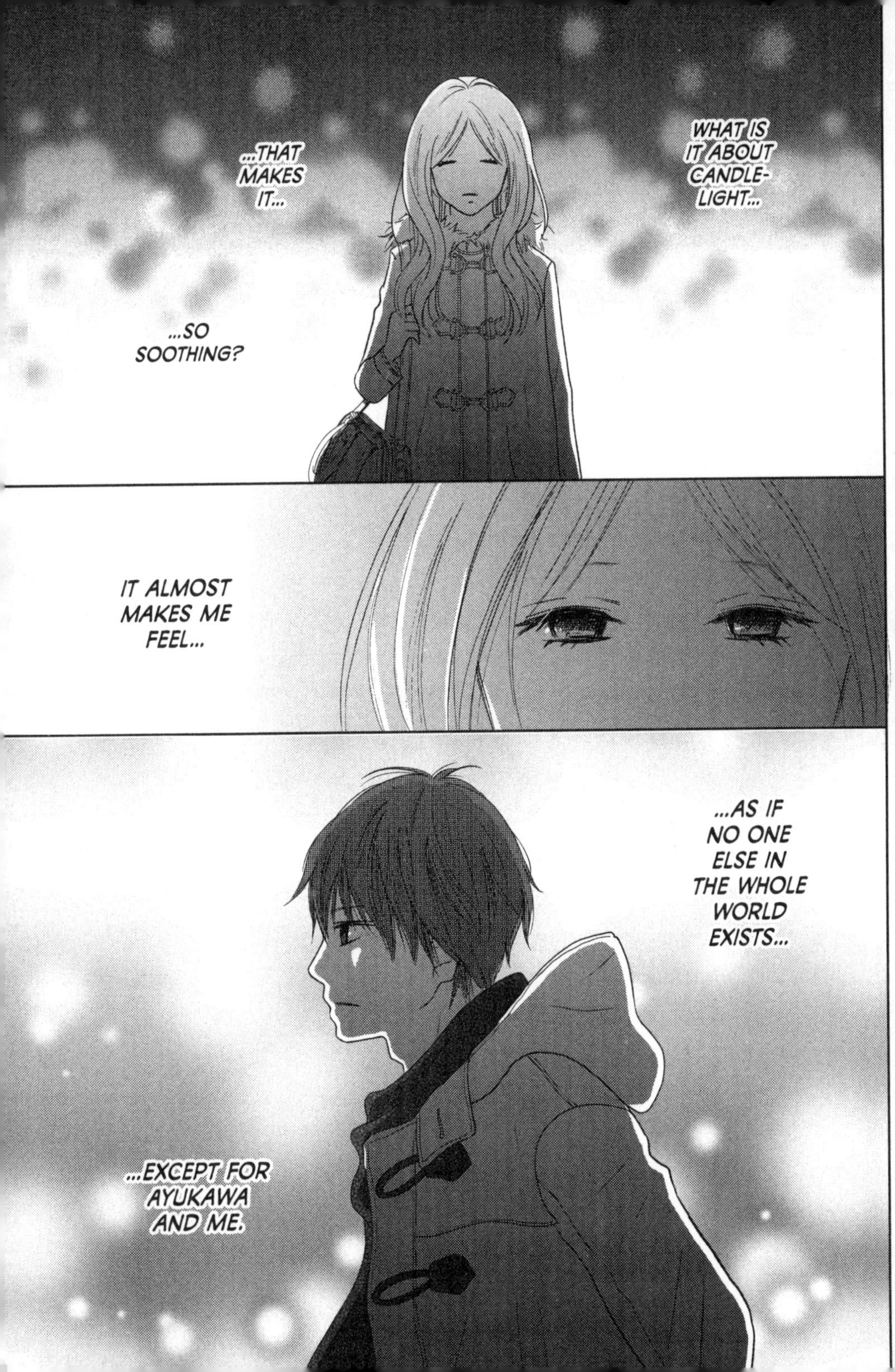
WHAT IS IT ABOUT CANDLE-LIGHT...
...THAT MAKES IT...
...SO SOOTHING?
IT ALMOST MAKES ME FEEL...
...AS IF NO ONE ELSE IN THE WHOLE WORLD EXISTS...
...EXCEPT FOR AYUKAWA AND ME.

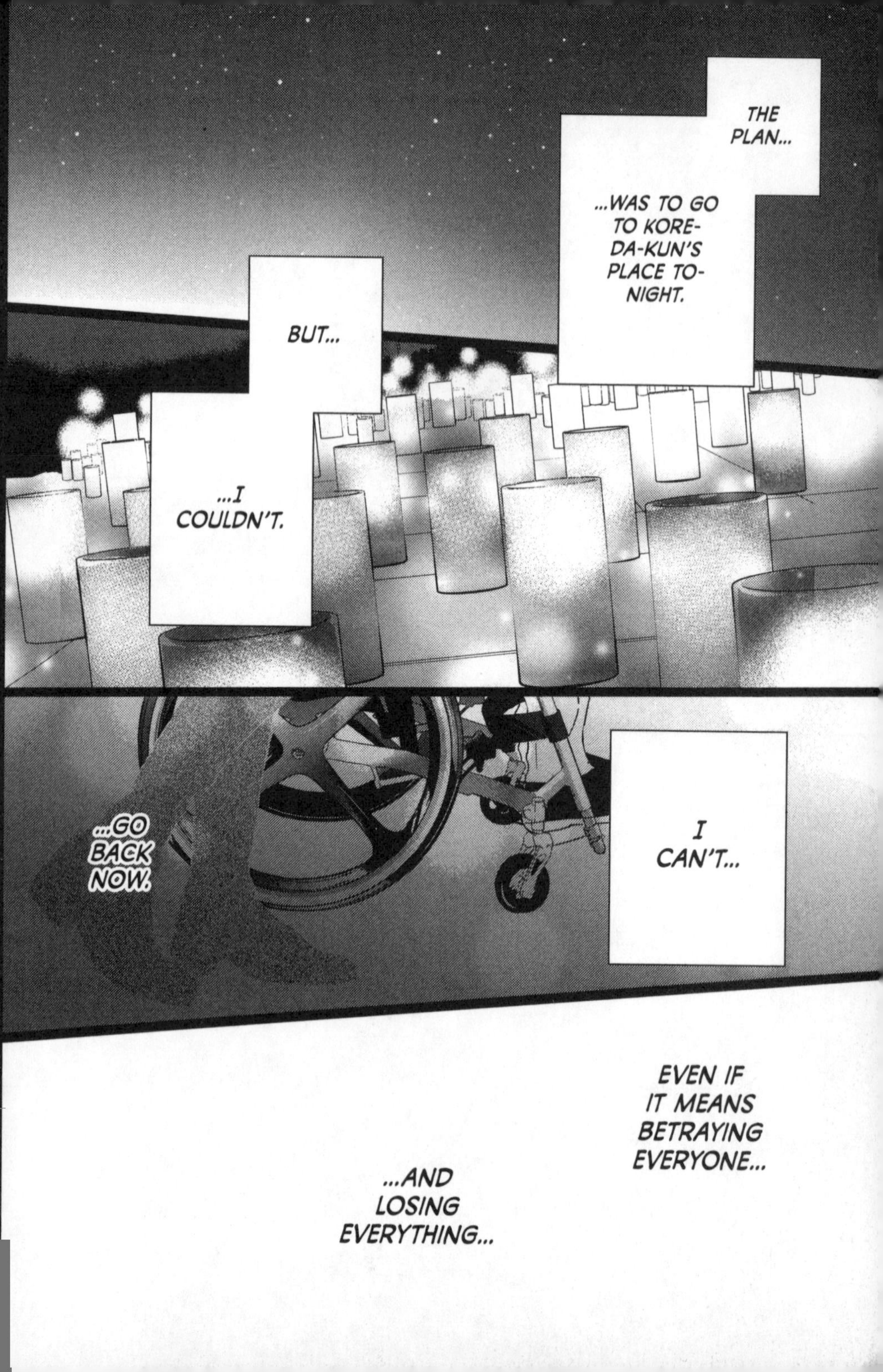
THE PLAN...
...WAS TO GO TO KOREDA-KUN'S PLACE TONIGHT.
BUT...
...I COULDN'T.
I CAN'T...
...GO BACK NOW.
EVEN IF IT MEANS BETRAYING EVERYONE...
...AND LOSING EVERYTHING...

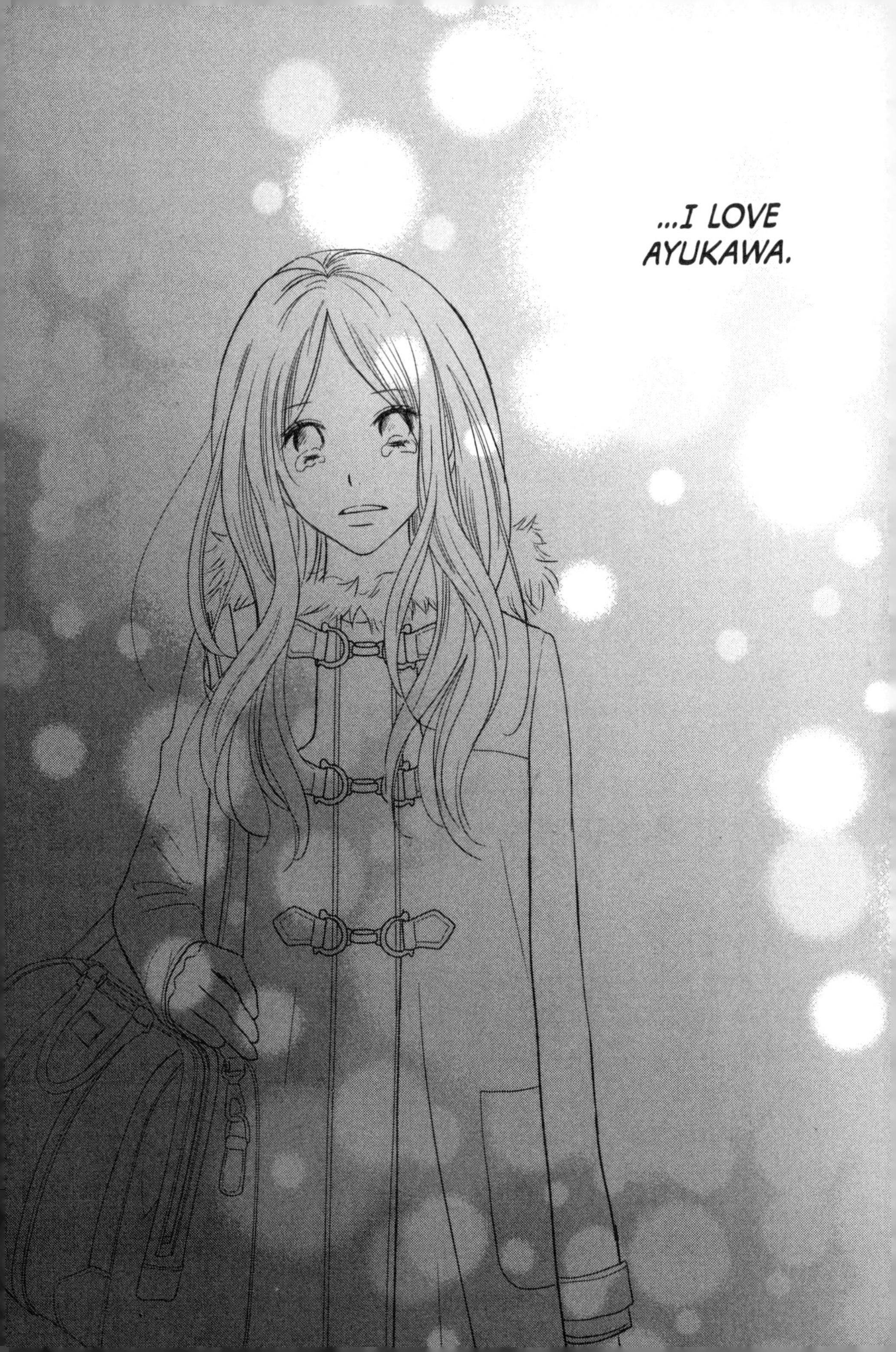
...I LOVE AYUKAWA.

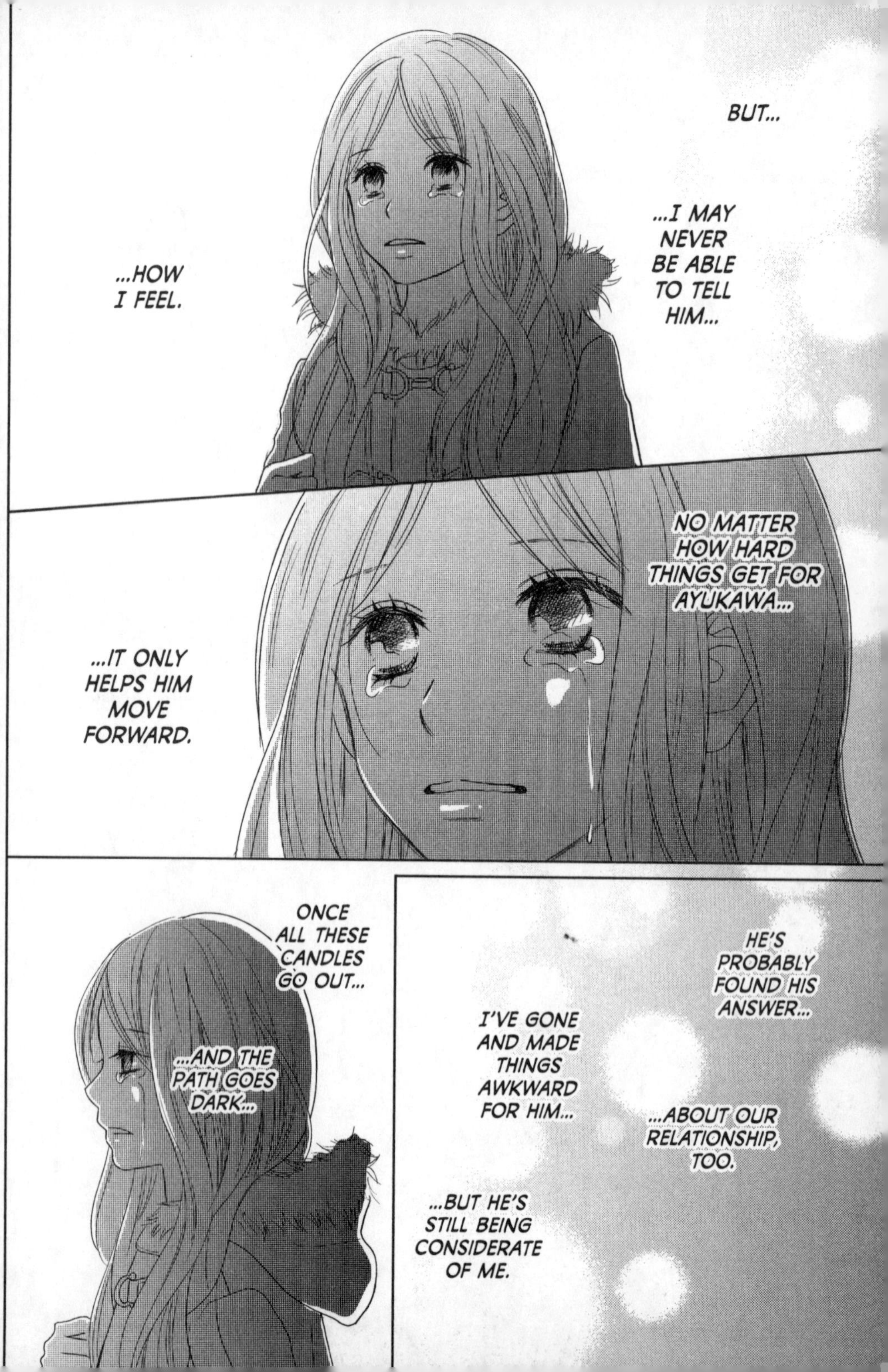
BUT...
...I MAY NEVER BE ABLE TO TELL HIM...
...HOW I FEEL.
NO MATTER HOW HARD THINGS GET FOR AYUKAWA...
...IT ONLY HELPS HIM MOVE FORWARD.
HE'S PROBABLY FOUND HIS ANSWER...
...ABOUT OUR RELATIONSHIP, TOO.
I'VE GONE AND MADE THINGS AWKWARD FOR HIM...
...BUT HE'S STILL BEING CONSIDERATE OF ME.
ONCE ALL THESE CANDLES GO OUT...
...AND THE PATH GOES DARK...

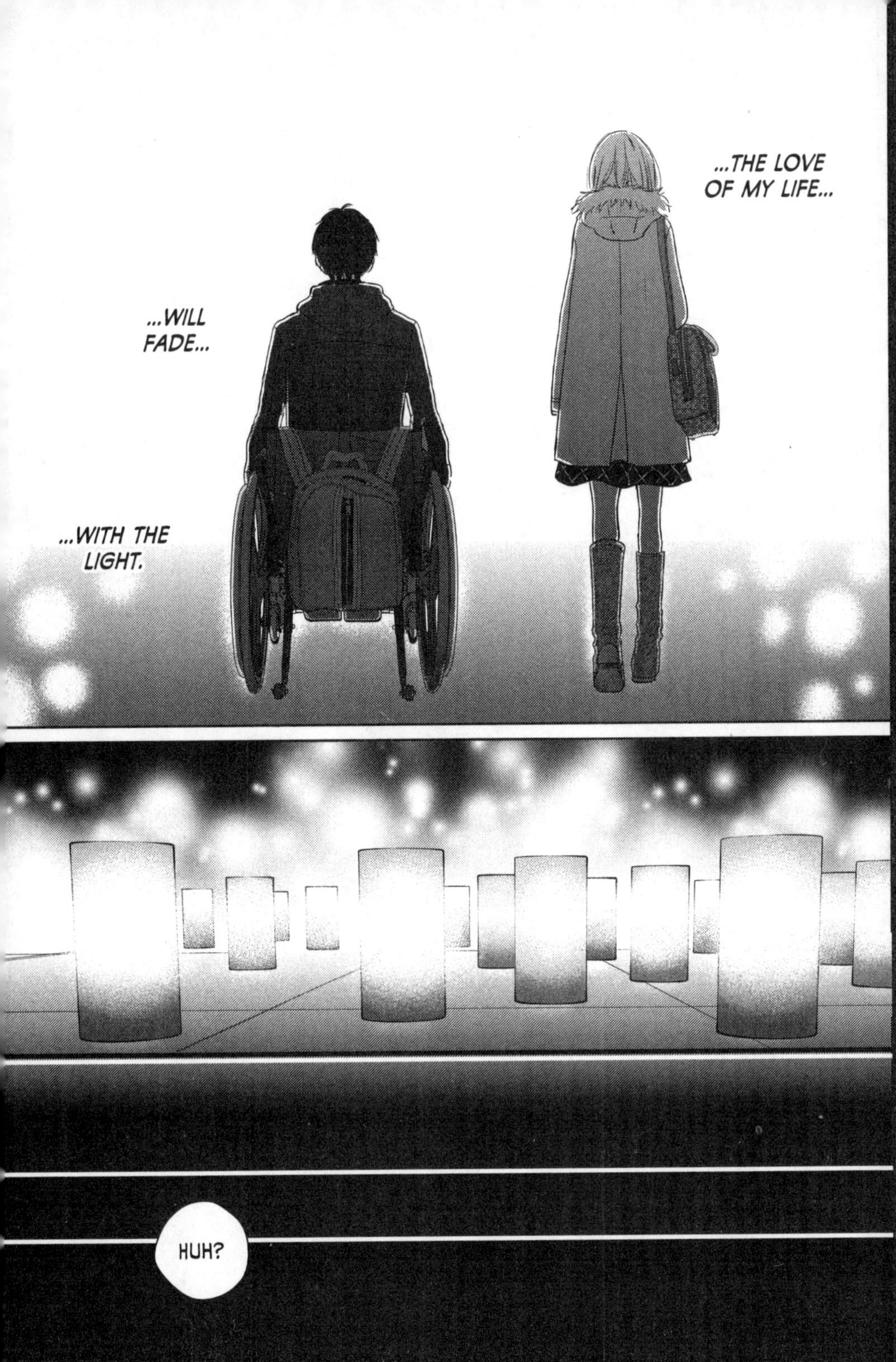
...THE LOVE OF MY LIFE...
...WILL FADE...
...WITH THE LIGHT.
HUH?

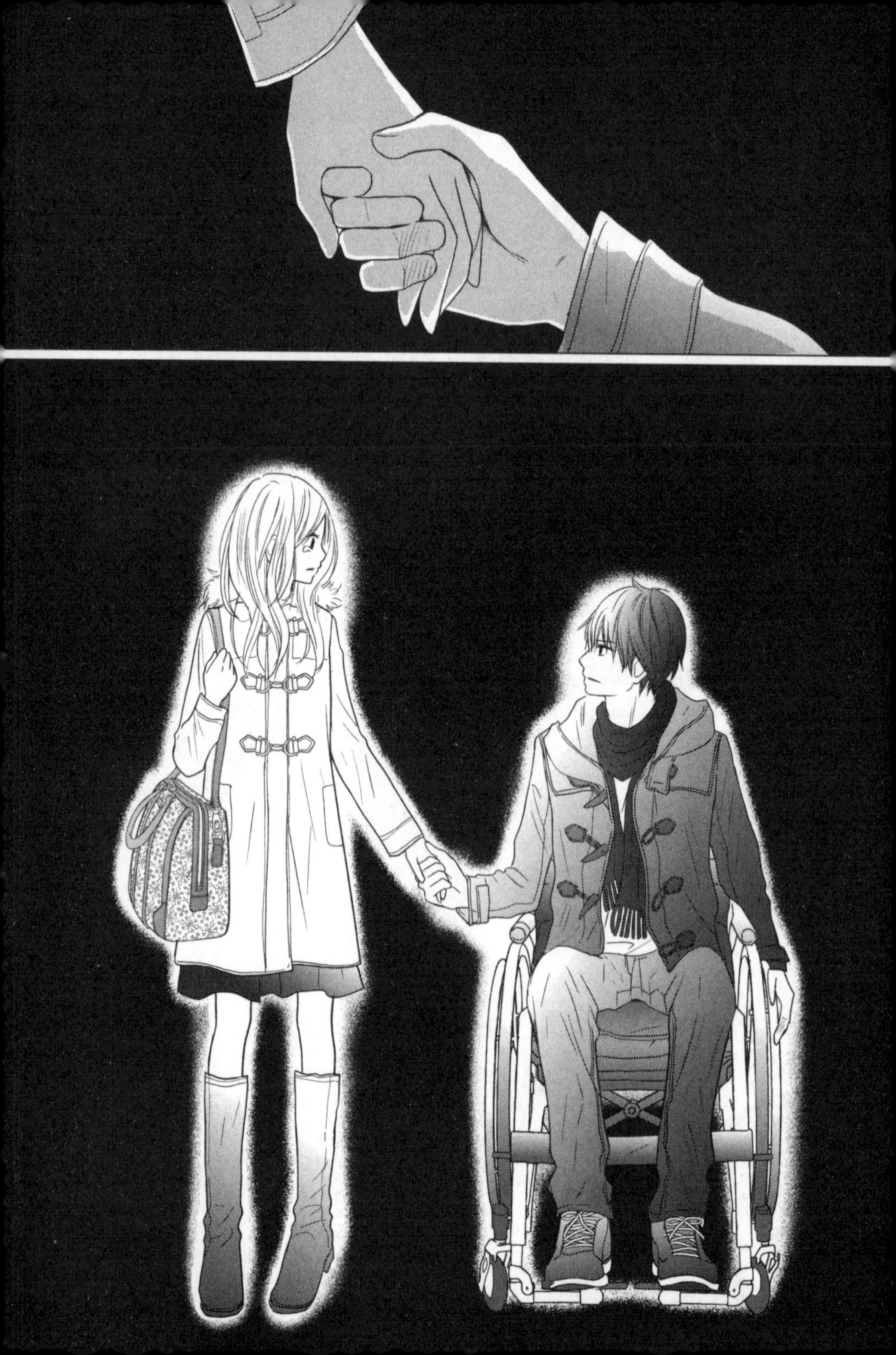

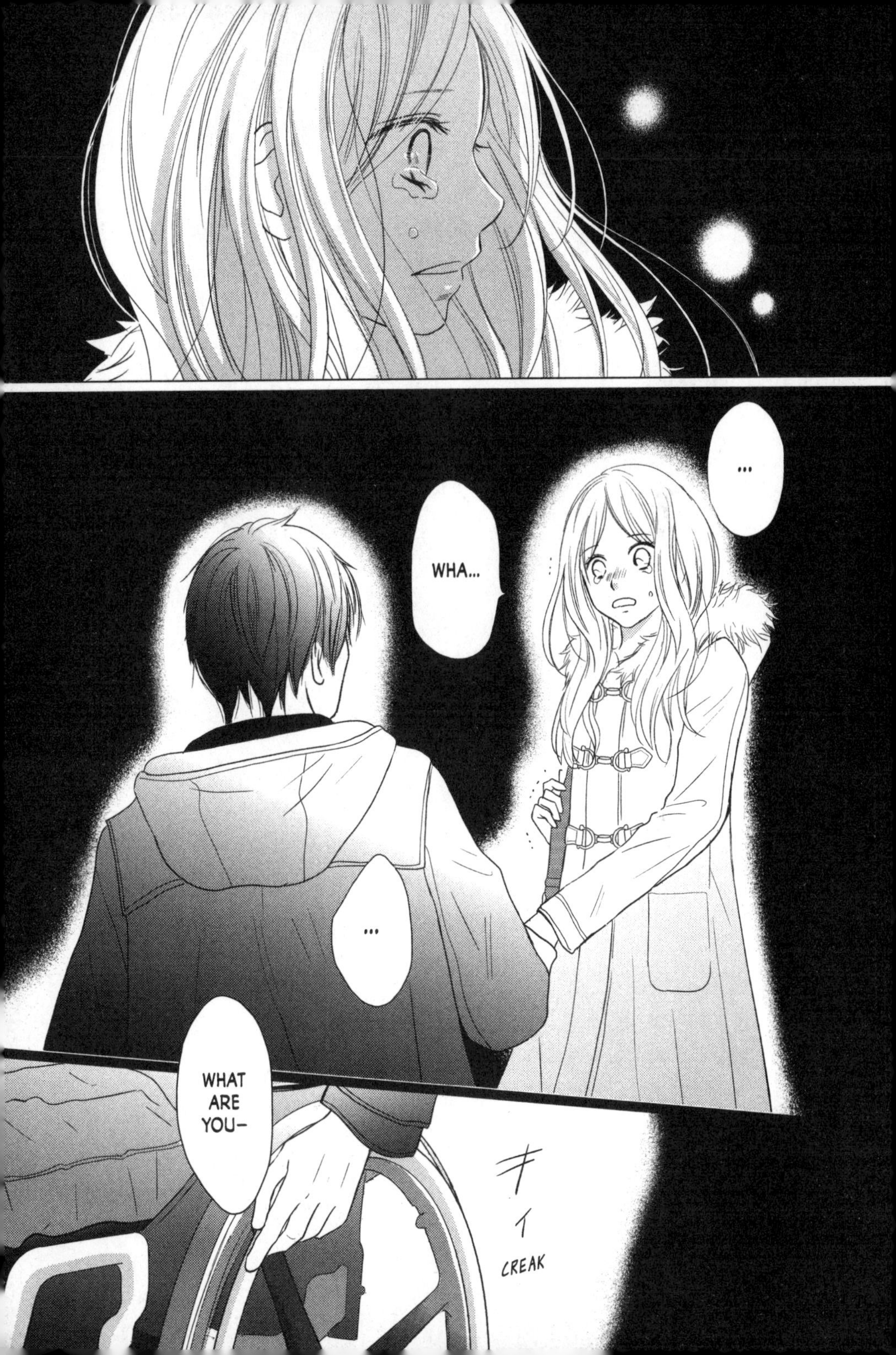
...
WHA...
...
WHAT ARE YOU–
キイ
CREAK

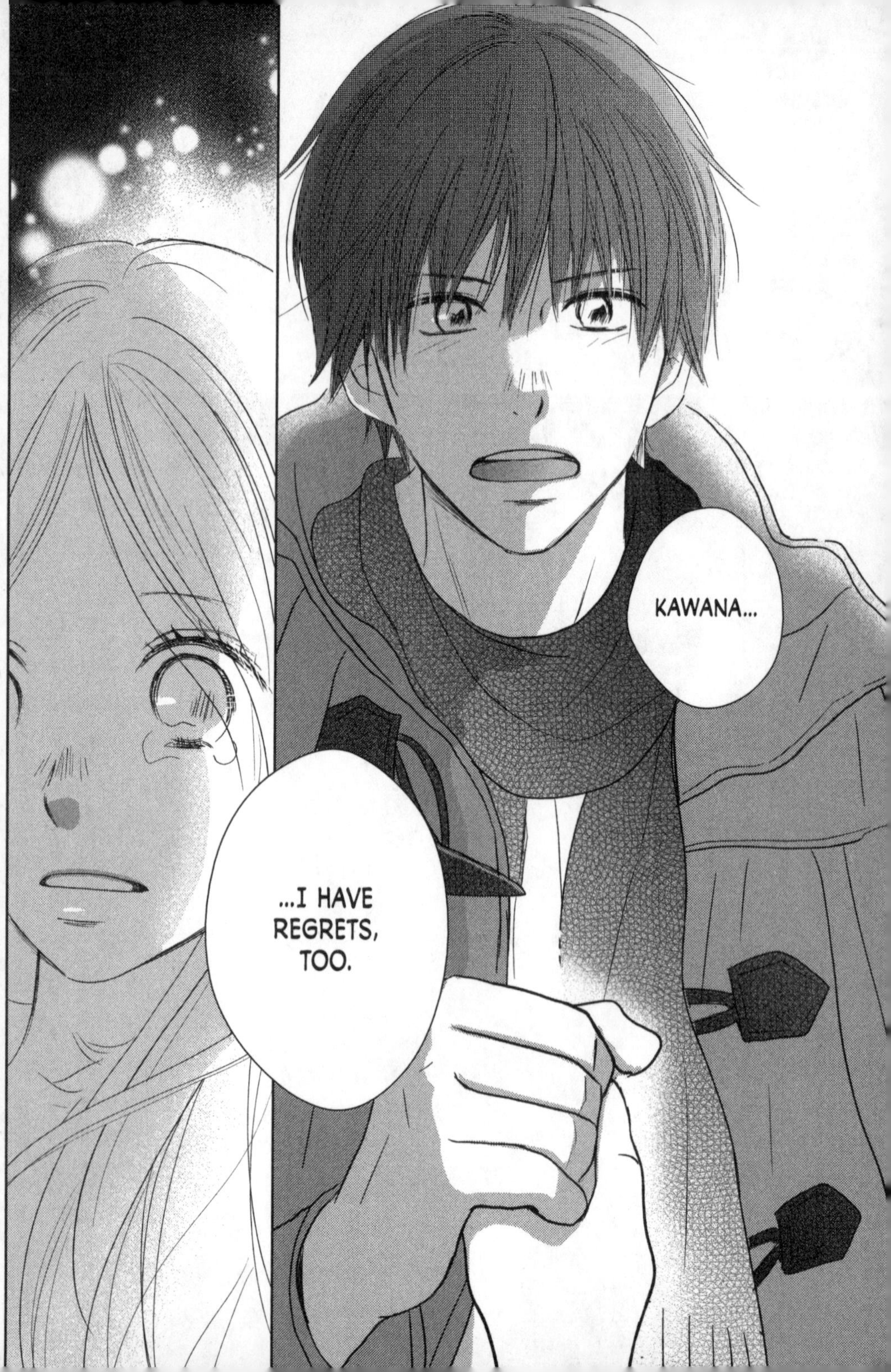
KAWANA...
...I HAVE REGRETS, TOO.

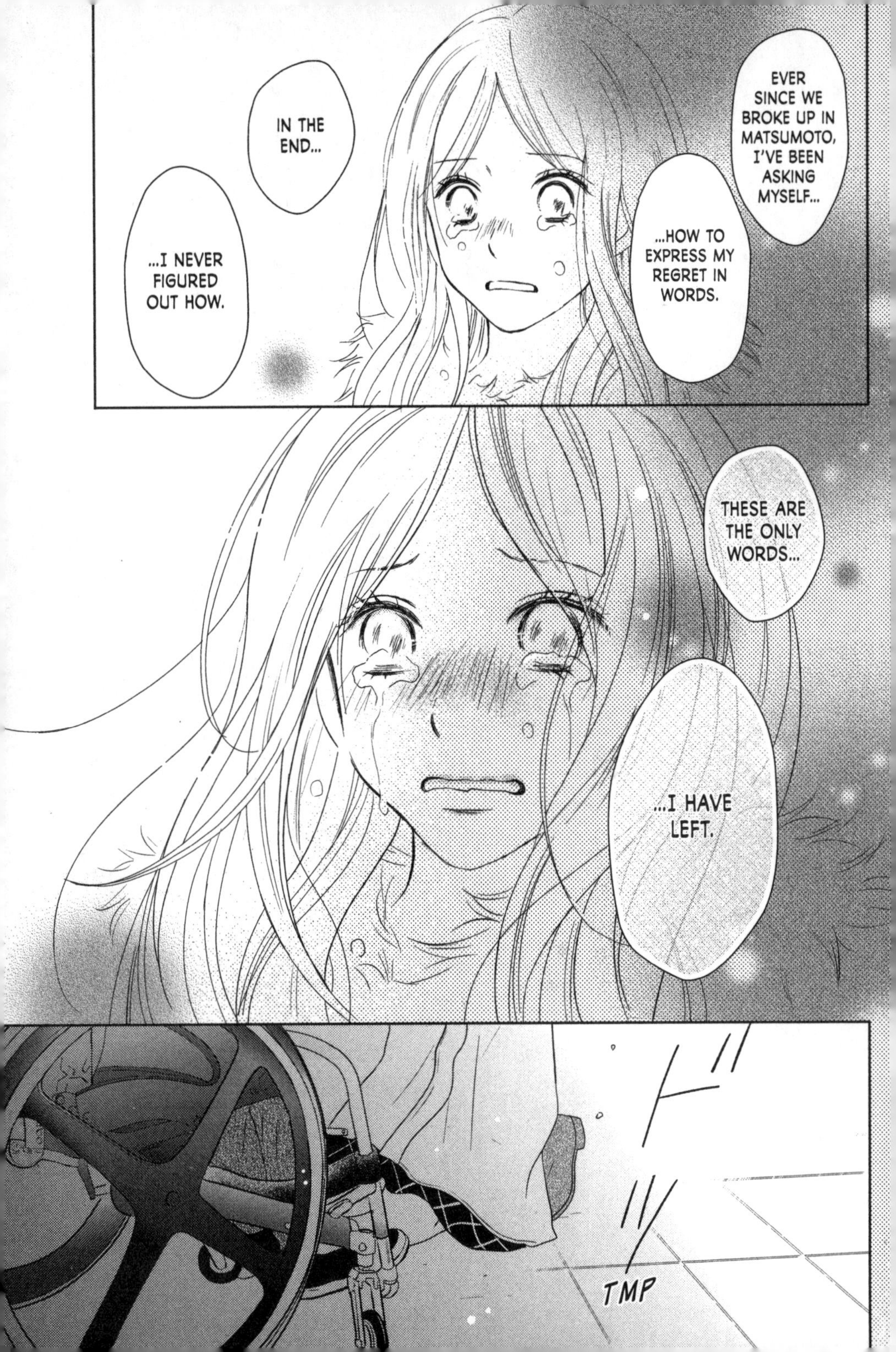
EVER SINCE WE BROKE UP IN MATSUMOTO, I'VE BEEN ASKING MYSELF...
...HOW TO EXPRESS MY REGRET IN WORDS.
IN THE END...
...I NEVER FIGURED OUT HOW.
THESE ARE THE ONLY WORDS...
...I HAVE LEFT.
TMP

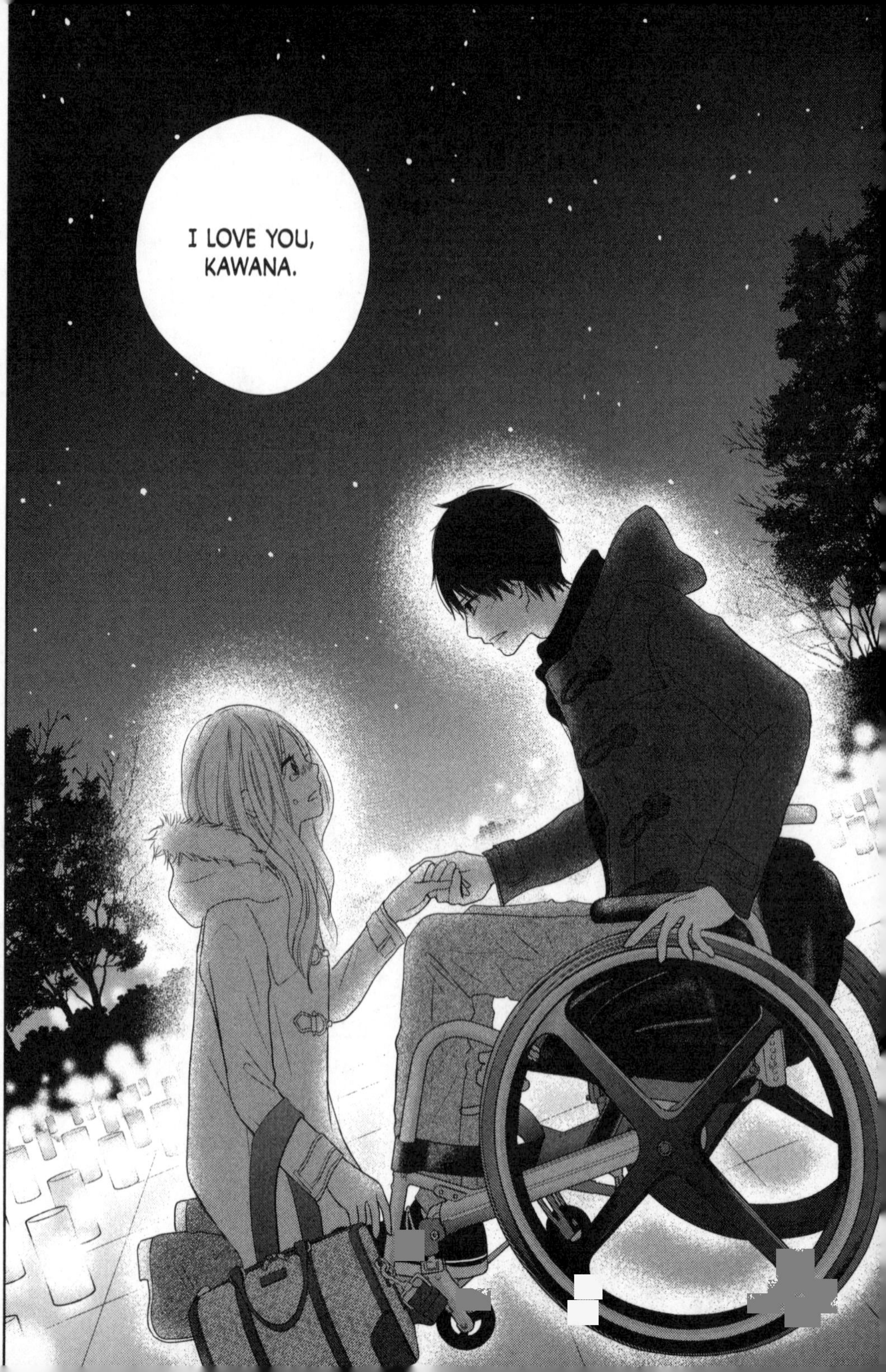
I LOVE YOU, KAWANA.

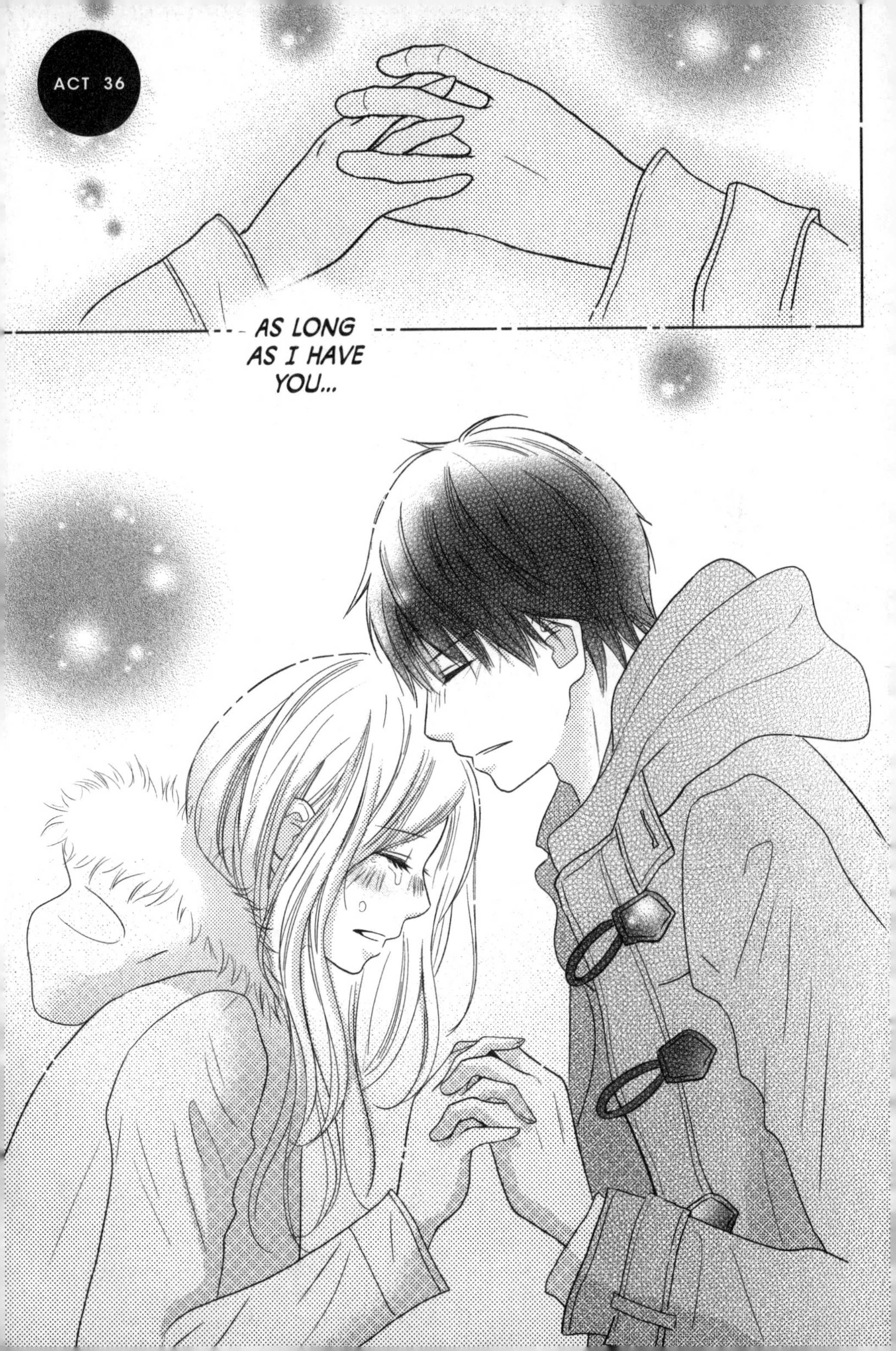
ACT 36
AS LONG AS I HAVE YOU...

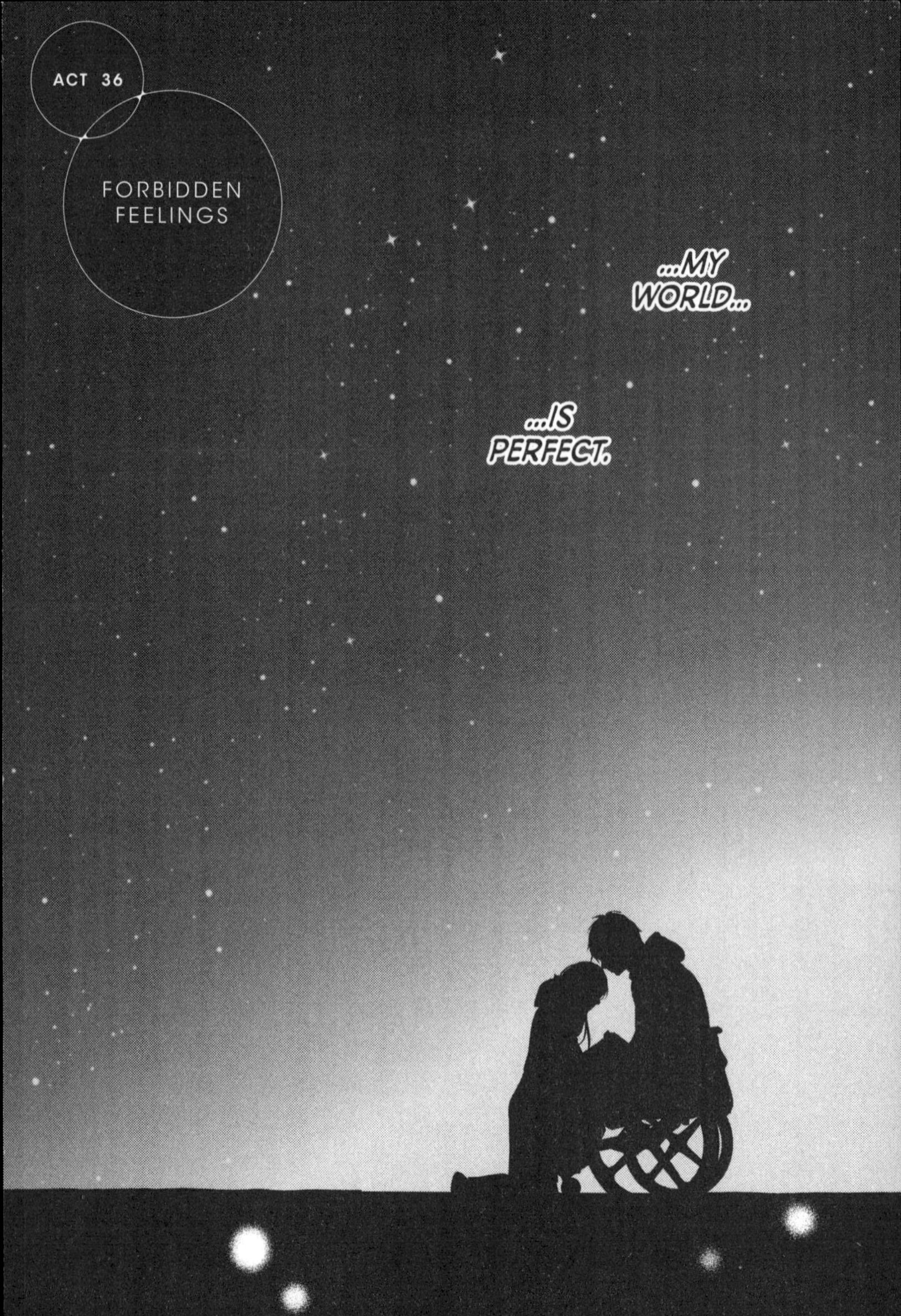
ACT 36
FORBIDDEN FEELINGS
...MY WORLD...
...IS PERFECT.

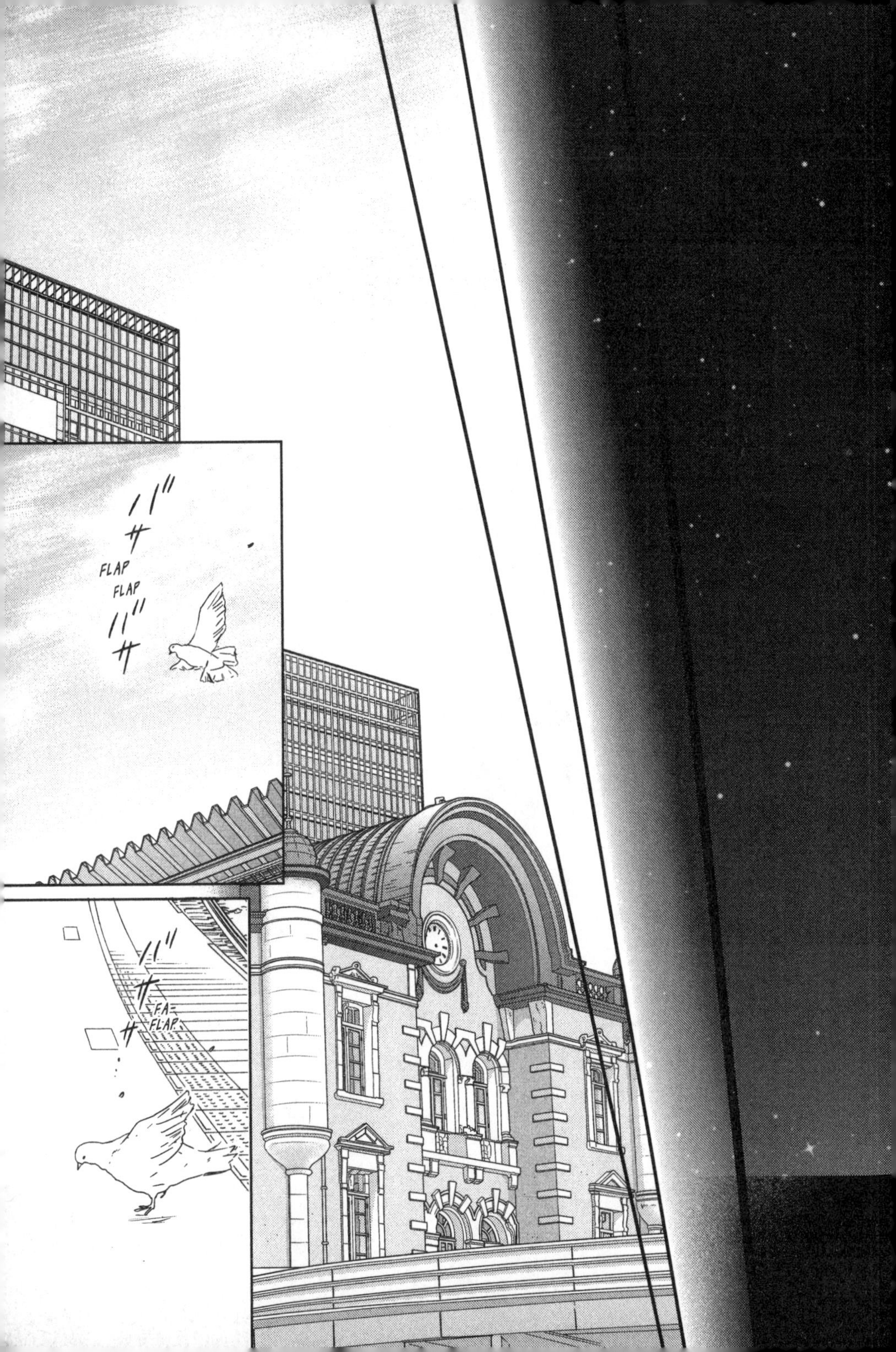
バサ
FLAP
FLAP
バサ
バサ
FA-
FLAP
サ

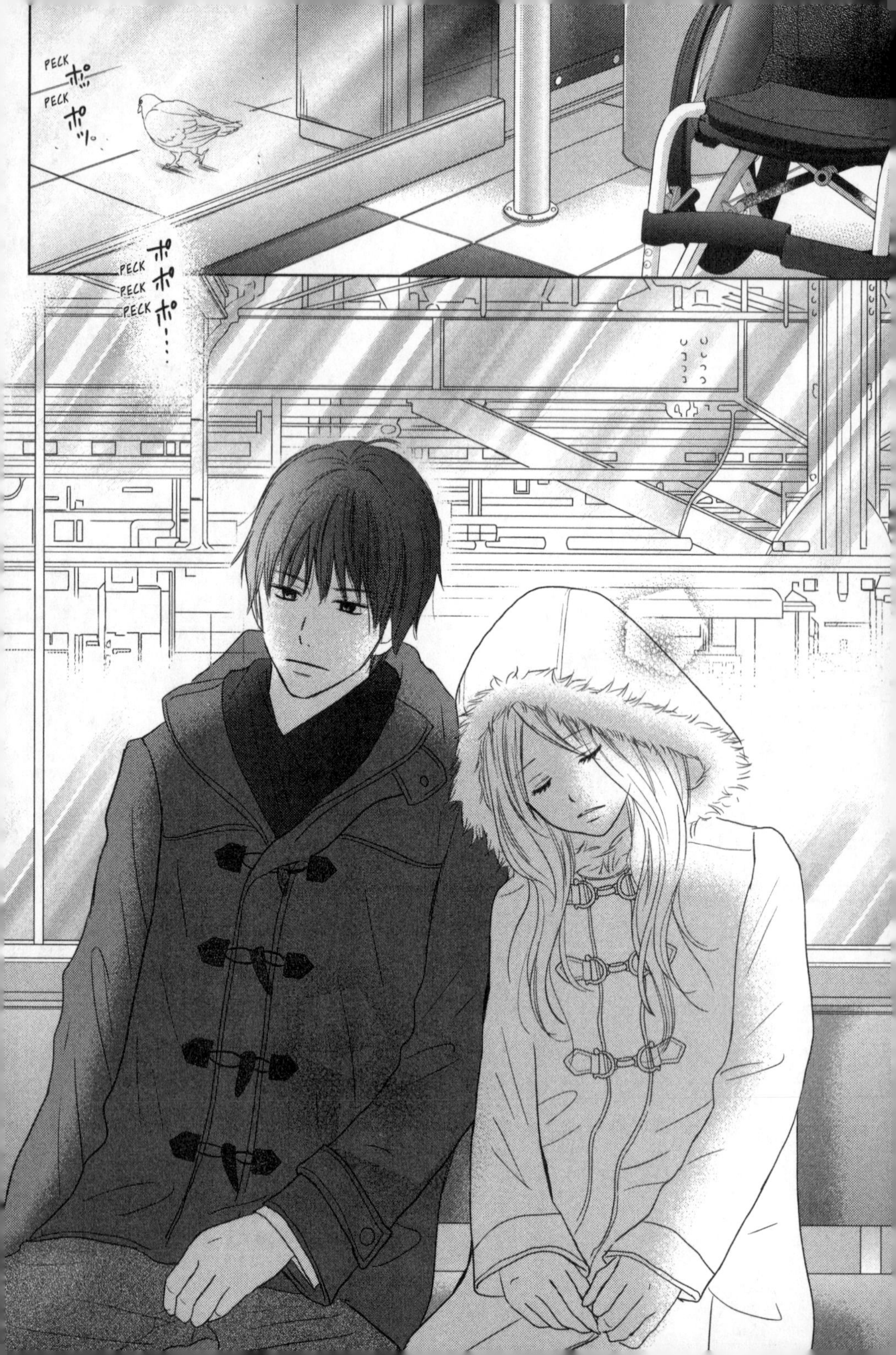
PECK
ポ
PECK
ポッ。
PECK
PECK
PECK
ポポポ…

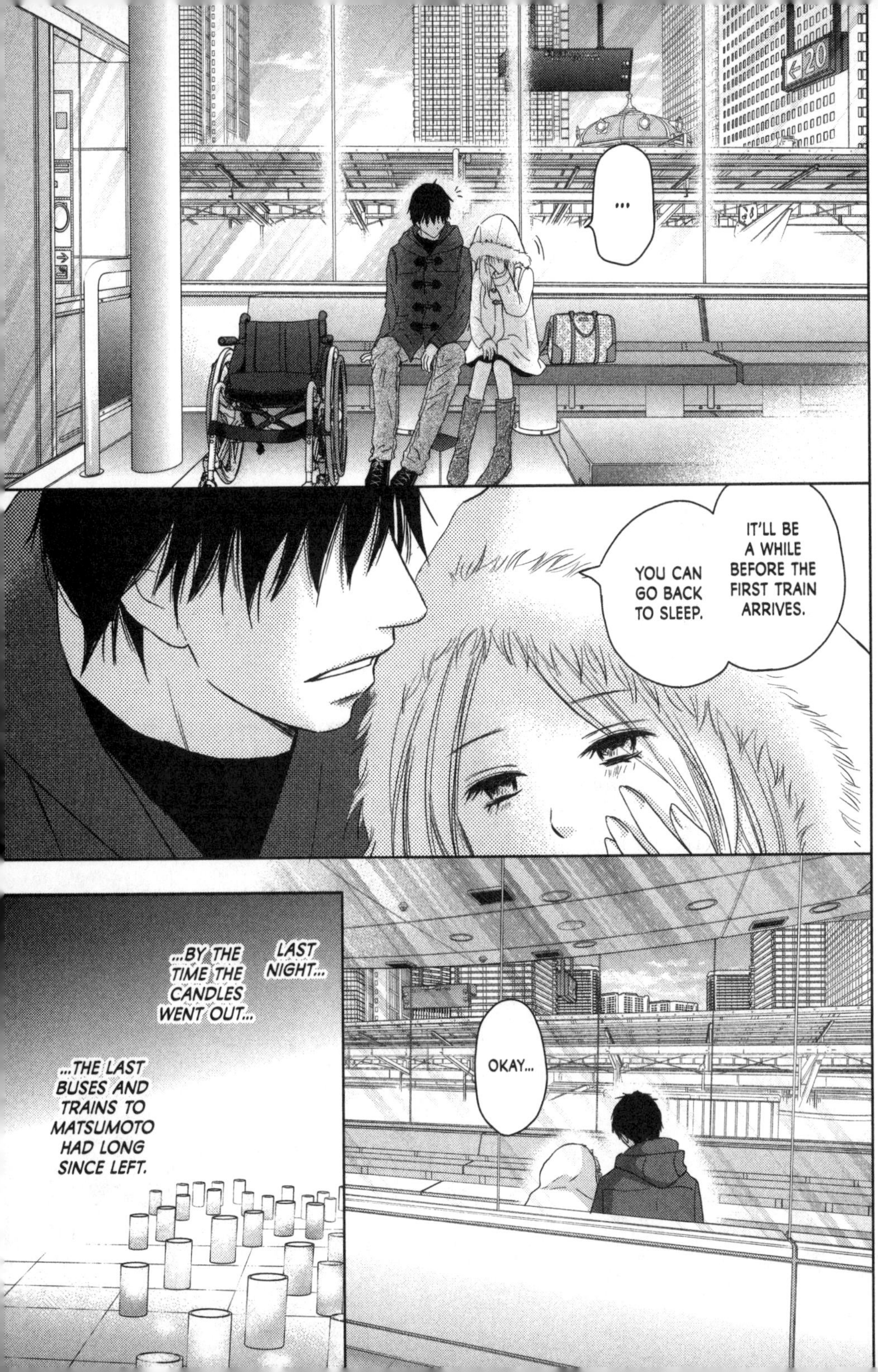
20
...
IT'LL BE A WHILE BEFORE THE FIRST TRAIN ARRIVES.
YOU CAN GO BACK TO SLEEP.
OKAY...
LAST NIGHT...
...BY THE TIME THE CANDLES WENT OUT...
...THE LAST BUSES AND TRAINS TO MATSUMOTO HAD LONG SINCE LEFT.

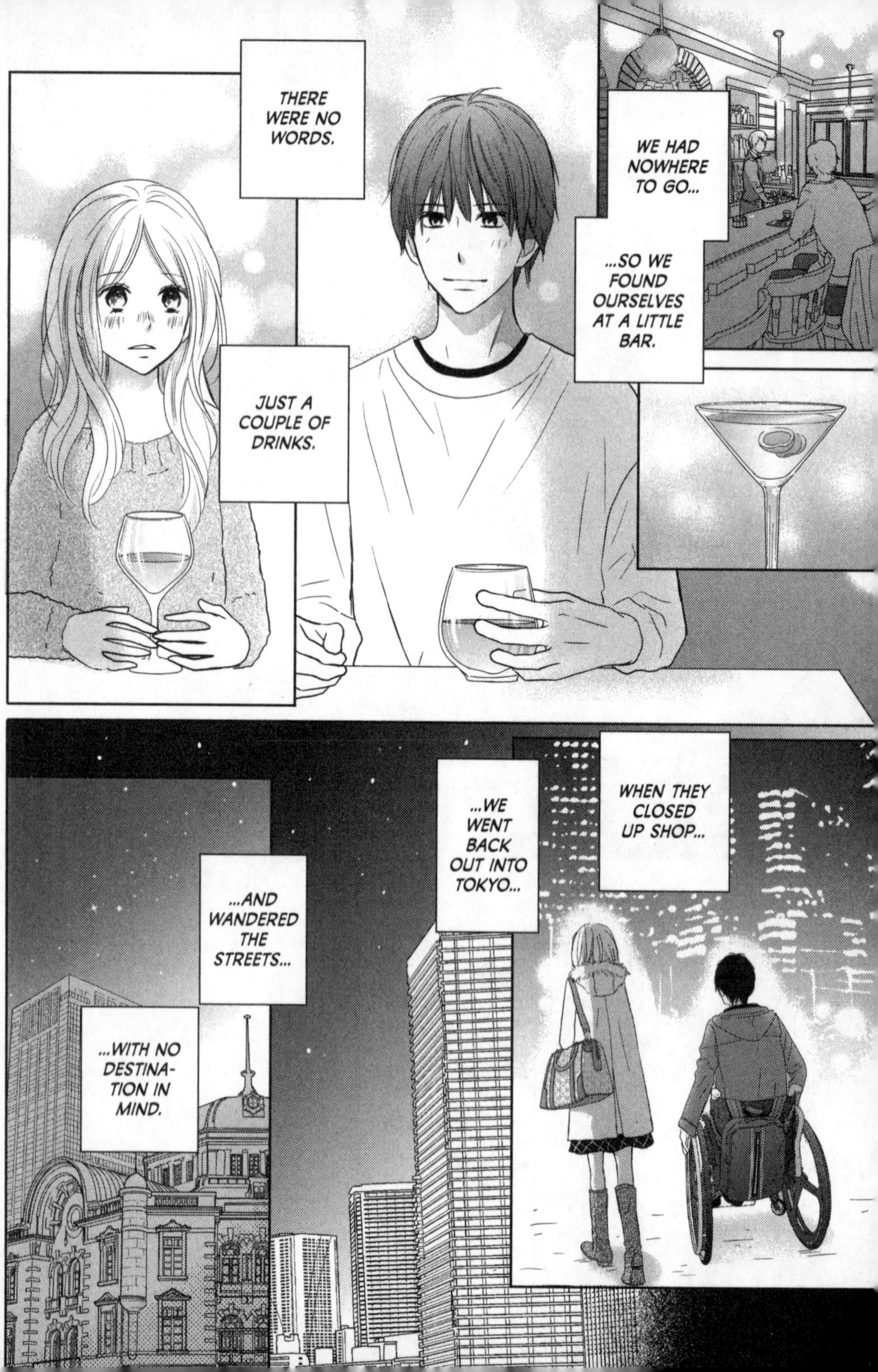
WE HAD NOWHERE TO GO...
...SO WE FOUND OURSELVES AT A LITTLE BAR.
THERE WERE NO WORDS.
JUST A COUPLE OF DRINKS.
WHEN THEY CLOSED UP SHOP...
...WE WENT BACK OUT INTO TOKYO...
...AND WANDERED THE STREETS...
...WITH NO DESTINATION IN MIND.

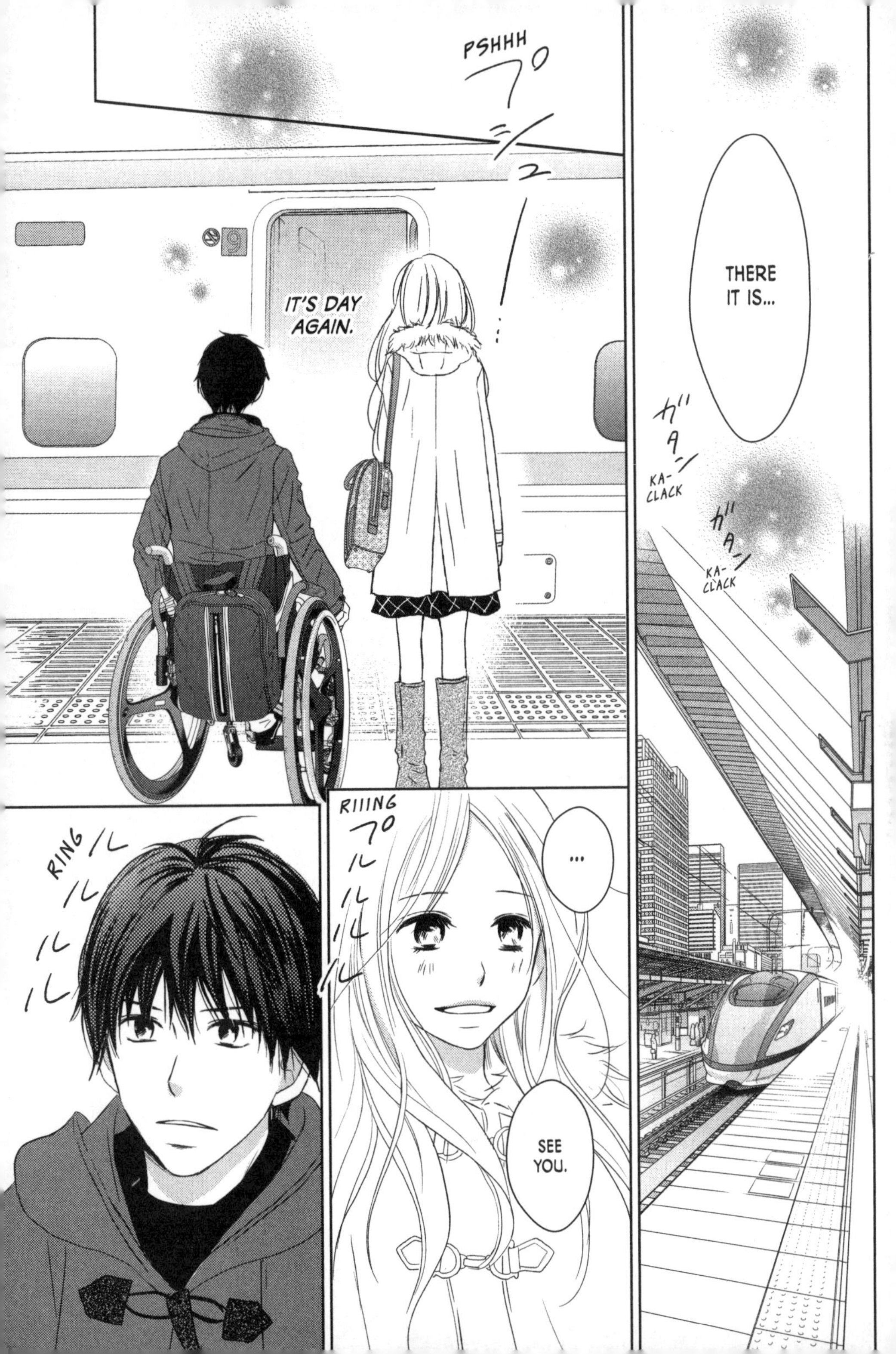
THERE IT IS...
KA-CLACK
KA-CLACK
PSHHH
IT'S DAY AGAIN.
RIIING
...
SEE YOU.
RING

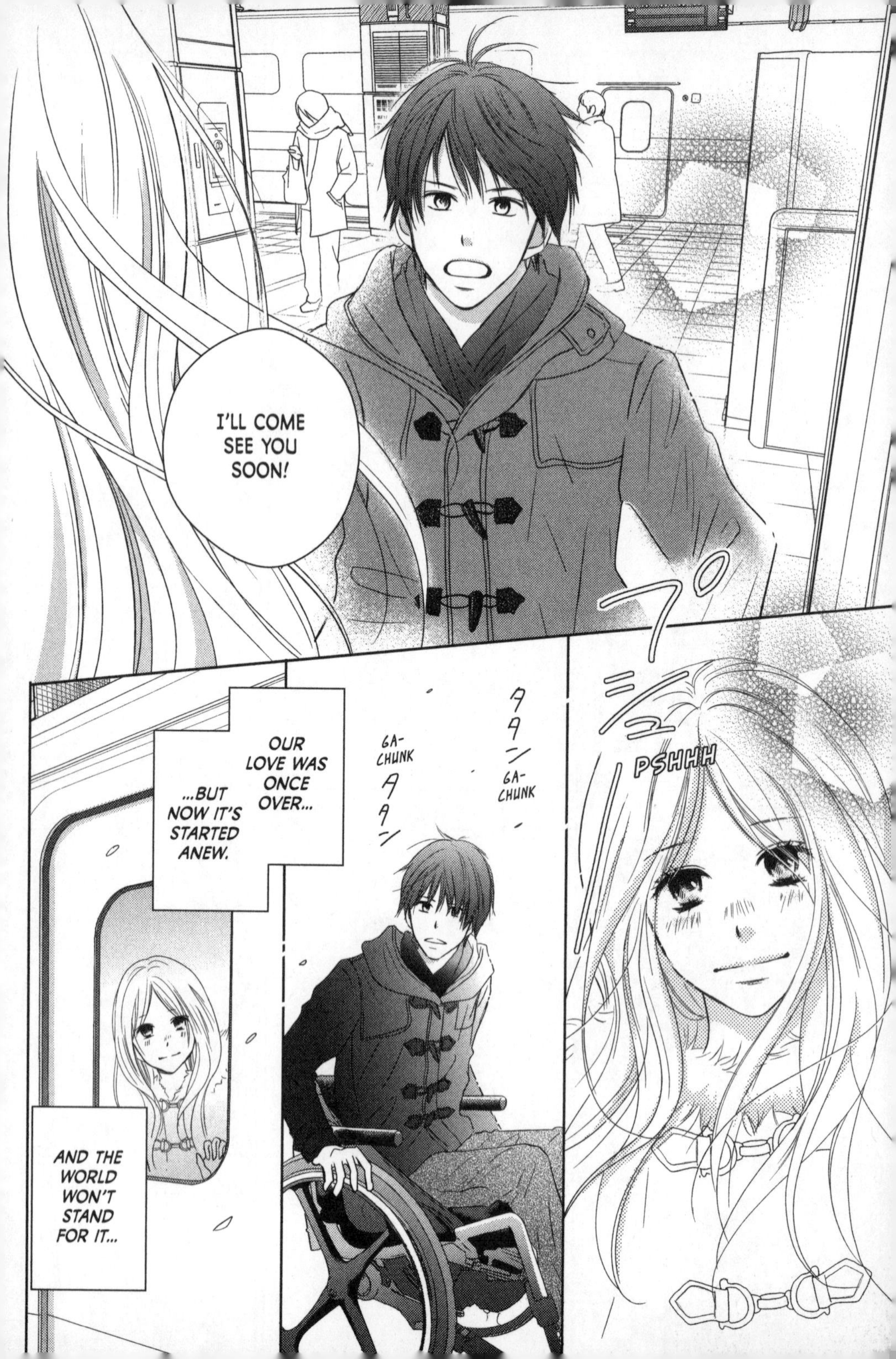
I'LL COME SEE YOU SOON!
プ
シュ
PSHHH
タタン
GA-CHUNK
タタン
GA-CHUNK
OUR LOVE WAS ONCE OVER...
...BUT NOW IT'S STARTED ANEW.
AND THE WORLD WON'T STAND FOR IT...

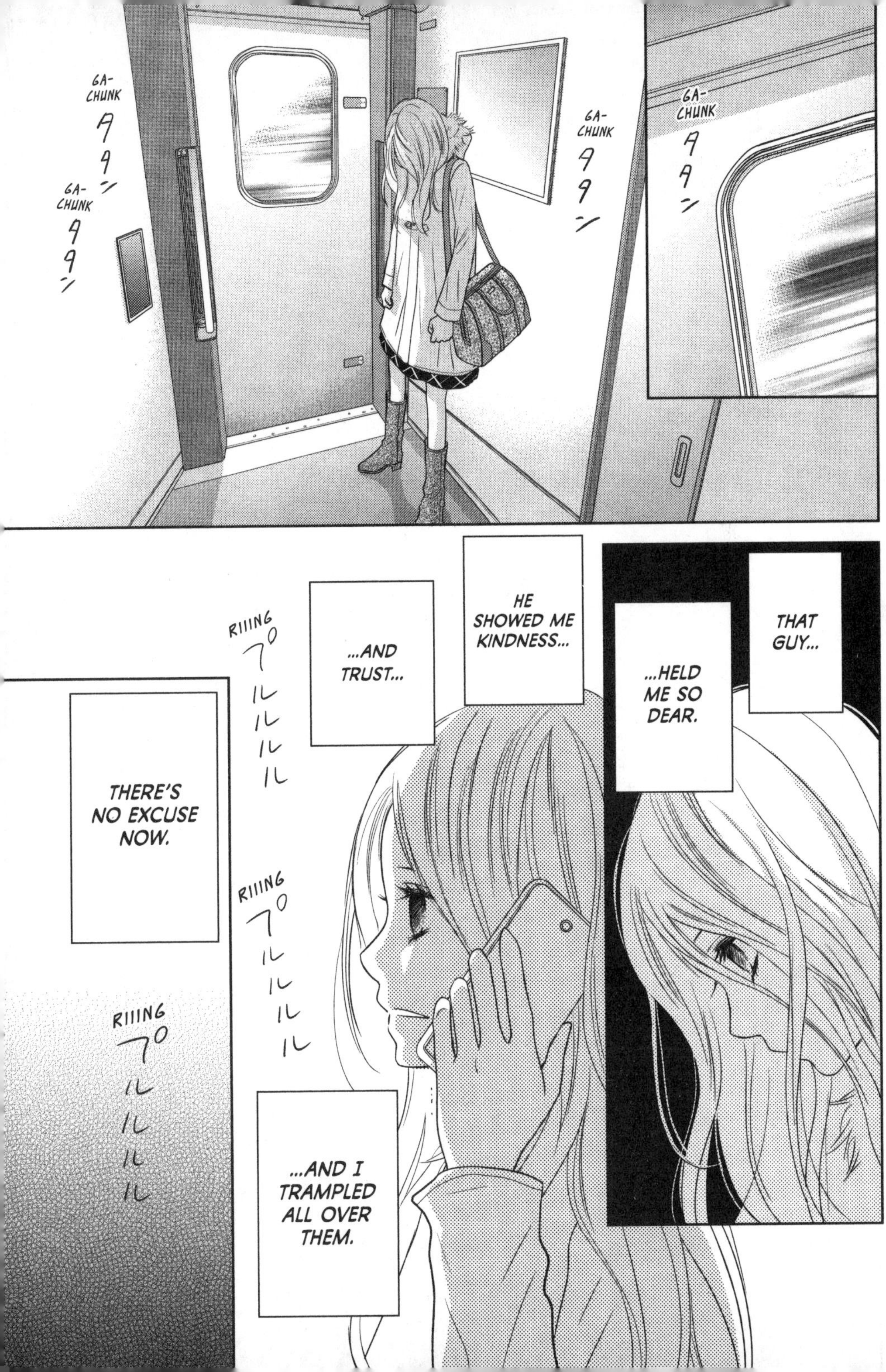
GA-CHUNK
タタン
GA-CHUNK
タタン
GA-CHUNK
タタン
GA-CHUNK
タタン
THAT GUY...
...HELD ME SO DEAR.
HE SHOWED ME KINDNESS...
...AND TRUST...
RIIING
プルルルル
...AND I TRAMPLED ALL OVER THEM.
RIIING
プルルルル
THERE'S NO EXCUSE NOW.
RIIING
プルルルル

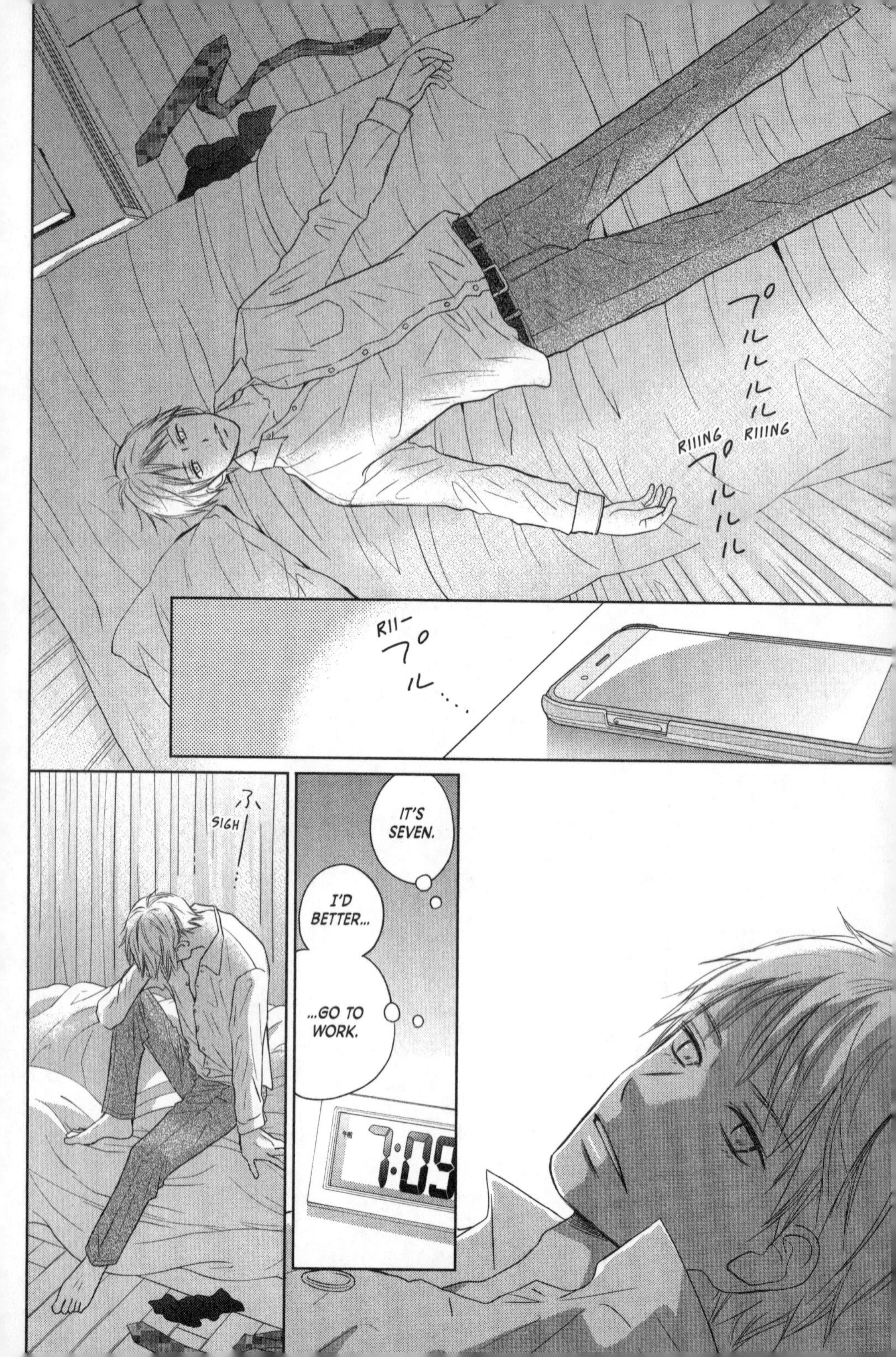
プルルルル
RIIING
プルルル
RIIING
RII-
プル…
IT'S SEVEN.
I'D BETTER...
...GO TO WORK.
ふ
SIGH

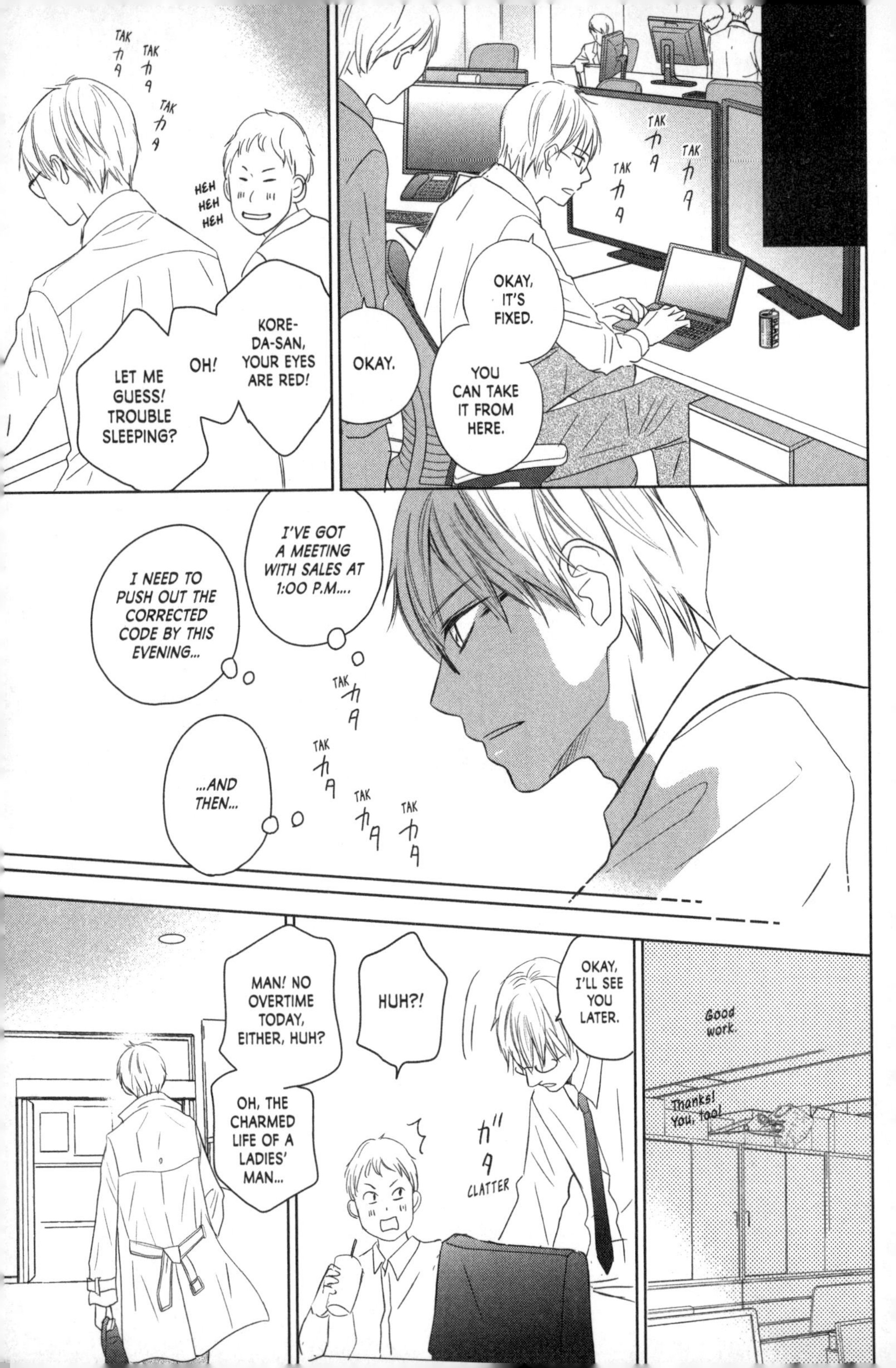
TAK
TAK
TAK
OKAY, IT'S FIXED.
YOU CAN TAKE IT FROM HERE.
OKAY.
TAK
TAK
TAK
HEH HEH HEH
KORE-DA-SAN, YOUR EYES ARE RED!
OH!
LET ME GUESS! TROUBLE SLEEPING?
I'VE GOT A MEETING WITH SALES AT 1:00 P.M....
I NEED TO PUSH OUT THE CORRECTED CODE BY THIS EVENING...
TAK
TAK
TAK
TAK
...AND THEN...
Good work.
Thanks! You, too!
OKAY, I'LL SEE YOU LATER.
HUH?!
MAN! NO OVERTIME TODAY, EITHER, HUH?
OH, THE CHARMED LIFE OF A LADIES' MAN...
CLATTER

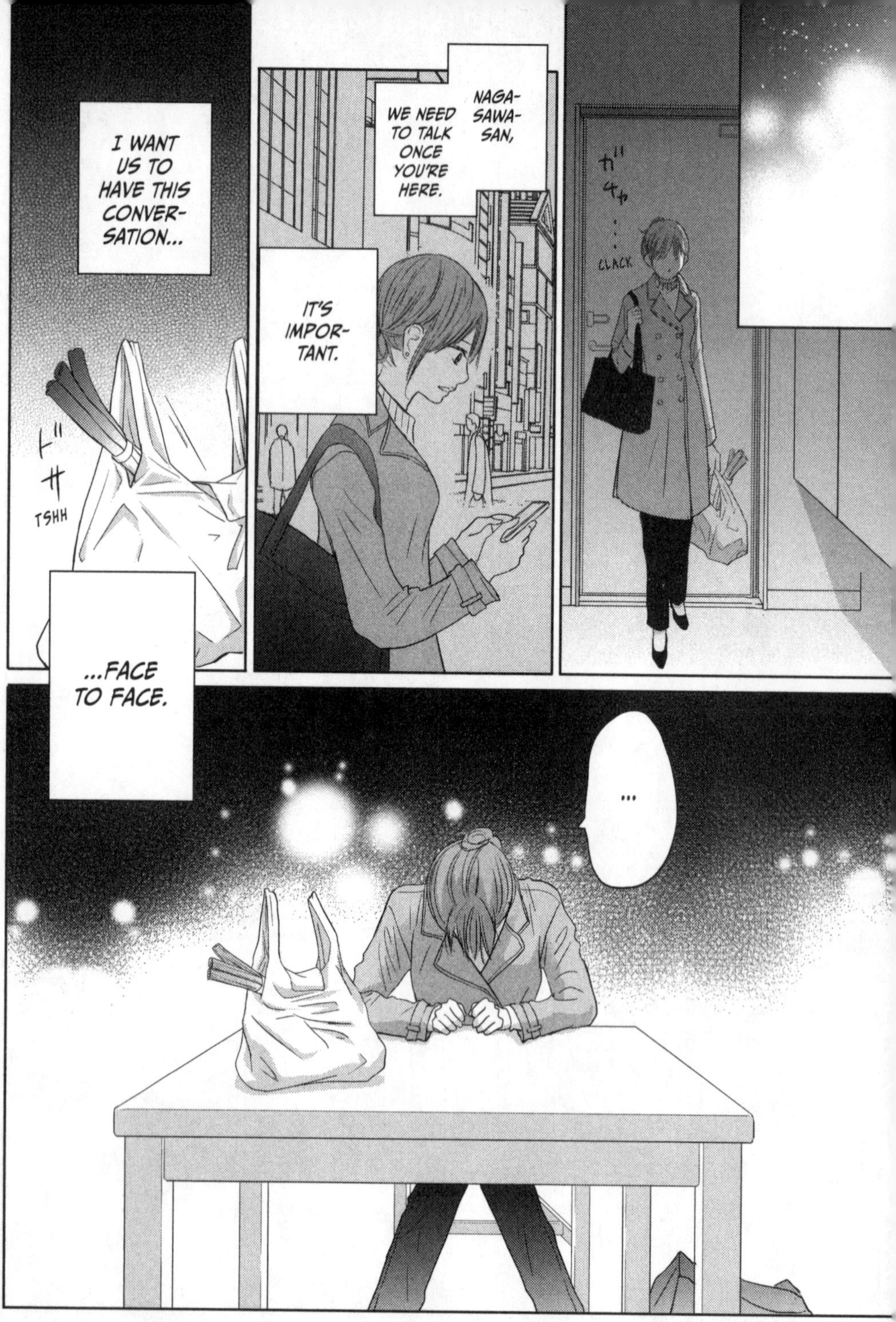
ガチャ
CLACK
NAGA-SAWA-SAN,
WE NEED TO TALK ONCE YOU'RE HERE.
IT'S IMPORTANT.
I WANT US TO HAVE THIS CONVER-SATION...
ドサ
TSHH
...FACE TO FACE.
...

I JUST GOT HERE, ITSUKI-KUN.

LET'S HAVE HOT POT WITH CHICKEN MEATBALLS FOR DINNER TONIGHT.

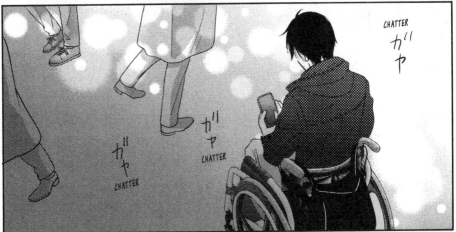

CHATTER
ガ
ヤ

ガ
ヤ
CHATTER

ガ
ヤ
CHATTER

C'mon! Let's go in already!

HA HA HA HA!

CHATTER
ガ
ヤ
CHATTER
ガ
ヤ

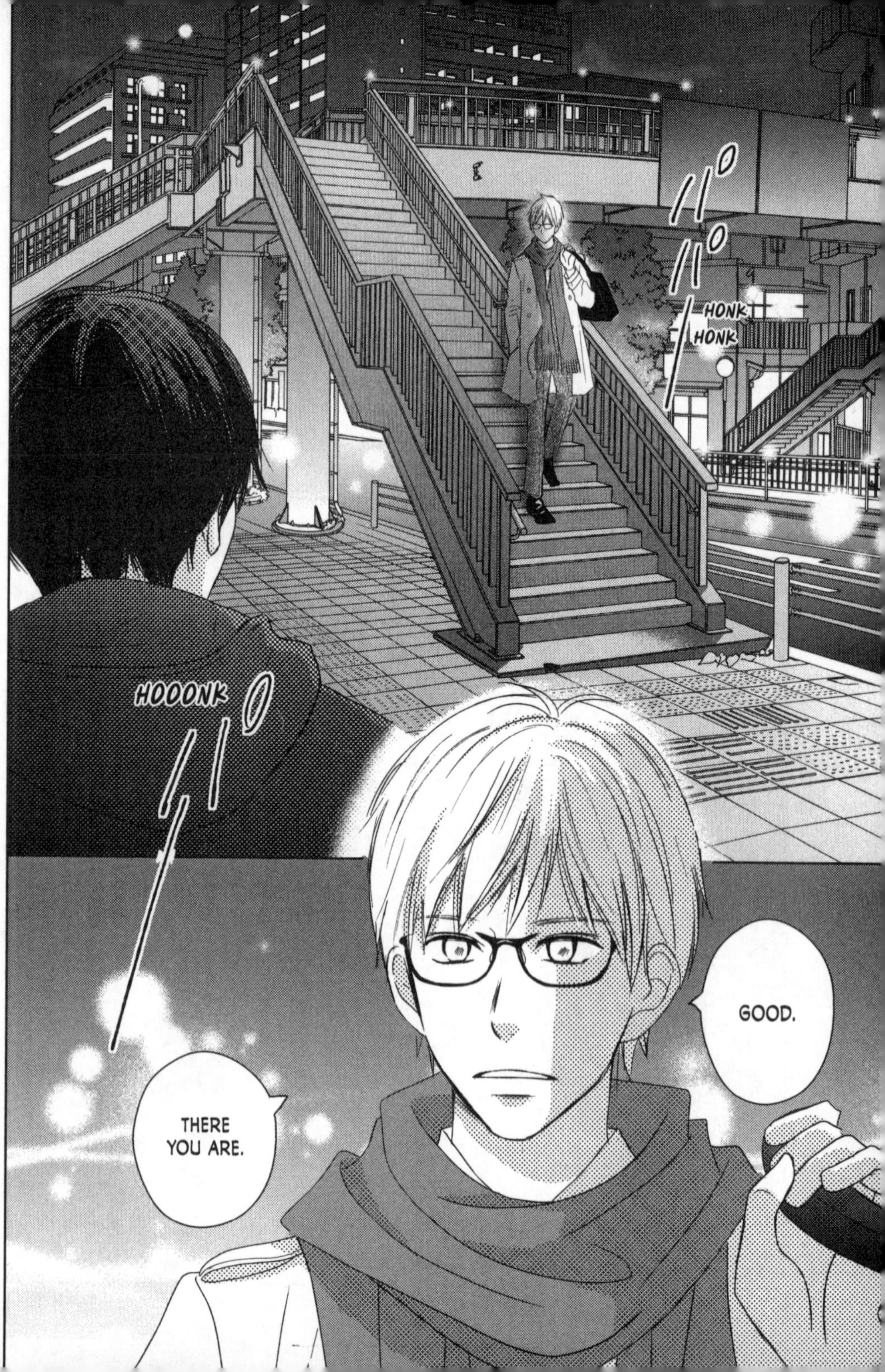
HONK
HONK
HOOONK
GOOD.
THERE YOU ARE.

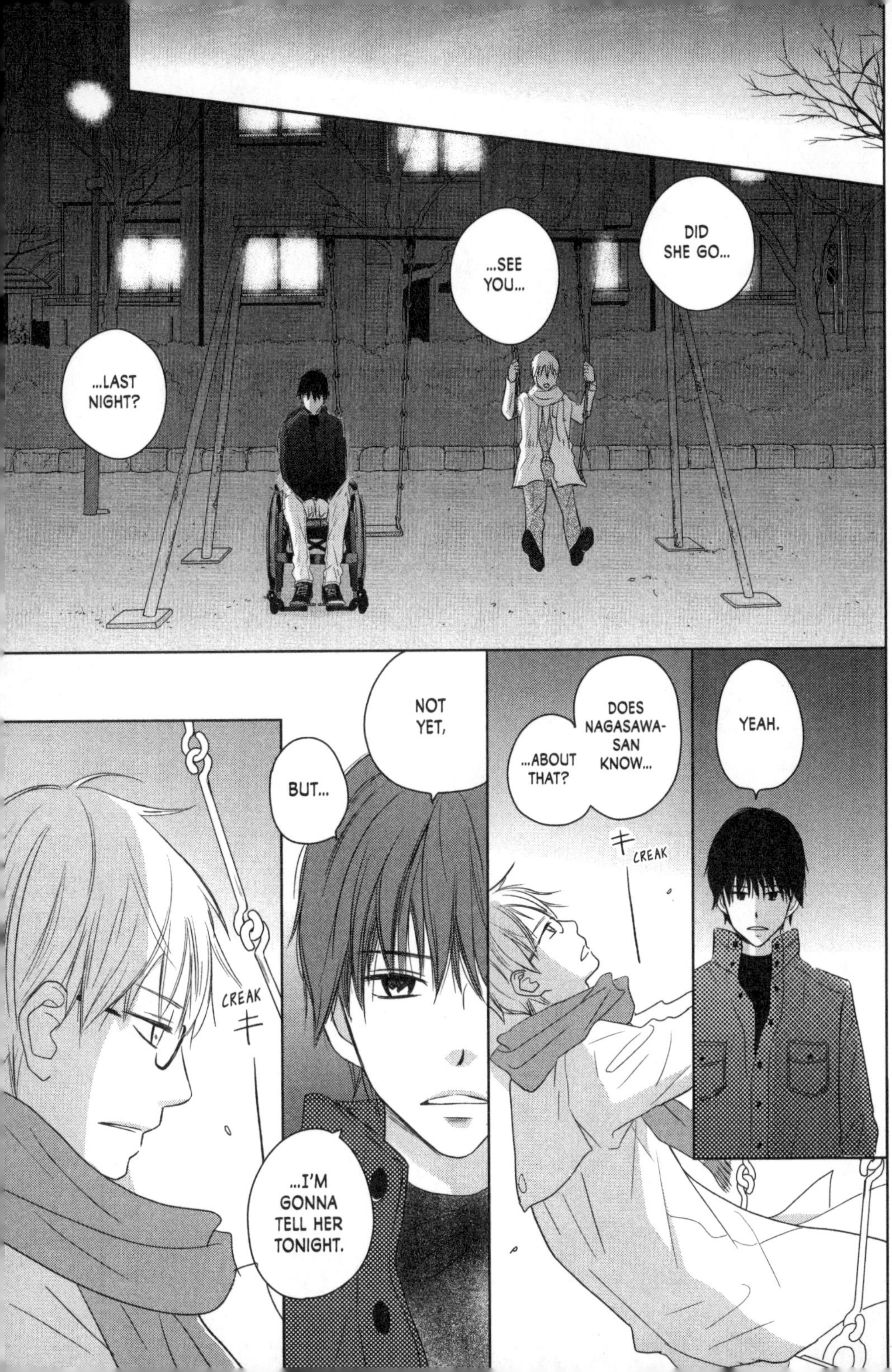
DID SHE GO...
...SEE YOU...
...LAST NIGHT?
YEAH.
DOES NAGASAWA-SAN KNOW...
...ABOUT THAT?
CREAK
NOT YET,
BUT...
CREAK
...I'M GONNA TELL HER TONIGHT.

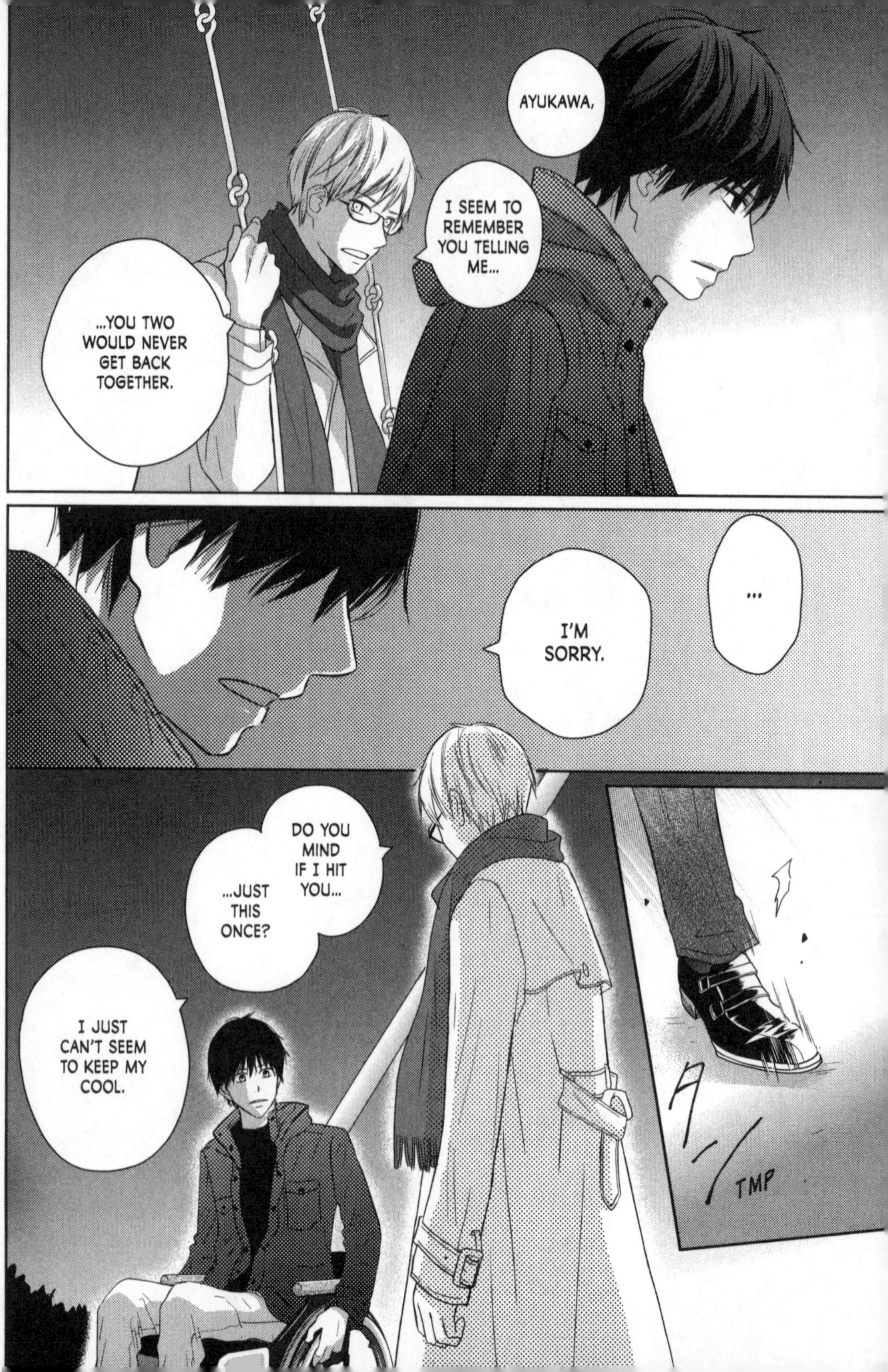
AYUKAWA,
I SEEM TO REMEMBER YOU TELLING ME...
...YOU TWO WOULD NEVER GET BACK TOGETHER.
...
I'M SORRY.
TMP
DO YOU MIND IF I HIT YOU...
...JUST THIS ONCE?
I JUST CAN'T SEEM TO KEEP MY COOL.

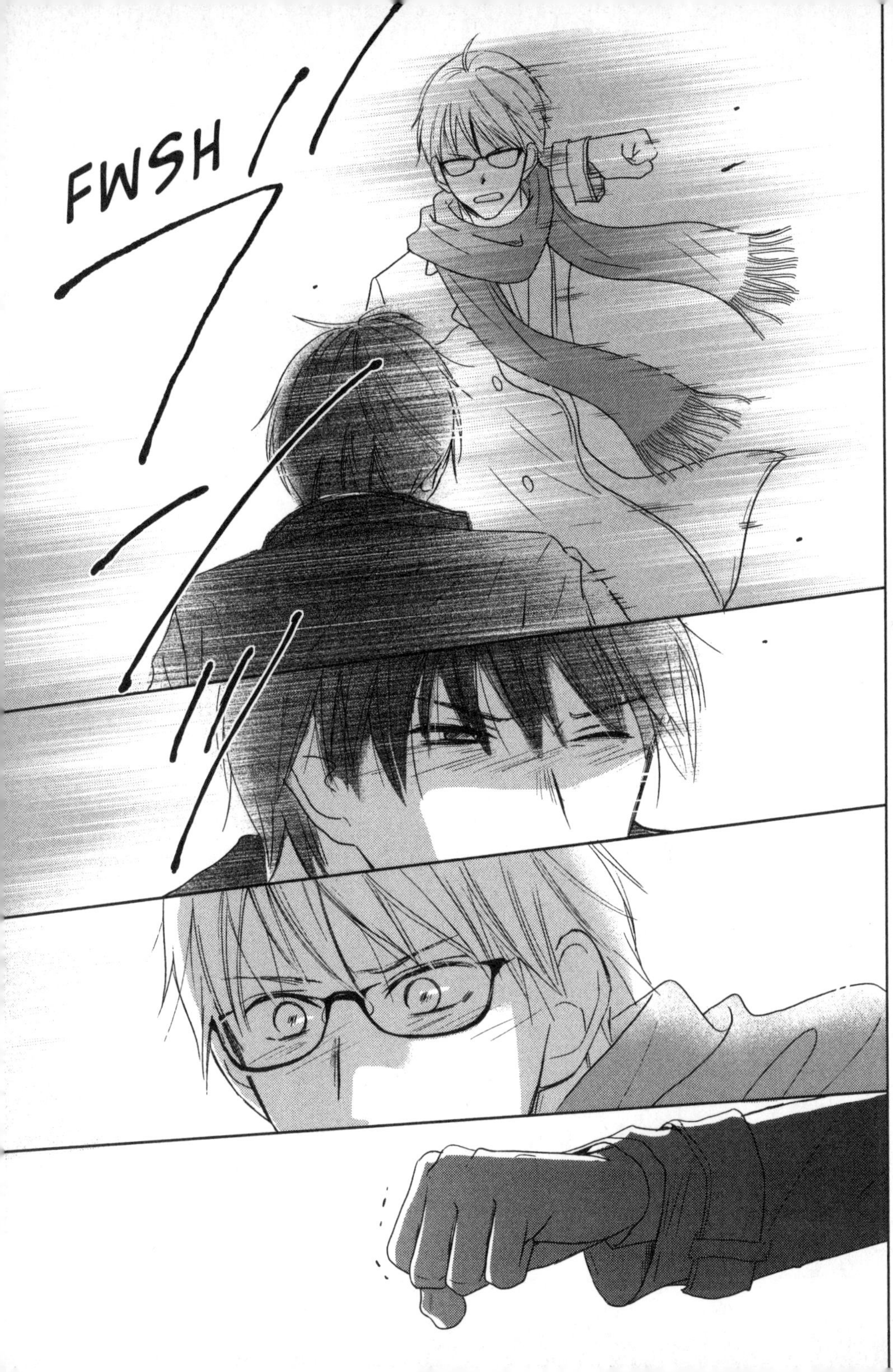
FWSH

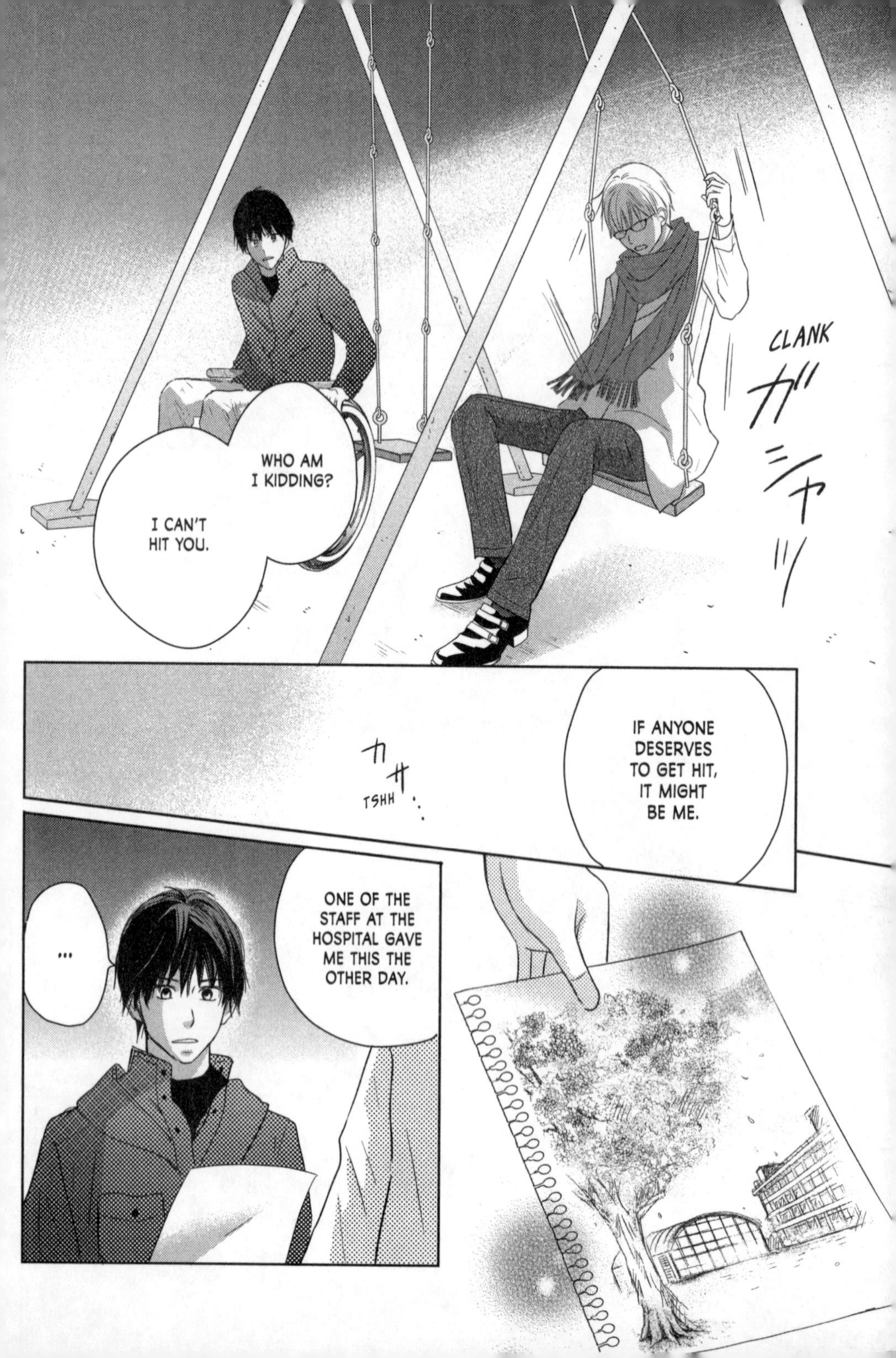
CLANK
ガシャッ
WHO AM I KIDDING?
I CAN'T HIT YOU.
IF ANYONE DESERVES TO GET HIT, IT MIGHT BE ME.
カサ
TSHH
ONE OF THE STAFF AT THE HOSPITAL GAVE ME THIS THE OTHER DAY.
...

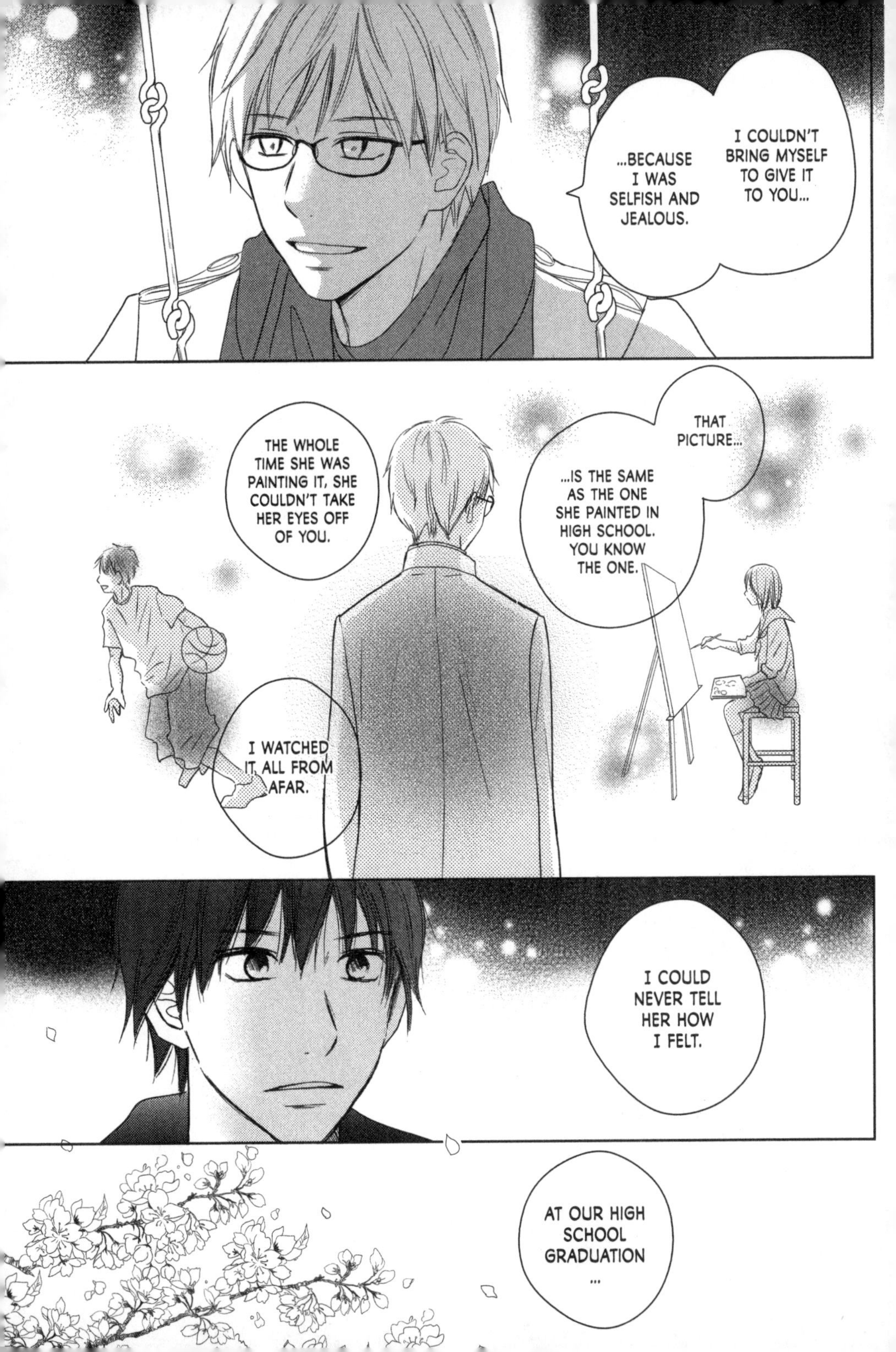
I COULDN'T BRING MYSELF TO GIVE IT TO YOU...
...BECAUSE I WAS SELFISH AND JEALOUS.
THAT PICTURE...
...IS THE SAME AS THE ONE SHE PAINTED IN HIGH SCHOOL. YOU KNOW THE ONE.
THE WHOLE TIME SHE WAS PAINTING IT, SHE COULDN'T TAKE HER EYES OFF OF YOU.
I WATCHED IT ALL FROM AFAR.
I COULD NEVER TELL HER HOW I FELT.
AT OUR HIGH SCHOOL GRADUATION...

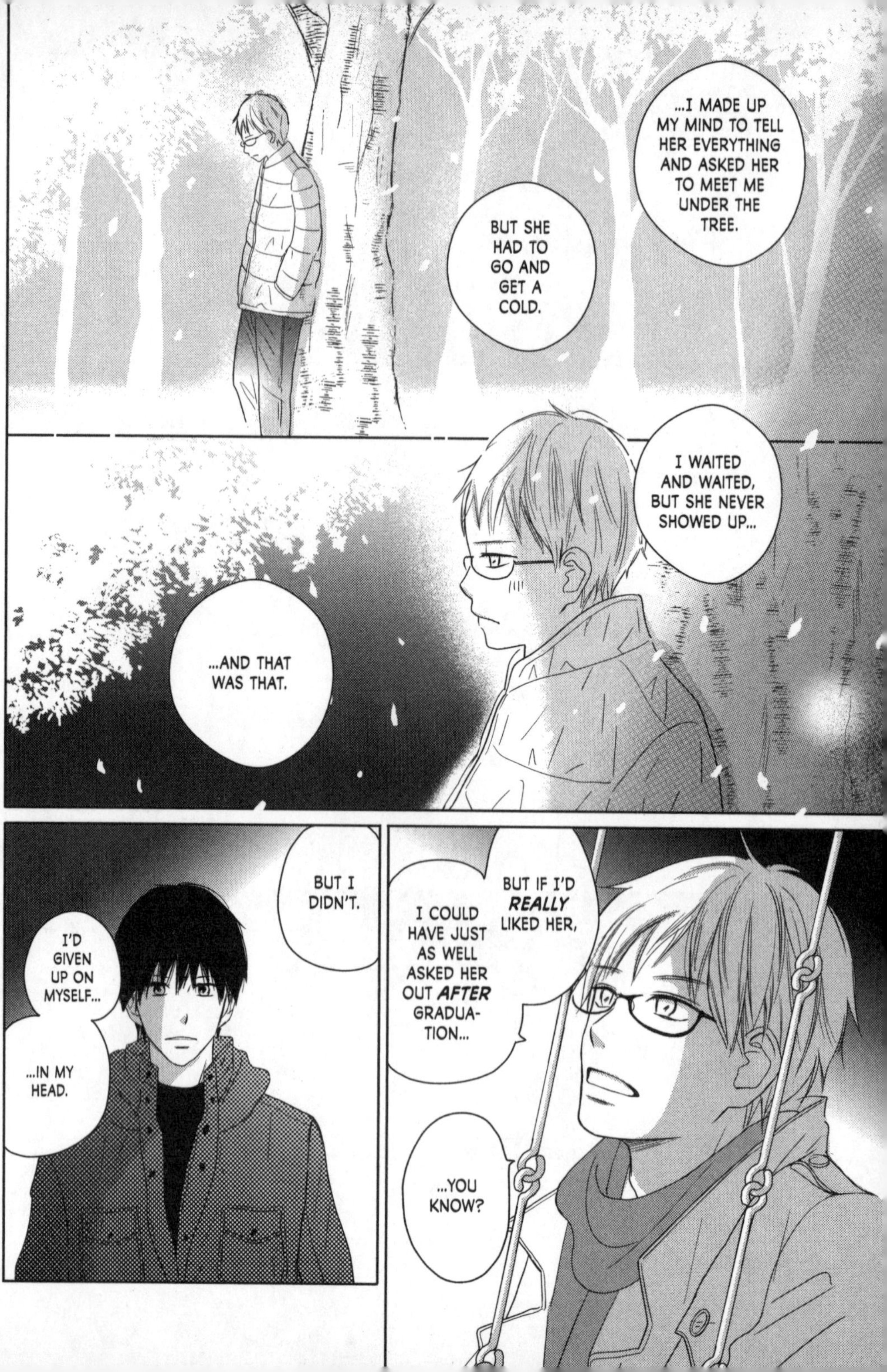
...I MADE UP MY MIND TO TELL HER EVERYTHING AND ASKED HER TO MEET ME UNDER THE TREE.
BUT SHE HAD TO GO AND GET A COLD.
I WAITED AND WAITED, BUT SHE NEVER SHOWED UP...
...AND THAT WAS THAT.
BUT IF I'D *REALLY* LIKED HER,
I COULD HAVE JUST AS WELL ASKED HER OUT *AFTER* GRADUATION...
...YOU KNOW?
BUT I DIDN'T.
I'D GIVEN UP ON MYSELF...
...IN MY HEAD.

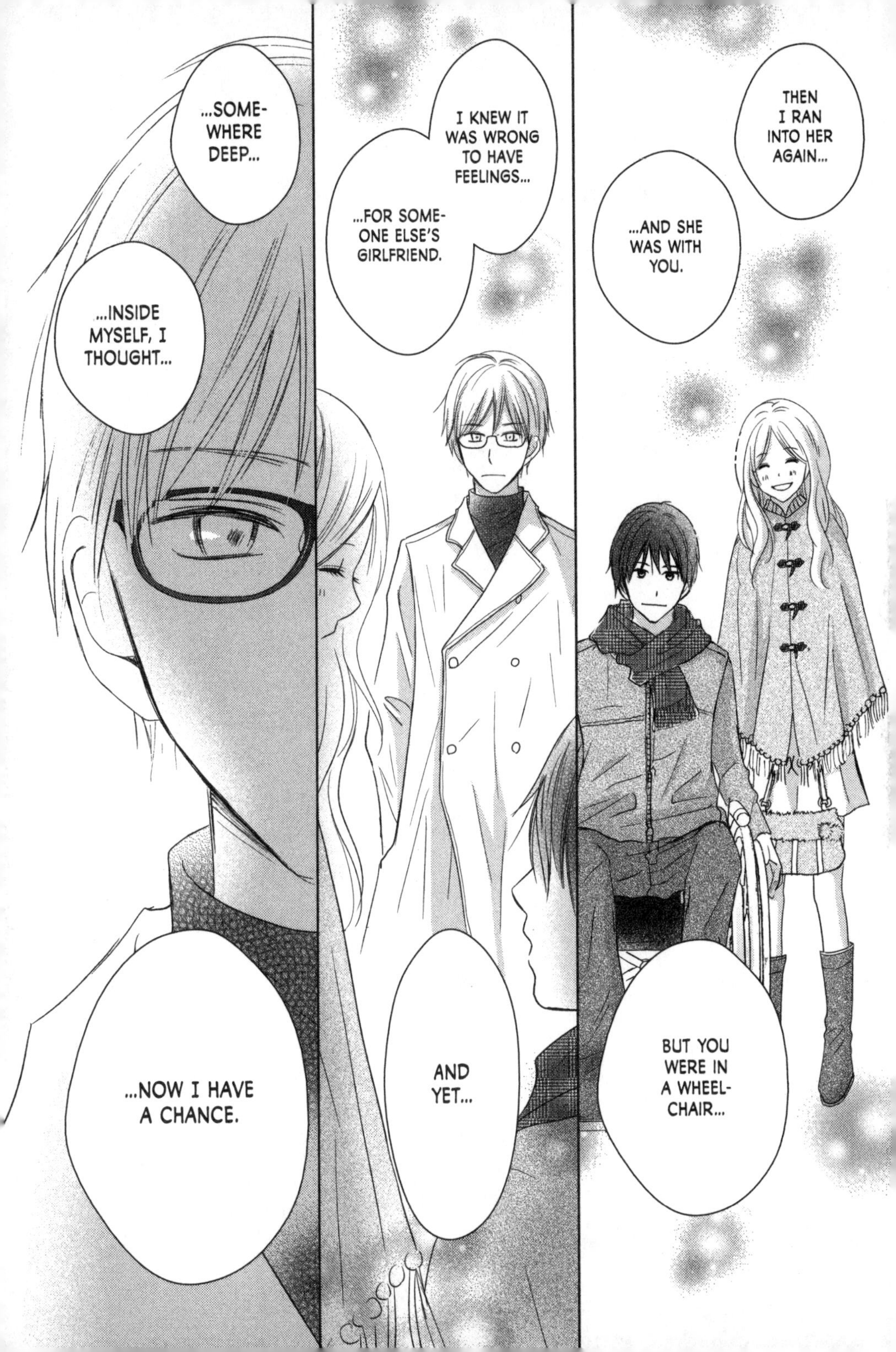
THEN I RAN INTO HER AGAIN...
...AND SHE WAS WITH YOU.
BUT YOU WERE IN A WHEEL-CHAIR...
I KNEW IT WAS WRONG TO HAVE FEELINGS...
...FOR SOME-ONE ELSE'S GIRLFRIEND.
AND YET...
...SOME-WHERE DEEP...
...INSIDE MYSELF, I THOUGHT...
...NOW I HAVE A CHANCE.

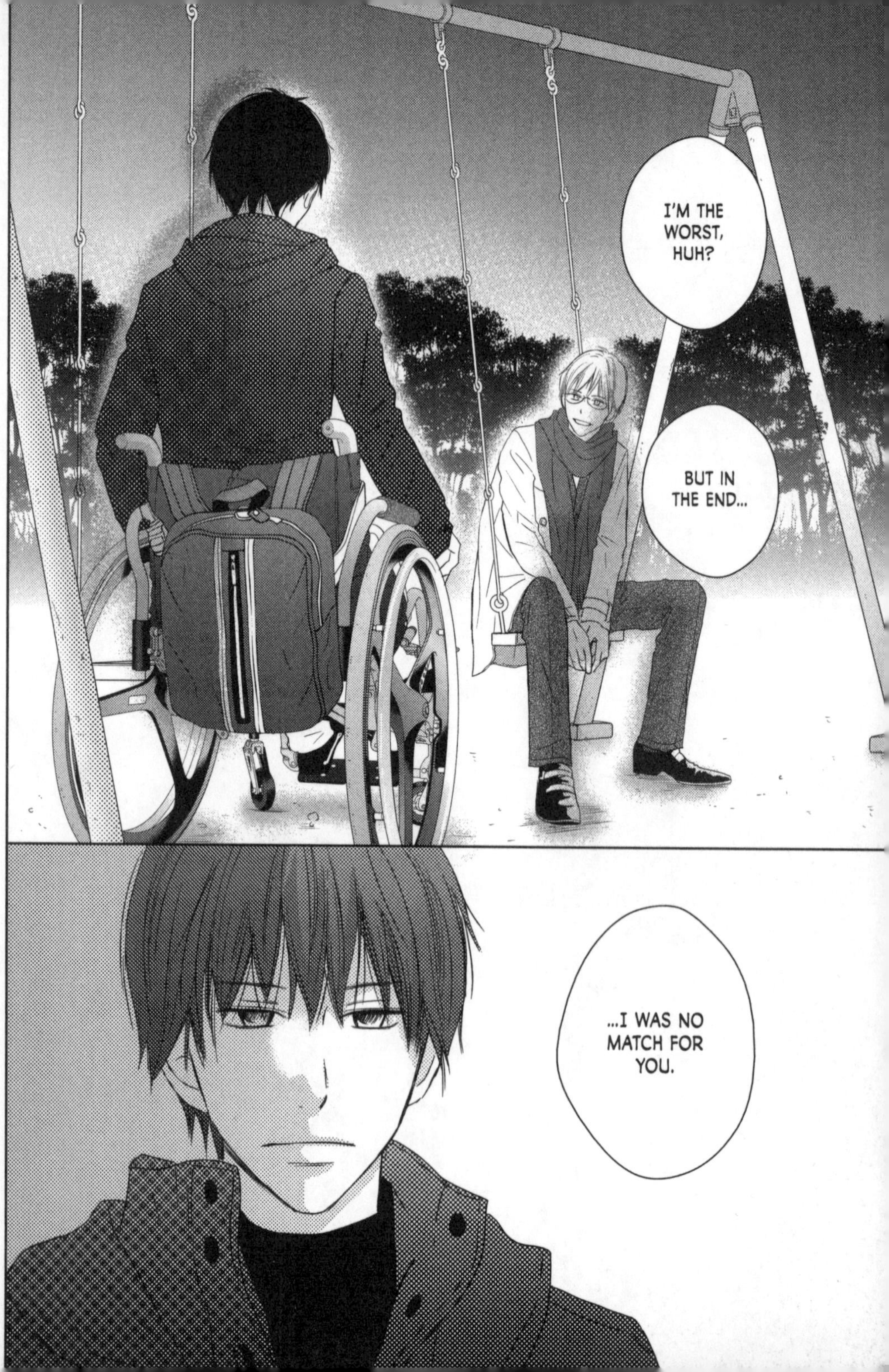
I'M THE WORST, HUH?
BUT IN THE END...
...I WAS NO MATCH FOR YOU.

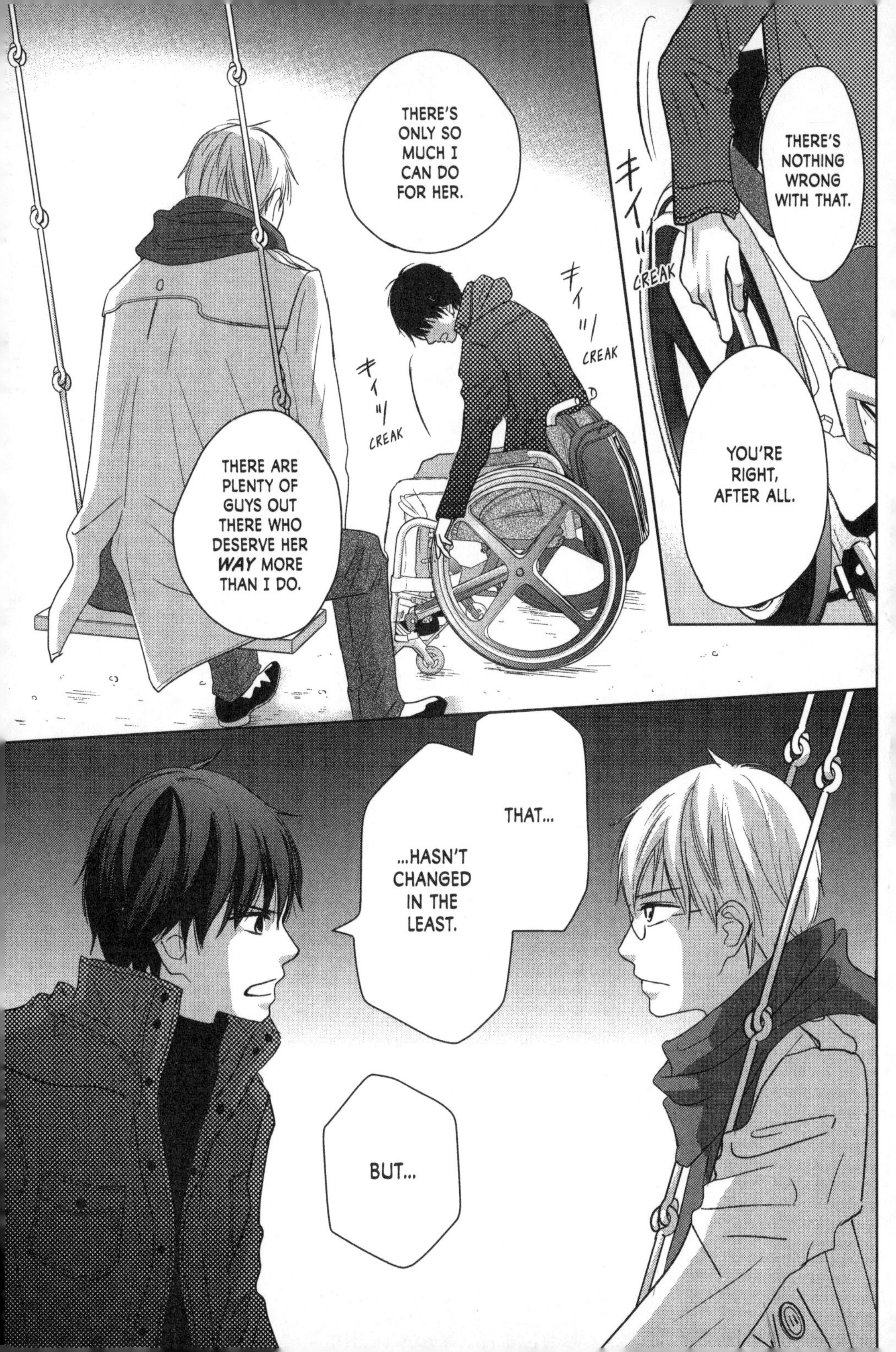

THERE'S NOTHING WRONG WITH THAT.
CREAK
YOU'RE RIGHT, AFTER ALL.
THERE'S ONLY SO MUCH I CAN DO FOR HER.
CREAK
CREAK
THERE ARE PLENTY OF GUYS OUT THERE WHO DESERVE HER *WAY* MORE THAN I DO.
THAT...
...HASN'T CHANGED IN THE LEAST.
BUT...

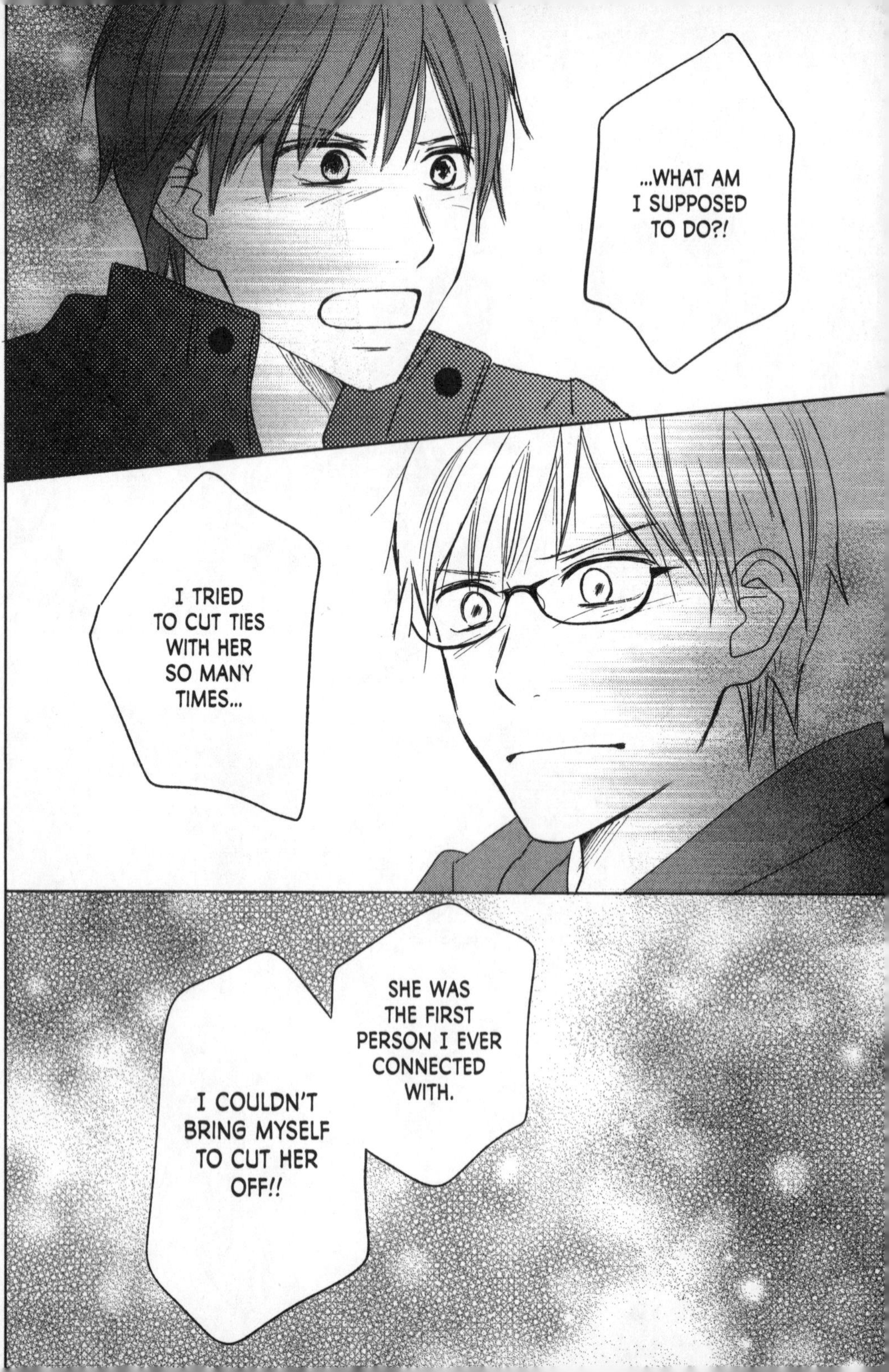
...WHAT AM I SUPPOSED TO DO?!
I TRIED TO CUT TIES WITH HER SO MANY TIMES...
SHE WAS THE FIRST PERSON I EVER CONNECTED WITH.
I COULDN'T BRING MYSELF TO CUT HER OFF!!

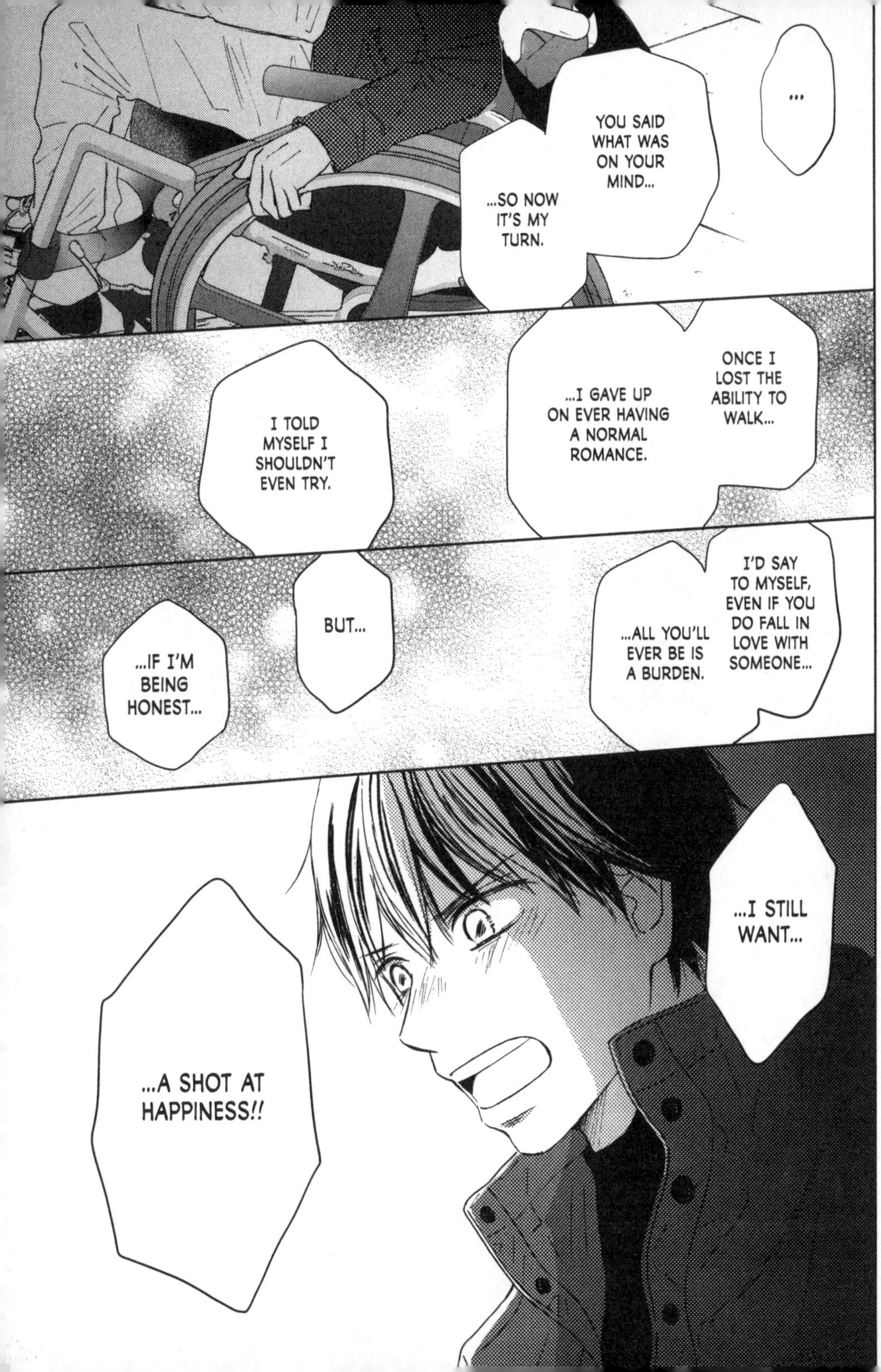
...
YOU SAID WHAT WAS ON YOUR MIND...
...SO NOW IT'S MY TURN.
ONCE I LOST THE ABILITY TO WALK...
...I GAVE UP ON EVER HAVING A NORMAL ROMANCE.
I TOLD MYSELF I SHOULDN'T EVEN TRY.
I'D SAY TO MYSELF, EVEN IF YOU DO FALL IN LOVE WITH SOMEONE...
...ALL YOU'LL EVER BE IS A BURDEN.
BUT...
...IF I'M BEING HONEST...
...I STILL WANT...
...A SHOT AT HAPPINESS!!

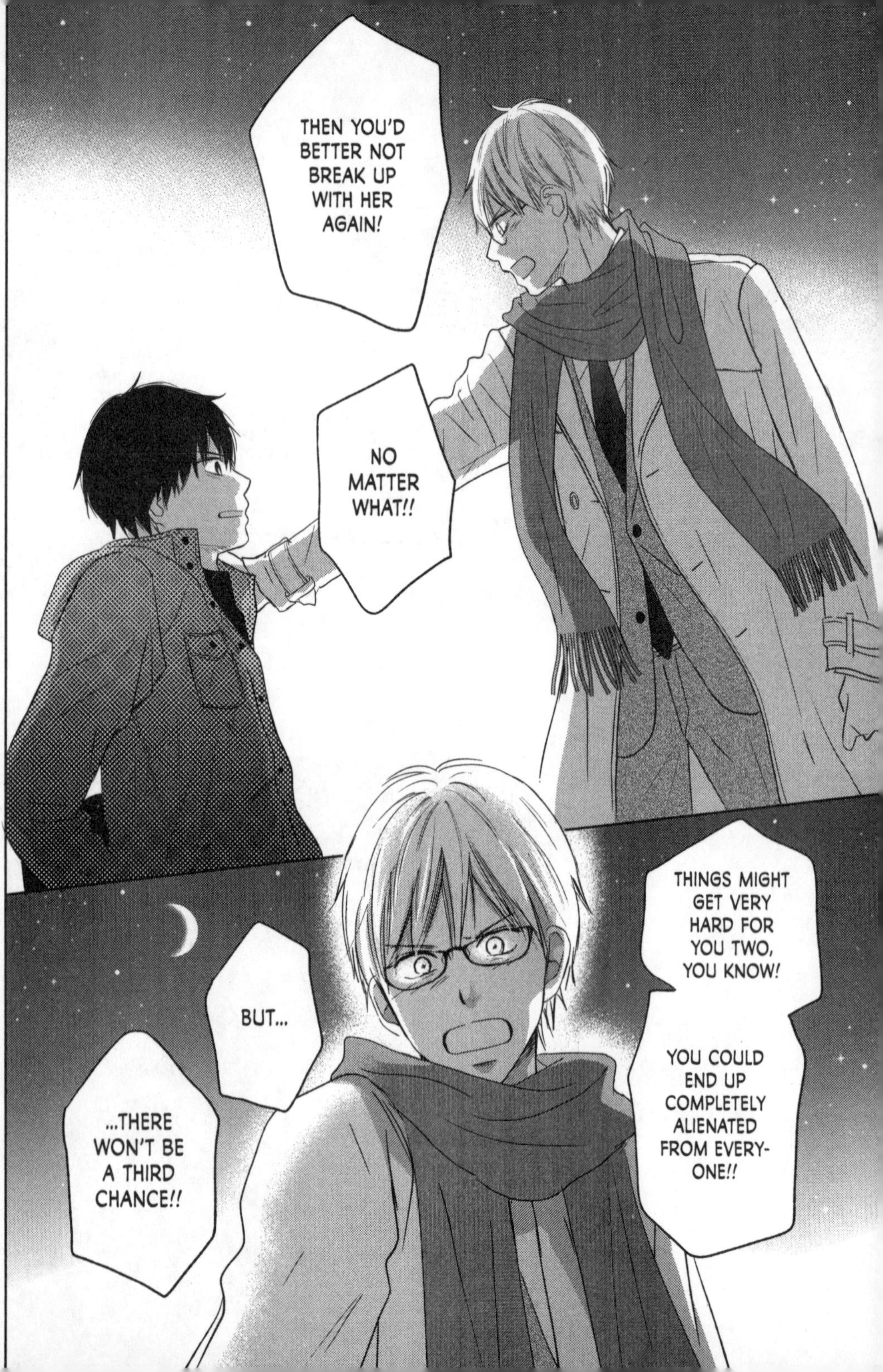
THEN YOU'D BETTER NOT BREAK UP WITH HER AGAIN!
NO MATTER WHAT!!
THINGS MIGHT GET VERY HARD FOR YOU TWO, YOU KNOW!
YOU COULD END UP COMPLETELY ALIENATED FROM EVERY-ONE!!
BUT...
...THERE WON'T BE A THIRD CHANCE!!

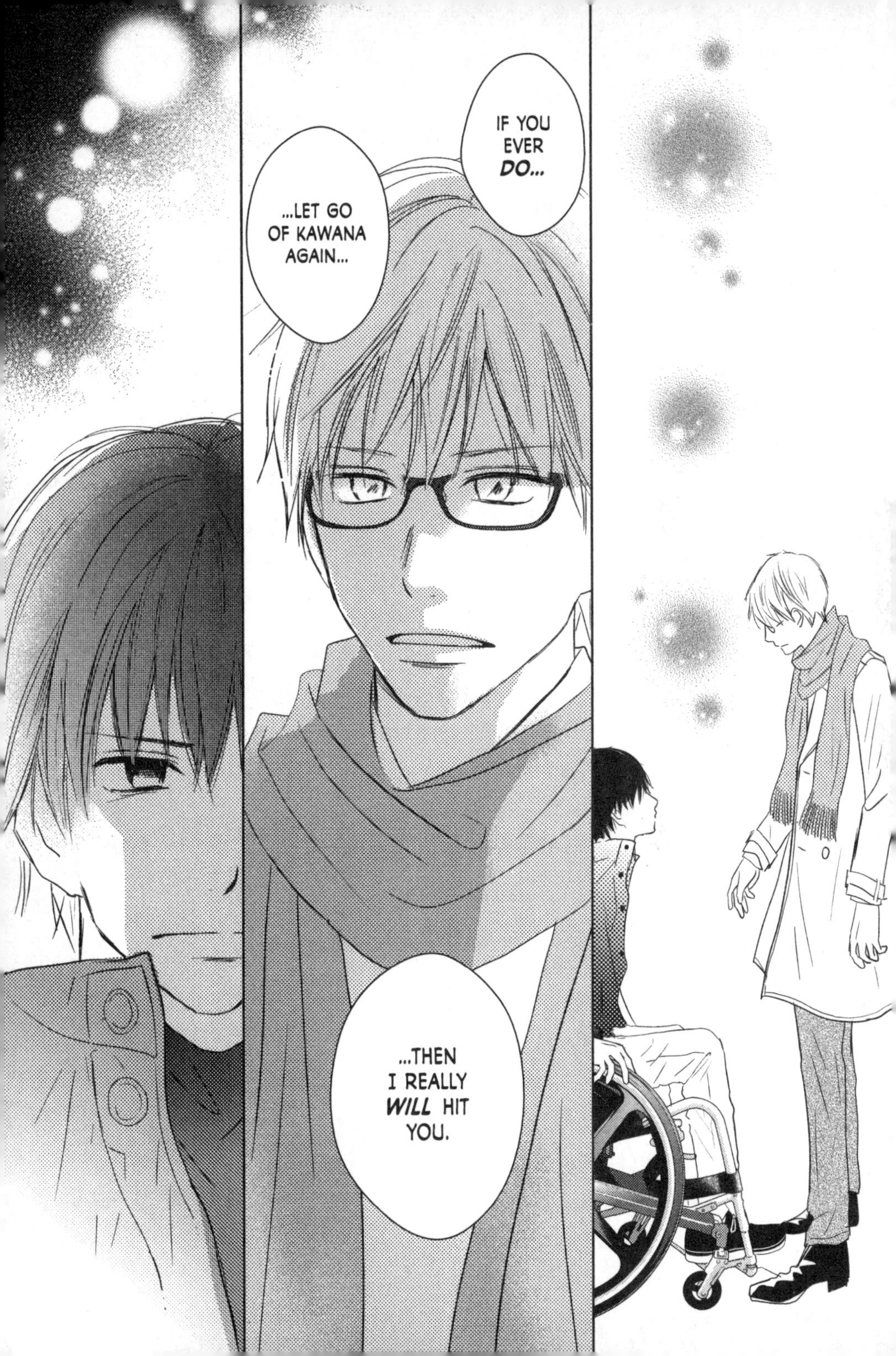
IF YOU EVER *DO*...
...LET GO OF KAWANA AGAIN...
...THEN I REALLY *WILL* HIT YOU.

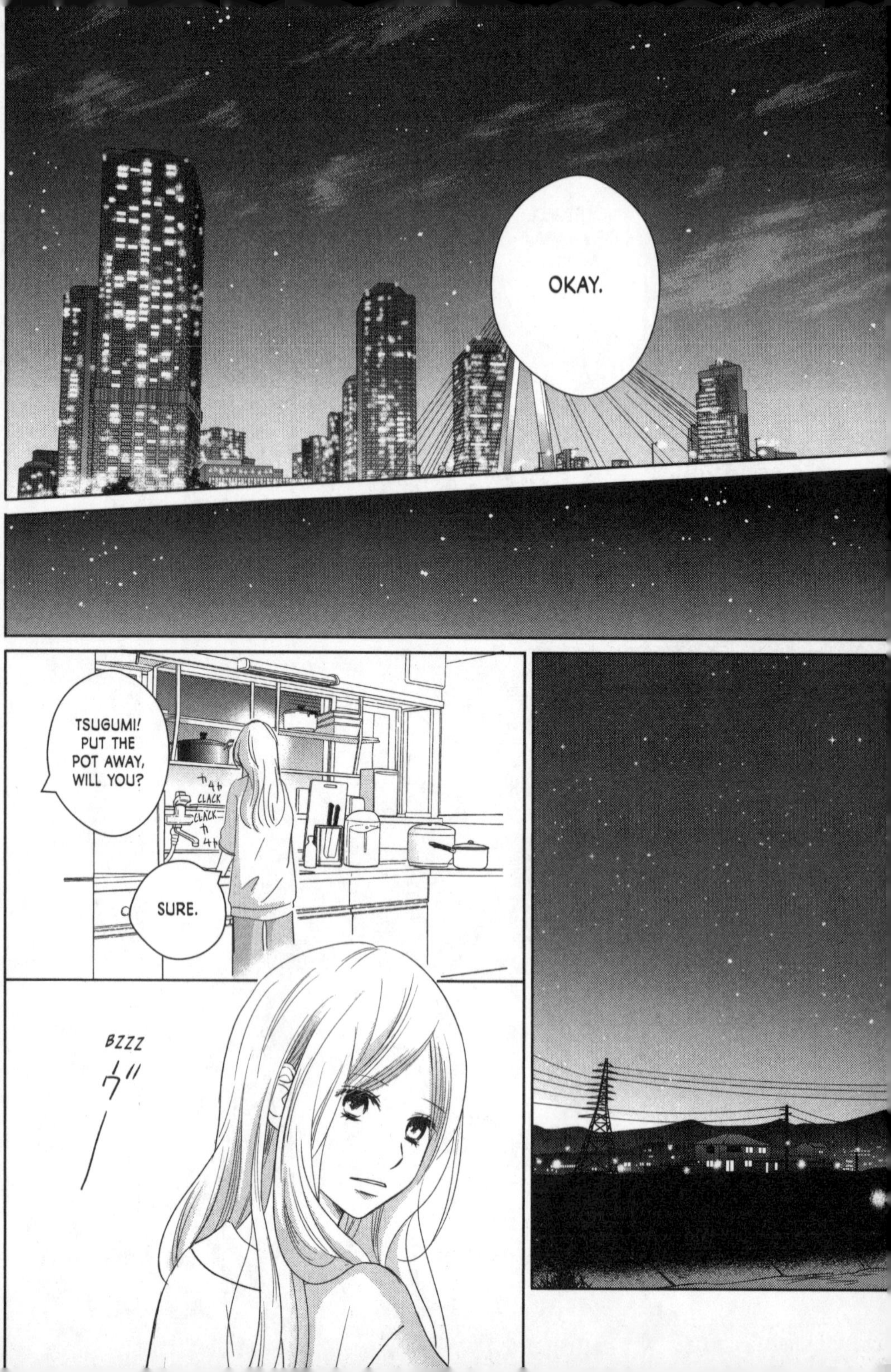
OKAY.
TSUGUMI! PUT THE POT AWAY, WILL YOU?
CLACK
CLACK
SURE.
BZZZ

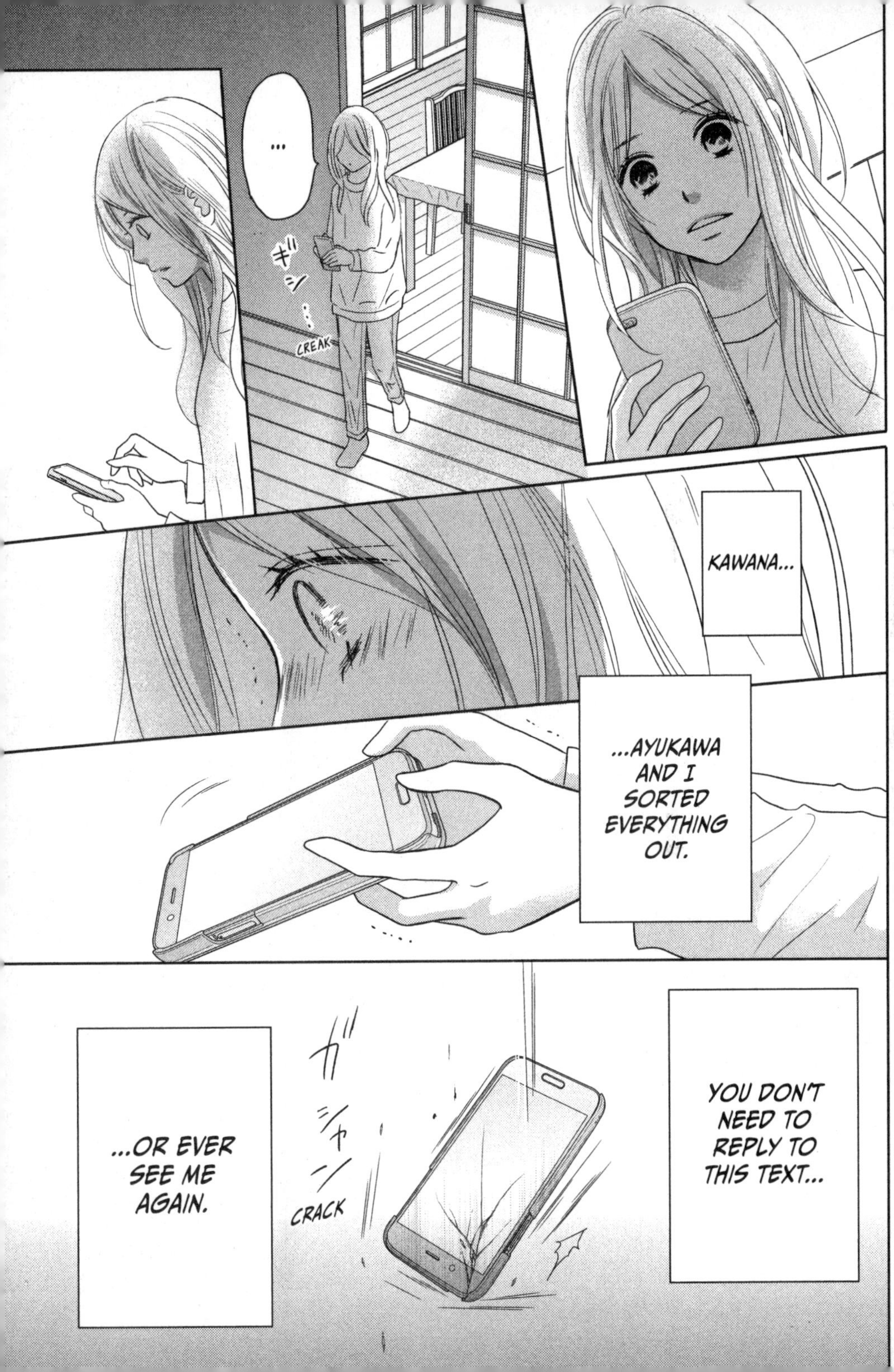
...
ギシ
CREAK
KAWANA...
...AYUKAWA AND I SORTED EVERYTHING OUT.
YOU DON'T NEED TO REPLY TO THIS TEXT...
ガシャーン
CRACK
...OR EVER SEE ME AGAIN.

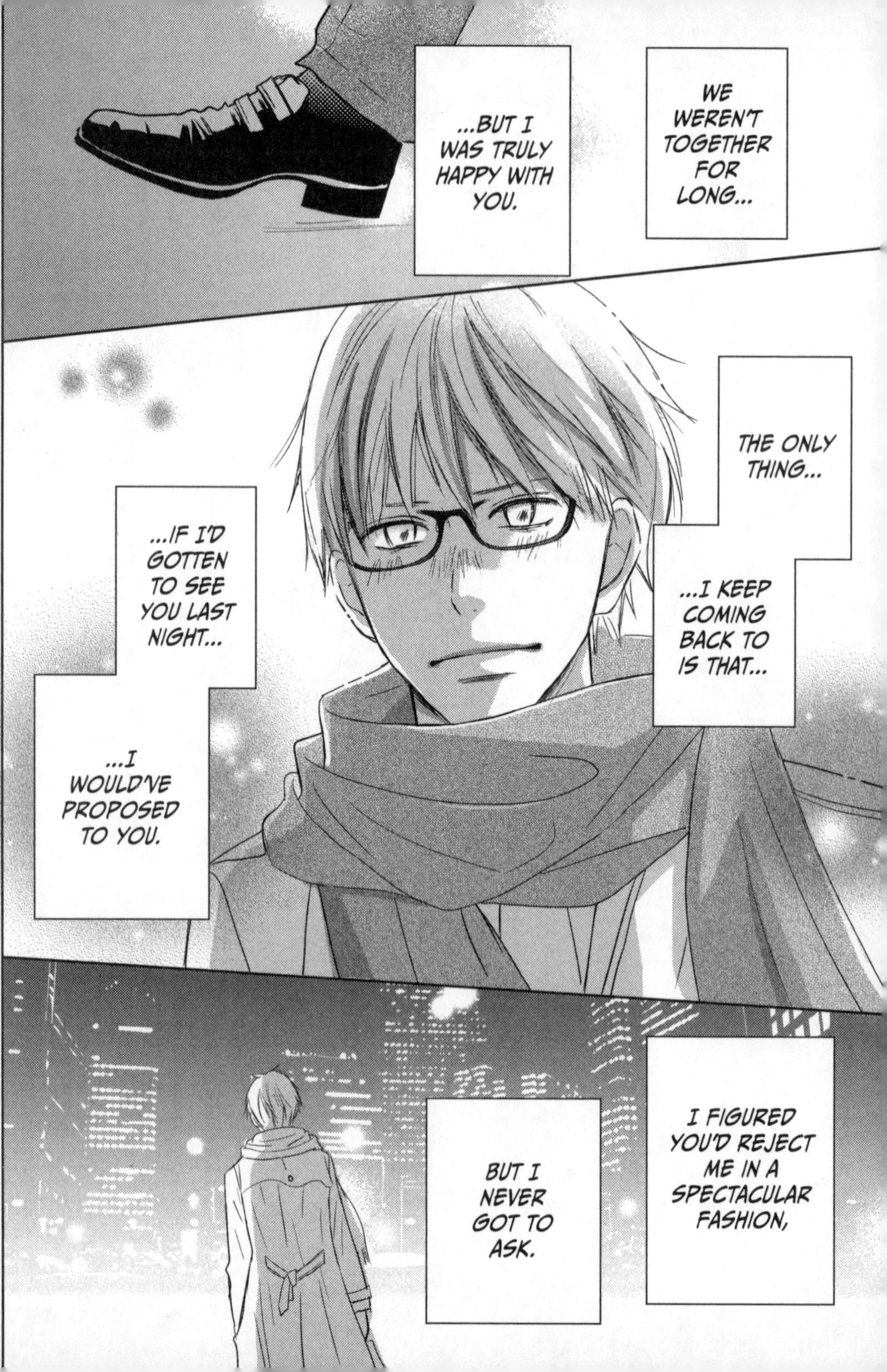
WE WEREN'T TOGETHER FOR LONG...
...BUT I WAS TRULY HAPPY WITH YOU.
THE ONLY THING...
...I KEEP COMING BACK TO IS THAT...
...IF I'D GOTTEN TO SEE YOU LAST NIGHT...
...I WOULD'VE PROPOSED TO YOU.
I FIGURED YOU'D REJECT ME IN A SPECTACULAR FASHION,
BUT I NEVER GOT TO ASK.

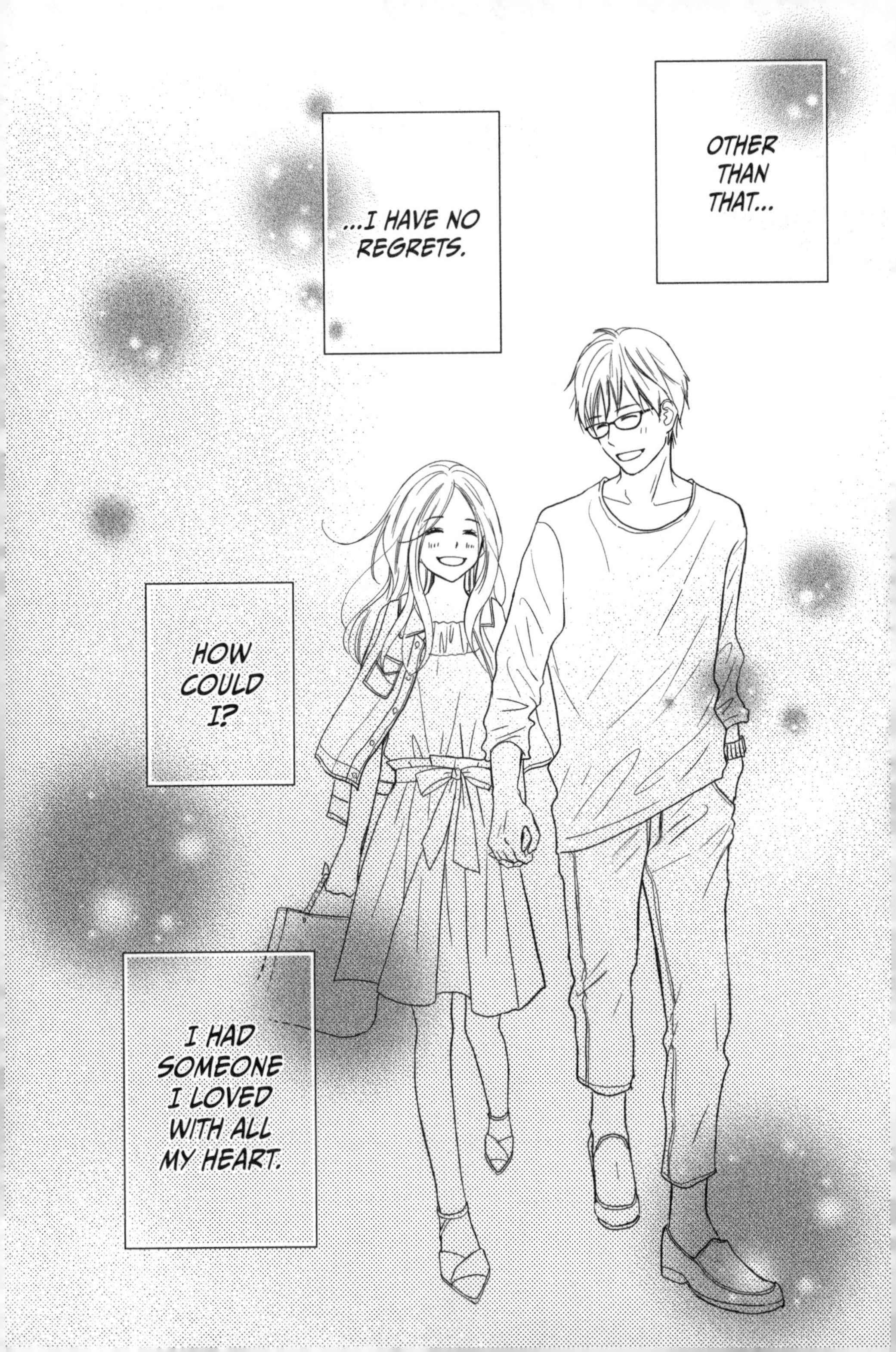
OTHER THAN THAT...
...I HAVE NO REGRETS.
HOW COULD I?
I HAD SOMEONE I LOVED WITH ALL MY HEART.

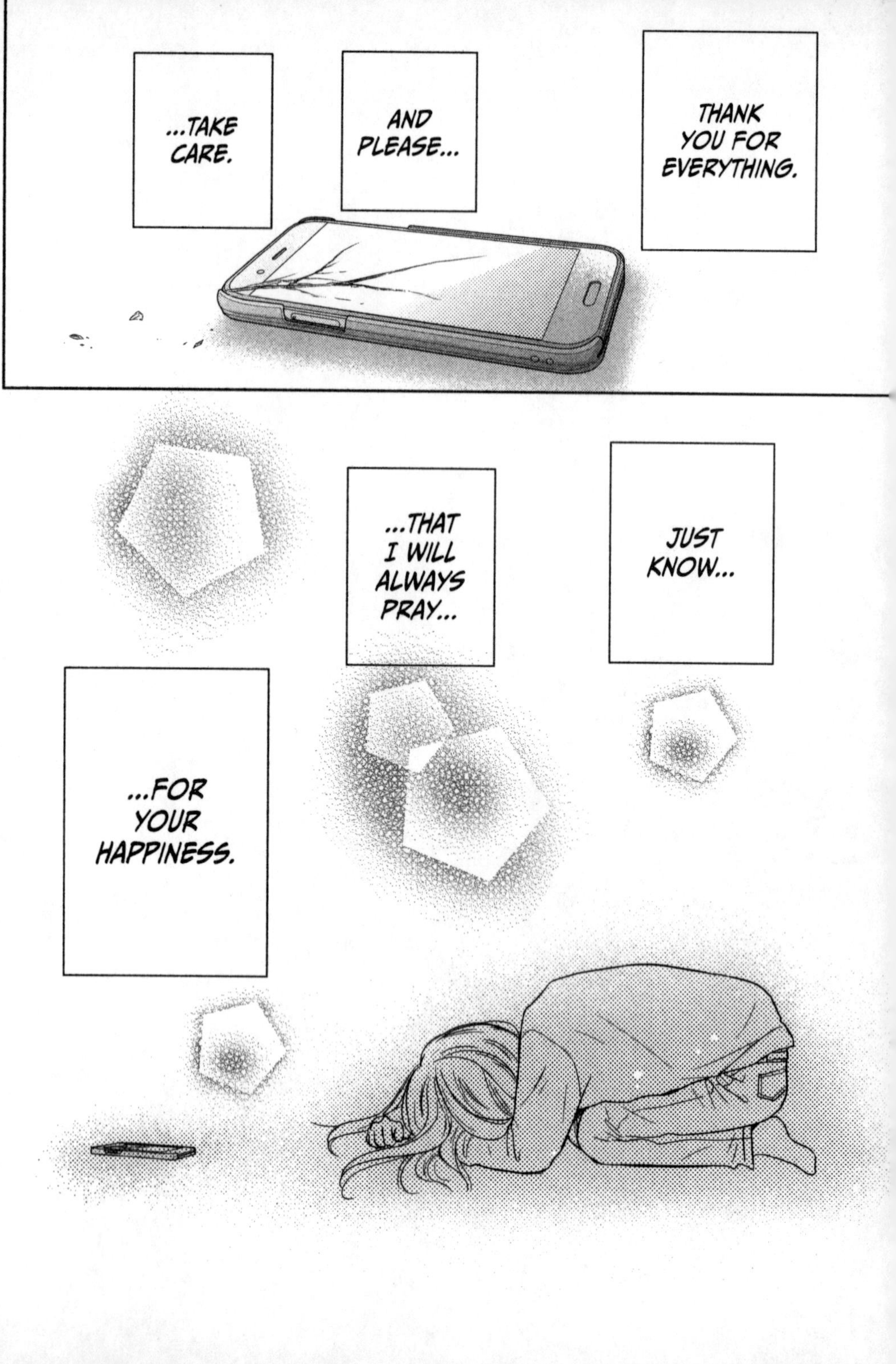
THANK YOU FOR EVERYTHING.
AND PLEASE...
...TAKE CARE.
JUST KNOW...
...THAT I WILL ALWAYS PRAY...
...FOR YOUR HAPPINESS.

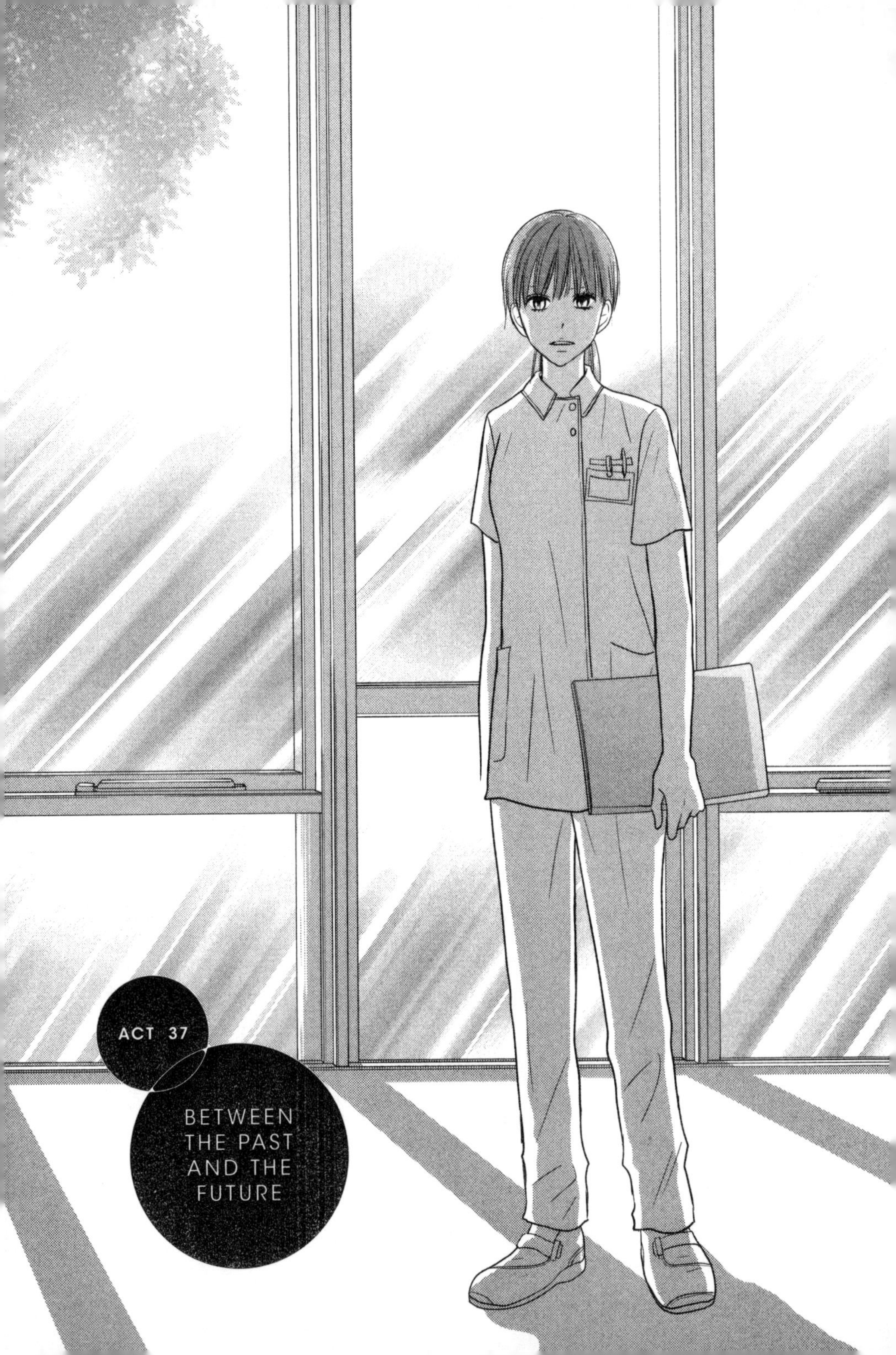
ACT 37
BETWEEN THE PAST AND THE FUTURE

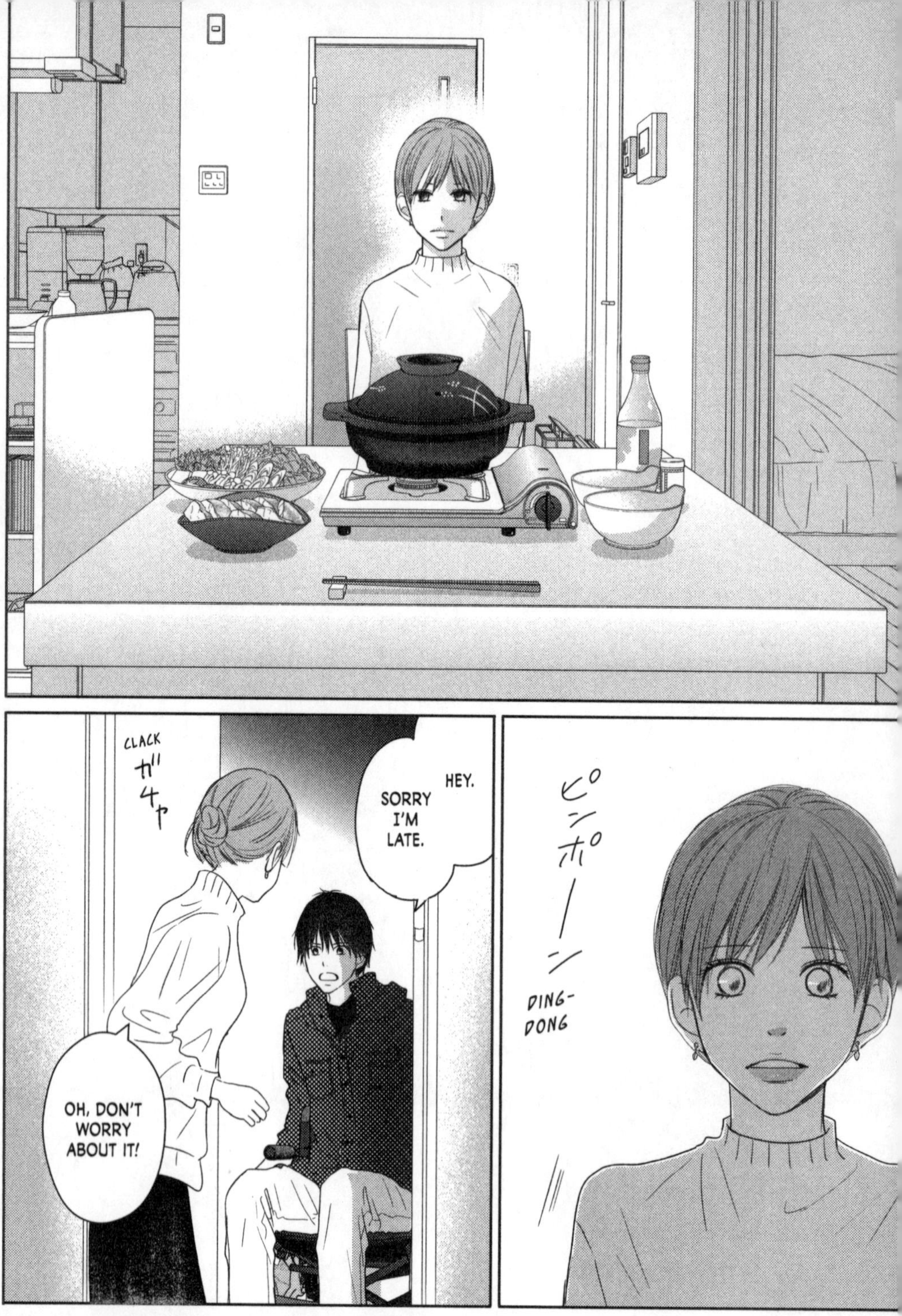
ピンポーン
DING-DONG
CLACK
ガチャ
HEY.
SORRY I'M LATE.
OH, DON'T WORRY ABOUT IT!

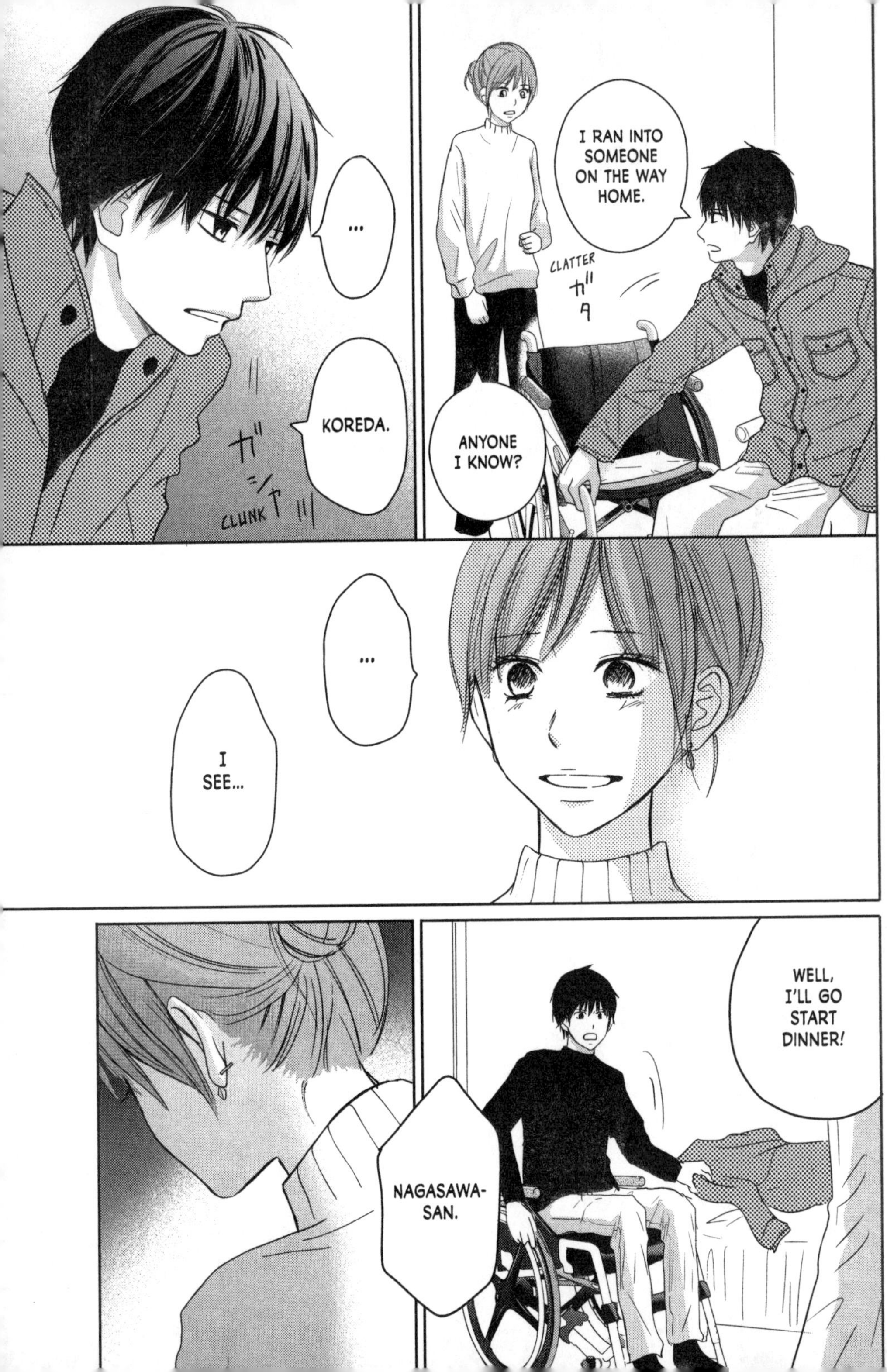
I RAN INTO SOMEONE ON THE WAY HOME.
CLATTER
ガタ
ANYONE I KNOW?
...
KOREDA.
ガシャ
CLUNK
...
I SEE...
WELL, I'LL GO START DINNER!
NAGASAWA-SAN.

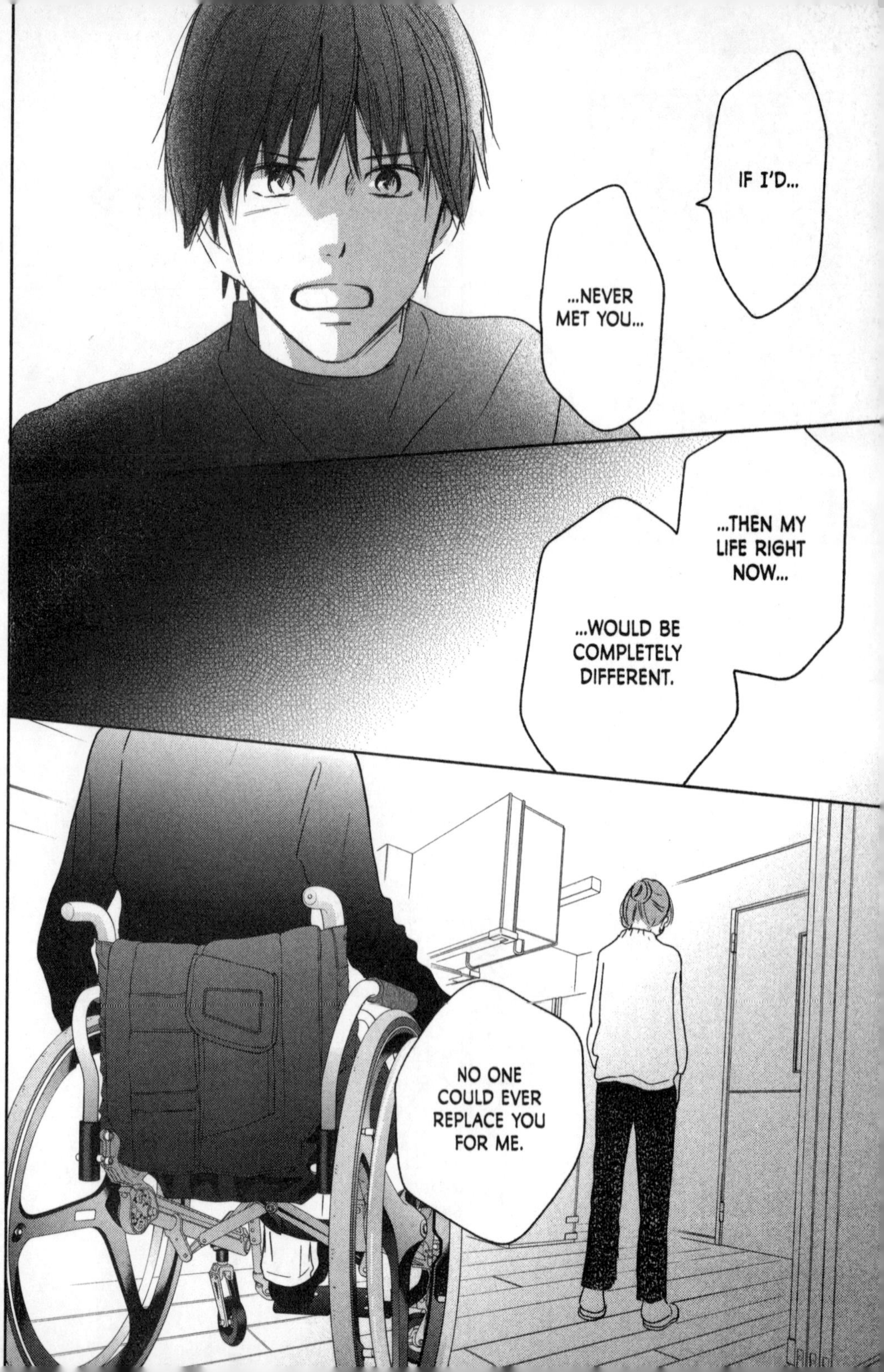
IF I'D...
...NEVER MET YOU...
...THEN MY LIFE RIGHT NOW...
...WOULD BE COMPLETELY DIFFERENT.
NO ONE COULD EVER REPLACE YOU FOR ME.

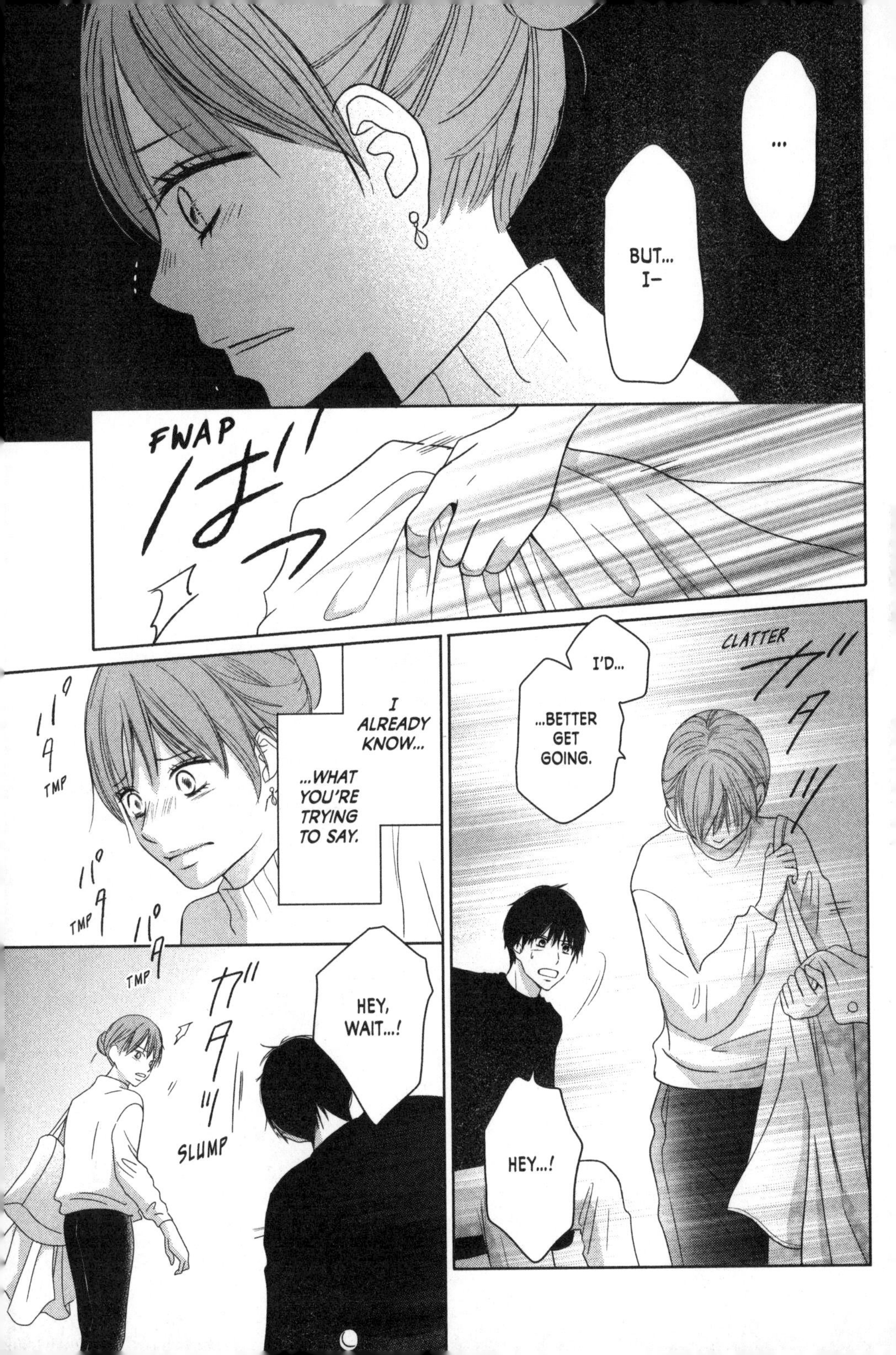
...
BUT... I–
FWAP
ばっ
CLATTER
ガタッ
I'D...
...BETTER GET GOING.
HEY...!
I ALREADY KNOW...
...WHAT YOU'RE TRYING TO SAY.
パタ
TMP
パタ
TMP
パタ
TMP
HEY, WAIT...!
ガタッ
SLUMP

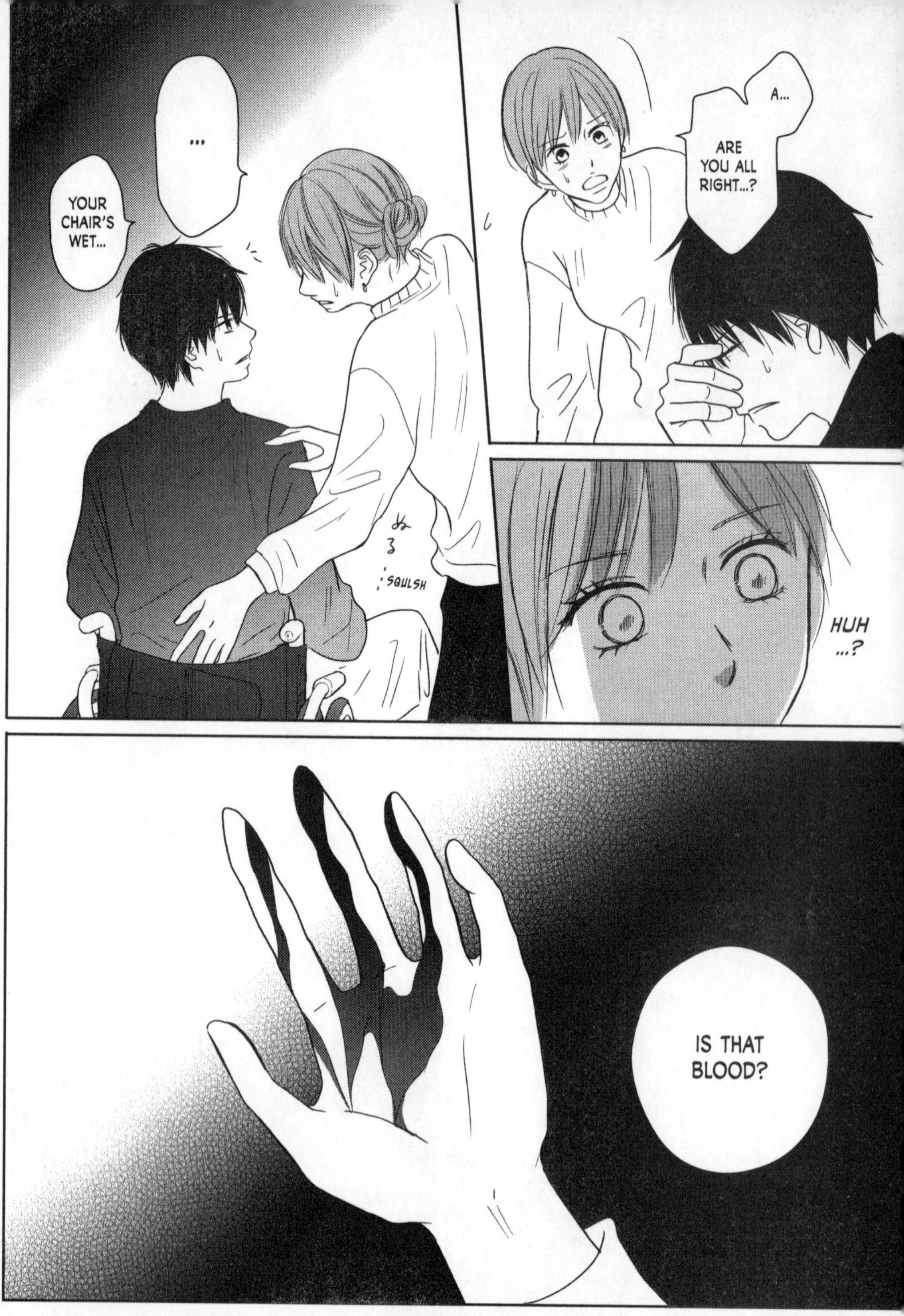
A...
ARE YOU ALL RIGHT...?
HUH ...?
...
YOUR CHAIR'S WET...
ぬる
SQULSH
IS THAT BLOOD?

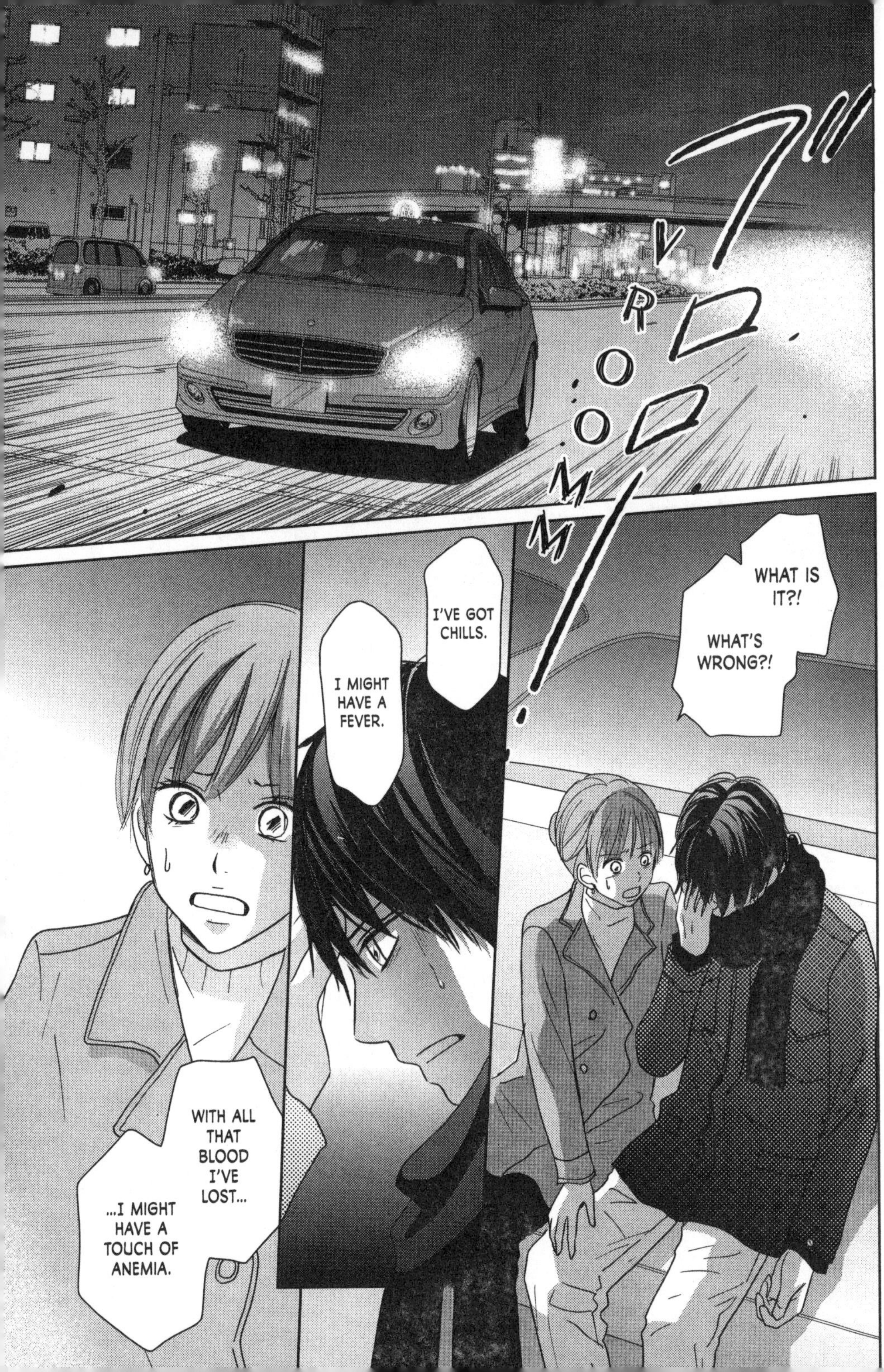
VROOMM
WHAT IS IT?!
WHAT'S WRONG?!
I'VE GOT CHILLS.
I MIGHT HAVE A FEVER.
WITH ALL THAT BLOOD I'VE LOST...
...I MIGHT HAVE A TOUCH OF ANEMIA.

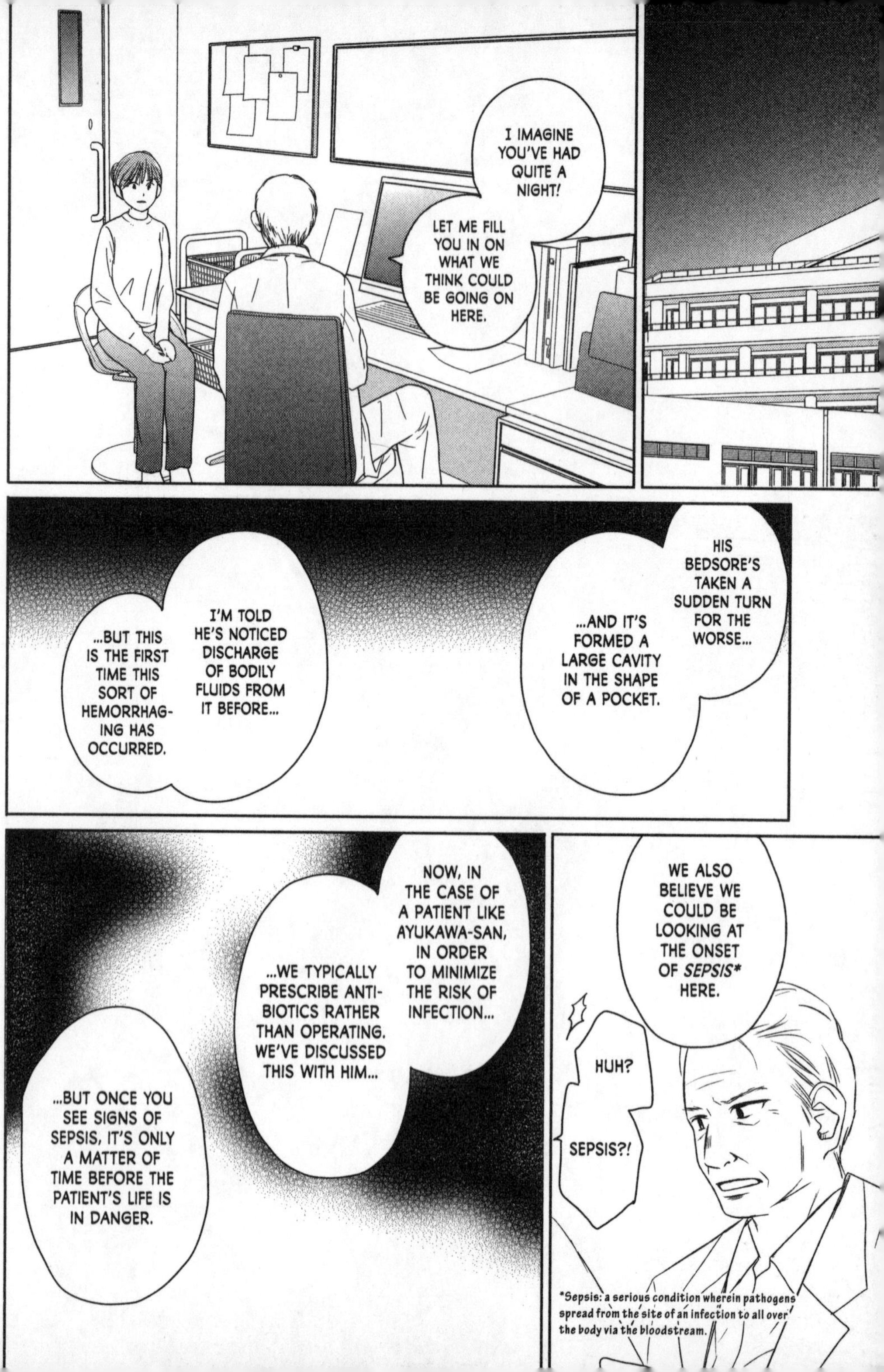
I IMAGINE YOU'VE HAD QUITE A NIGHT!
LET ME FILL YOU IN ON WHAT WE THINK COULD BE GOING ON HERE.
HIS BEDSORE'S TAKEN A SUDDEN TURN FOR THE WORSE...
...AND IT'S FORMED A LARGE CAVITY IN THE SHAPE OF A POCKET.
I'M TOLD HE'S NOTICED DISCHARGE OF BODILY FLUIDS FROM IT BEFORE...
...BUT THIS IS THE FIRST TIME THIS SORT OF HEMORRHAGING HAS OCCURRED.
WE ALSO BELIEVE WE COULD BE LOOKING AT THE ONSET OF *SEPSIS** HERE.
HUH?
SEPSIS?!
*Sepsis: a serious condition wherein pathogens spread from the site of an infection to all over the body via the bloodstream.
NOW, IN THE CASE OF A PATIENT LIKE AYUKAWA-SAN, IN ORDER TO MINIMIZE THE RISK OF INFECTION...
...WE TYPICALLY PRESCRIBE ANTIBIOTICS RATHER THAN OPERATING. WE'VE DISCUSSED THIS WITH HIM...
...BUT ONCE YOU SEE SIGNS OF SEPSIS, IT'S ONLY A MATTER OF TIME BEFORE THE PATIENT'S LIFE IS IN DANGER.

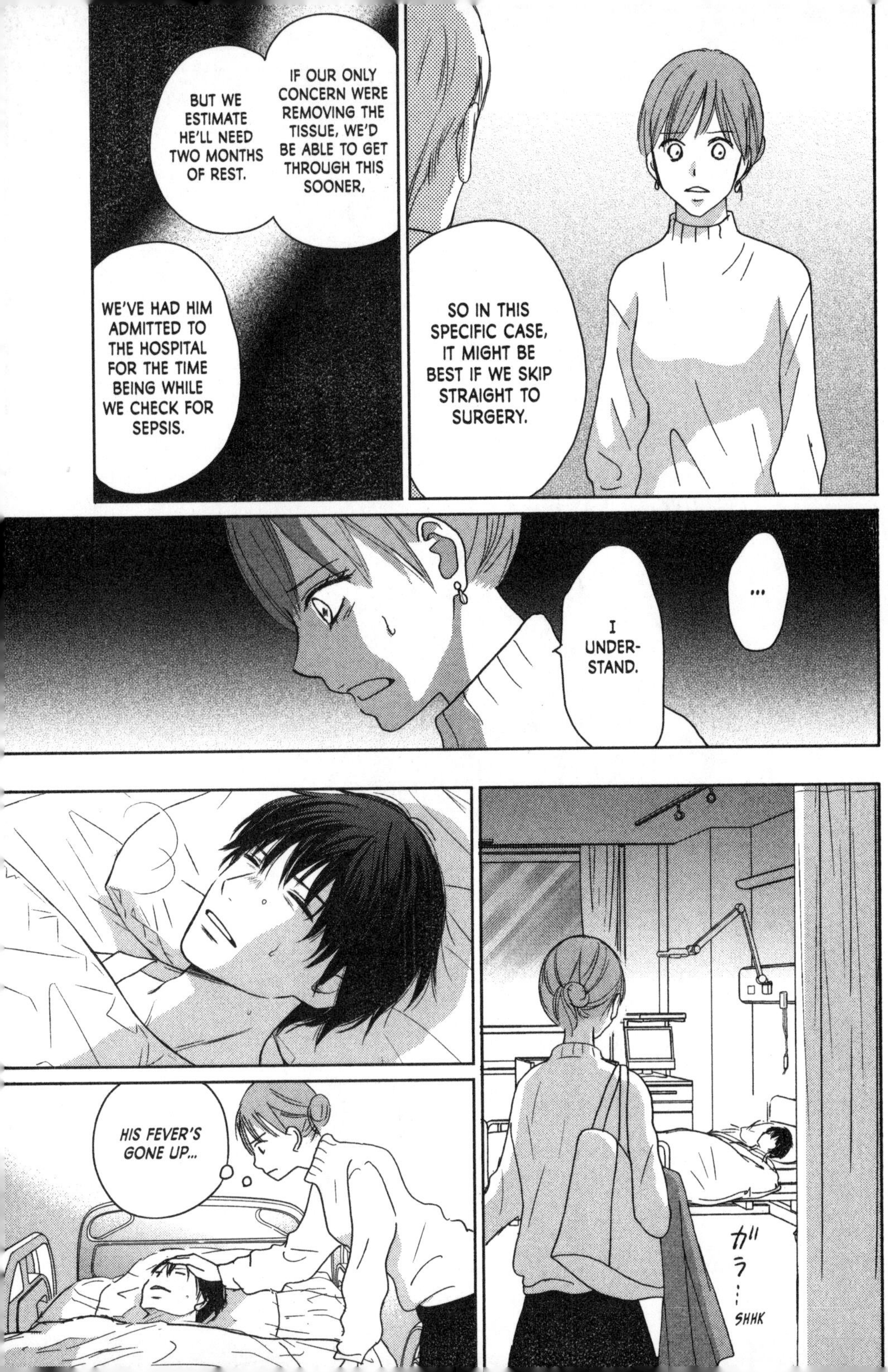

SO IN THIS SPECIFIC CASE, IT MIGHT BE BEST IF WE SKIP STRAIGHT TO SURGERY.
IF OUR ONLY CONCERN WERE REMOVING THE TISSUE, WE'D BE ABLE TO GET THROUGH THIS SOONER,
BUT WE ESTIMATE HE'LL NEED TWO MONTHS OF REST.
WE'VE HAD HIM ADMITTED TO THE HOSPITAL FOR THE TIME BEING WHILE WE CHECK FOR SEPSIS.
...
I UNDERSTAND.
ガラ…
SHHK
HIS FEVER'S GONE UP...

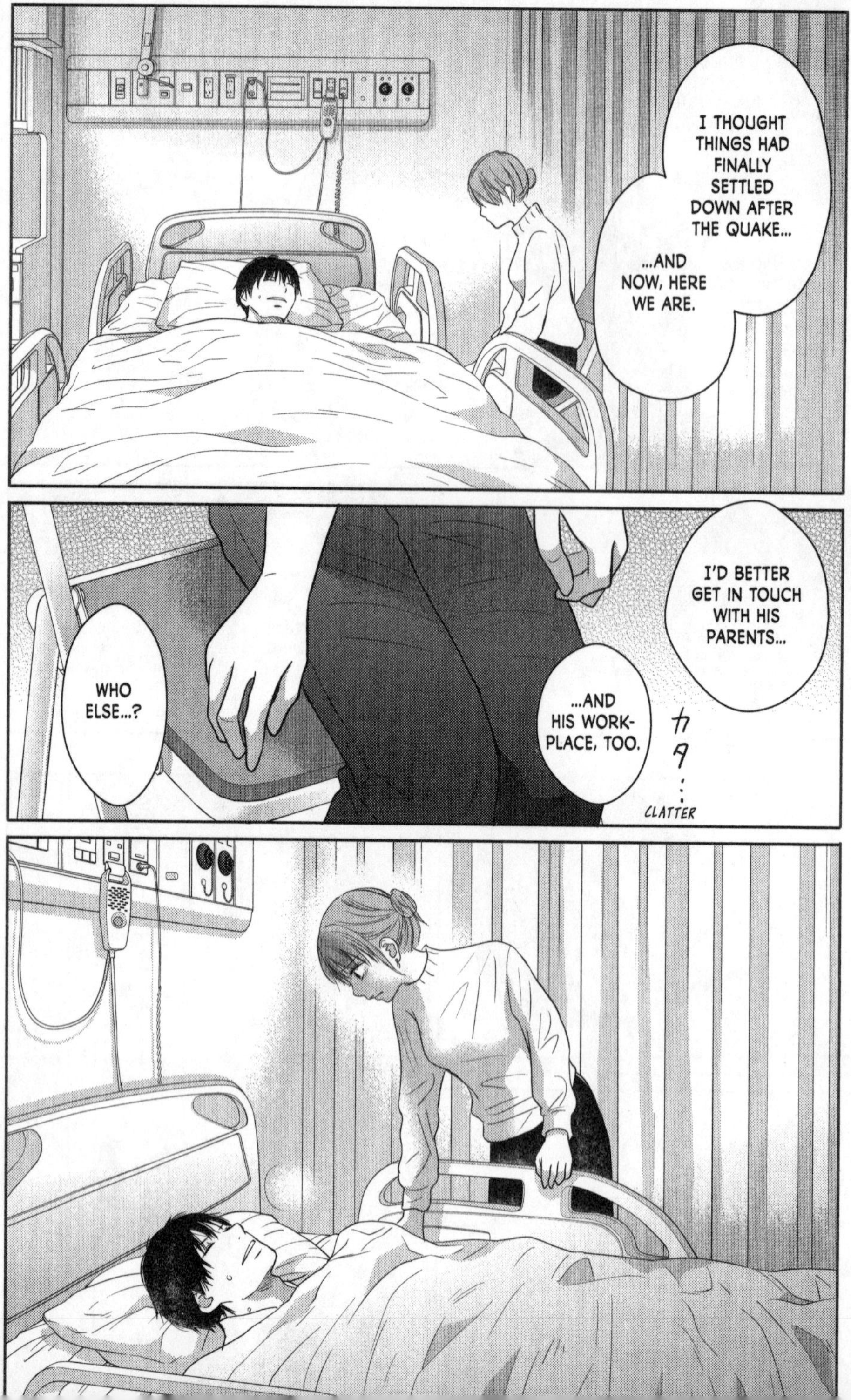
I THOUGHT THINGS HAD FINALLY SETTLED DOWN AFTER THE QUAKE...
...AND NOW, HERE WE ARE.
I'D BETTER GET IN TOUCH WITH HIS PARENTS...
...AND HIS WORK-PLACE, TOO.
カタ…
CLATTER
WHO ELSE...?

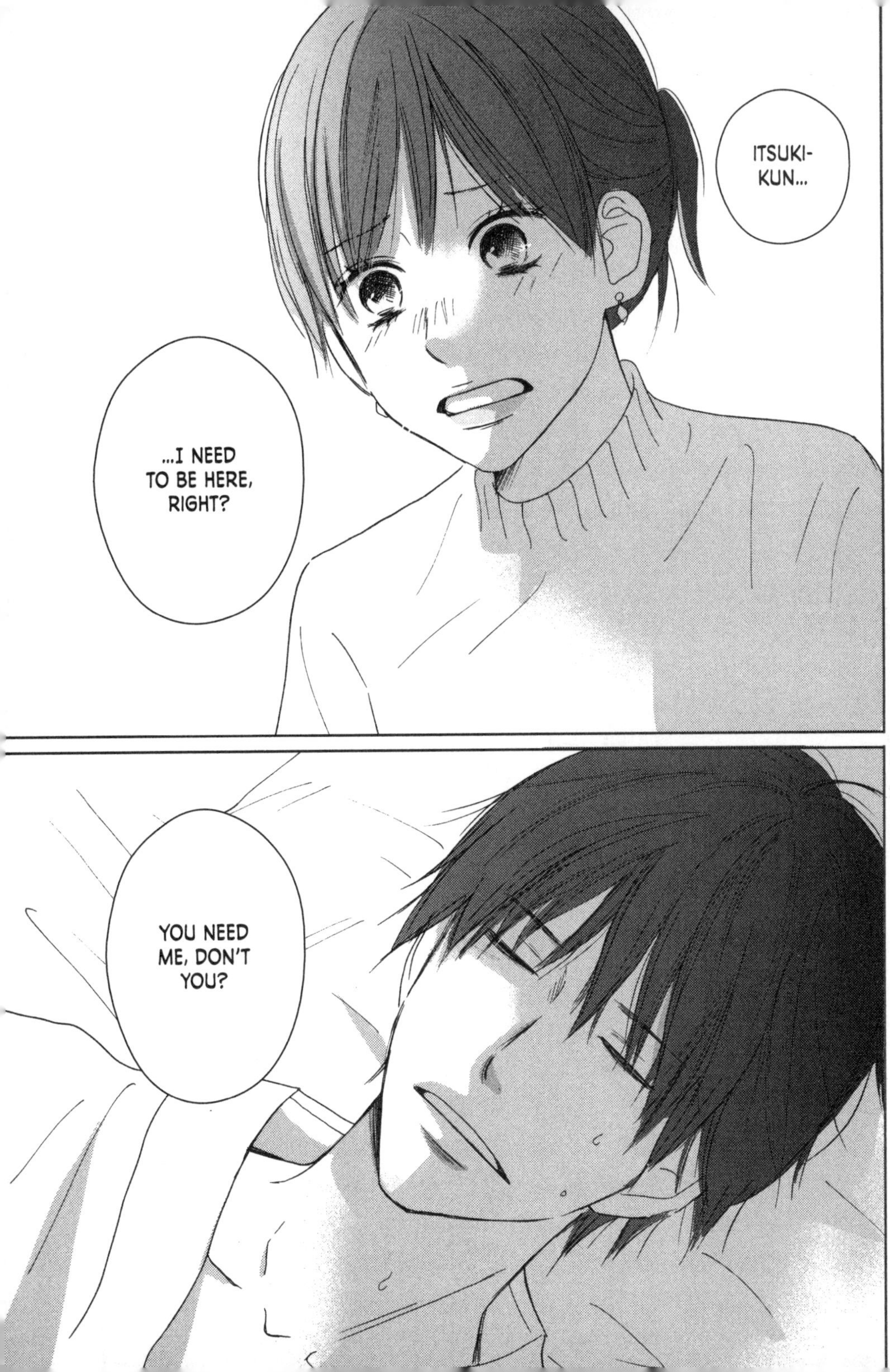
ITSUKI-KUN...
...I NEED TO BE HERE, RIGHT?
YOU NEED ME, DON'T YOU?

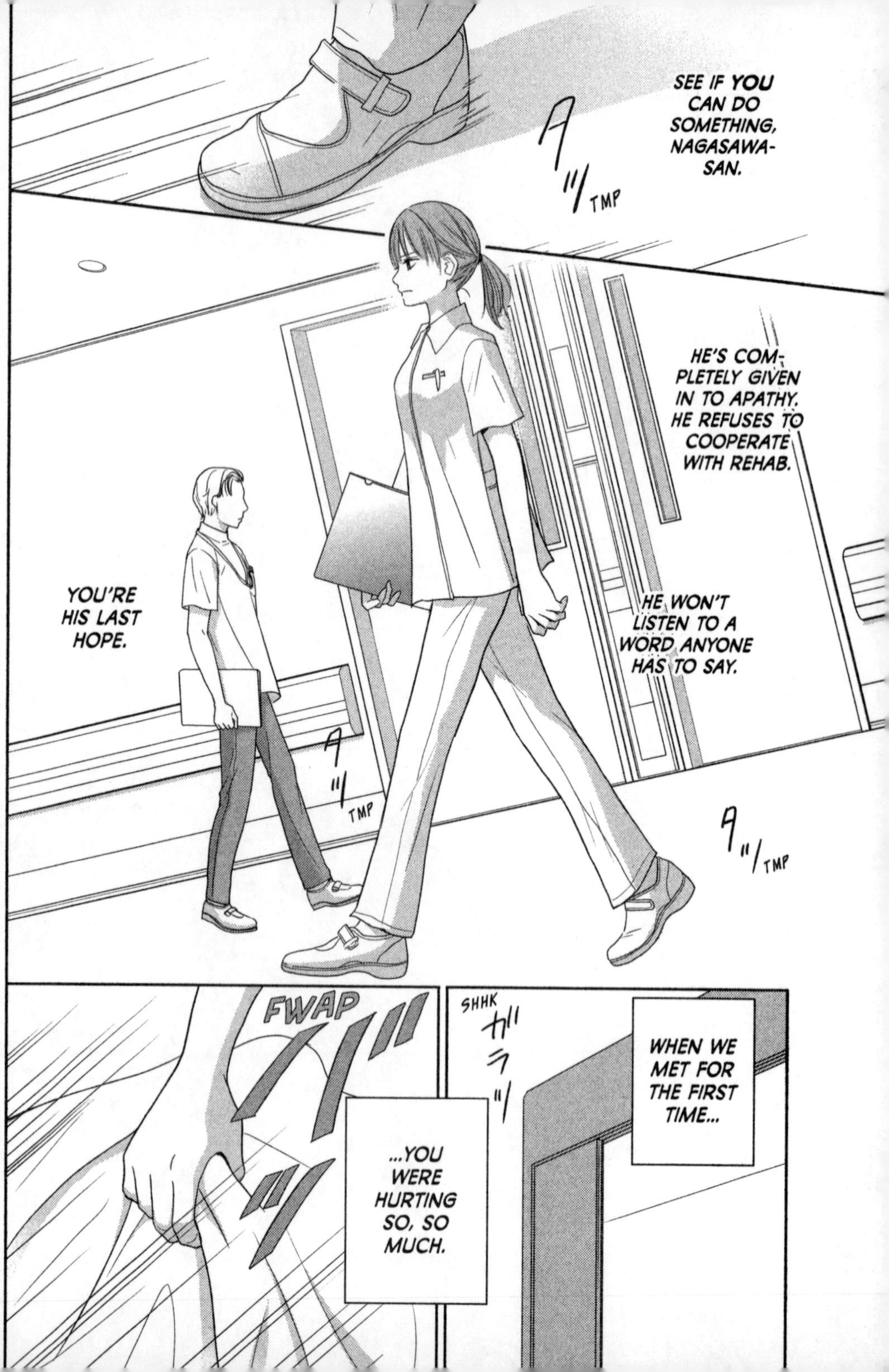
SEE IF YOU CAN DO SOMETHING, NAGASAWA-SAN.
TMP
HE'S COMPLETELY GIVEN IN TO APATHY. HE REFUSES TO COOPERATE WITH REHAB.
HE WON'T LISTEN TO A WORD ANYONE HAS TO SAY.
TMP
YOU'RE HIS LAST HOPE.
TMP
SHHK
WHEN WE MET FOR THE FIRST TIME...
FWAP
...YOU WERE HURTING SO, SO MUCH.

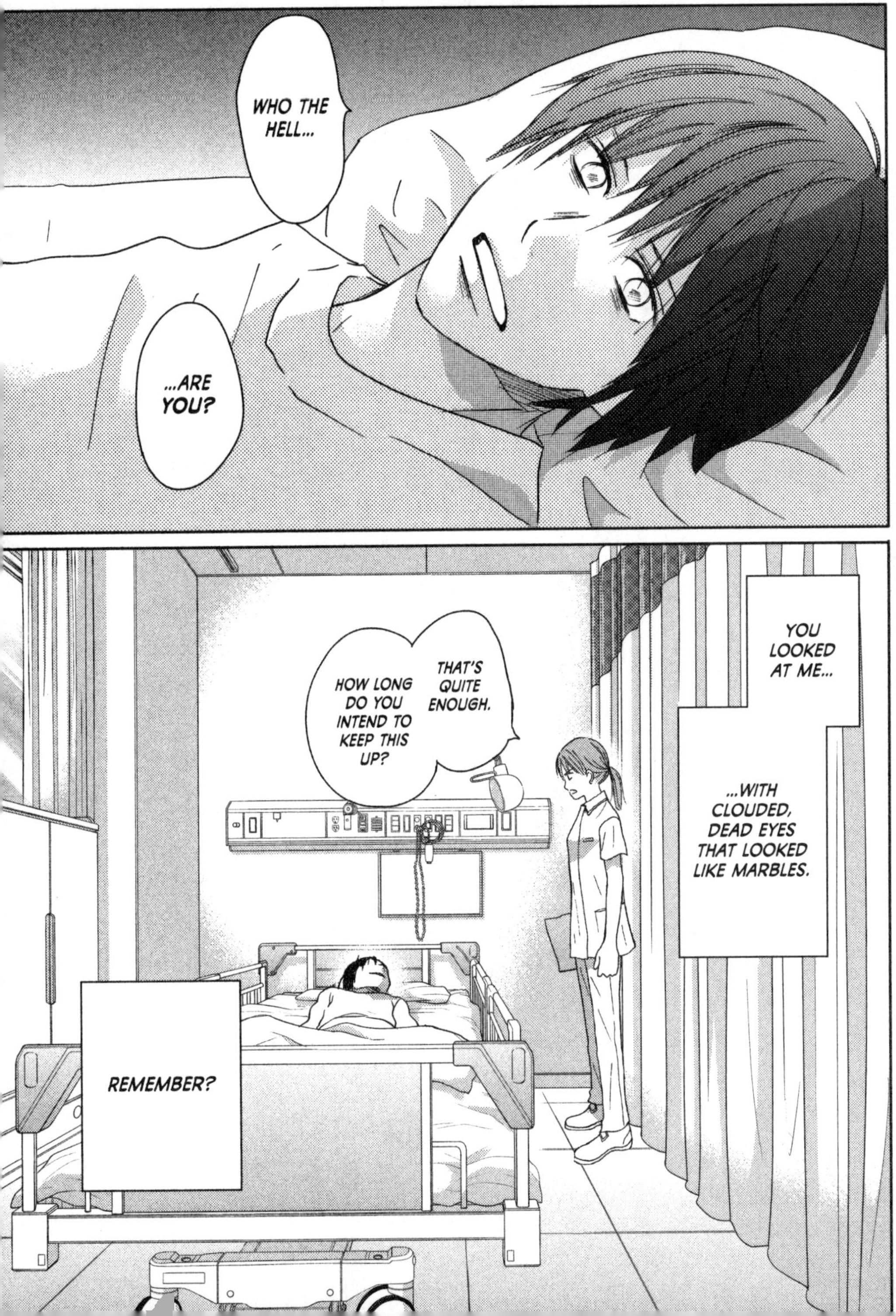
WHO THE HELL...
...ARE YOU?
YOU LOOKED AT ME...
...WITH CLOUDED, DEAD EYES THAT LOOKED LIKE MARBLES.
THAT'S QUITE ENOUGH.
HOW LONG DO YOU INTEND TO KEEP THIS UP?
REMEMBER?

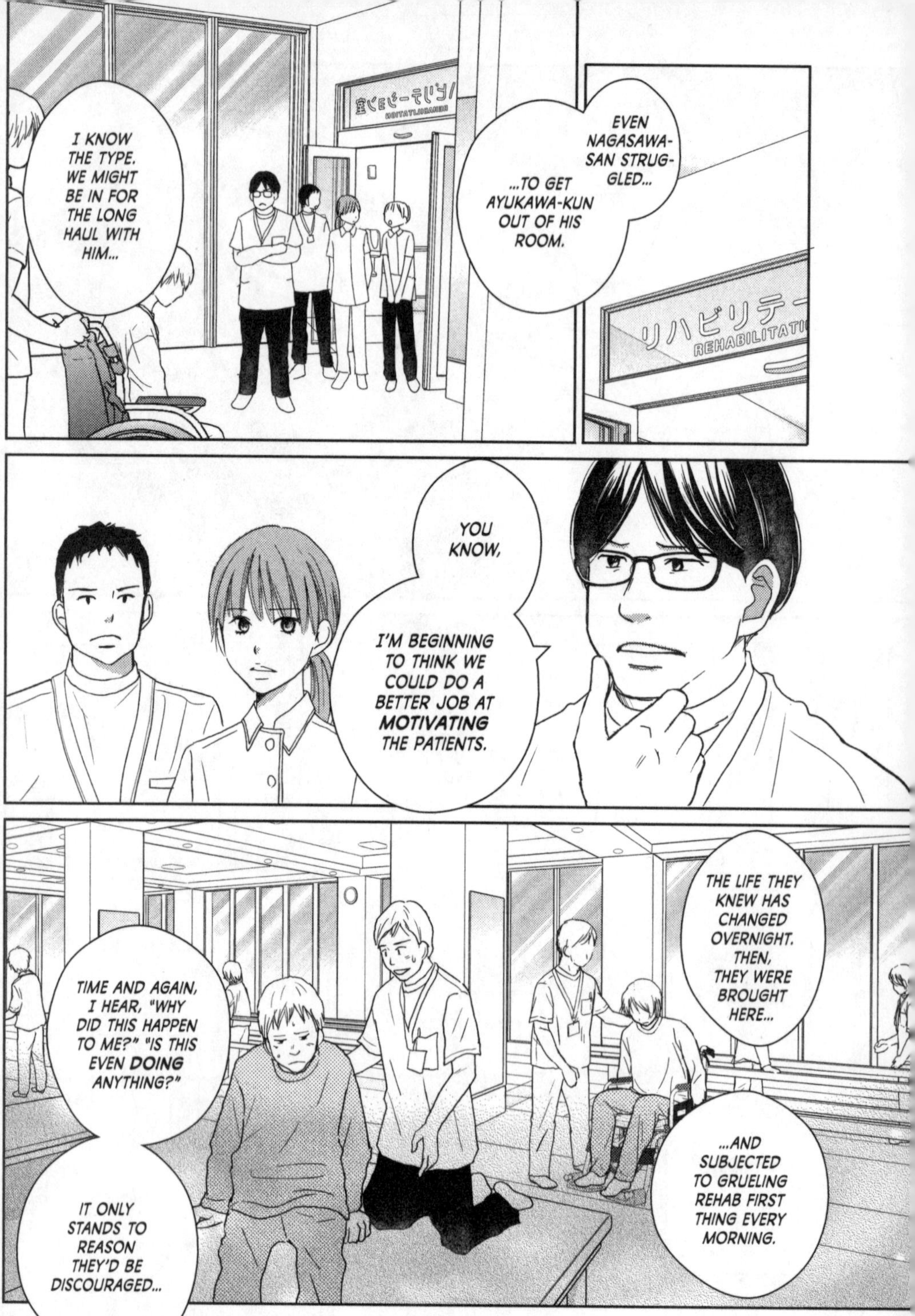
EVEN NAGASAWA-SAN STRUGGLED...
...TO GET AYUKAWA-KUN OUT OF HIS ROOM.
I KNOW THE TYPE. WE MIGHT BE IN FOR THE LONG HAUL WITH HIM...
YOU KNOW,
I'M BEGINNING TO THINK WE COULD DO A BETTER JOB AT **MOTIVATING** THE PATIENTS.
THE LIFE THEY KNEW HAS CHANGED OVERNIGHT. THEN, THEY WERE BROUGHT HERE...
...AND SUBJECTED TO GRUELING REHAB FIRST THING EVERY MORNING.
TIME AND AGAIN, I HEAR, "WHY DID THIS HAPPEN TO ME?" "IS THIS EVEN **DOING** ANYTHING?"
IT ONLY STANDS TO REASON THEY'D BE DISCOURAGED...

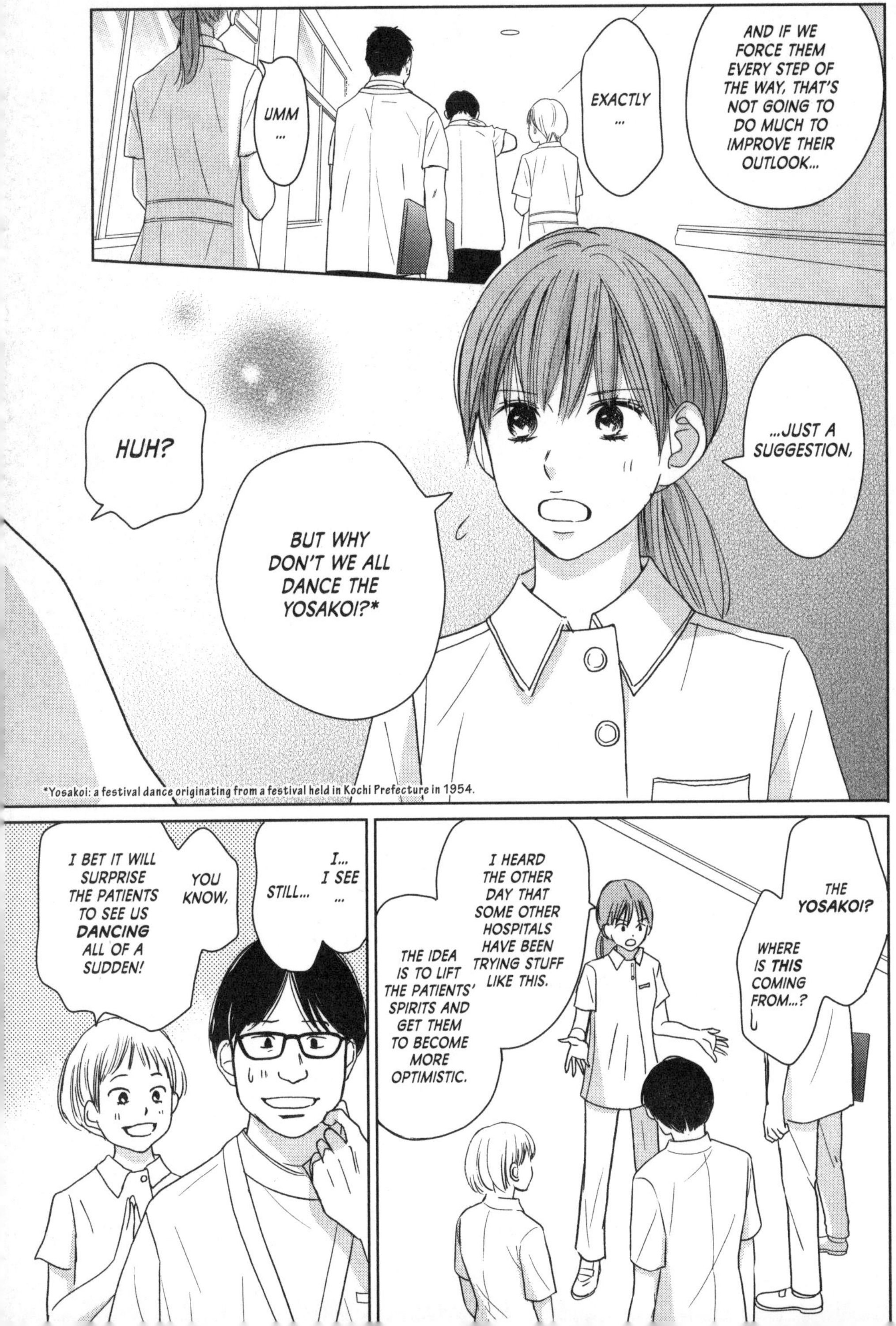
AND IF WE FORCE THEM EVERY STEP OF THE WAY, THAT'S NOT GOING TO DO MUCH TO IMPROVE THEIR OUTLOOK...
EXACTLY ...
UMM ...
...JUST A SUGGESTION,
BUT WHY DON'T WE ALL DANCE THE YOSAKOI?*
HUH?
THE YOSAKOI?
WHERE IS THIS COMING FROM...?
I HEARD THE OTHER DAY THAT SOME OTHER HOSPITALS HAVE BEEN TRYING STUFF LIKE THIS.
THE IDEA IS TO LIFT THE PATIENTS' SPIRITS AND GET THEM TO BECOME MORE OPTIMISTIC.
I... I SEE ...
STILL...
YOU KNOW,
I BET IT WILL SURPRISE THE PATIENTS TO SEE US DANCING ALL OF A SUDDEN!

*Yosakoi: a festival dance originating from a festival held in Kochi Prefecture in 1954.

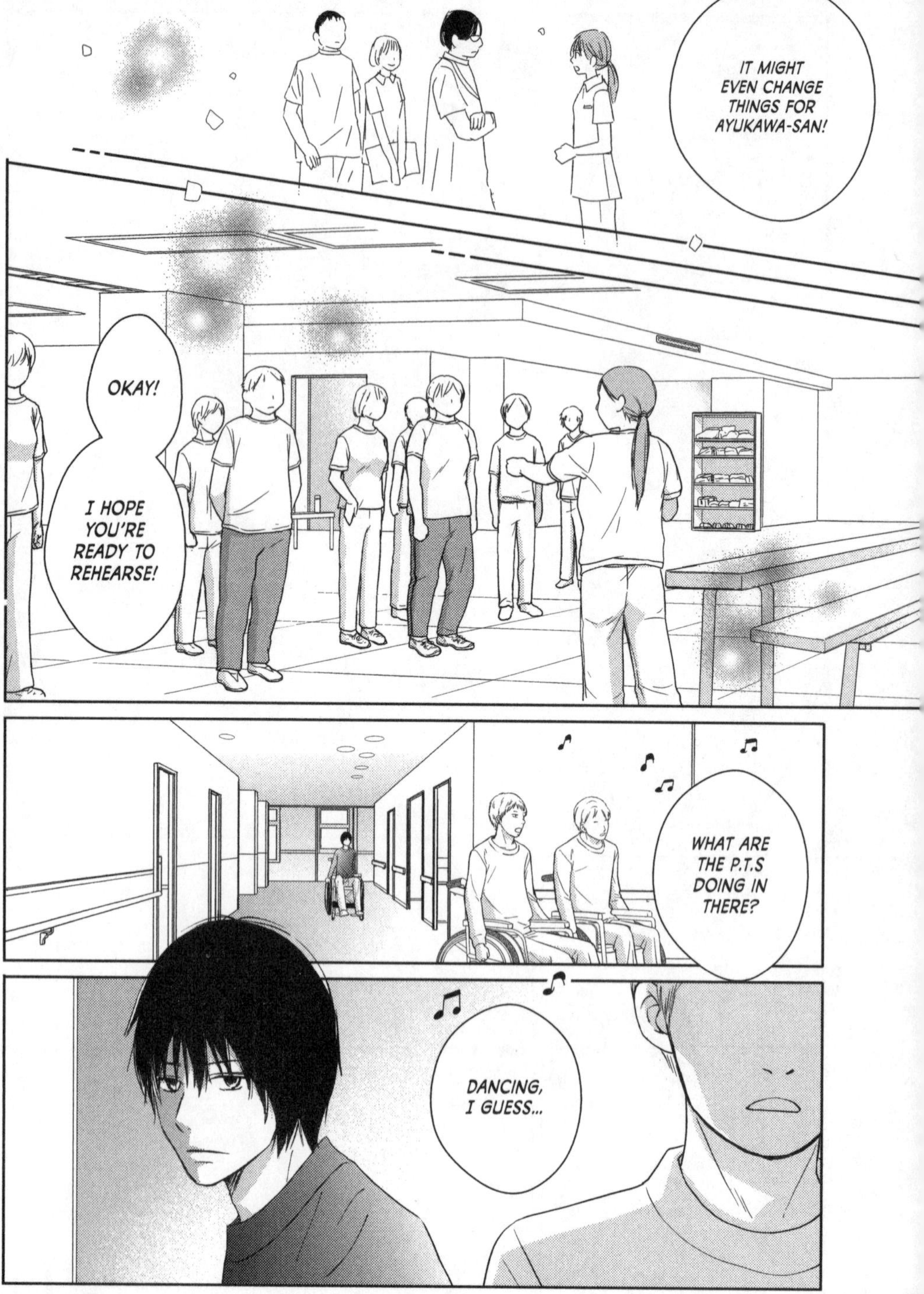
IT MIGHT EVEN CHANGE THINGS FOR AYUKAWA-SAN!
OKAY!
I HOPE YOU'RE READY TO REHEARSE!
WHAT ARE THE P.T.S DOING IN THERE?
DANCING, I GUESS...

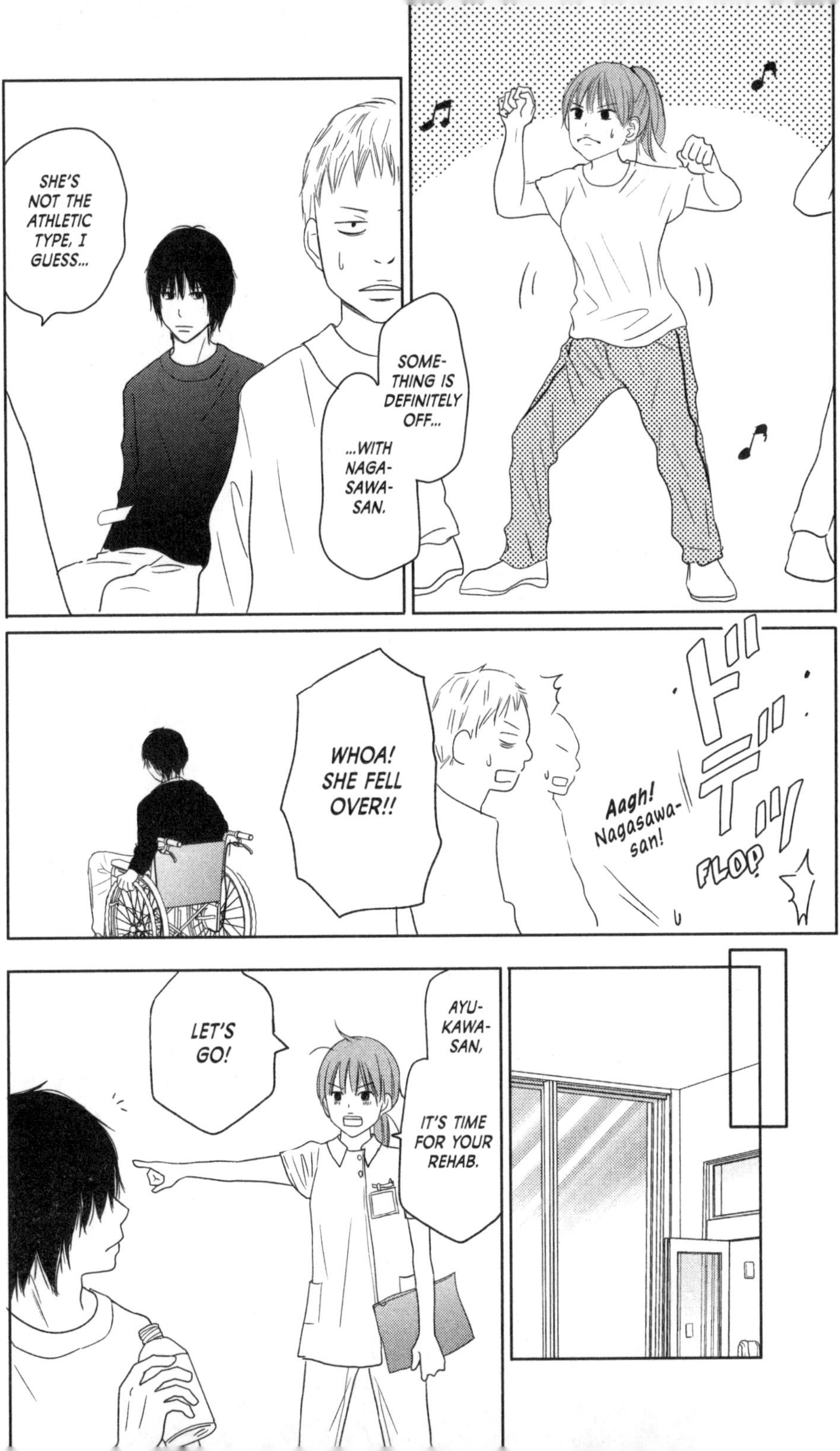
SHE'S NOT THE ATHLETIC TYPE, I GUESS...
SOMETHING IS DEFINITELY OFF...
...WITH NAGASAWA-SAN.
ドデッ
FLOP
Aagh! Nagasawa-san!
WHOA! SHE FELL OVER!!
AYUKAWA-SAN,
IT'S TIME FOR YOUR REHAB.
LET'S GO!

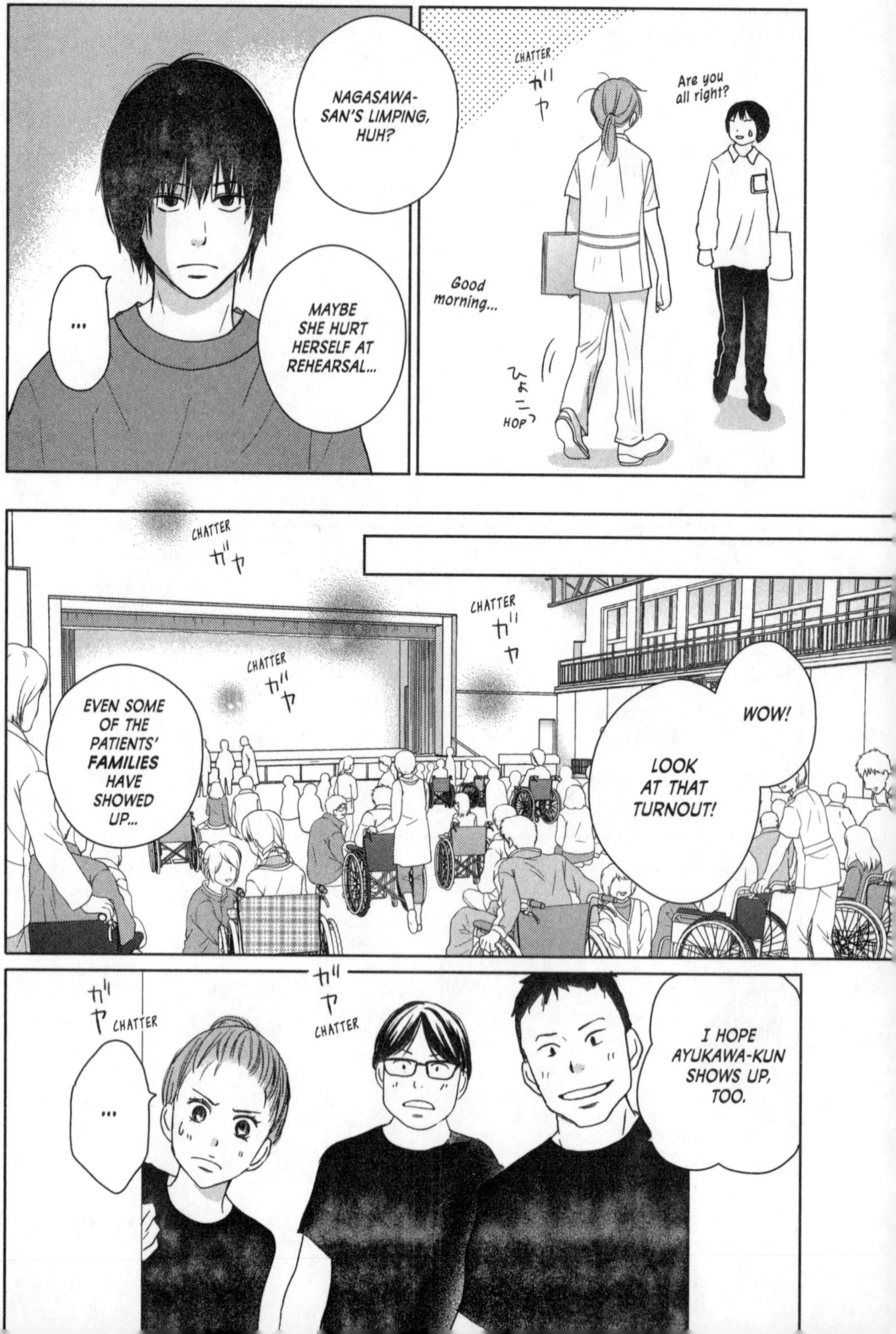
Are you all right?
CHATTER ガヤ
Good morning...
ひょこっ HOP
NAGASAWA-SAN'S LIMPING, HUH?
MAYBE SHE HURT HERSELF AT REHEARSAL...
...
WOW!
LOOK AT THAT TURNOUT!
CHATTER ガヤ
CHATTER ガヤ
CHATTER ガヤ
EVEN SOME OF THE PATIENTS' **FAMILIES** HAVE SHOWED UP...
I HOPE AYUKAWA-KUN SHOWS UP, TOO.
ガヤ CHATTER
ガヤ CHATTER
...

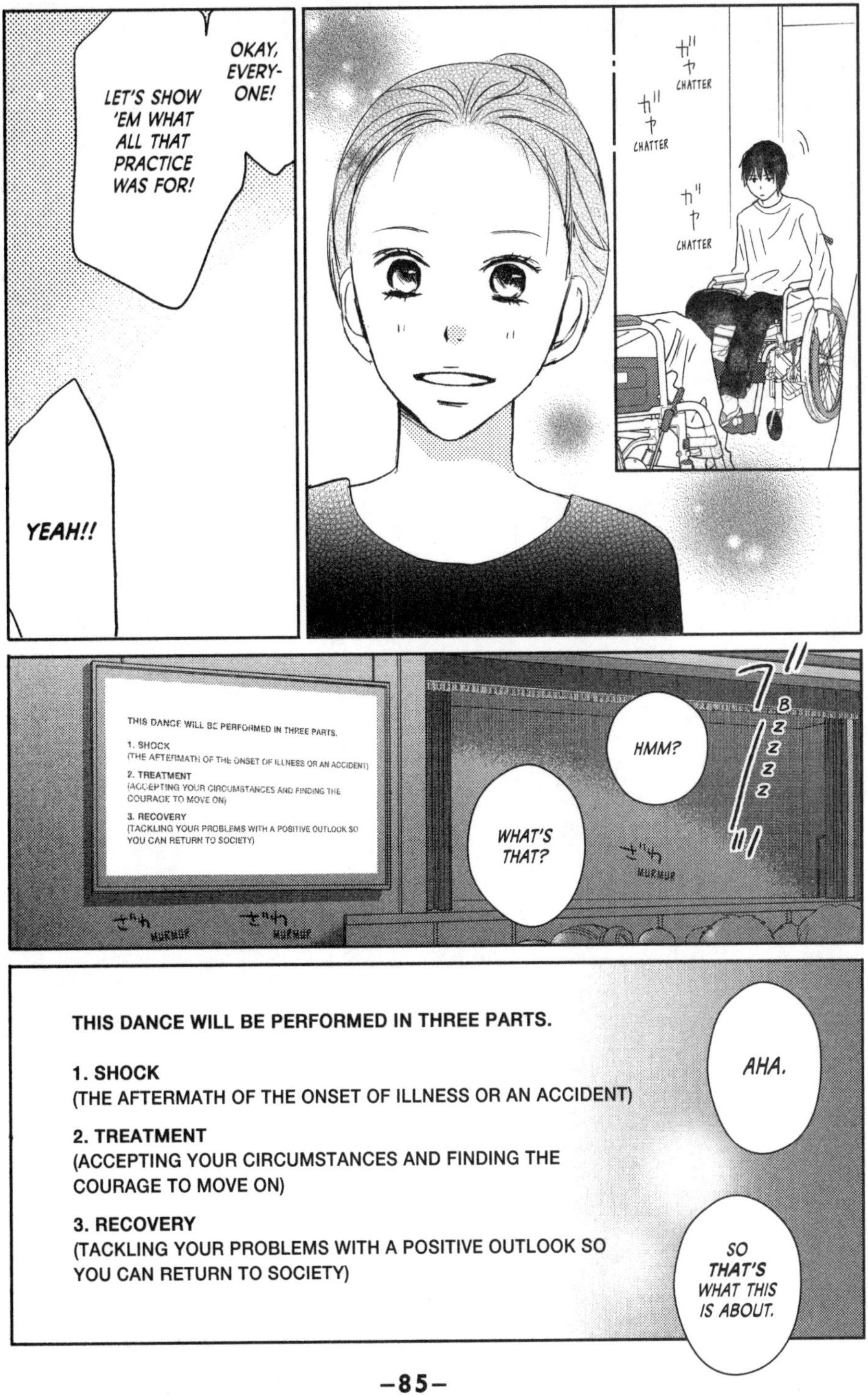
ガヤ
CHATTER
ガヤ
CHATTER
ガヤ
CHATTER
OKAY, EVERYONE!
LET'S SHOW 'EM WHAT ALL THAT PRACTICE WAS FOR!
YEAH!!
BZZZZ
HMM?
WHAT'S THAT?
ざわ
MURMUR
THIS DANCE WILL BE PERFORMED IN THREE PARTS.
1. SHOCK
(THE AFTERMATH OF THE ONSET OF ILLNESS OR AN ACCIDENT)
2. TREATMENT
(ACCEPTING YOUR CIRCUMSTANCES AND FINDING THE COURAGE TO MOVE ON)
3. RECOVERY
(TACKLING YOUR PROBLEMS WITH A POSITIVE OUTLOOK SO YOU CAN RETURN TO SOCIETY)
ざわ
MURMUR
ざわ
MURMUR
AHA.
SO THAT'S WHAT THIS IS ABOUT.
THIS DANCE WILL BE PERFORMED IN THREE PARTS.
1. SHOCK
(THE AFTERMATH OF THE ONSET OF ILLNESS OR AN ACCIDENT)
2. TREATMENT
(ACCEPTING YOUR CIRCUMSTANCES AND FINDING THE COURAGE TO MOVE ON)
3. RECOVERY
(TACKLING YOUR PROBLEMS WITH A POSITIVE OUTLOOK SO YOU CAN RETURN TO SOCIETY)

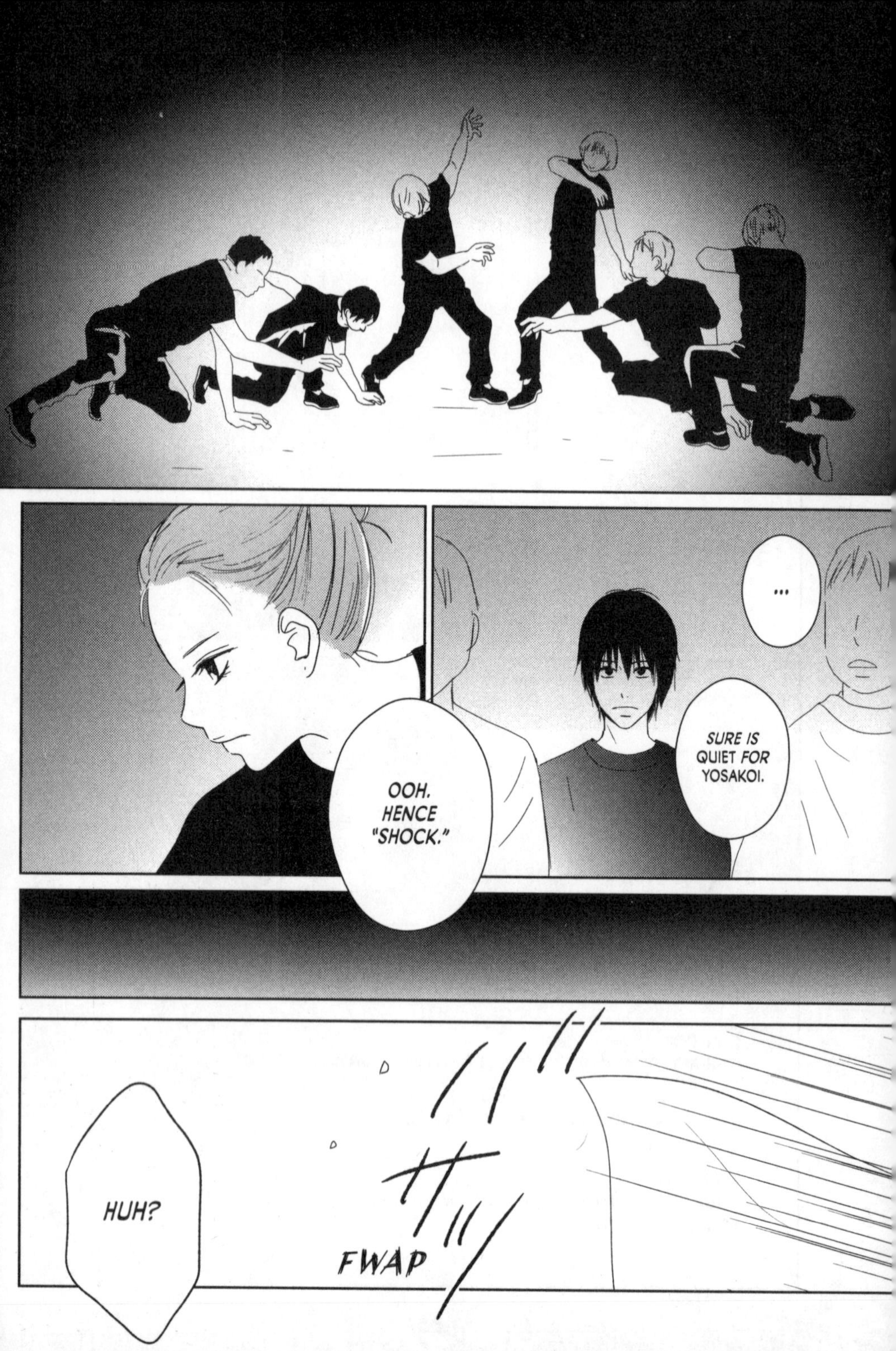
...
SURE IS QUIET FOR YOSAKOI.
OOH. HENCE "SHOCK."
FWAP
HUH?

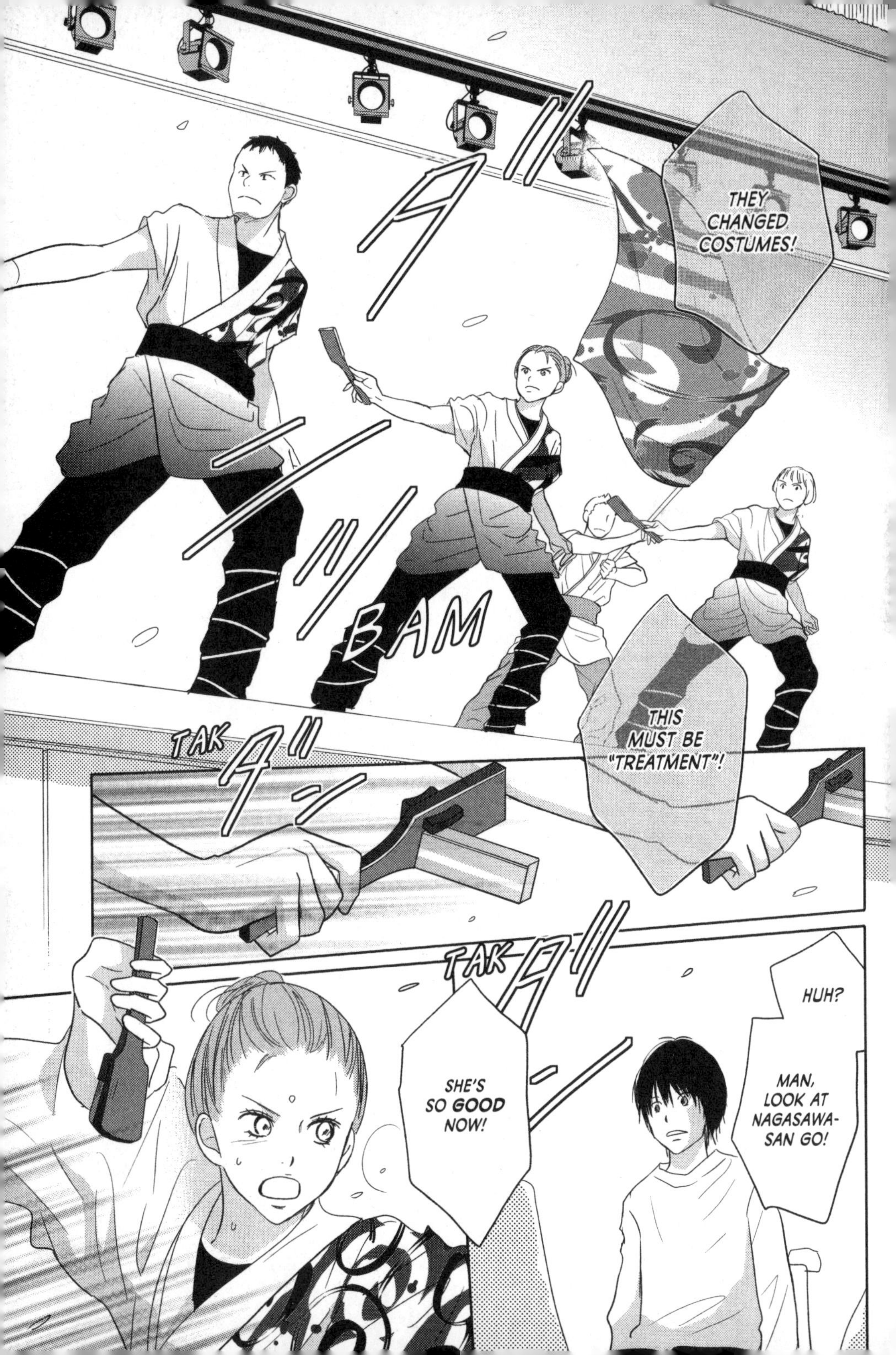
THEY CHANGED COSTUMES!
BAM
THIS MUST BE "TREATMENT"!
TAK
TAK
HUH?
MAN, LOOK AT NAGASAWA-SAN GO!
SHE'S SO GOOD NOW!

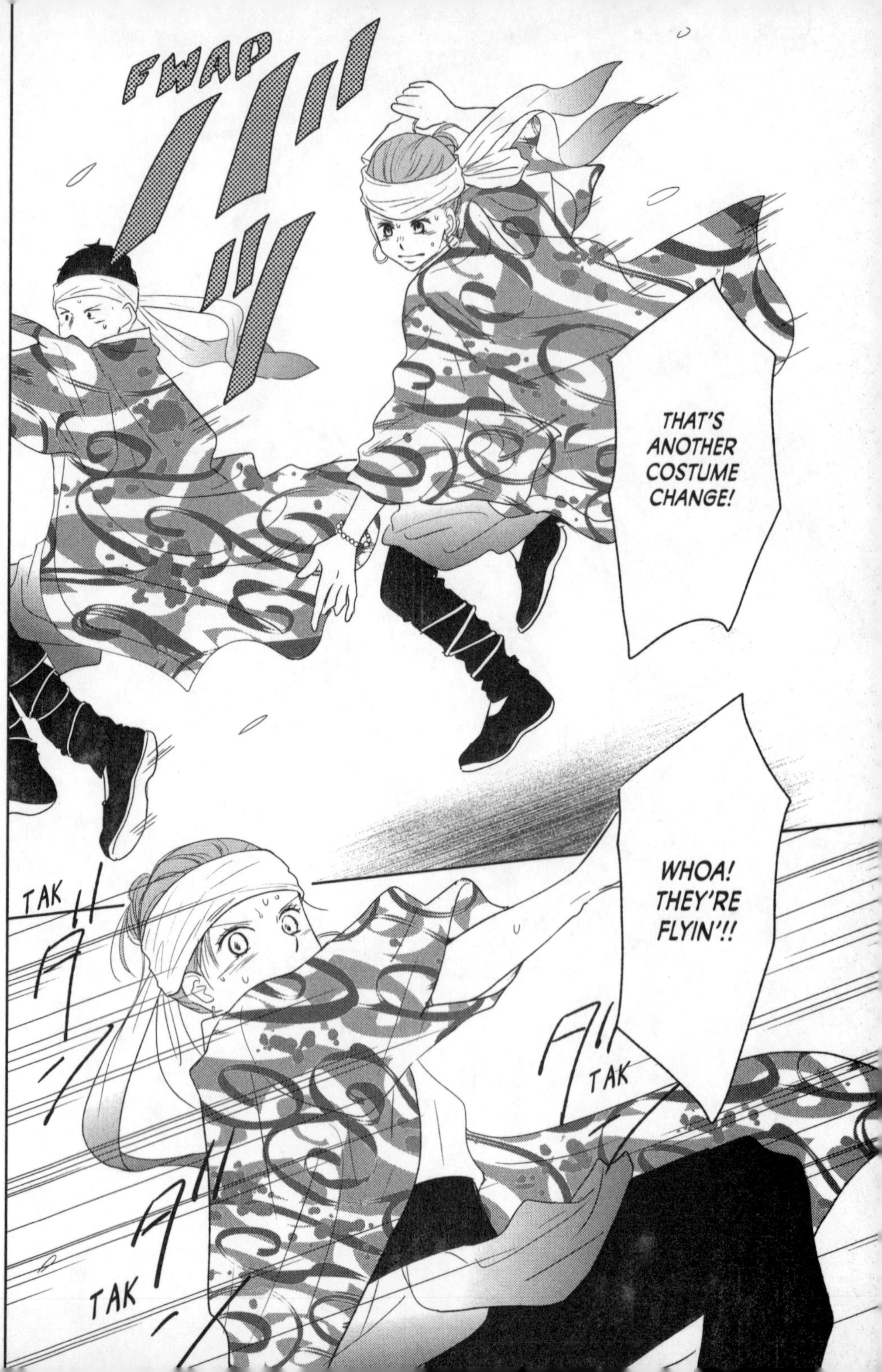
THAT'S ANOTHER COSTUME CHANGE!
FWAP
WHOA! THEY'RE FLYIN'!!
TAK
TAK
TAK

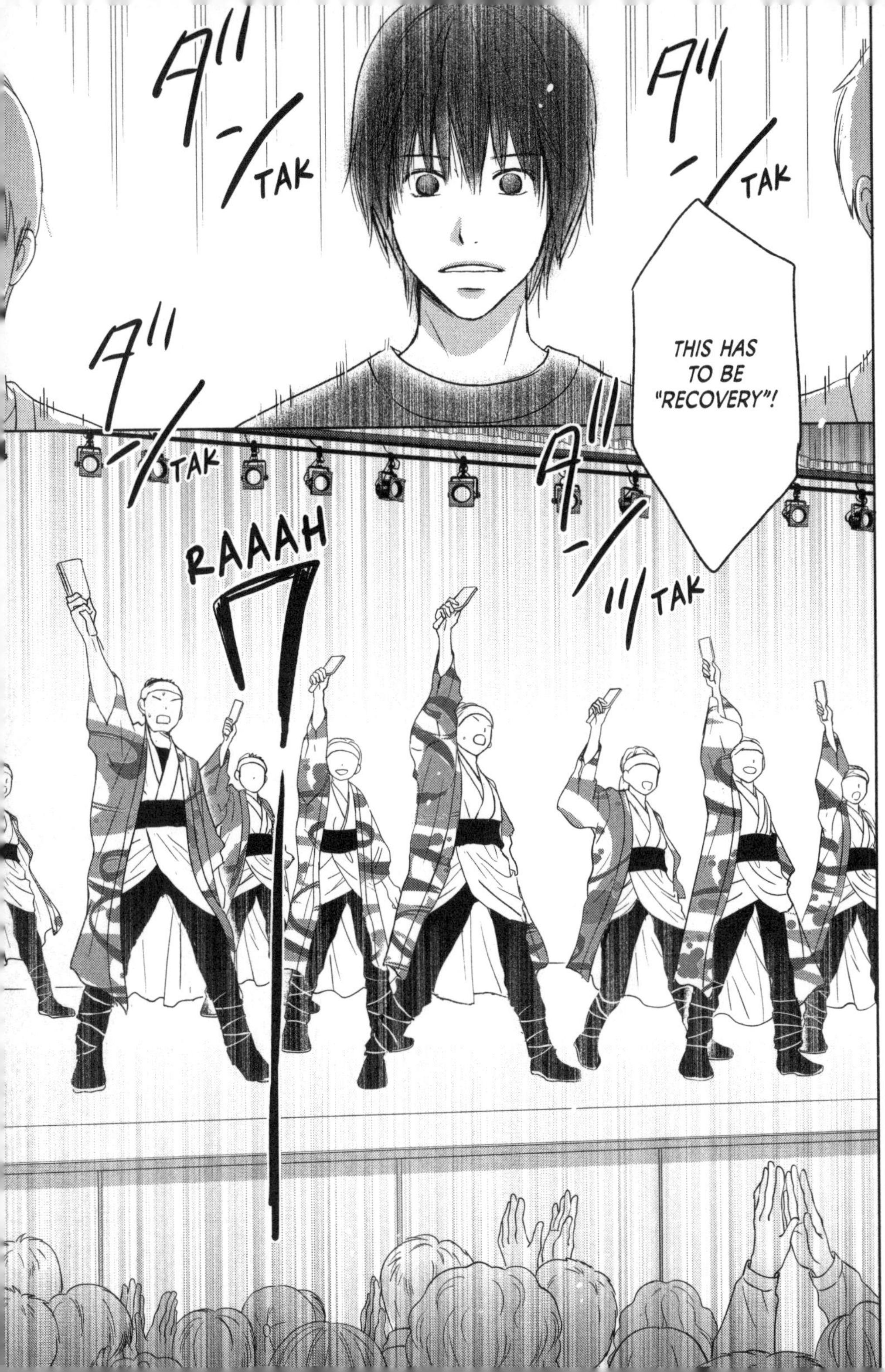
ダーン
TAK
THIS HAS TO BE "RECOVERY"!
ダーン
TAK
ダーンッ
TAK
ダーン
TAK
RAAAH
ワ

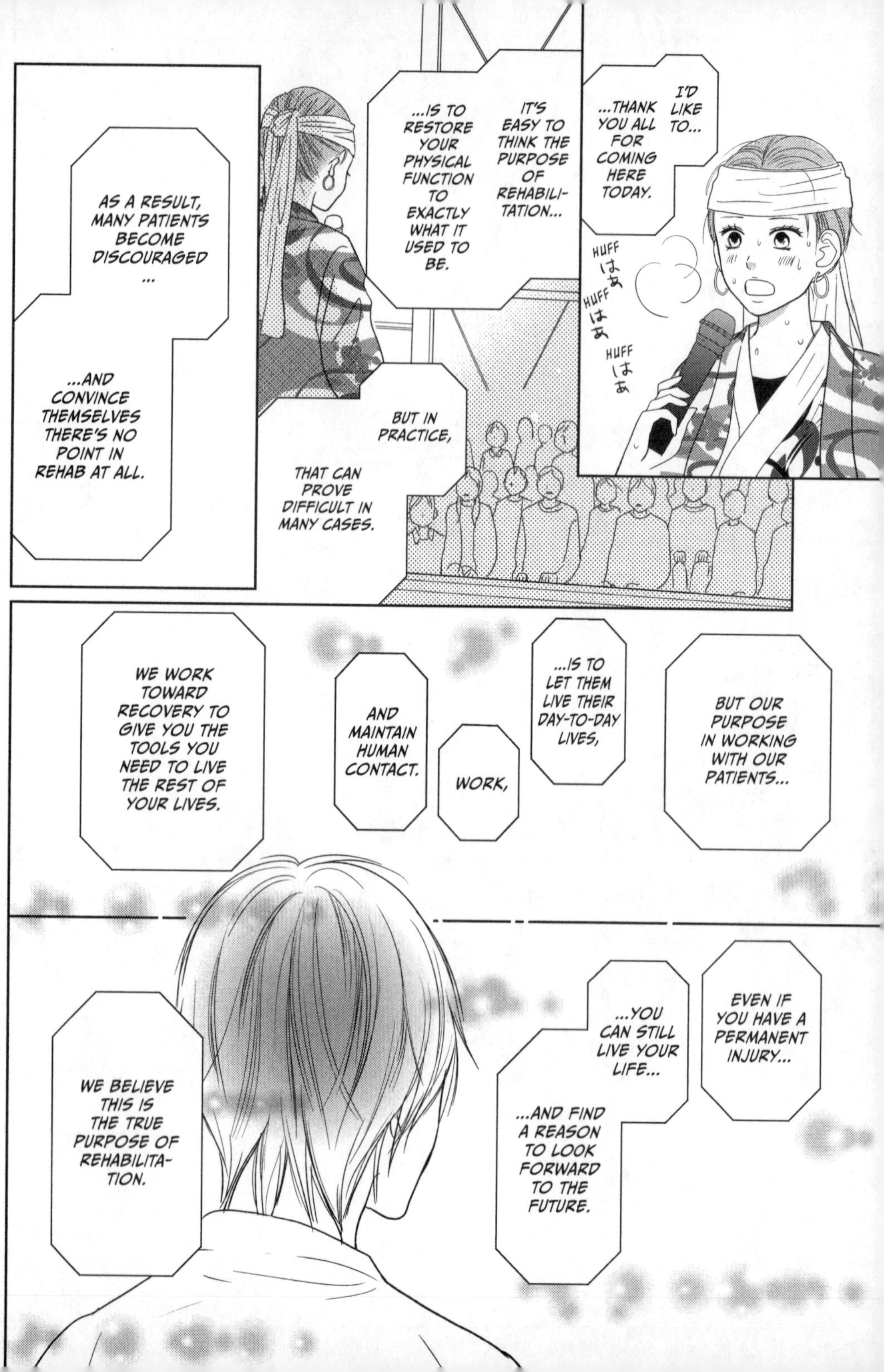
I'D LIKE TO...
...THANK YOU ALL FOR COMING HERE TODAY.
HUFF はあ
HUFF はあ
HUFF はあ
IT'S EASY TO THINK THE PURPOSE OF REHABILITATION...
...IS TO RESTORE YOUR PHYSICAL FUNCTION TO EXACTLY WHAT IT USED TO BE.
BUT IN PRACTICE,
THAT CAN PROVE DIFFICULT IN MANY CASES.
AS A RESULT, MANY PATIENTS BECOME DISCOURAGED...
...AND CONVINCE THEMSELVES THERE'S NO POINT IN REHAB AT ALL.
BUT OUR PURPOSE IN WORKING WITH OUR PATIENTS...
...IS TO LET THEM LIVE THEIR DAY-TO-DAY LIVES,
WORK,
AND MAINTAIN HUMAN CONTACT.
WE WORK TOWARD RECOVERY TO GIVE YOU THE TOOLS YOU NEED TO LIVE THE REST OF YOUR LIVES.
EVEN IF YOU HAVE A PERMANENT INJURY...
...YOU CAN STILL LIVE YOUR LIFE...
...AND FIND A REASON TO LOOK FORWARD TO THE FUTURE.
WE BELIEVE THIS IS THE TRUE PURPOSE OF REHABILITATION.

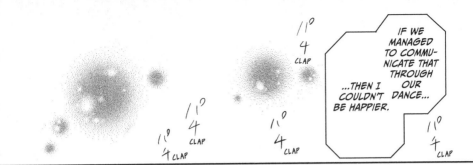

IF WE MANAGED TO COMMUNICATE THAT THROUGH OUR DANCE... ...THEN I COULDN'T BE HAPPIER.

パ 4 CLAP

パ 4 CLAP

パ 4 CLAP

パ 4 CLAP

パ 4 CLAP

パ 4 CLAP

JUST A LITTLE MORE, AYUKAWA-KUN!

HUFF は あ

HUFF は あ

GSHH

AAH!

ARE YOU ALL RIGHT?!

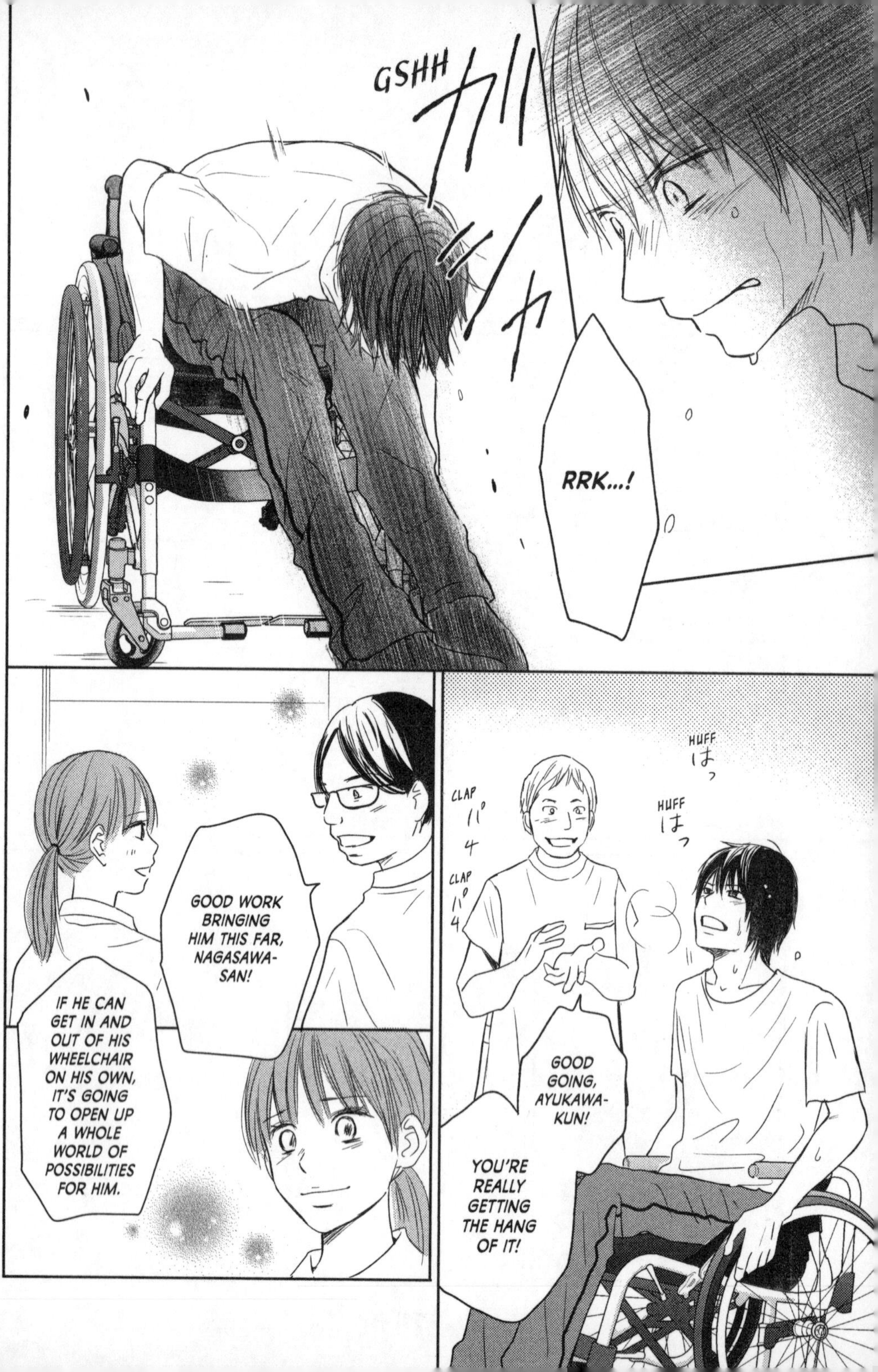
RRK...!
GSHH
HUFF
はっ
HUFF
はっ
CLAP
CLAP
GOOD GOING, AYUKAWA-KUN!
YOU'RE REALLY GETTING THE HANG OF IT!
GOOD WORK BRINGING HIM THIS FAR, NAGASAWA-SAN!
IF HE CAN GET IN AND OUT OF HIS WHEELCHAIR ON HIS OWN, IT'S GOING TO OPEN UP A WHOLE WORLD OF POSSIBILITIES FOR HIM.

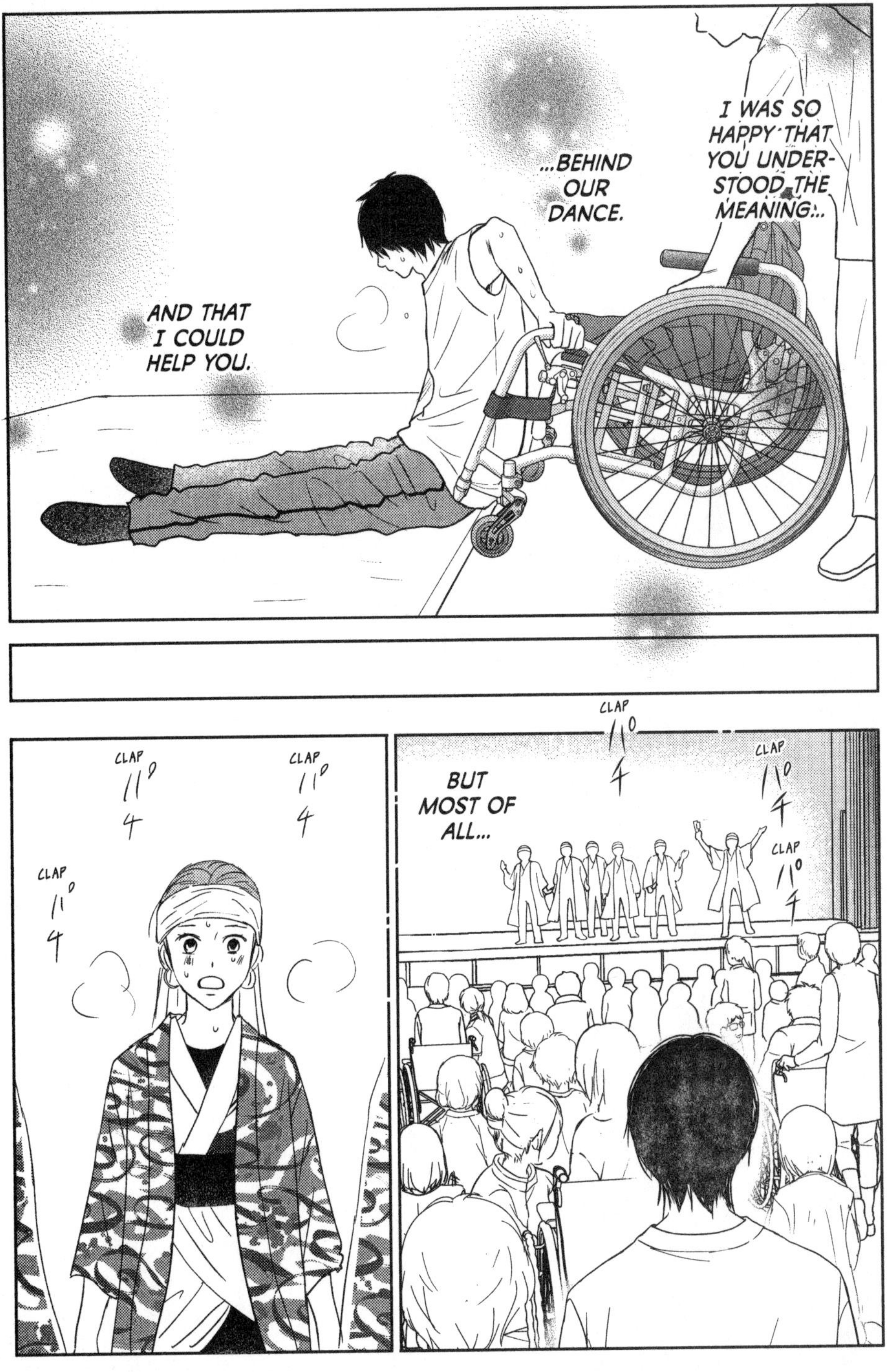
I WAS SO HAPPY THAT YOU UNDER-STOOD THE MEANING...
...BEHIND OUR DANCE.
AND THAT I COULD HELP YOU.
CLAP
CLAP
BUT MOST OF ALL...
CLAP
CLAP
CLAP
CLAP

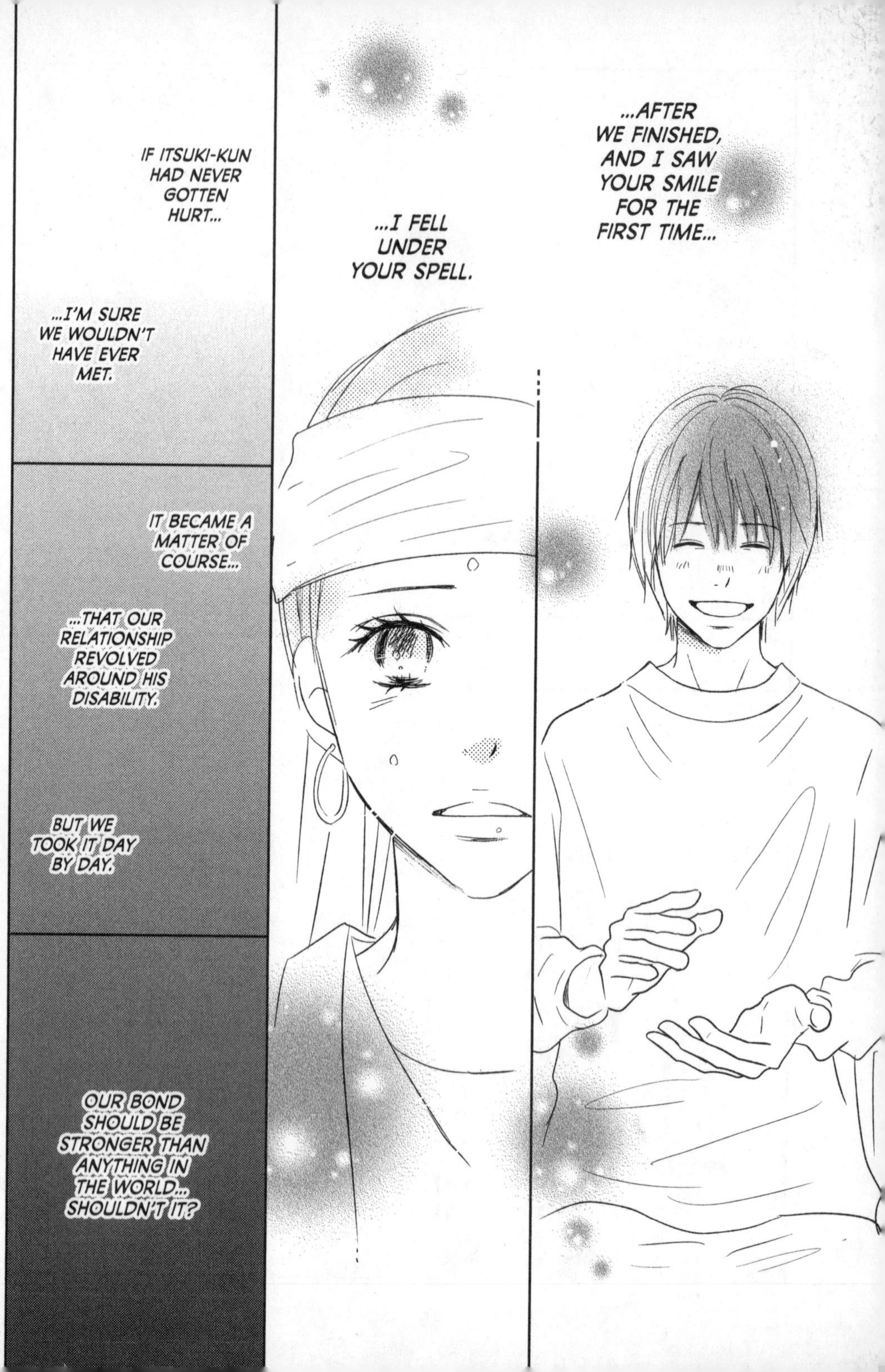
...AFTER WE FINISHED, AND I SAW YOUR SMILE FOR THE FIRST TIME...
...I FELL UNDER YOUR SPELL.
IF ITSUKI-KUN HAD NEVER GOTTEN HURT...
...I'M SURE WE WOULDN'T HAVE EVER MET.
IT BECAME A MATTER OF COURSE...
...THAT OUR RELATIONSHIP REVOLVED AROUND HIS DISABILITY.
BUT WE TOOK IT DAY BY DAY.
OUR BOND SHOULD BE STRONGER THAN ANYTHING IN THE WORLD... SHOULDN'T IT?

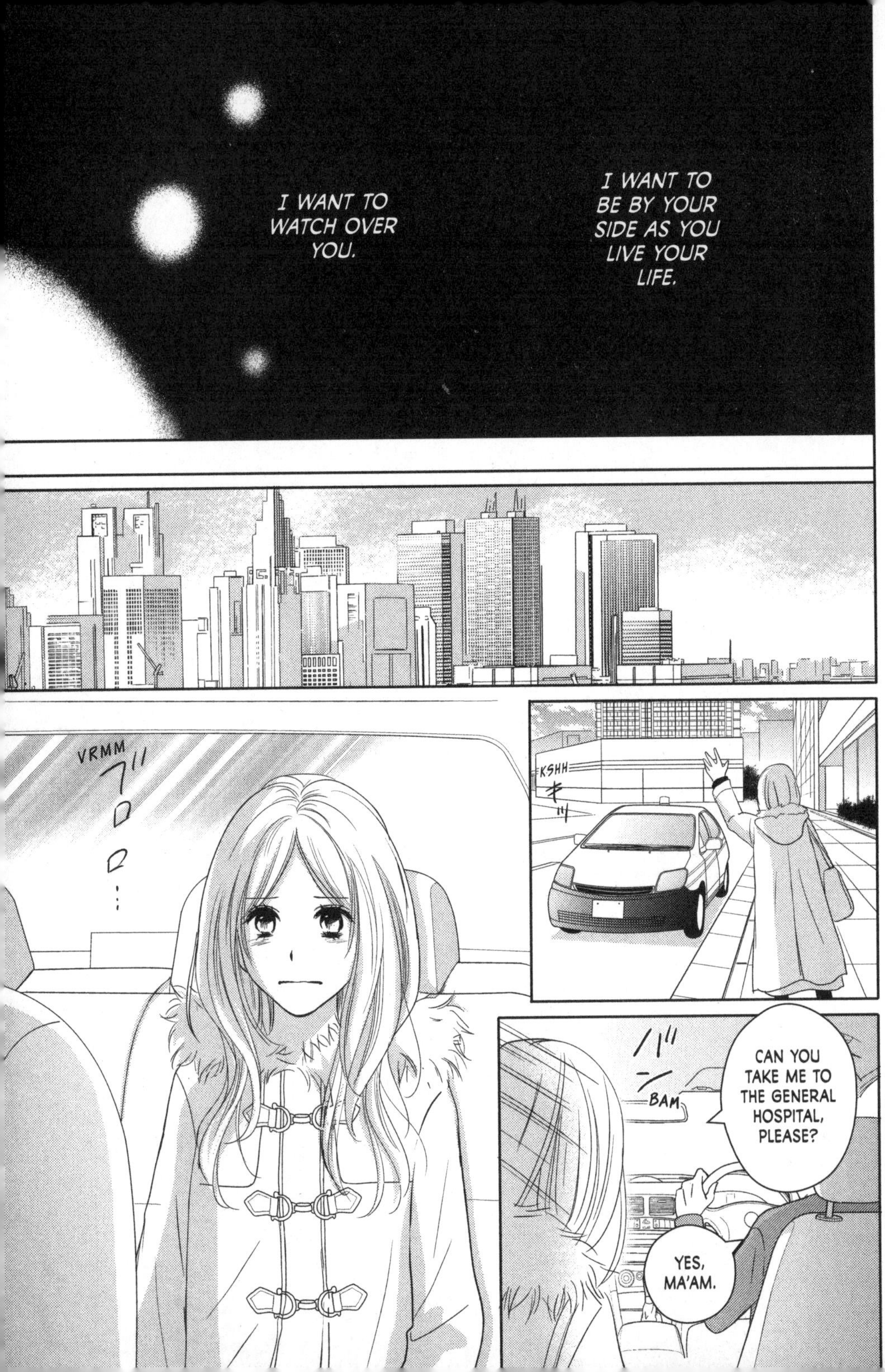
I WANT TO BE BY YOUR SIDE AS YOU LIVE YOUR LIFE.
I WANT TO WATCH OVER YOU.
KSHH
BAM
CAN YOU TAKE ME TO THE GENERAL HOSPITAL, PLEASE?
YES, MA'AM.
VRMM

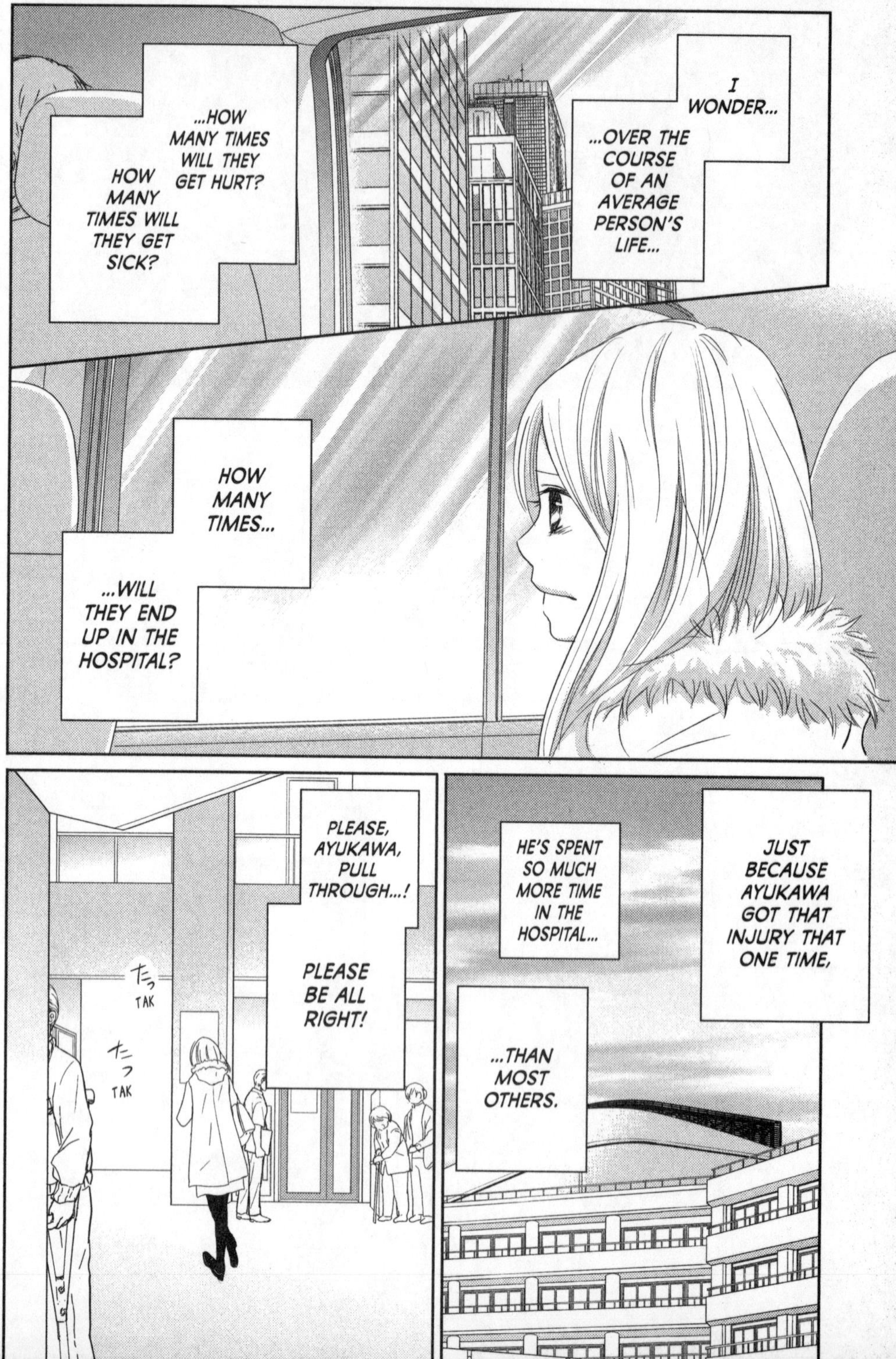
I WONDER...
...OVER THE COURSE OF AN AVERAGE PERSON'S LIFE...
...HOW MANY TIMES WILL THEY GET HURT?
HOW MANY TIMES WILL THEY GET SICK?
HOW MANY TIMES...
...WILL THEY END UP IN THE HOSPITAL?
JUST BECAUSE AYUKAWA GOT THAT INJURY THAT ONE TIME,
HE'S SPENT SO MUCH MORE TIME IN THE HOSPITAL...
...THAN MOST OTHERS.
PLEASE, AYUKAWA, PULL THROUGH...!
PLEASE BE ALL RIGHT!
たっ
TAK
たっ
TAK

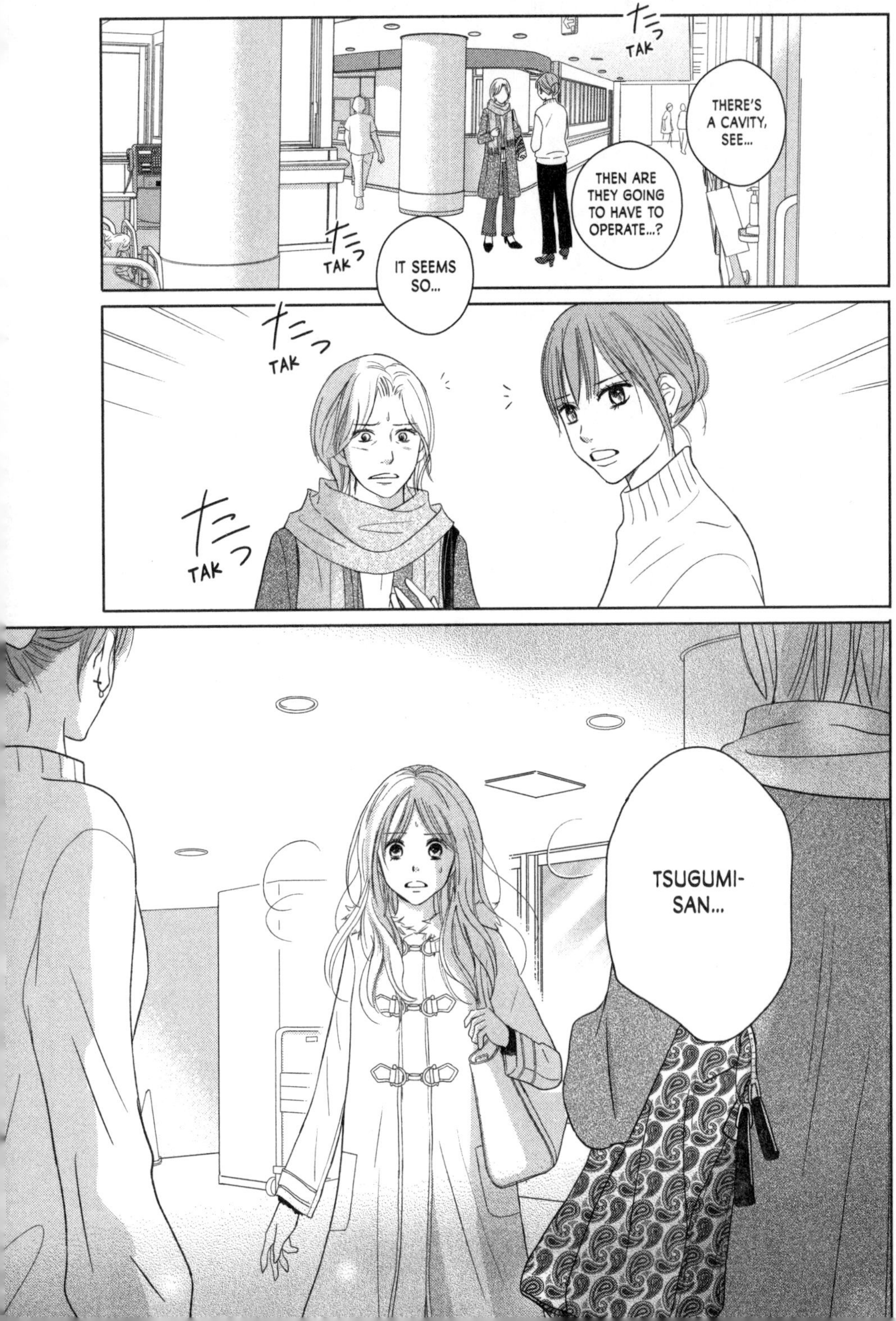
TAK
THERE'S A CAVITY, SEE...
THEN ARE THEY GOING TO HAVE TO OPERATE...?
IT SEEMS SO...
TAK
TAK
TAK
TSUGUMI-SAN...

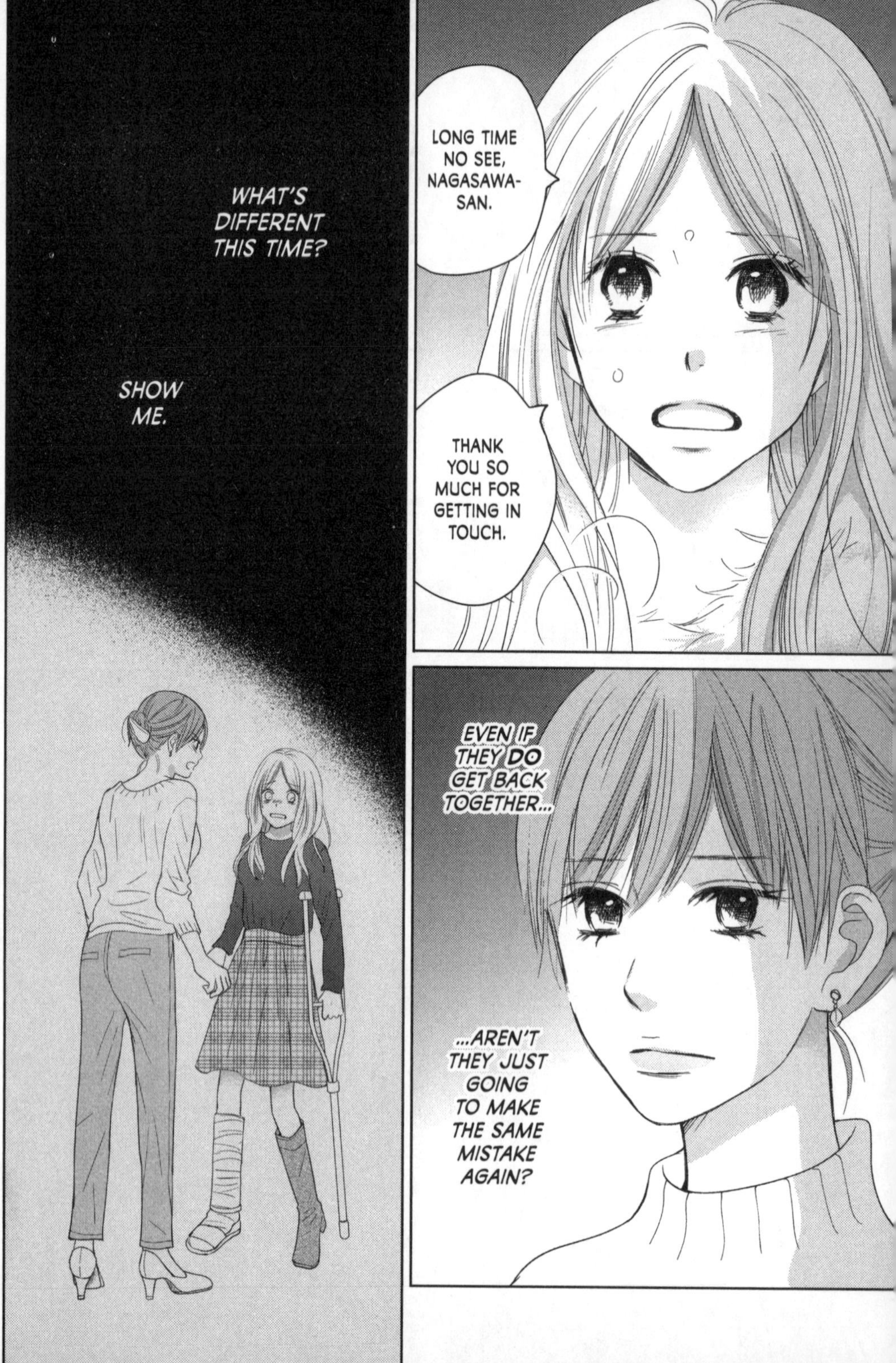
LONG TIME NO SEE, NAGASAWA-SAN.
THANK YOU SO MUCH FOR GETTING IN TOUCH.
EVEN IF THEY DO GET BACK TOGETHER...
...AREN'T THEY JUST GOING TO MAKE THE SAME MISTAKE AGAIN?
WHAT'S DIFFERENT THIS TIME?
SHOW ME.

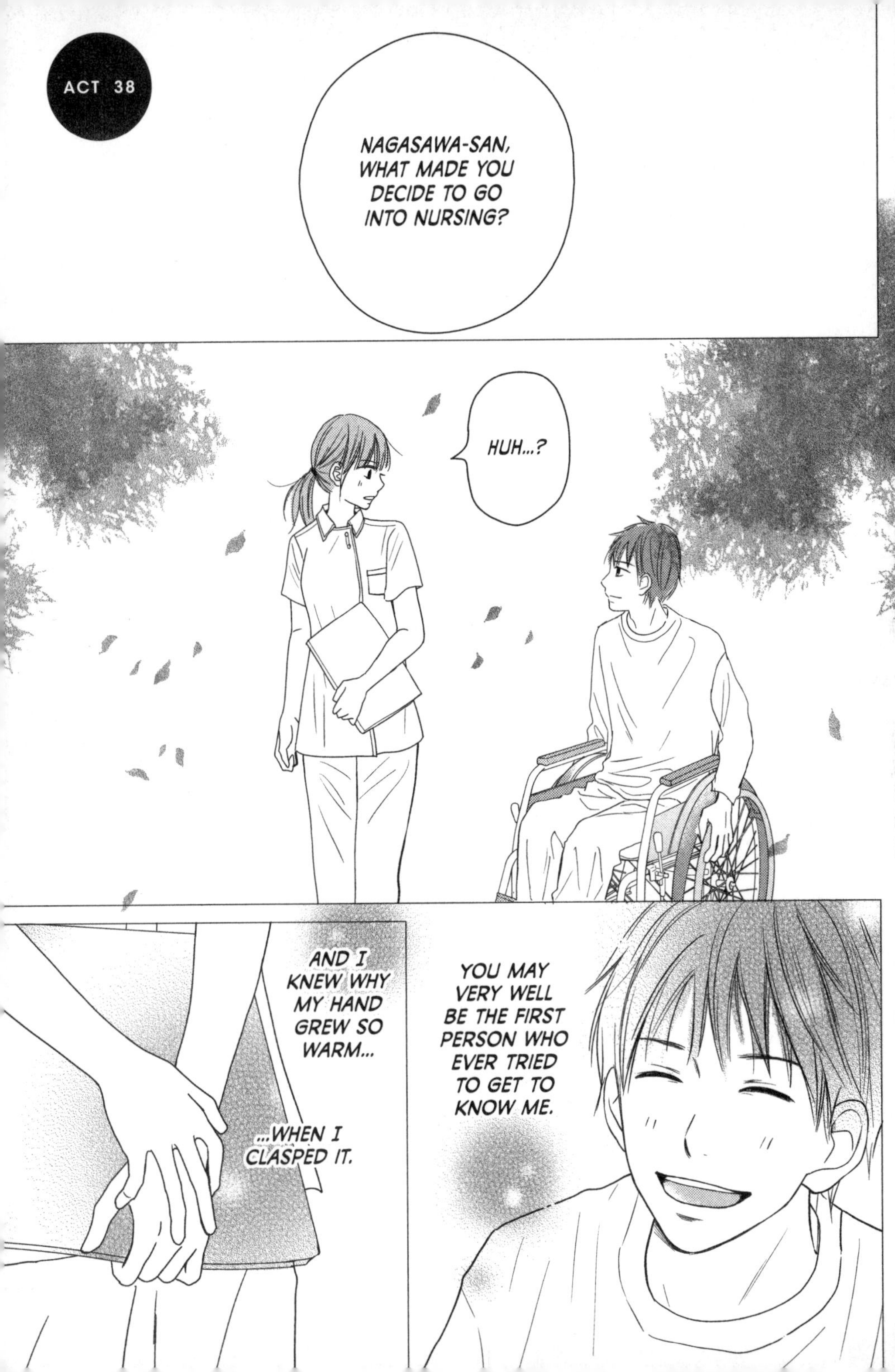
ACT 38
NAGASAWA-SAN, WHAT MADE YOU DECIDE TO GO INTO NURSING?
HUH...?
YOU MAY VERY WELL BE THE FIRST PERSON WHO EVER TRIED TO GET TO KNOW ME.
AND I KNEW WHY MY HAND GREW SO WARM...
...WHEN I CLASPED IT.

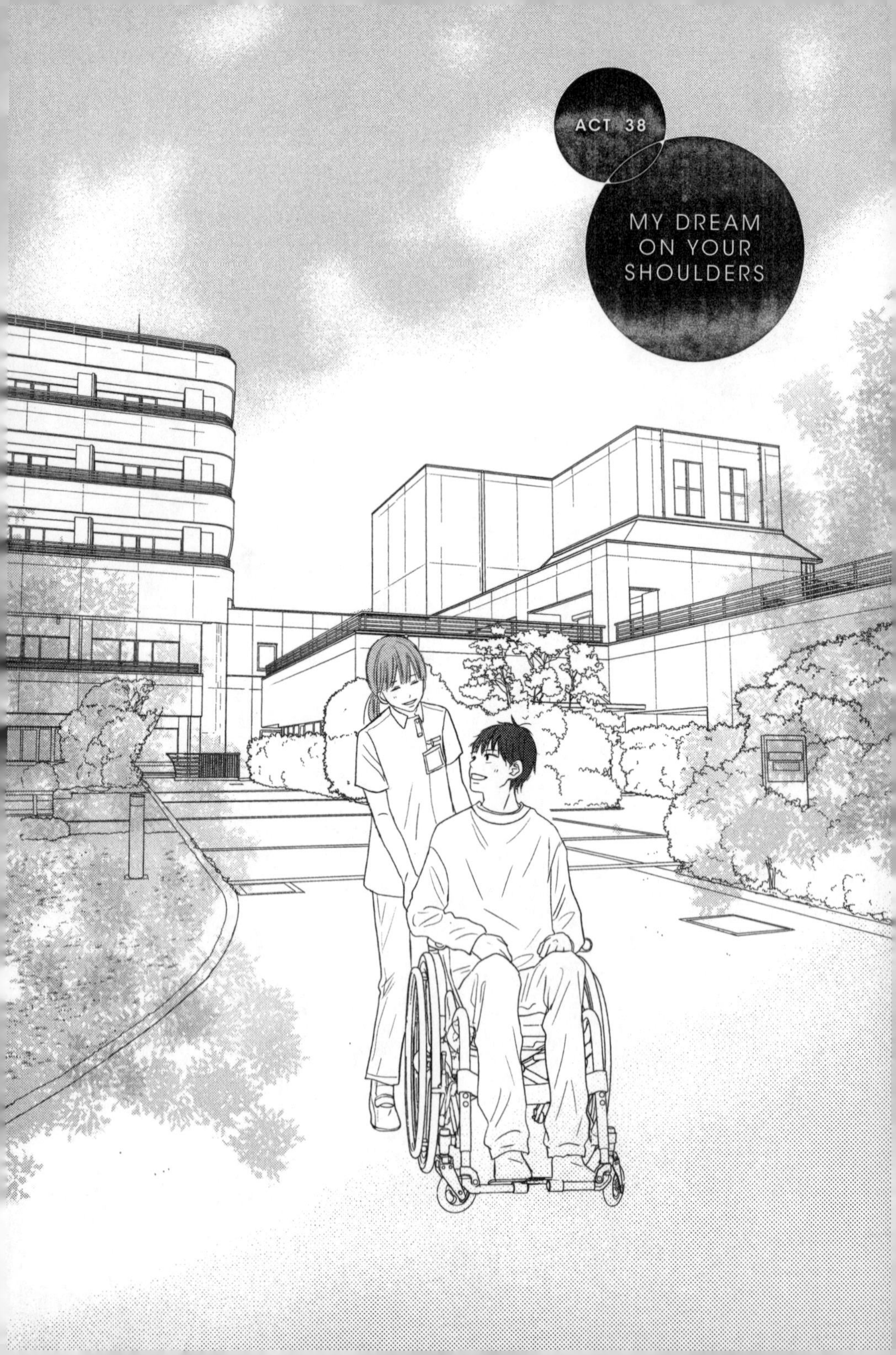
ACT 38
MY DREAM ON YOUR SHOULDERS

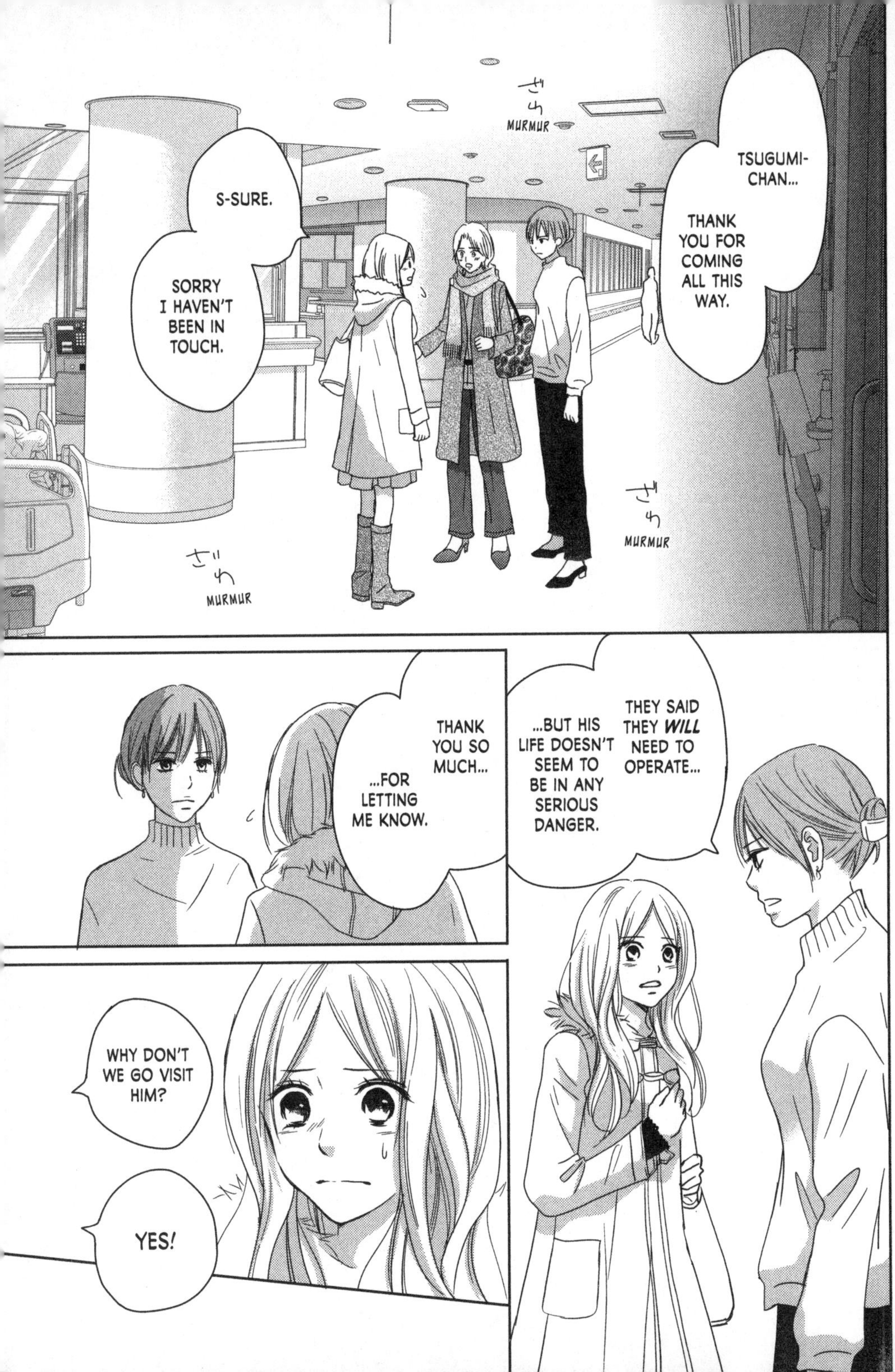
ざわ
MURMUR
TSUGUMI-CHAN...
THANK YOU FOR COMING ALL THIS WAY.
S-SURE.
SORRY I HAVEN'T BEEN IN TOUCH.
ざわ
MURMUR
ざわ
MURMUR
THEY SAID THEY *WILL* NEED TO OPERATE...
...BUT HIS LIFE DOESN'T SEEM TO BE IN ANY SERIOUS DANGER.
THANK YOU SO MUCH...
...FOR LETTING ME KNOW.
WHY DON'T WE GO VISIT HIM?
YES!

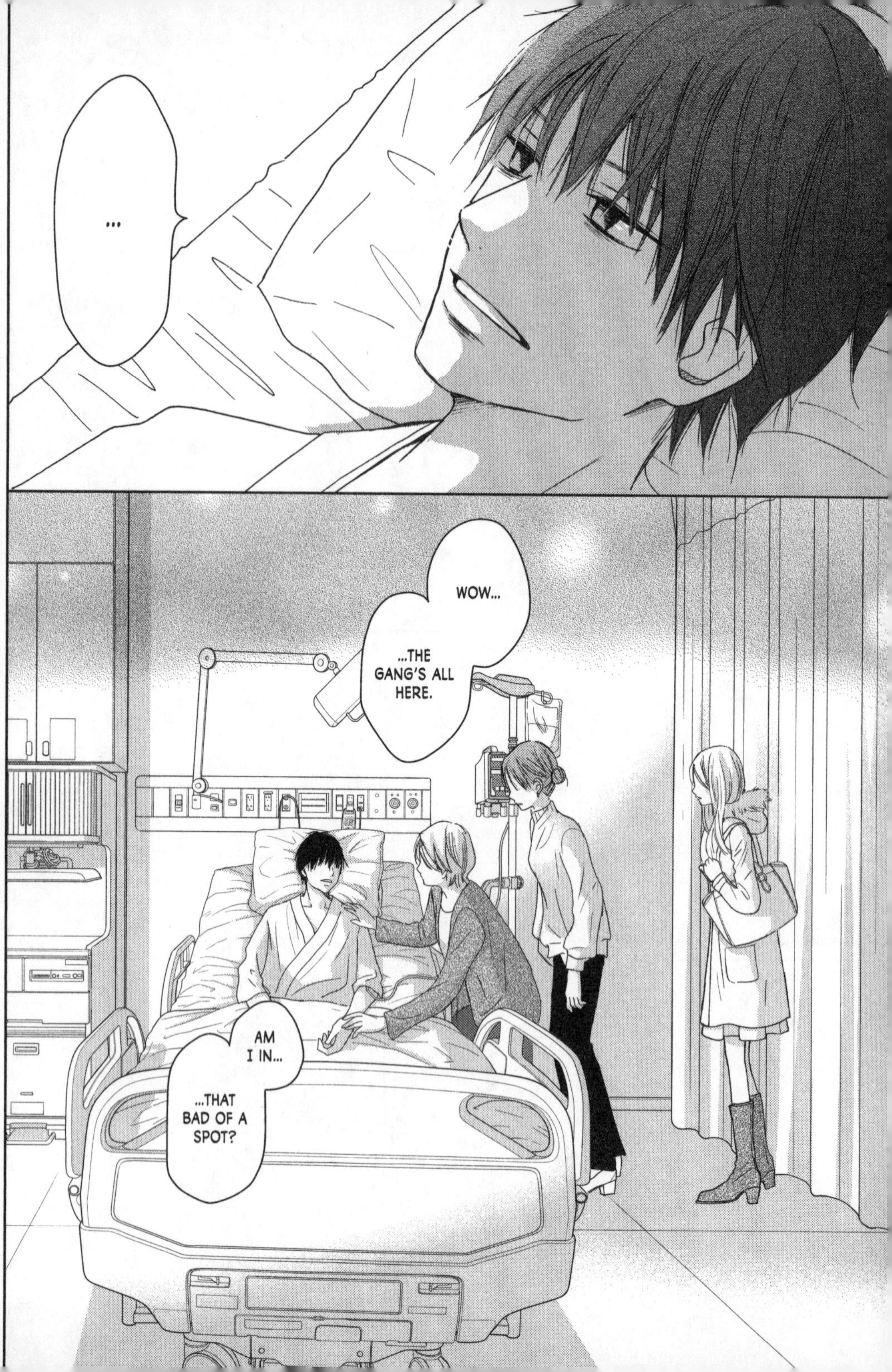
...
WOW...
...THE GANG'S ALL HERE.
AM I IN...
...THAT BAD OF A SPOT?

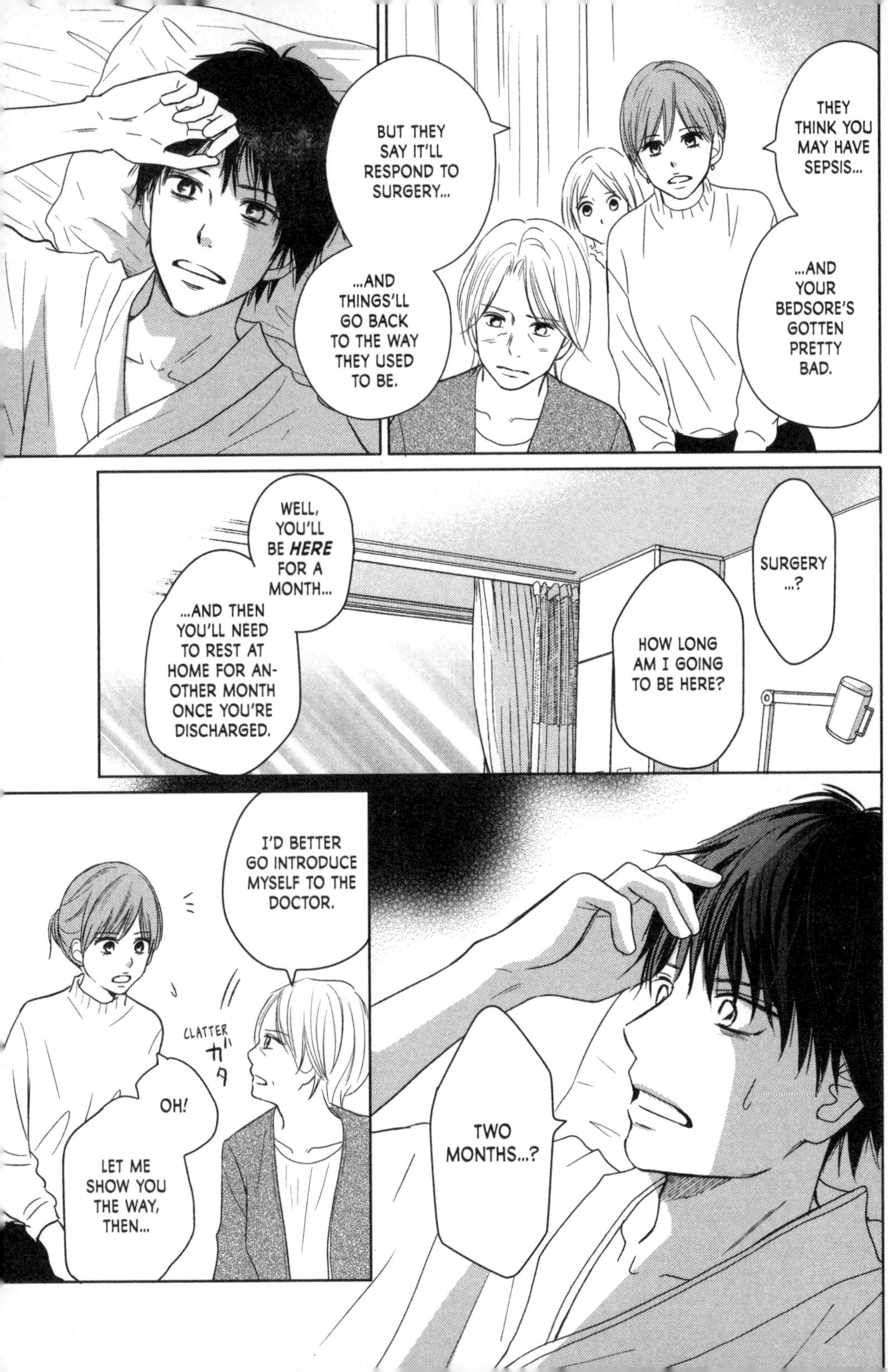
THEY THINK YOU MAY HAVE SEPSIS...
...AND YOUR BEDSORE'S GOTTEN PRETTY BAD.
BUT THEY SAY IT'LL RESPOND TO SURGERY...
...AND THINGS'LL GO BACK TO THE WAY THEY USED TO BE.
SURGERY ...?
HOW LONG AM I GOING TO BE HERE?
WELL, YOU'LL BE ***HERE*** FOR A MONTH...
...AND THEN YOU'LL NEED TO REST AT HOME FOR ANOTHER MONTH ONCE YOU'RE DISCHARGED.
TWO MONTHS...?
I'D BETTER GO INTRODUCE MYSELF TO THE DOCTOR.
CLATTER ガタ
OH!
LET ME SHOW YOU THE WAY, THEN...

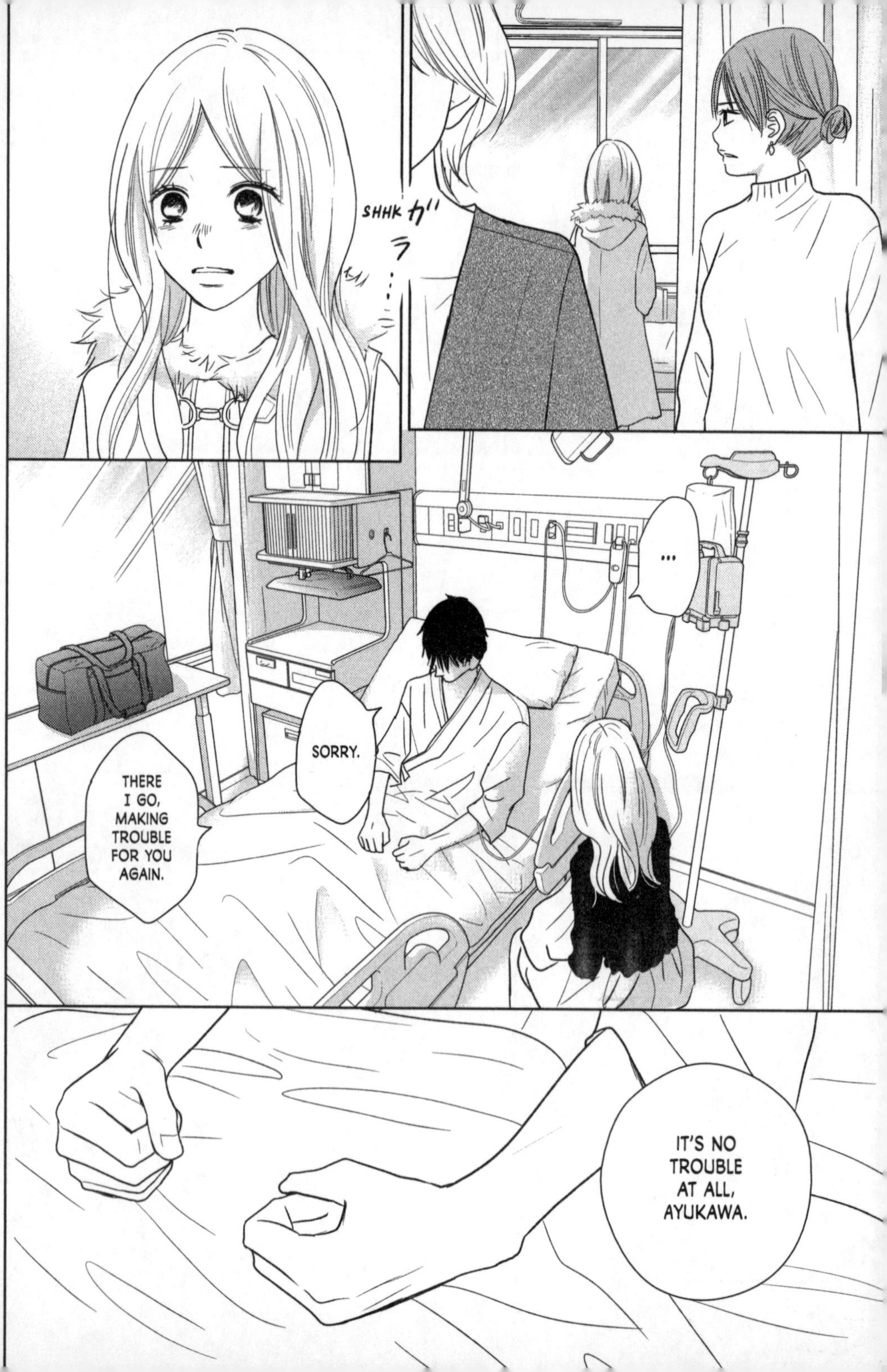
SHHK ガラ…
...
SORRY.
THERE I GO, MAKING TROUBLE FOR YOU AGAIN.
IT'S NO TROUBLE AT ALL, AYUKAWA.

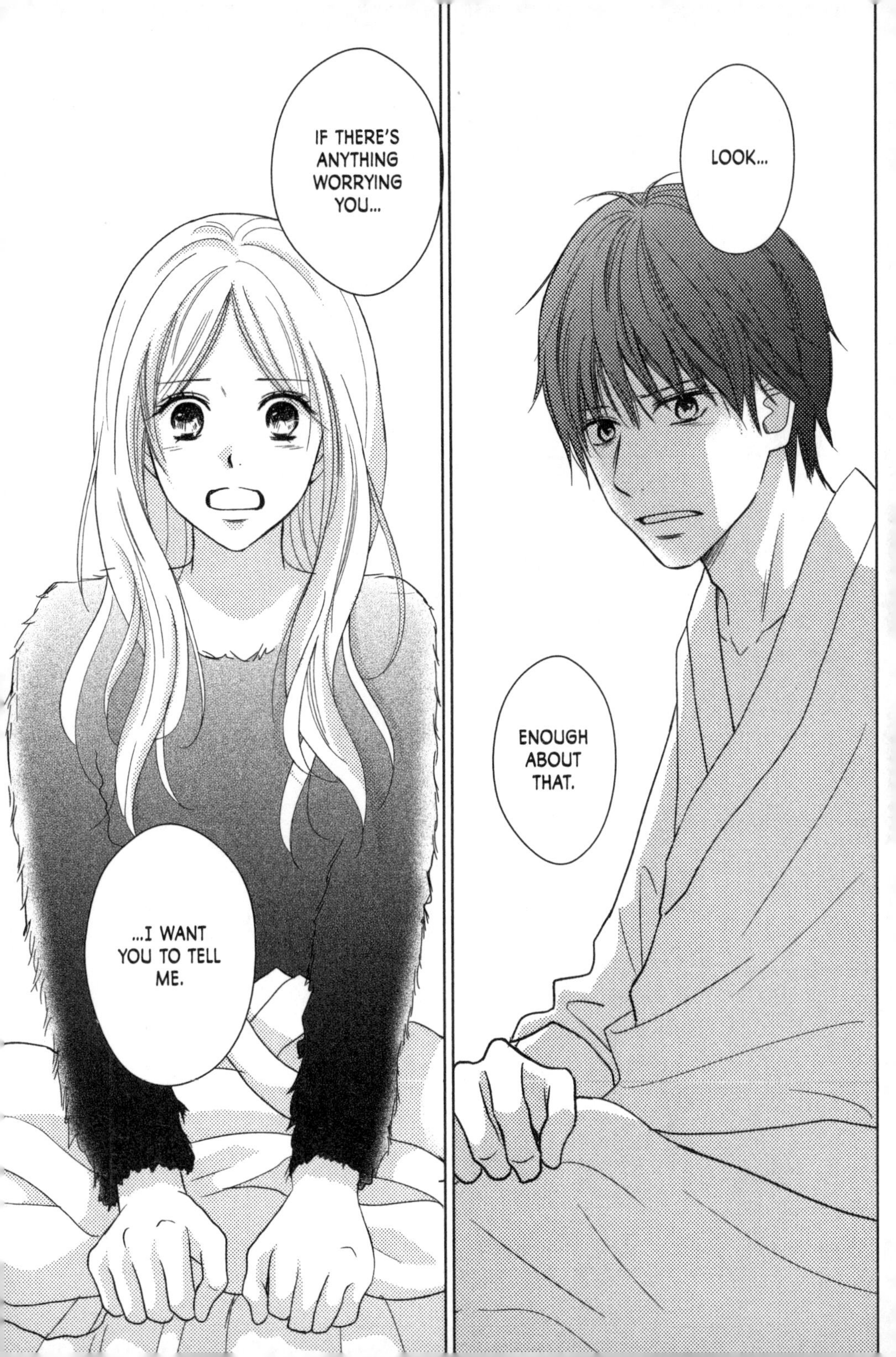
LOOK...
ENOUGH ABOUT THAT.
IF THERE'S ANYTHING WORRYING YOU...
...I WANT YOU TO TELL ME.

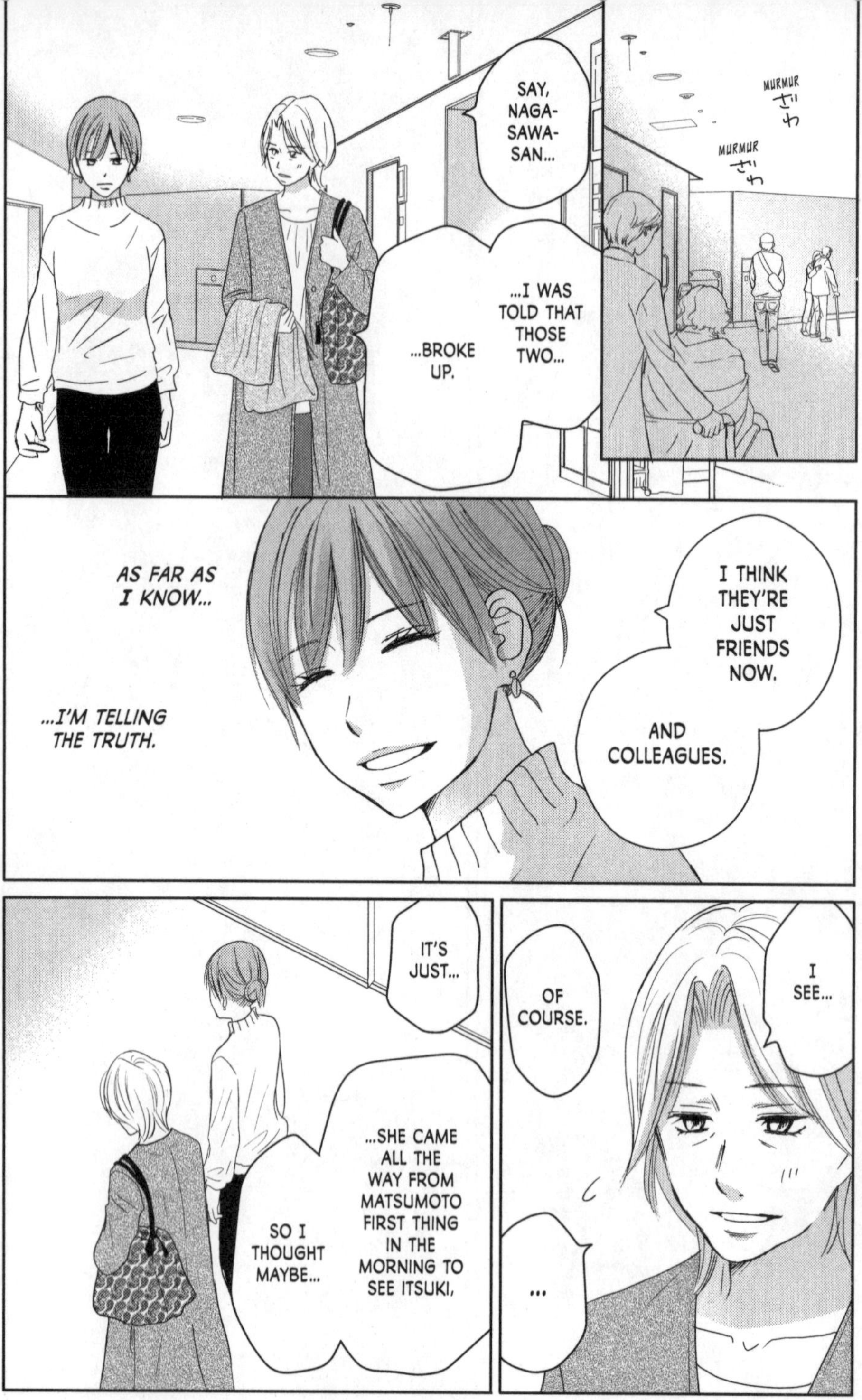
MURMUR ざわ
MURMUR ざわ
SAY, NAGA-SAWA-SAN...
...I WAS TOLD THAT THOSE TWO...
...BROKE UP.
I THINK THEY'RE JUST FRIENDS NOW.
AND COLLEAGUES.
AS FAR AS I KNOW...
...I'M TELLING THE TRUTH.
I SEE...
OF COURSE.
...
IT'S JUST...
...SHE CAME ALL THE WAY FROM MATSUMOTO FIRST THING IN THE MORNING TO SEE ITSUKI,
SO I THOUGHT MAYBE...

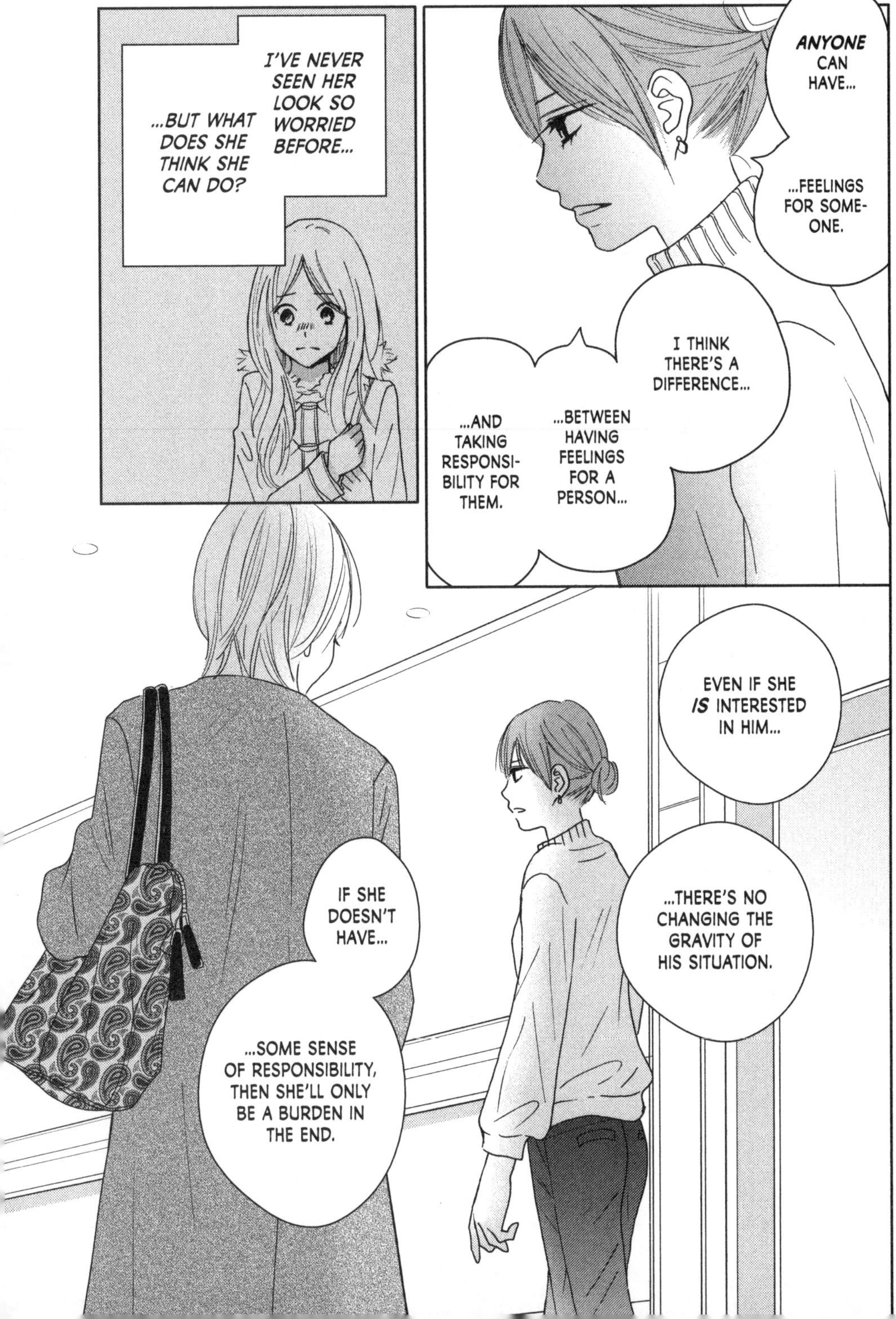
ANYONE CAN HAVE...
...FEELINGS FOR SOMEONE.
I THINK THERE'S A DIFFERENCE...
...BETWEEN HAVING FEELINGS FOR A PERSON...
...AND TAKING RESPONSIBILITY FOR THEM.
I'VE NEVER SEEN HER LOOK SO WORRIED BEFORE...
...BUT WHAT DOES SHE THINK SHE CAN DO?
EVEN IF SHE IS INTERESTED IN HIM...
...THERE'S NO CHANGING THE GRAVITY OF HIS SITUATION.
IF SHE DOESN'T HAVE...
...SOME SENSE OF RESPONSIBILITY, THEN SHE'LL ONLY BE A BURDEN IN THE END.

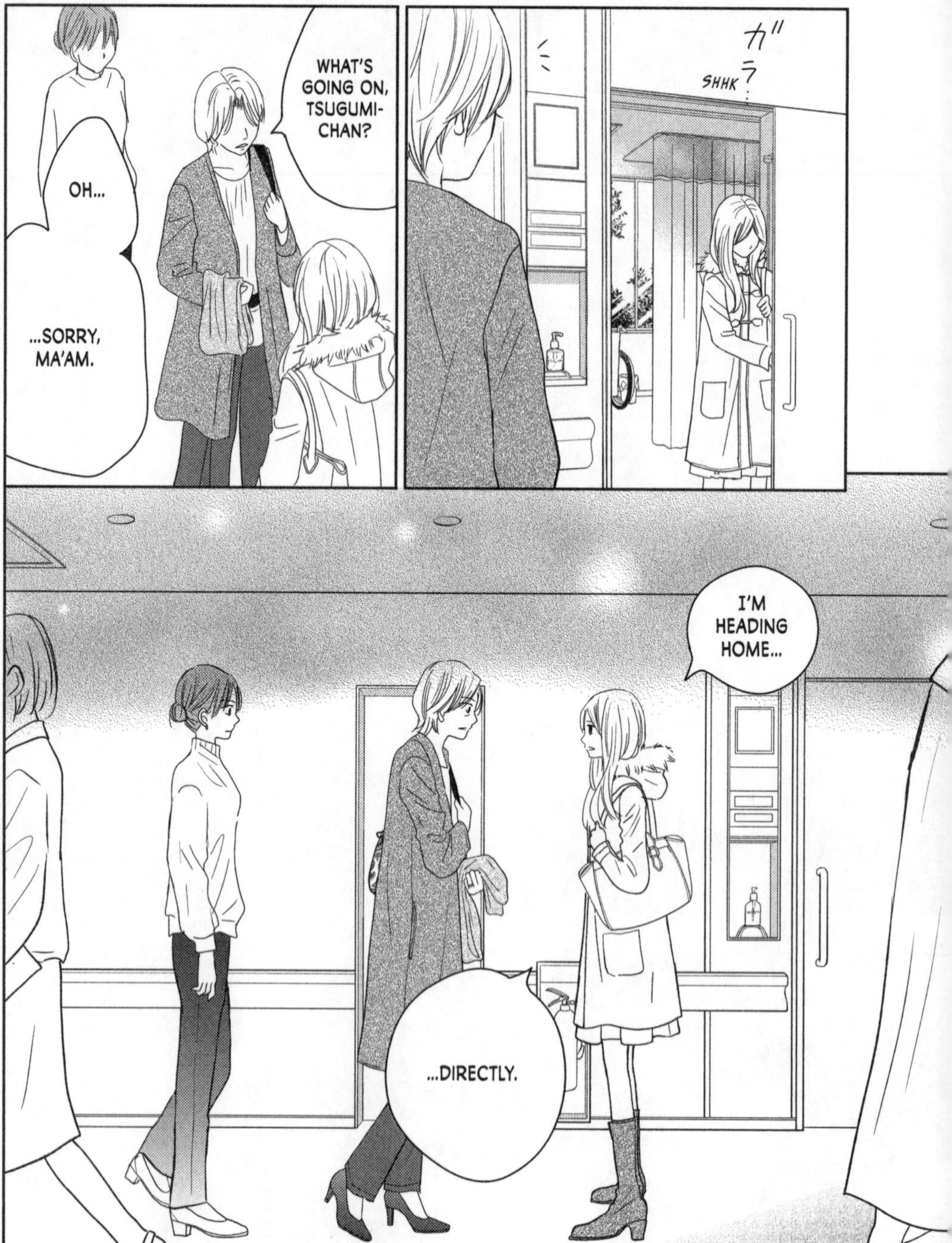
ガラ
SHHK
WHAT'S GOING ON, TSUGUMI-CHAN?
OH...
...SORRY, MA'AM.
I'M HEADING HOME...
...DIRECTLY.

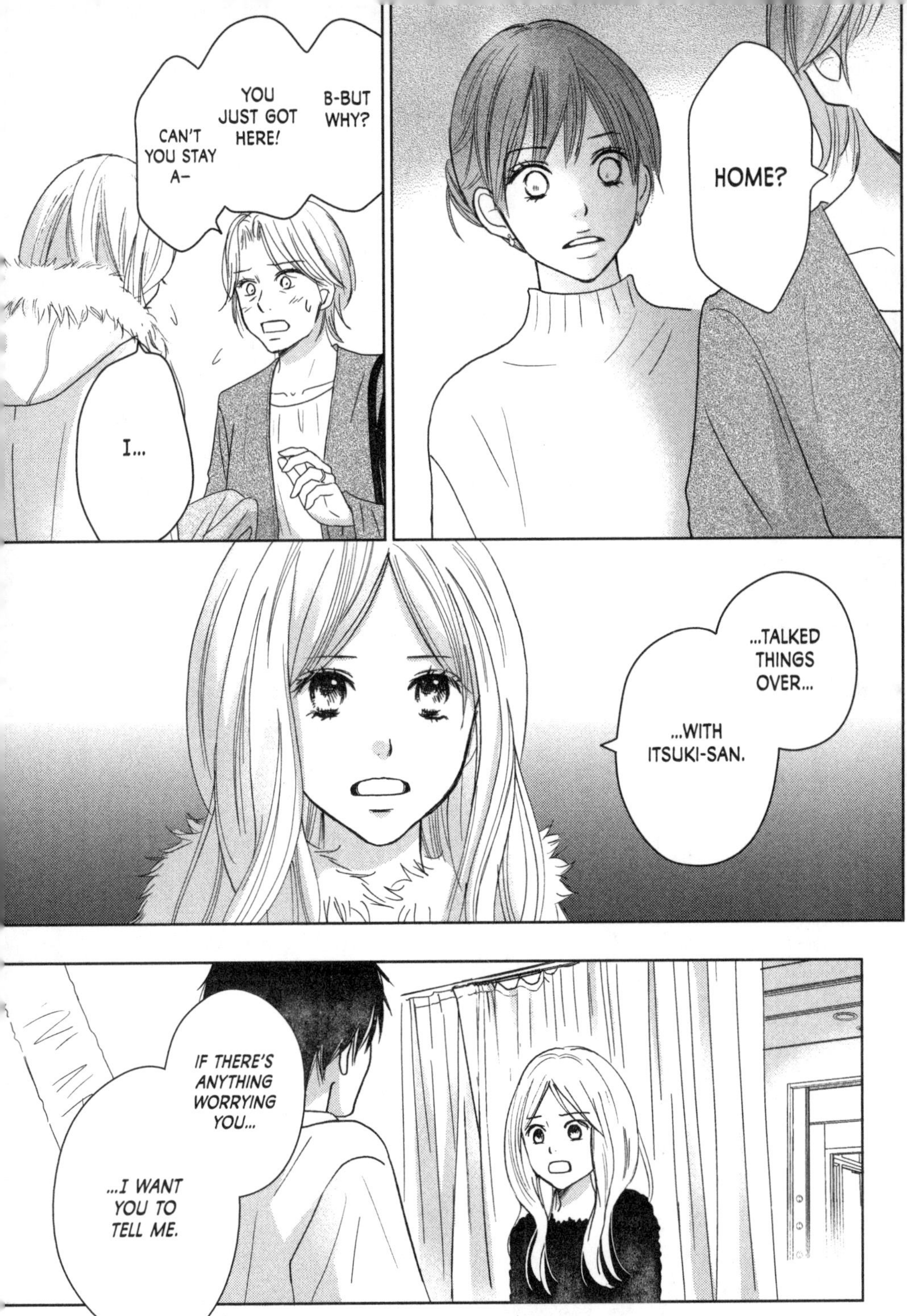
HOME?
B-BUT WHY?
YOU JUST GOT HERE!
CAN'T YOU STAY A-
I...
...TALKED THINGS OVER...
...WITH ITSUKI-SAN.
IF THERE'S ANYTHING WORRYING YOU...
...I WANT YOU TO TELL ME.

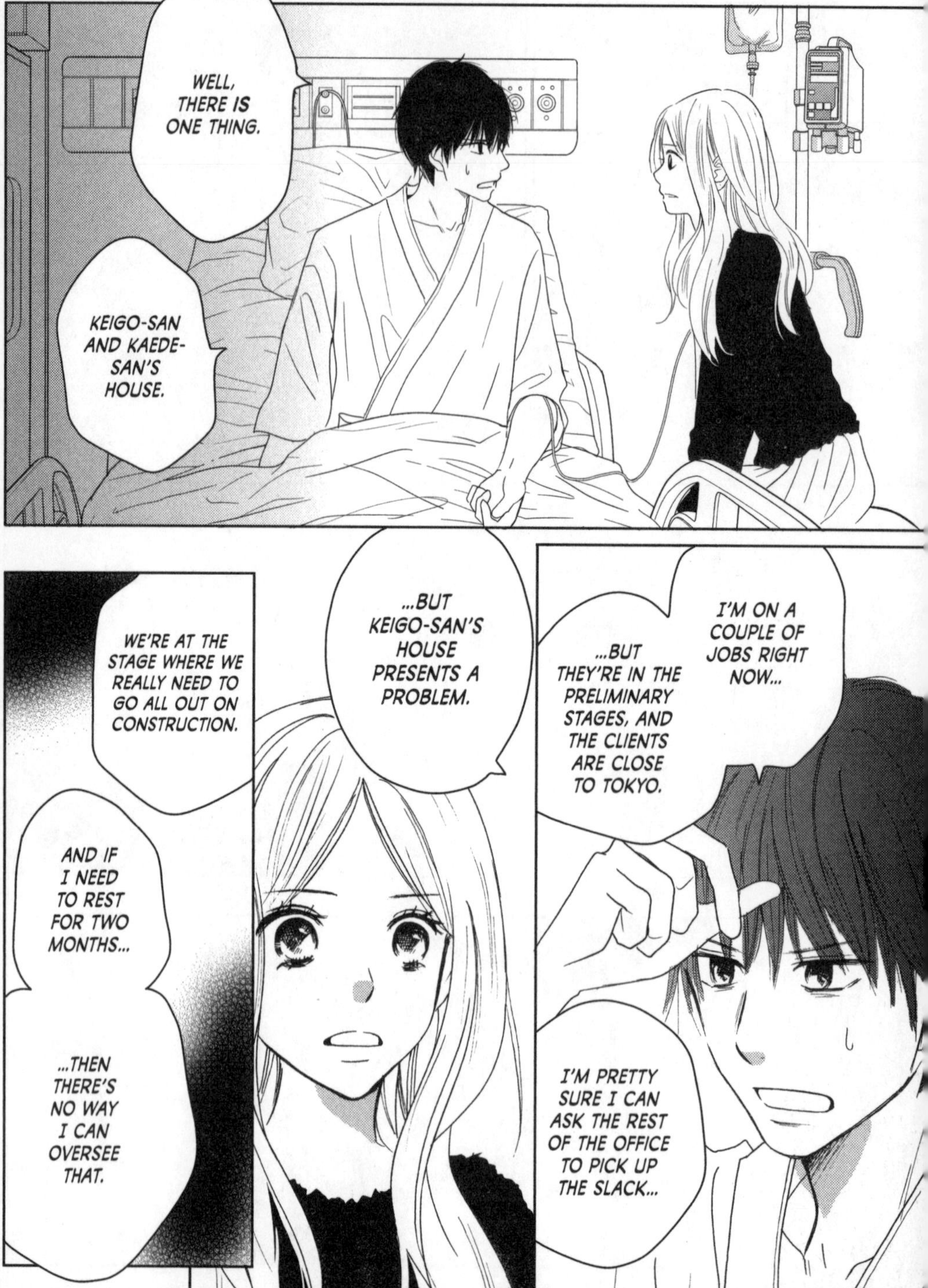
WELL, THERE IS ONE THING.
KEIGO-SAN AND KAEDE-SAN'S HOUSE.
I'M ON A COUPLE OF JOBS RIGHT NOW...
...BUT THEY'RE IN THE PRELIMINARY STAGES, AND THE CLIENTS ARE CLOSE TO TOKYO.
I'M PRETTY SURE I CAN ASK THE REST OF THE OFFICE TO PICK UP THE SLACK...
...BUT KEIGO-SAN'S HOUSE PRESENTS A PROBLEM.
WE'RE AT THE STAGE WHERE WE REALLY NEED TO GO ALL OUT ON CONSTRUCTION.
AND IF I NEED TO REST FOR TWO MONTHS...
...THEN THERE'S NO WAY I CAN OVERSEE THAT.

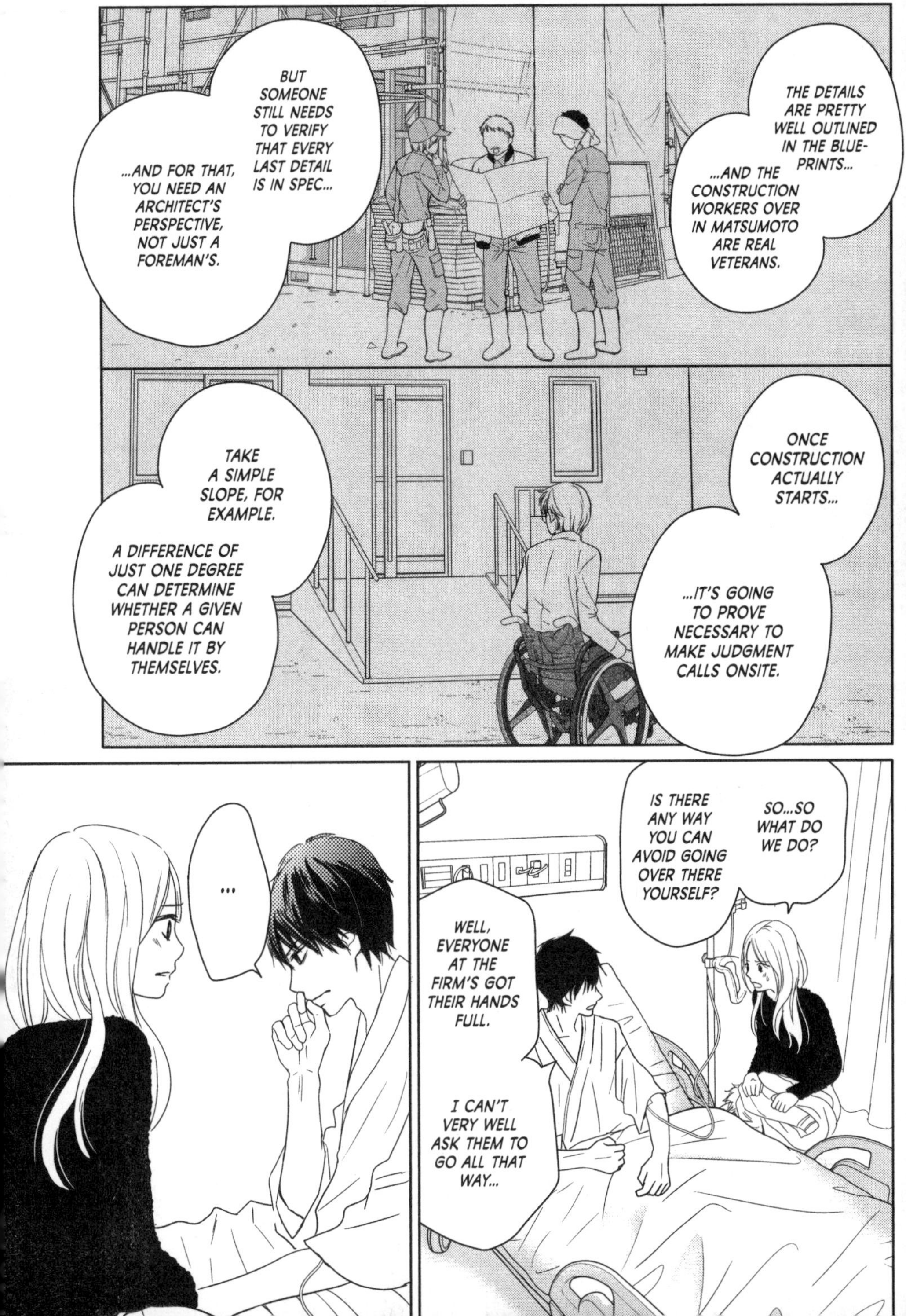
THE DETAILS ARE PRETTY WELL OUTLINED IN THE BLUE-PRINTS...
...AND THE CONSTRUCTION WORKERS OVER IN MATSUMOTO ARE REAL VETERANS.
BUT SOMEONE STILL NEEDS TO VERIFY THAT EVERY LAST DETAIL IS IN SPEC...
...AND FOR THAT, YOU NEED AN ARCHITECT'S PERSPECTIVE, NOT JUST A FOREMAN'S.
ONCE CONSTRUCTION ACTUALLY STARTS...
...IT'S GOING TO PROVE NECESSARY TO MAKE JUDGMENT CALLS ONSITE.
TAKE A SIMPLE SLOPE, FOR EXAMPLE.
A DIFFERENCE OF JUST ONE DEGREE CAN DETERMINE WHETHER A GIVEN PERSON CAN HANDLE IT BY THEMSELVES.
SO...SO WHAT DO WE DO?
IS THERE ANY WAY YOU CAN AVOID GOING OVER THERE YOURSELF?
WELL, EVERYONE AT THE FIRM'S GOT THEIR HANDS FULL.
I CAN'T VERY WELL ASK THEM TO GO ALL THAT WAY...
...

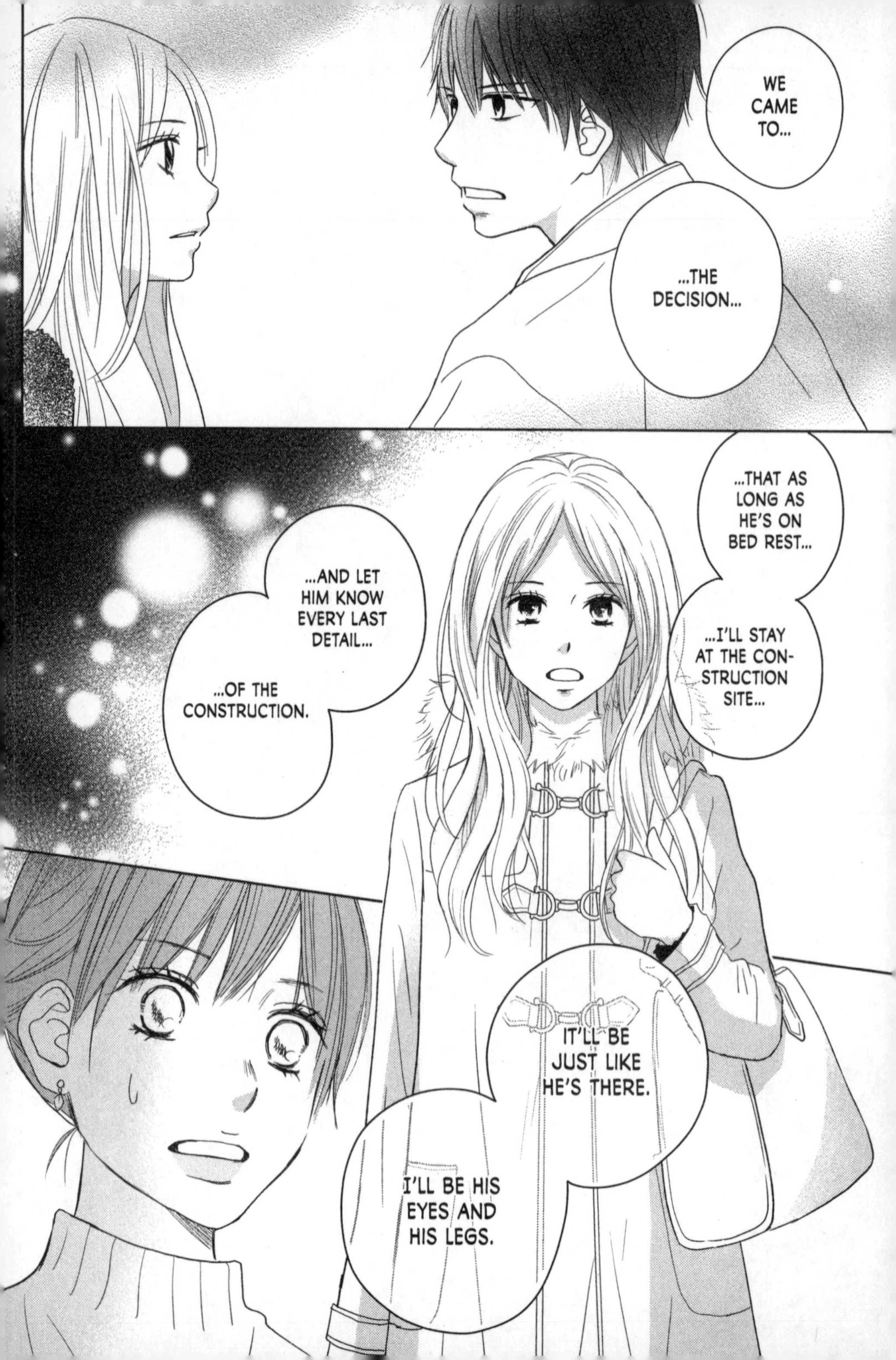

WE CAME TO...
...THE DECISION...
...THAT AS LONG AS HE'S ON BED REST...
...I'LL STAY AT THE CON-STRUCTION SITE...
...AND LET HIM KNOW EVERY LAST DETAIL...
...OF THE CONSTRUCTION.
IT'LL BE JUST LIKE HE'S THERE.
I'LL BE HIS EYES AND HIS LEGS.

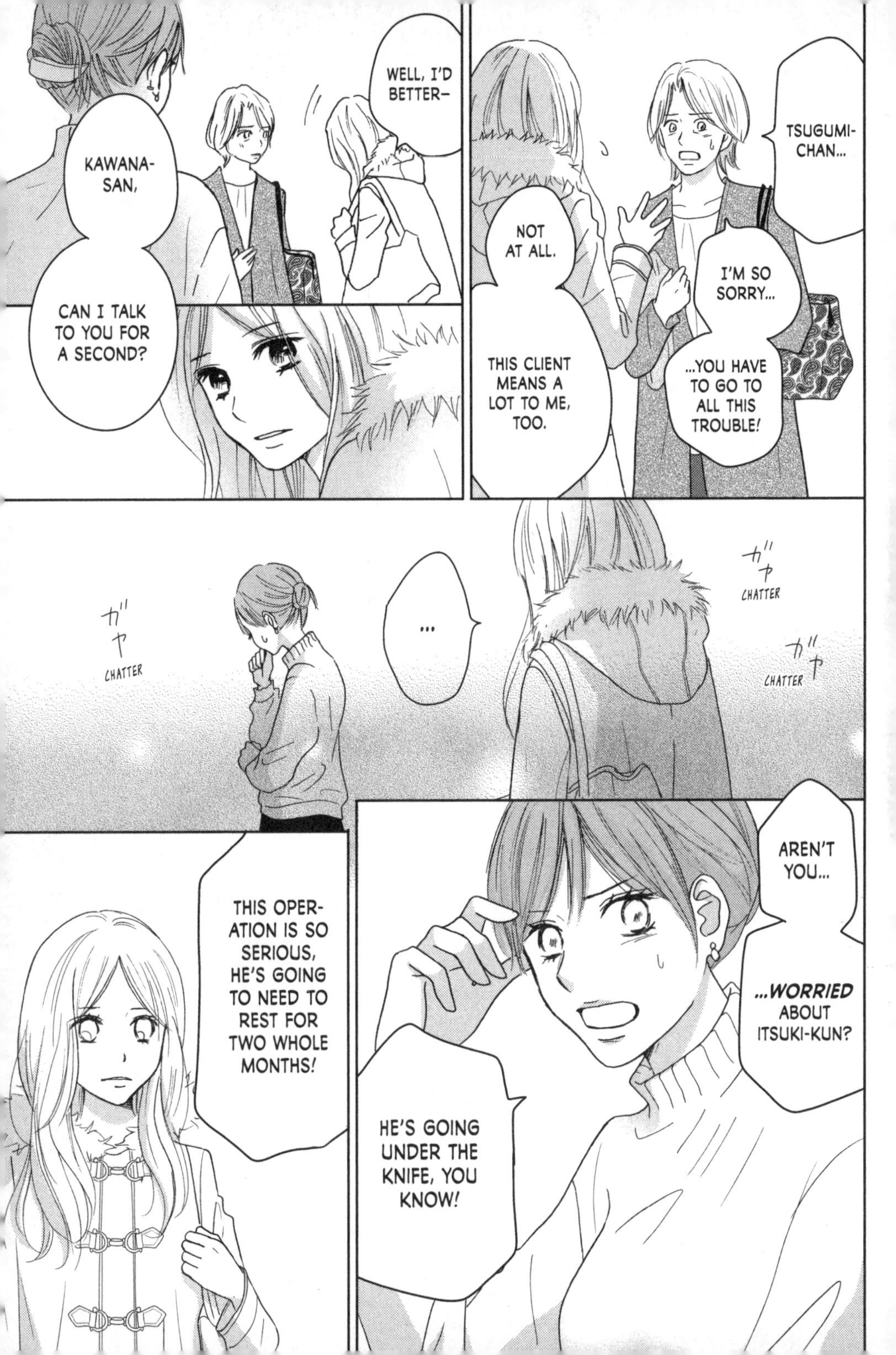
TSUGUMI-CHAN...
I'M SO SORRY...
...YOU HAVE TO GO TO ALL THIS TROUBLE!
NOT AT ALL.
THIS CLIENT MEANS A LOT TO ME, TOO.
WELL, I'D BETTER—
KAWANA-SAN,
CAN I TALK TO YOU FOR A SECOND?
ガヤ CHATTER
ガヤ CHATTER
...
ガヤ CHATTER
AREN'T YOU...
...WORRIED ABOUT ITSUKI-KUN?
HE'S GOING UNDER THE KNIFE, YOU KNOW!
THIS OPERATION IS SO SERIOUS, HE'S GOING TO NEED TO REST FOR TWO WHOLE MONTHS!

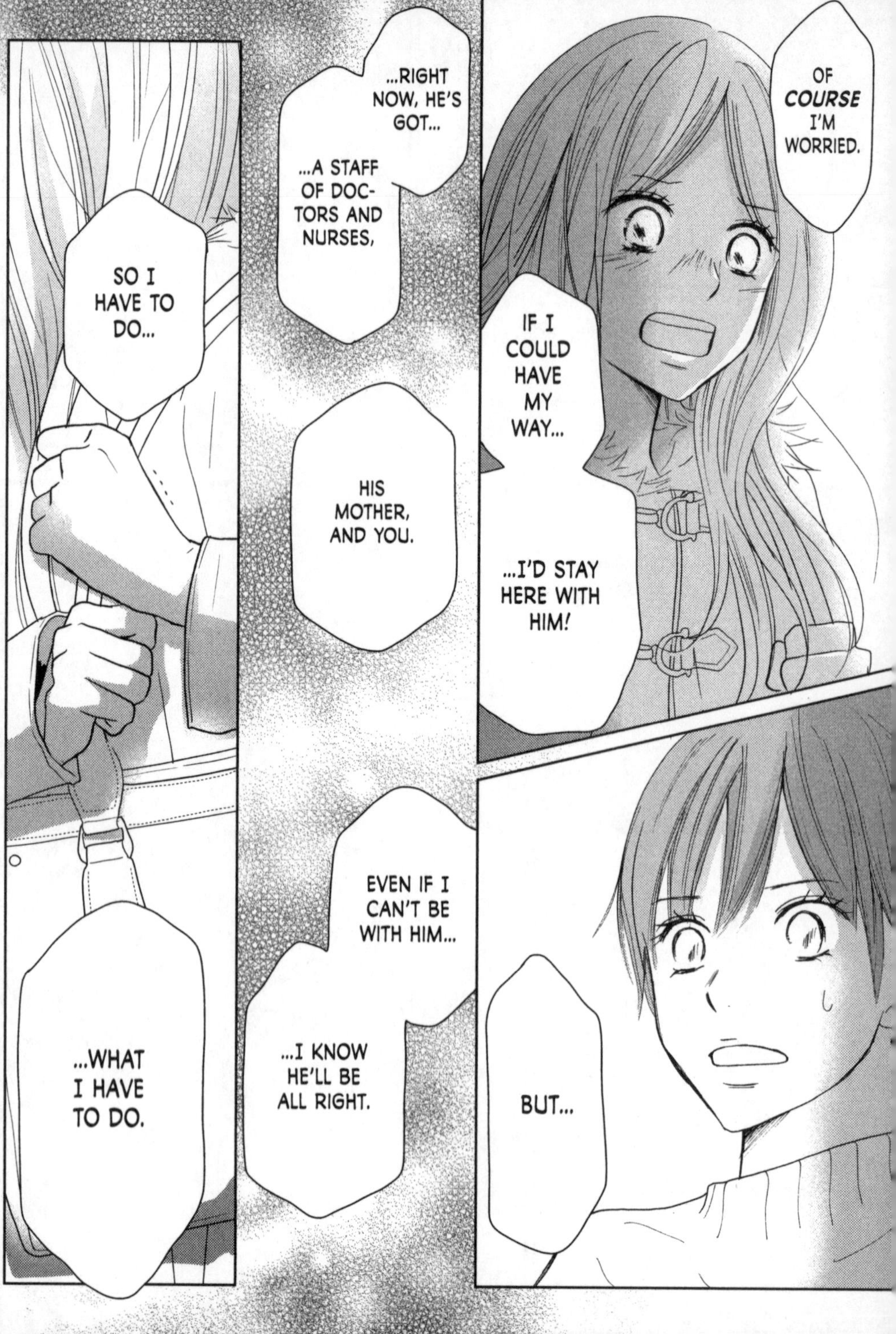
OF *COURSE* I'M WORRIED.
IF I COULD HAVE MY WAY...
...I'D STAY HERE WITH HIM!
BUT...
...RIGHT NOW, HE'S GOT...
...A STAFF OF DOC-TORS AND NURSES,
HIS MOTHER, AND YOU.
EVEN IF I CAN'T BE WITH HIM...
...I KNOW HE'LL BE ALL RIGHT.
SO I HAVE TO DO...
...WHAT I HAVE TO DO.

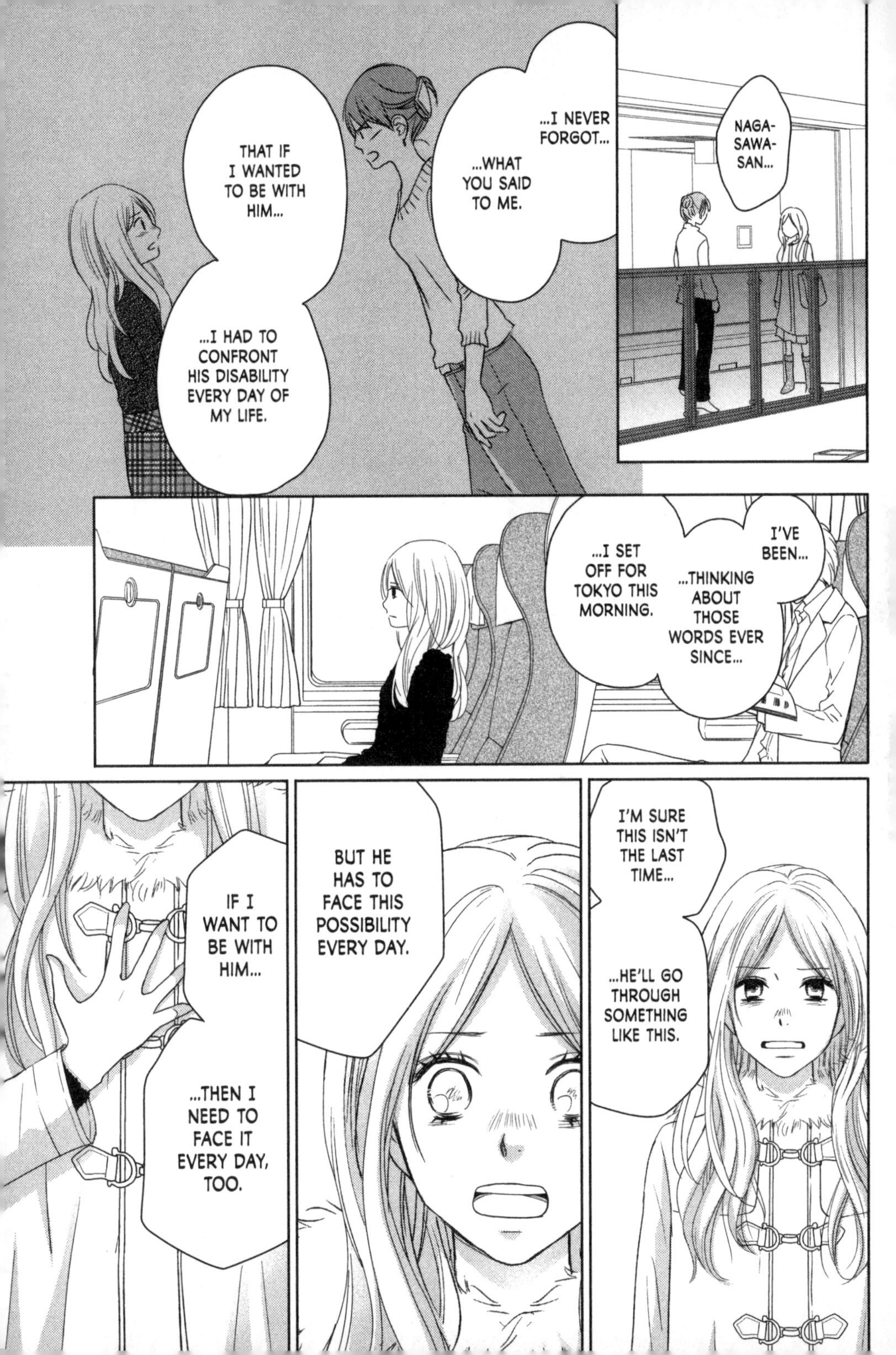
NAGA-SAWA-SAN...
...I NEVER FORGOT...
...WHAT YOU SAID TO ME.
THAT IF I WANTED TO BE WITH HIM...
...I HAD TO CONFRONT HIS DISABILITY EVERY DAY OF MY LIFE.
I'VE BEEN...
...THINKING ABOUT THOSE WORDS EVER SINCE...
...I SET OFF FOR TOKYO THIS MORNING.
I'M SURE THIS ISN'T THE LAST TIME...
...HE'LL GO THROUGH SOMETHING LIKE THIS.
BUT HE HAS TO FACE THIS POSSIBILITY EVERY DAY.
IF I WANT TO BE WITH HIM...
...THEN I NEED TO FACE IT EVERY DAY, TOO.

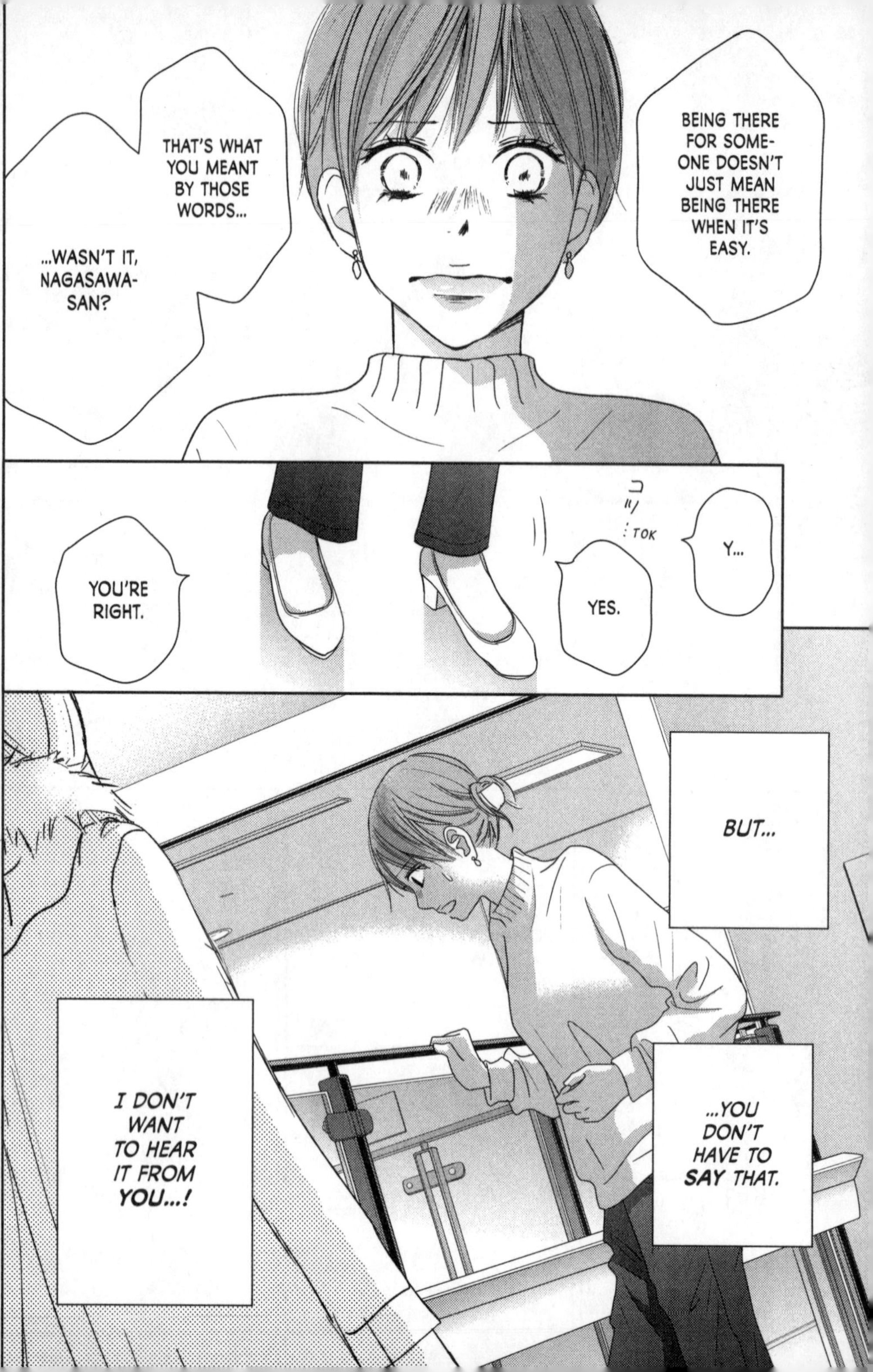
BEING THERE FOR SOME-ONE DOESN'T JUST MEAN BEING THERE WHEN IT'S EASY.
THAT'S WHAT YOU MEANT BY THOSE WORDS...
...WASN'T IT, NAGASAWA-SAN?
コツ TOK
Y...
YES.
YOU'RE RIGHT.
BUT...
...YOU DON'T HAVE TO **SAY** THAT.
I DON'T WANT TO HEAR IT FROM **YOU**...!

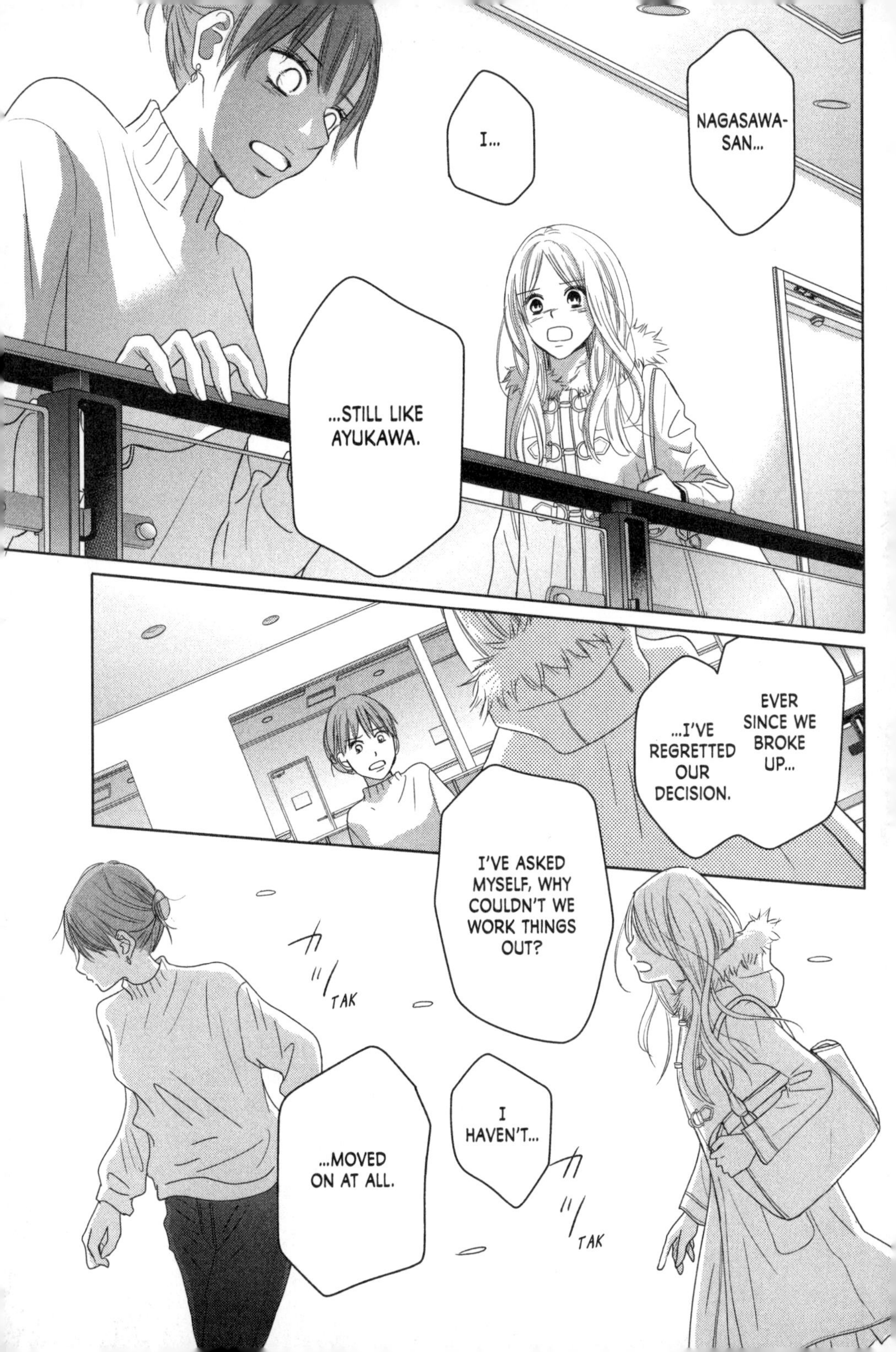
NAGASAWA-SAN...
I...
...STILL LIKE AYUKAWA.
EVER SINCE WE BROKE UP...
...I'VE REGRETTED OUR DECISION.
I'VE ASKED MYSELF, WHY COULDN'T WE WORK THINGS OUT?
TAK
I HAVEN'T...
...MOVED ON AT ALL.
TAK

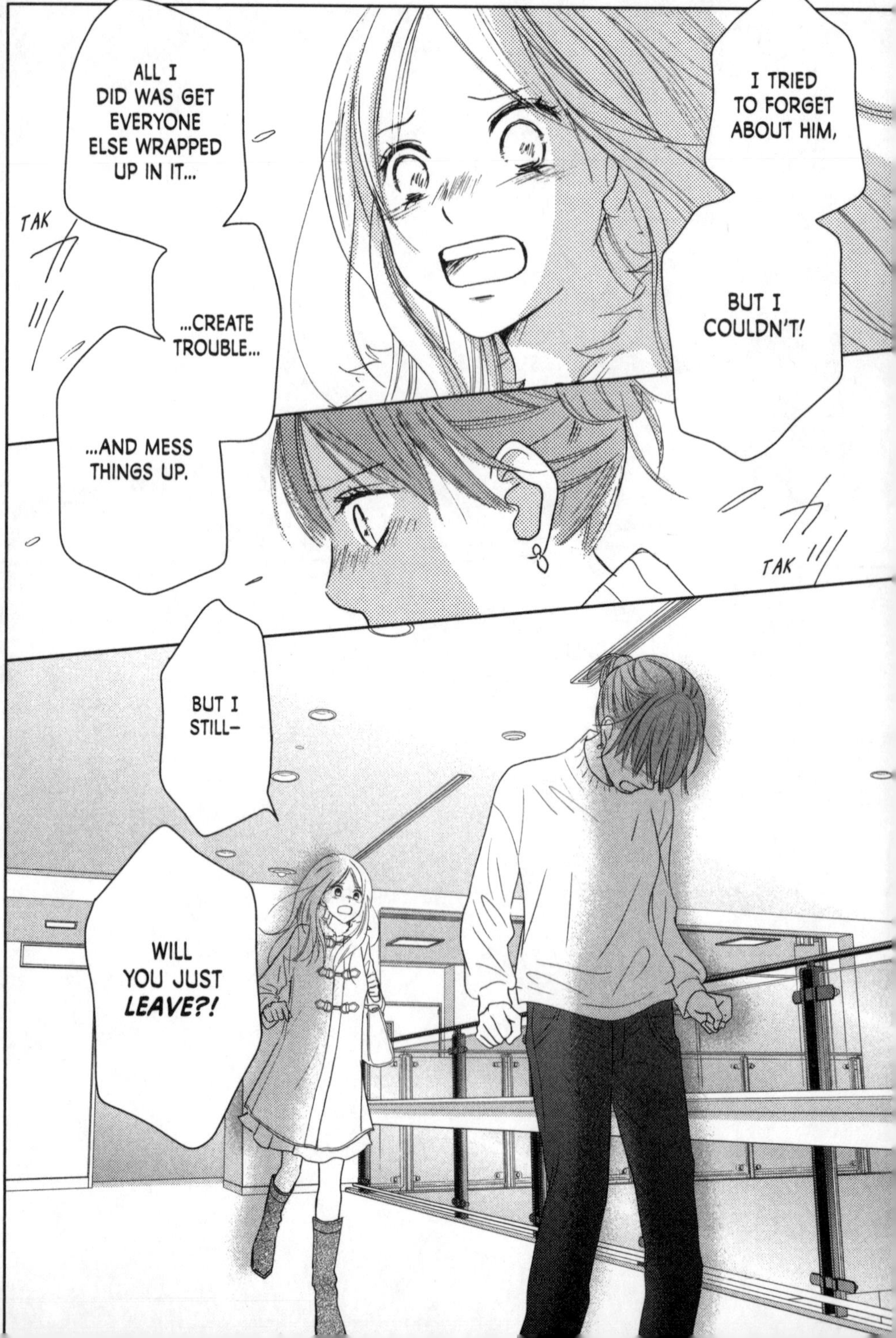
I TRIED TO FORGET ABOUT HIM,
BUT I COULDN'T!
ALL I DID WAS GET EVERYONE ELSE WRAPPED UP IN IT...
TAK
...CREATE TROUBLE...
TAK
...AND MESS THINGS UP.
BUT I STILL–
WILL YOU JUST *LEAVE?!*

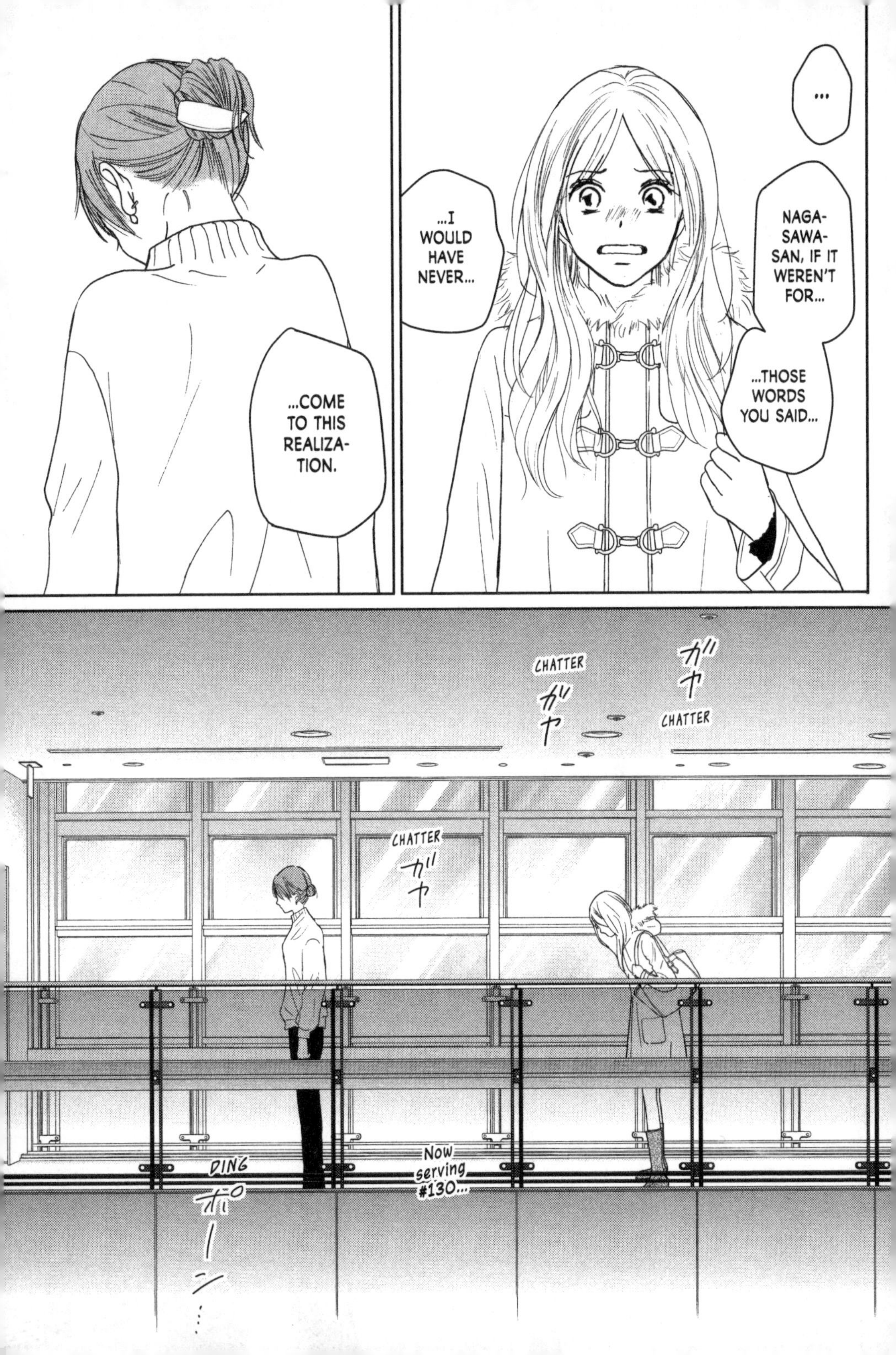
...
NAGA-SAWA-SAN, IF IT WEREN'T FOR...
...THOSE WORDS YOU SAID...
...I WOULD HAVE NEVER...
...COME TO THIS REALIZA-TION.
ガヤ
CHATTER
CHATTER
ガヤ
CHATTER
ガヤ
Now serving #130...
DING
ポーン...

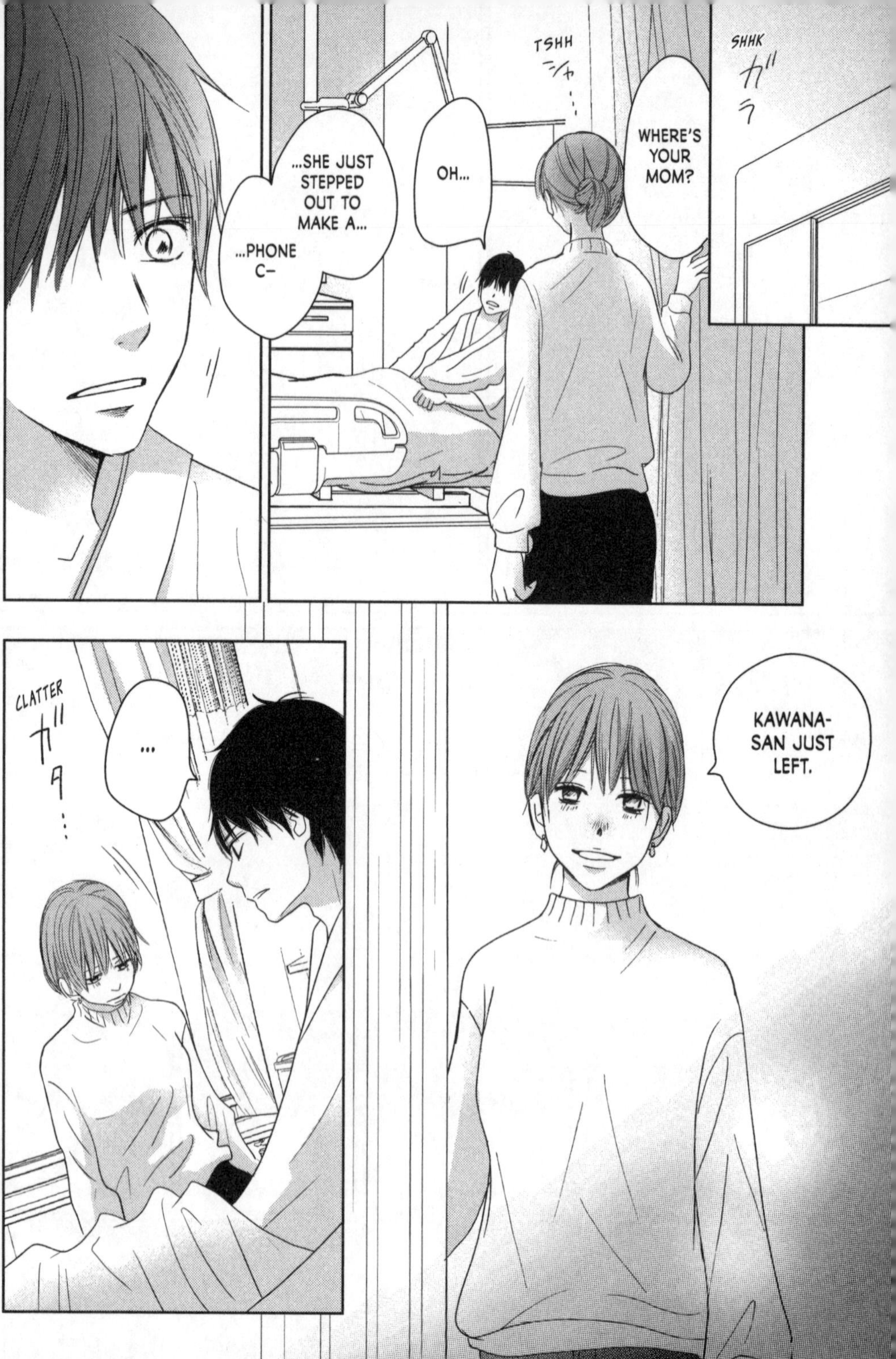
SHHK
ガラ
TSHH
シャ…
WHERE'S YOUR MOM?
OH...
...SHE JUST STEPPED OUT TO MAKE A...
...PHONE C–
KAWANA-SAN JUST LEFT.
CLATTER
ガタ…
...

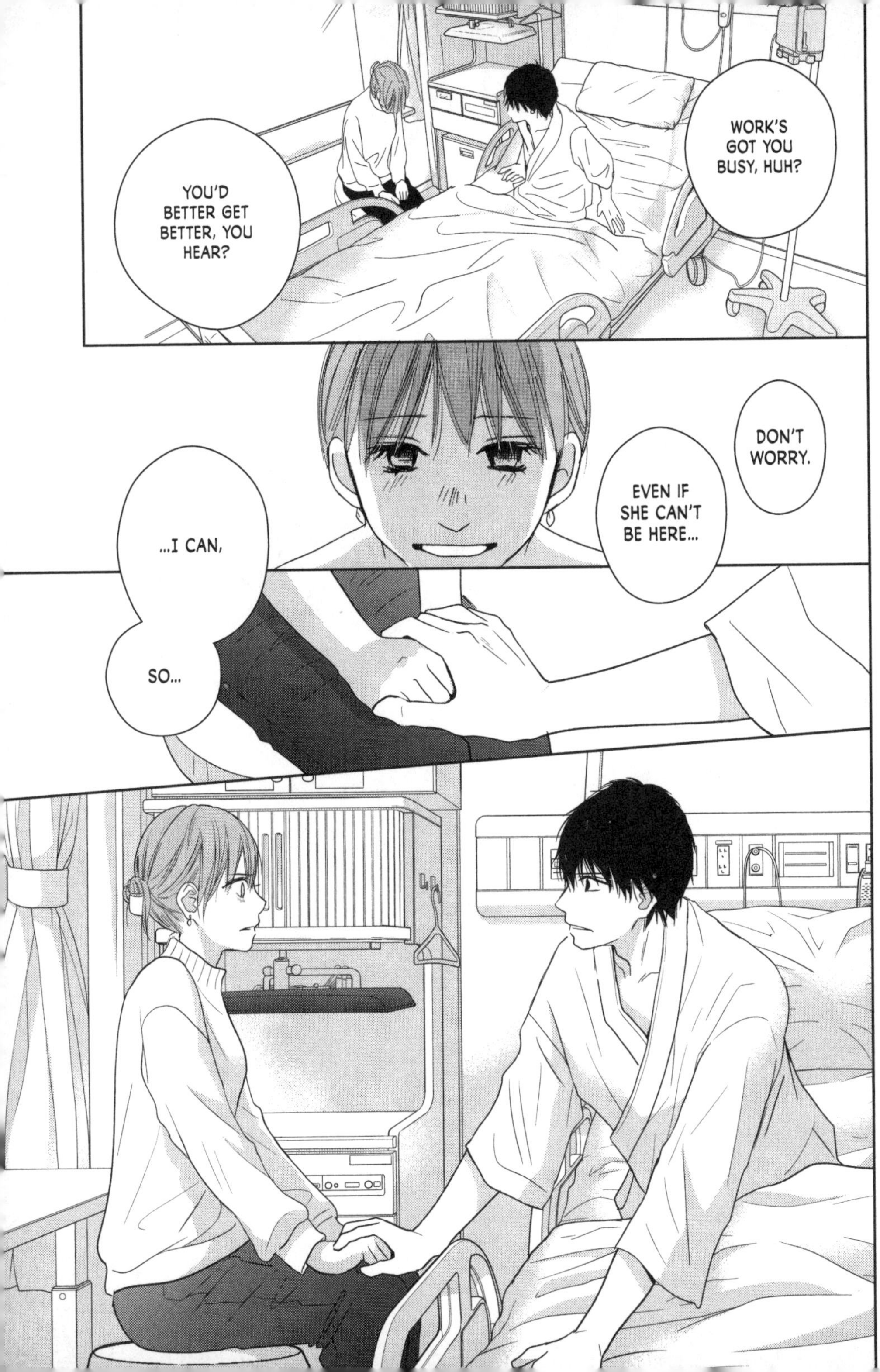
WORK'S GOT YOU BUSY, HUH?
YOU'D BETTER GET BETTER, YOU HEAR?
DON'T WORRY.
EVEN IF SHE CAN'T BE HERE...
...I CAN,
SO...

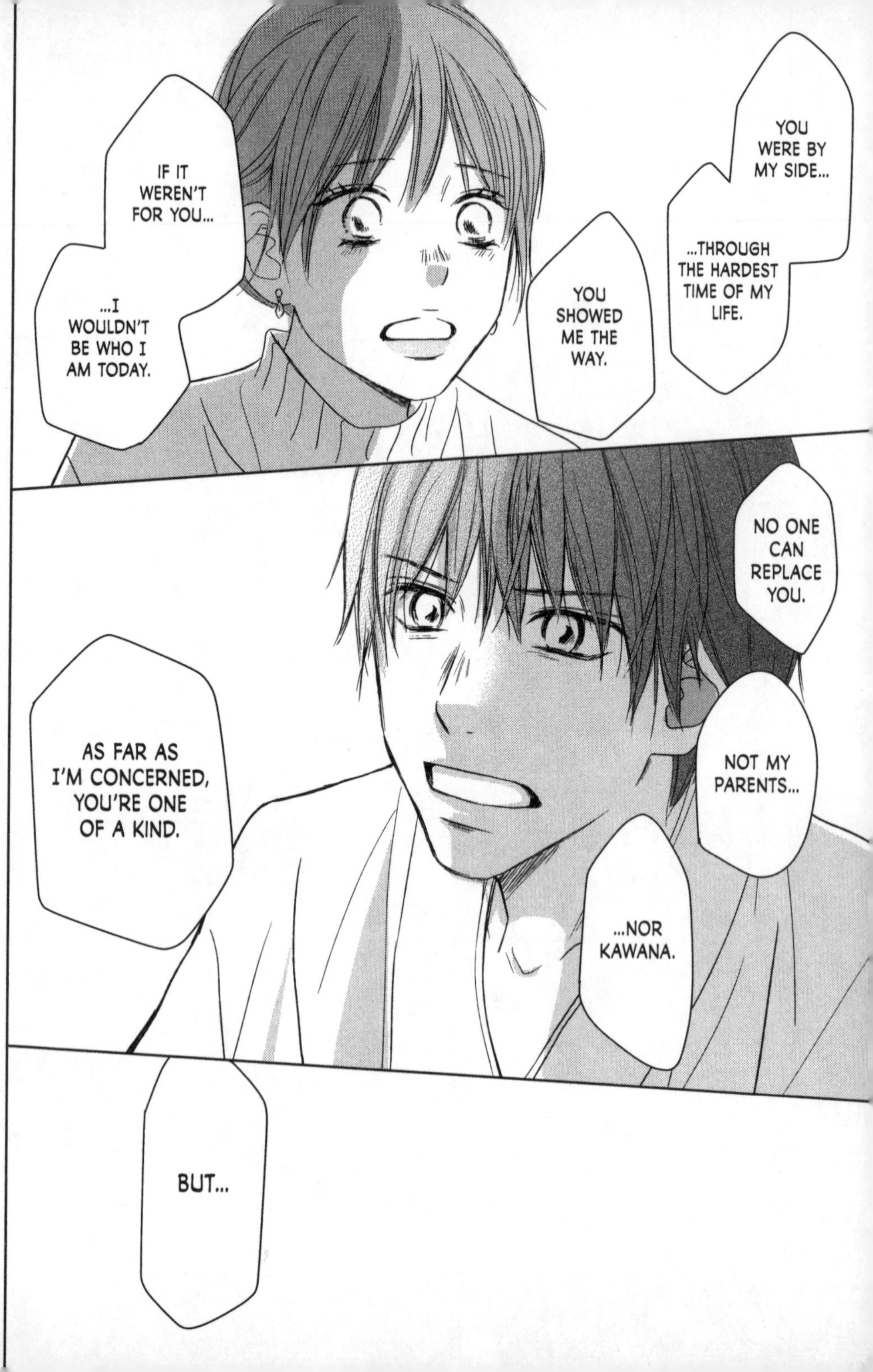
YOU WERE BY MY SIDE...
...THROUGH THE HARDEST TIME OF MY LIFE.
YOU SHOWED ME THE WAY.
IF IT WEREN'T FOR YOU...
...I WOULDN'T BE WHO I AM TODAY.
NO ONE CAN REPLACE YOU.
NOT MY PARENTS...
...NOR KAWANA.
AS FAR AS I'M CONCERNED, YOU'RE ONE OF A KIND.
BUT...

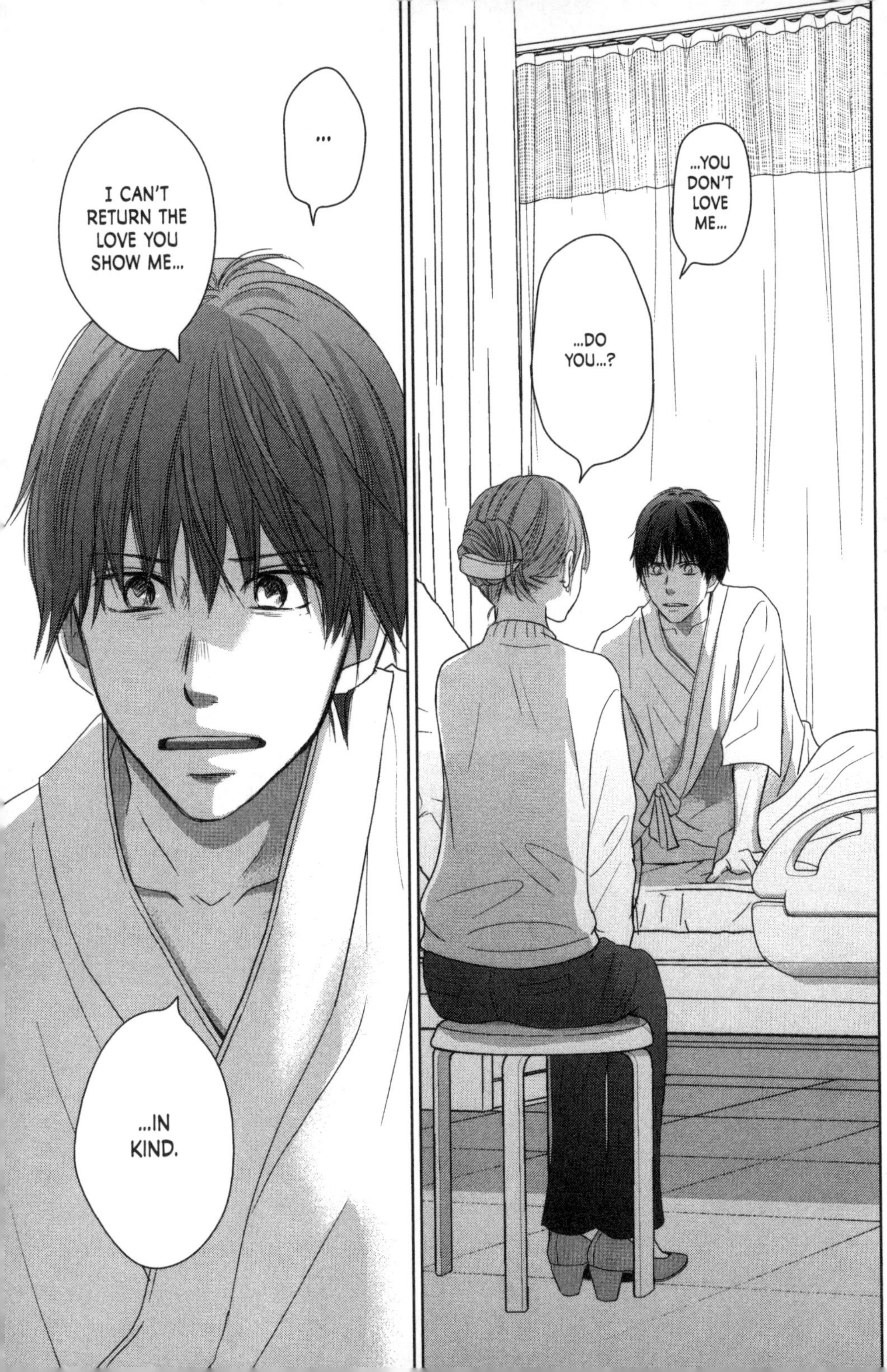
...YOU DON'T LOVE ME...
...DO YOU...?
...
I CAN'T RETURN THE LOVE YOU SHOW ME...
...IN KIND.

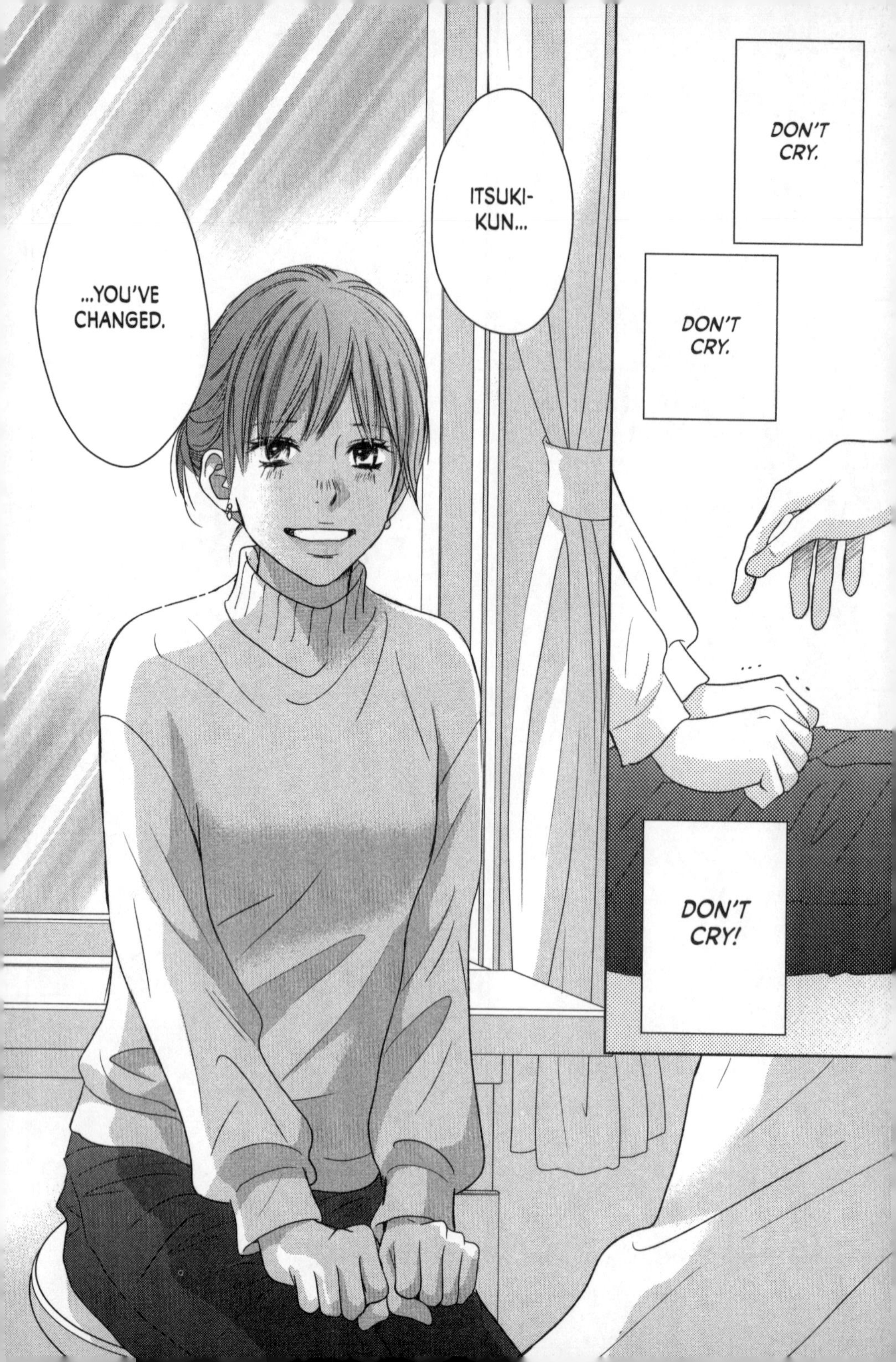
DON'T CRY.
DON'T CRY.
...
DON'T CRY!
ITSUKI-KUN...
...YOU'VE CHANGED.

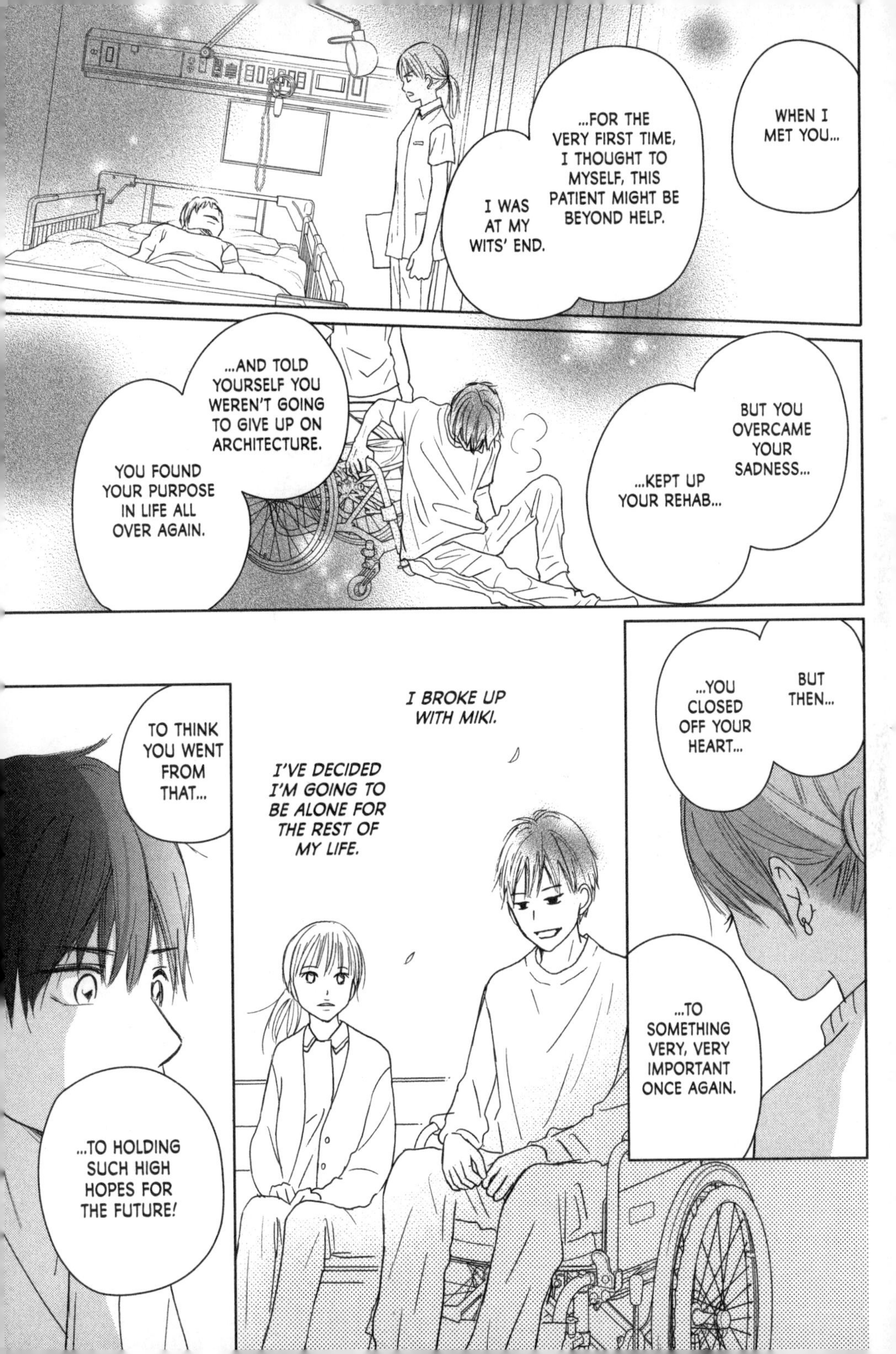
WHEN I MET YOU...
...FOR THE VERY FIRST TIME, I THOUGHT TO MYSELF, THIS PATIENT MIGHT BE BEYOND HELP.
I WAS AT MY WITS' END.
BUT YOU OVERCAME YOUR SADNESS...
...KEPT UP YOUR REHAB...
...AND TOLD YOURSELF YOU WEREN'T GOING TO GIVE UP ON ARCHITECTURE.
YOU FOUND YOUR PURPOSE IN LIFE ALL OVER AGAIN.
BUT THEN...
...YOU CLOSED OFF YOUR HEART...
...TO SOMETHING VERY, VERY IMPORTANT ONCE AGAIN.
I BROKE UP WITH MIKI.
I'VE DECIDED I'M GOING TO BE ALONE FOR THE REST OF MY LIFE.
TO THINK YOU WENT FROM THAT...
...TO HOLDING SUCH HIGH HOPES FOR THE FUTURE!

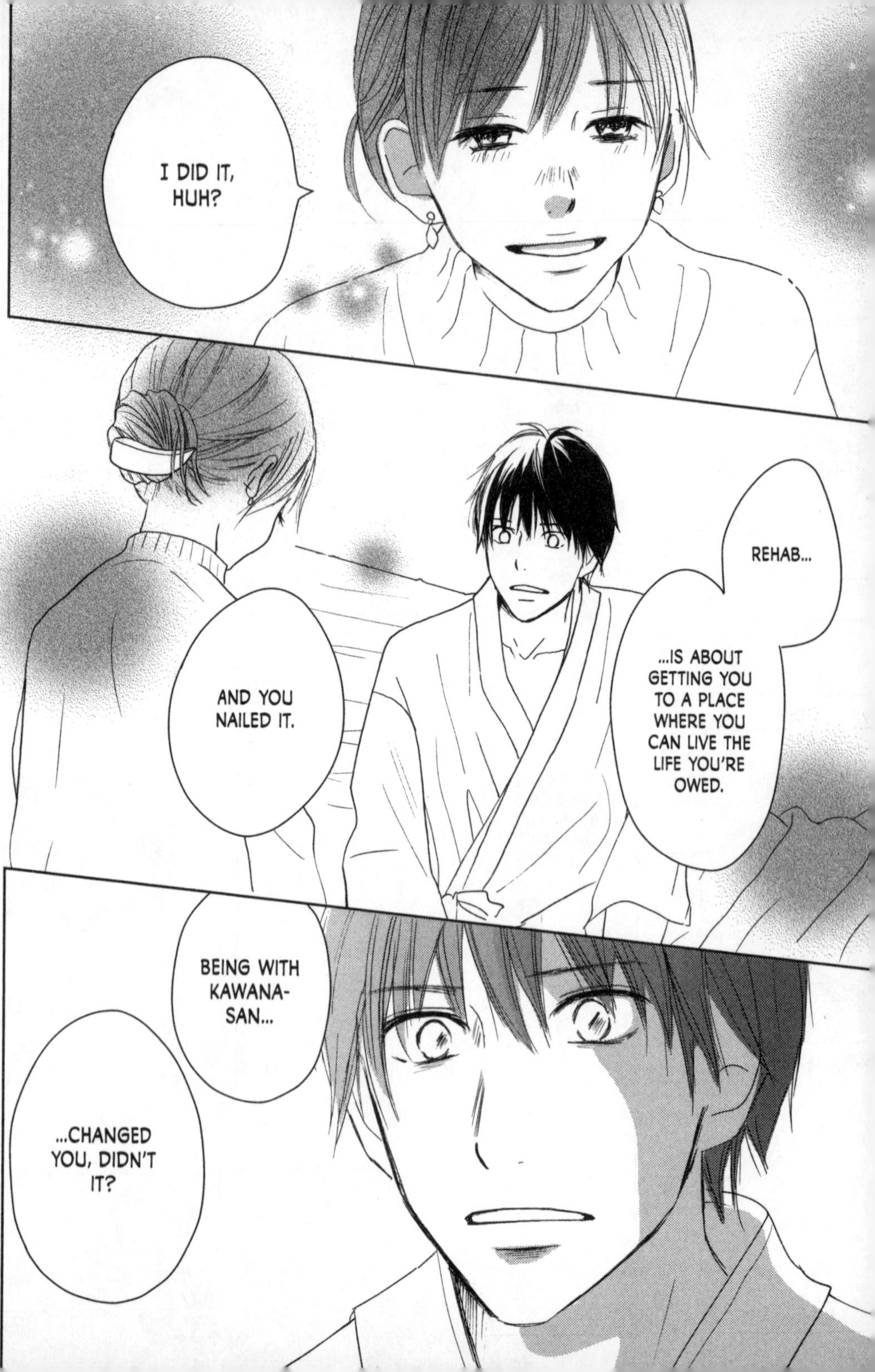
I DID IT, HUH?
REHAB...
...IS ABOUT GETTING YOU TO A PLACE WHERE YOU CAN LIVE THE LIFE YOU'RE OWED.
AND YOU NAILED IT.
BEING WITH KAWANA-SAN...
...CHANGED YOU, DIDN'T IT?

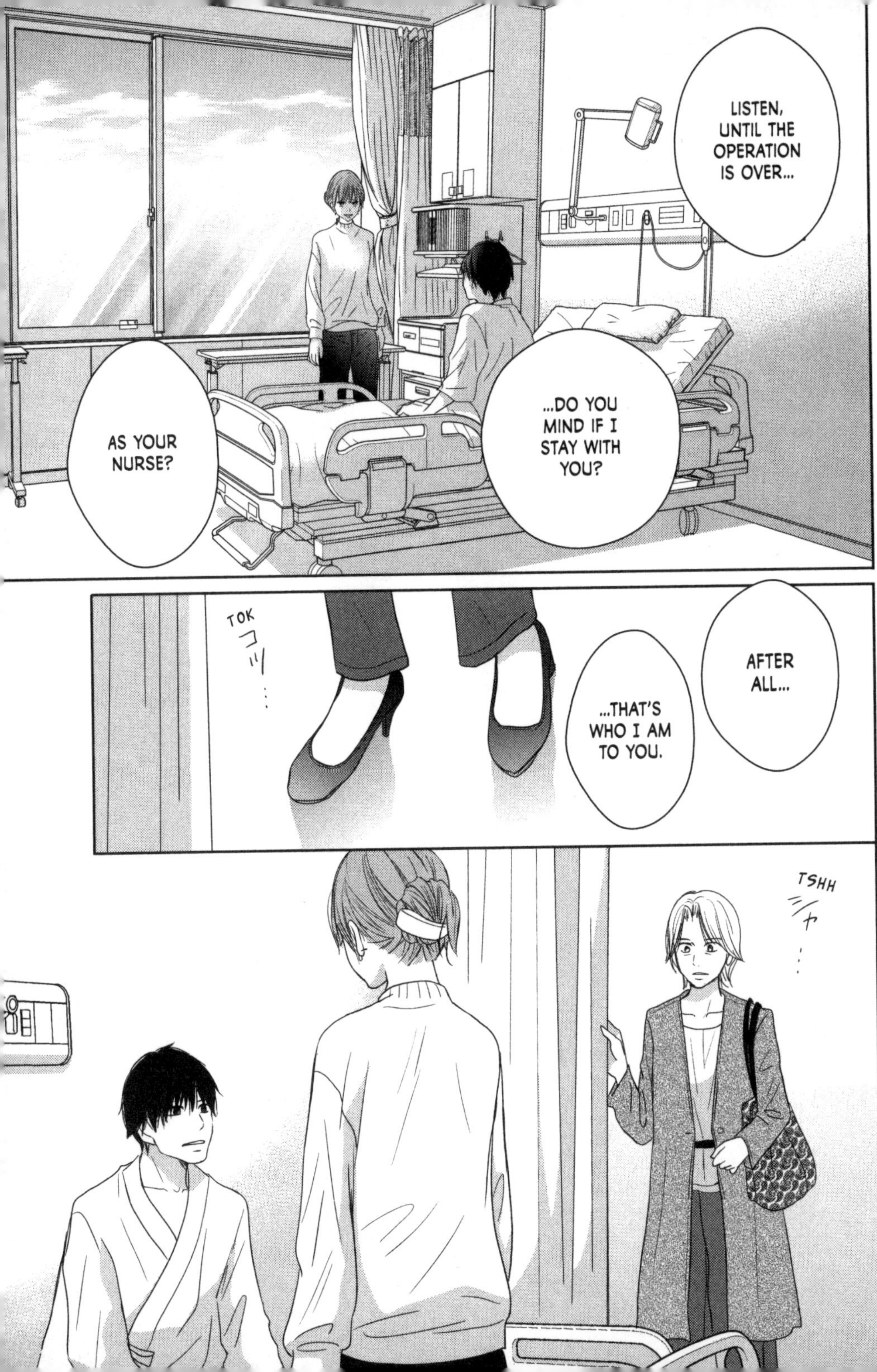
LISTEN, UNTIL THE OPERATION IS OVER...
...DO YOU MIND IF I STAY WITH YOU?
AS YOUR NURSE?
AFTER ALL...
...THAT'S WHO I AM TO YOU.
TOK
コツ…
TSHH
シャ…

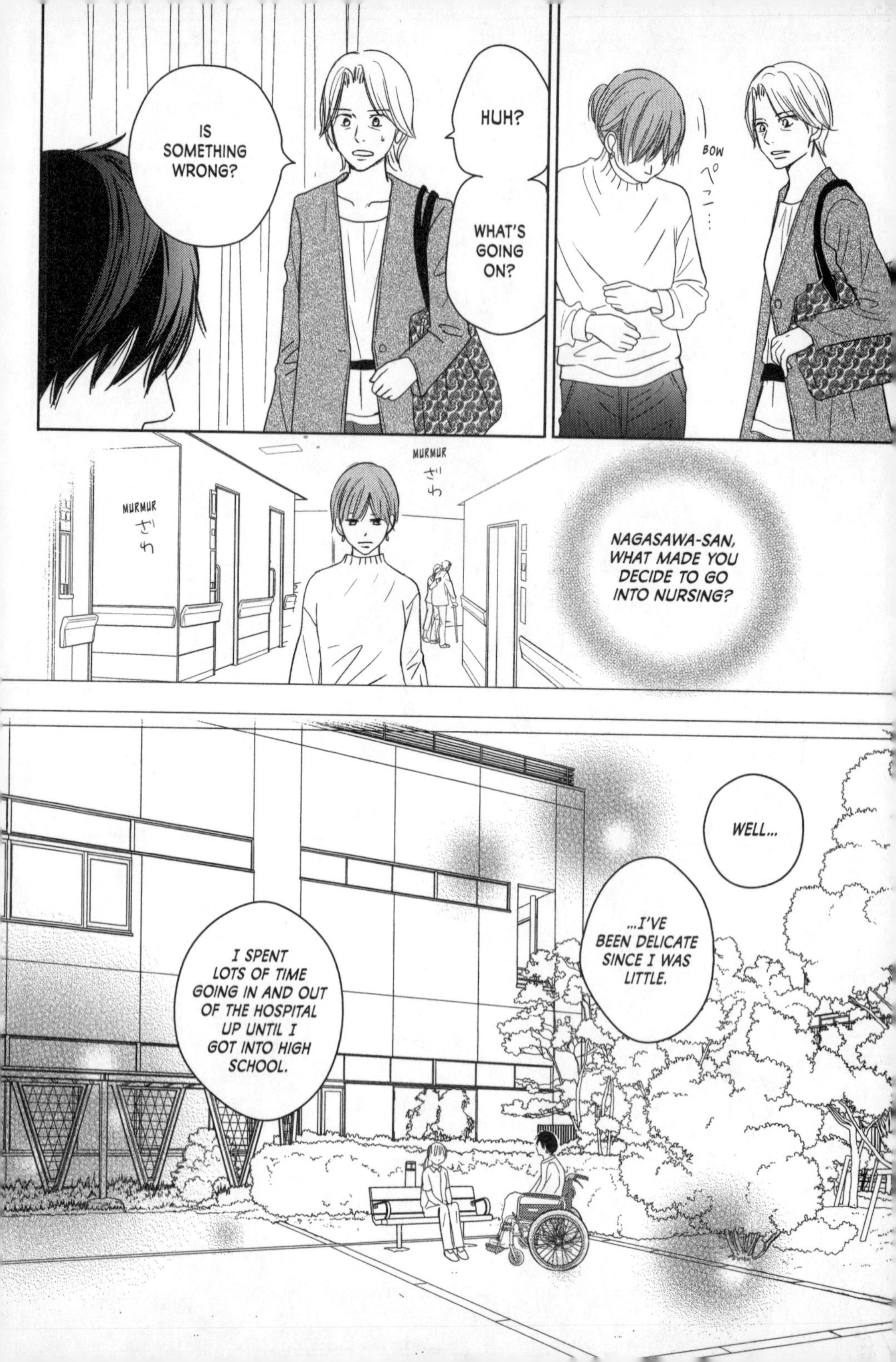
BOW
ペコ…
HUH?
WHAT'S GOING ON?
IS SOMETHING WRONG?
NAGASAWA-SAN, WHAT MADE YOU DECIDE TO GO INTO NURSING?
MURMUR
ざわ
MURMUR
ざわ
WELL...
...I'VE BEEN DELICATE SINCE I WAS LITTLE.
I SPENT LOTS OF TIME GOING IN AND OUT OF THE HOSPITAL UP UNTIL I GOT INTO HIGH SCHOOL.

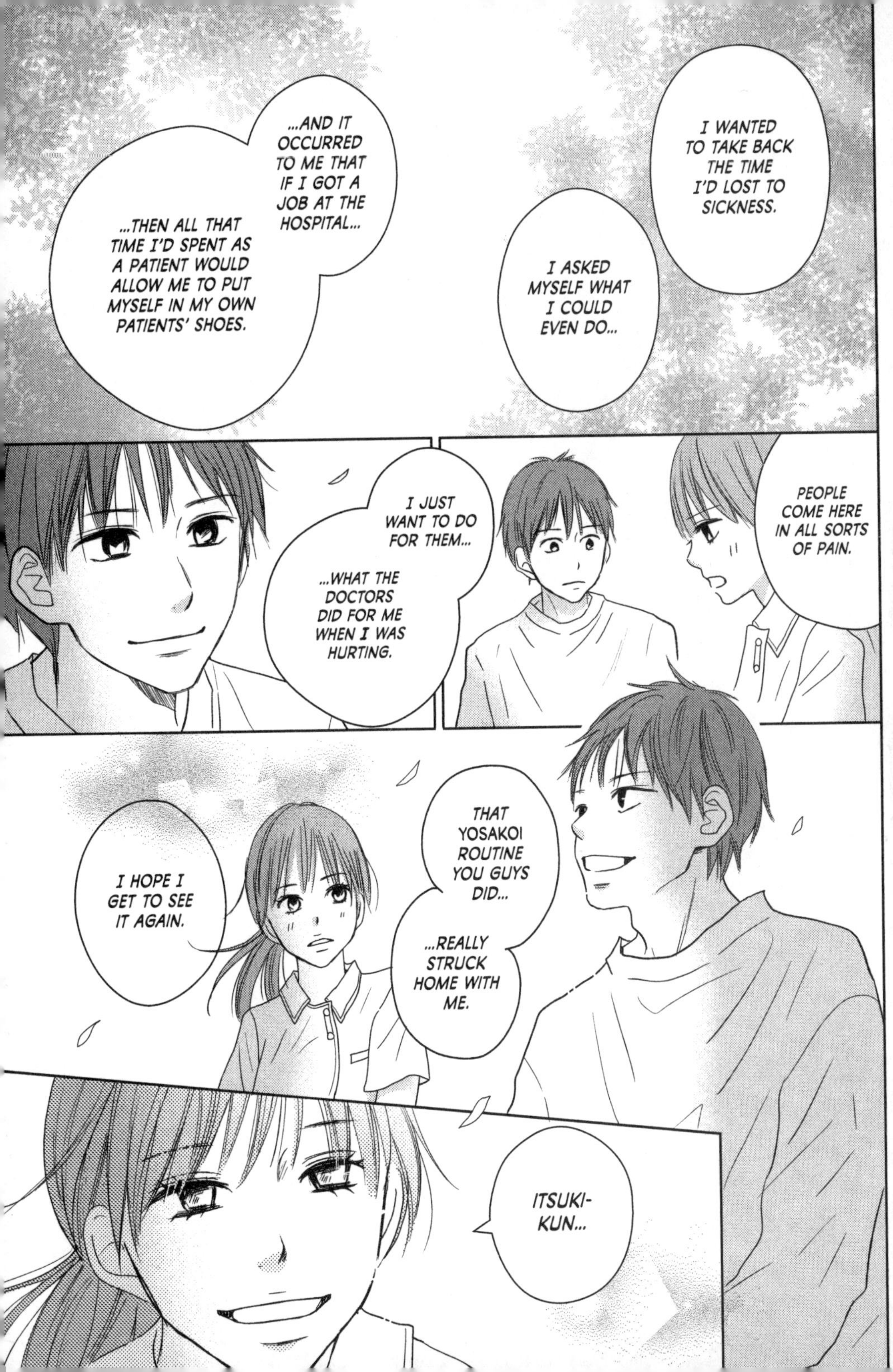
I WANTED TO TAKE BACK THE TIME I'D LOST TO SICKNESS.
I ASKED MYSELF WHAT I COULD EVEN DO...
...AND IT OCCURRED TO ME THAT IF I GOT A JOB AT THE HOSPITAL...
...THEN ALL THAT TIME I'D SPENT AS A PATIENT WOULD ALLOW ME TO PUT MYSELF IN MY OWN PATIENTS' SHOES.
PEOPLE COME HERE IN ALL SORTS OF PAIN.
I JUST WANT TO DO FOR THEM...
...WHAT THE DOCTORS DID FOR ME WHEN I WAS HURTING.
THAT YOSAKOI ROUTINE YOU GUYS DID...
...REALLY STRUCK HOME WITH ME.
I HOPE I GET TO SEE IT AGAIN.
ITSUKI-KUN...

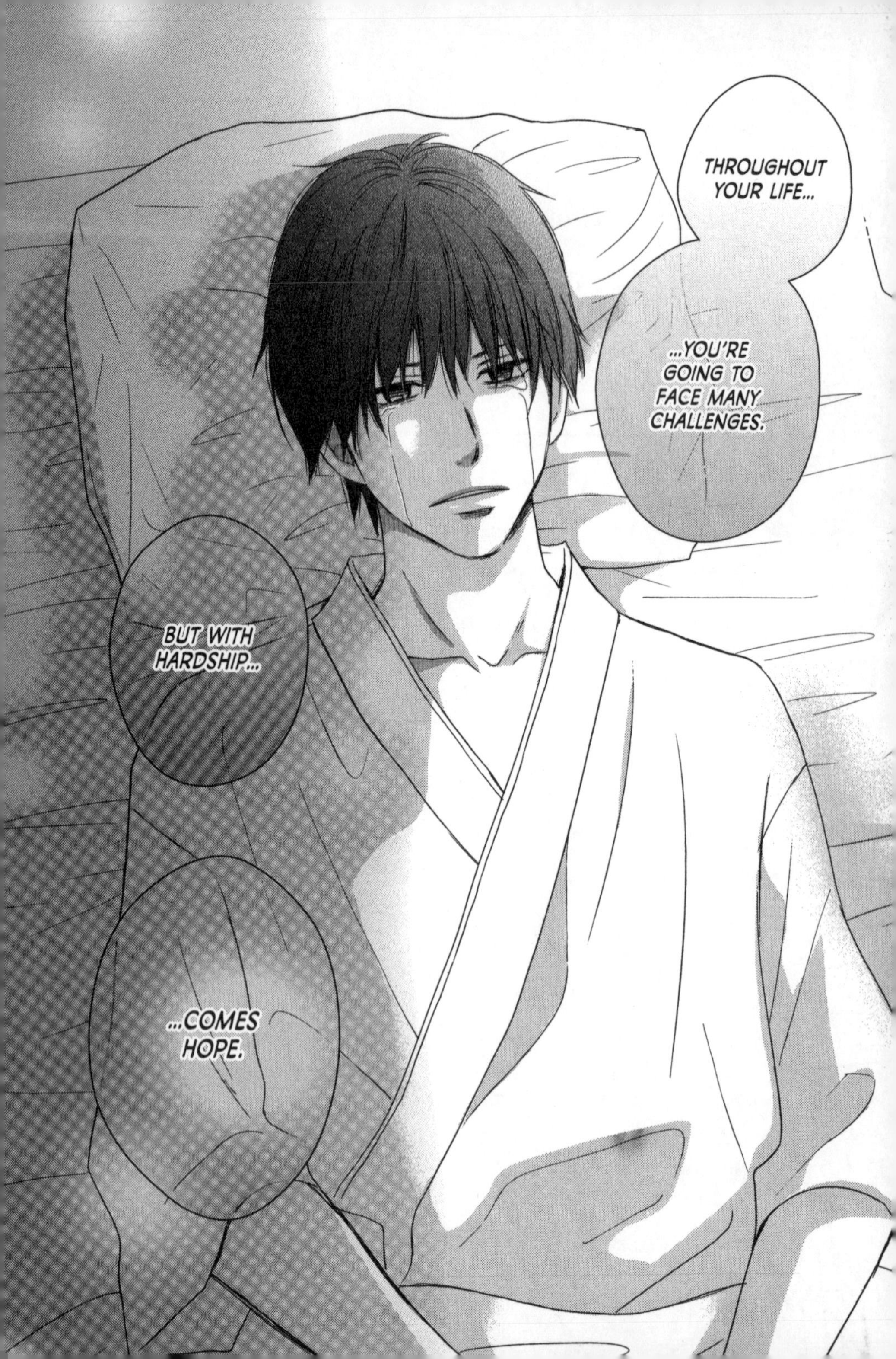
THROUGHOUT YOUR LIFE...
...YOU'RE GOING TO FACE MANY CHALLENGES.
BUT WITH HARDSHIP...
...COMES HOPE.

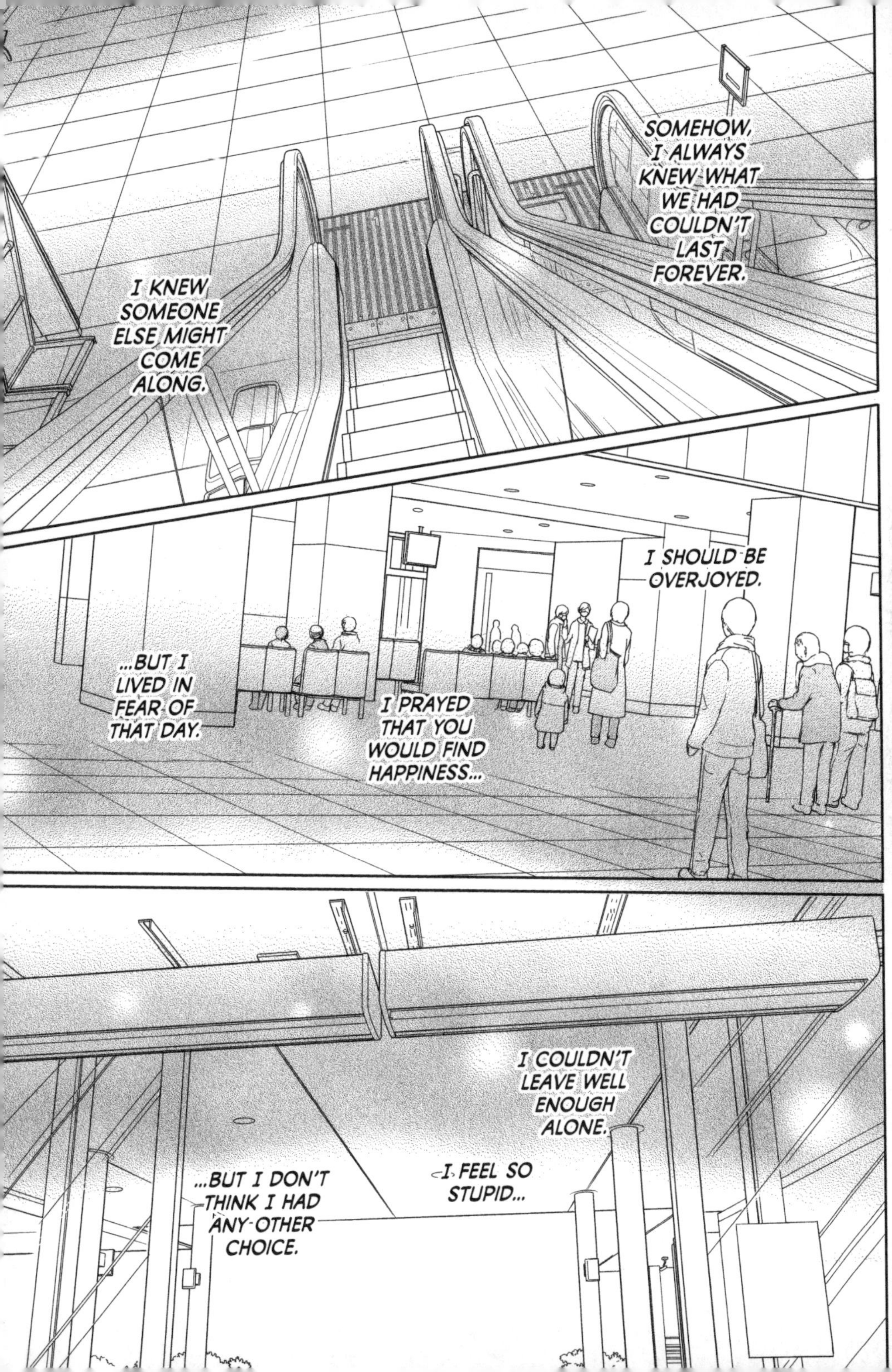
SOMEHOW, I ALWAYS KNEW WHAT WE HAD COULDN'T LAST FOREVER.
I KNEW SOMEONE ELSE MIGHT COME ALONG.
I SHOULD BE OVERJOYED.
I PRAYED THAT YOU WOULD FIND HAPPINESS...
...BUT I LIVED IN FEAR OF THAT DAY.
I COULDN'T LEAVE WELL ENOUGH ALONE.
I FEEL SO STUPID...
...BUT I DON'T THINK I HAD ANY OTHER CHOICE.

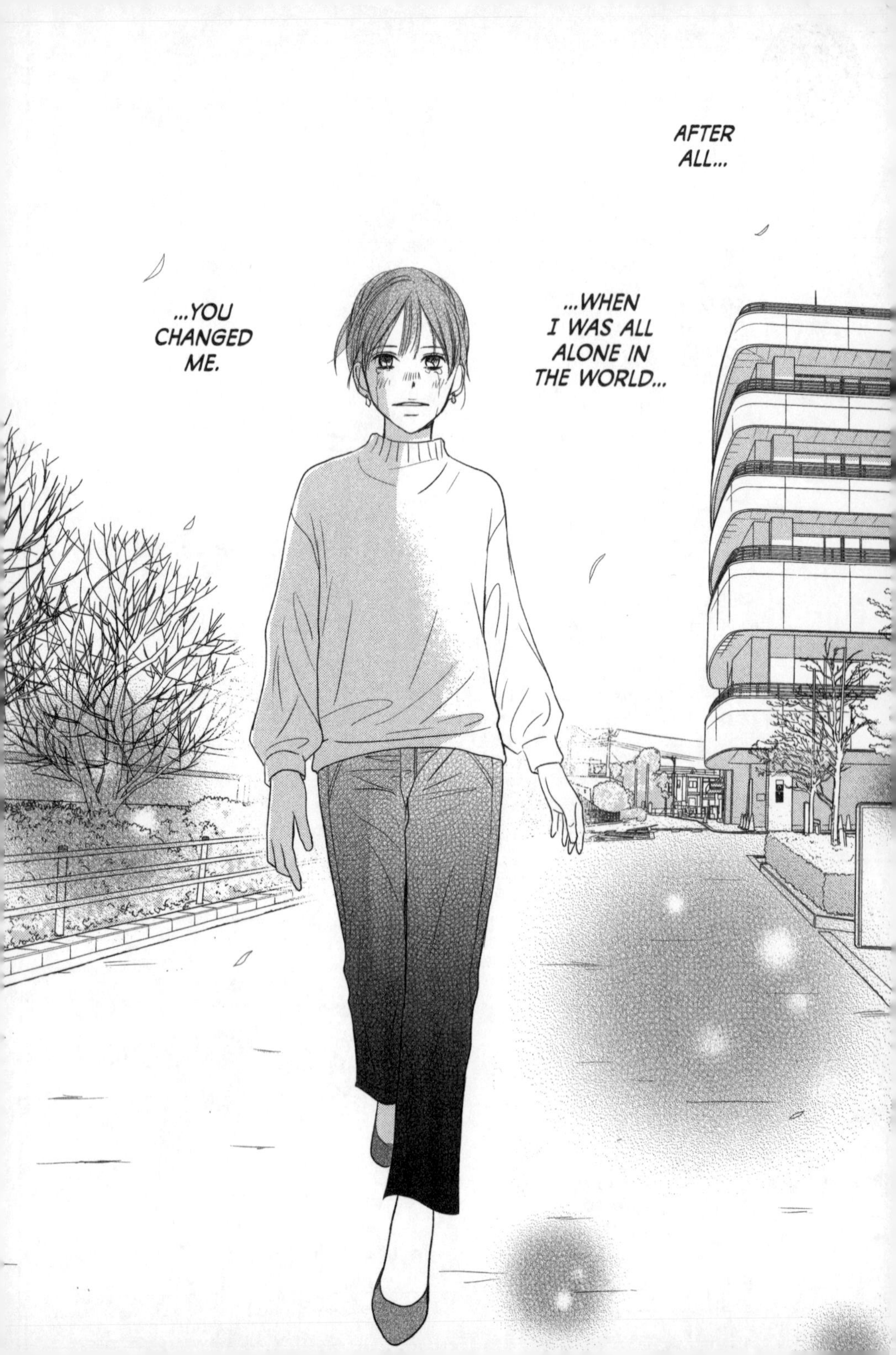
AFTER ALL...
...WHEN I WAS ALL ALONE IN THE WORLD...
...YOU CHANGED ME.

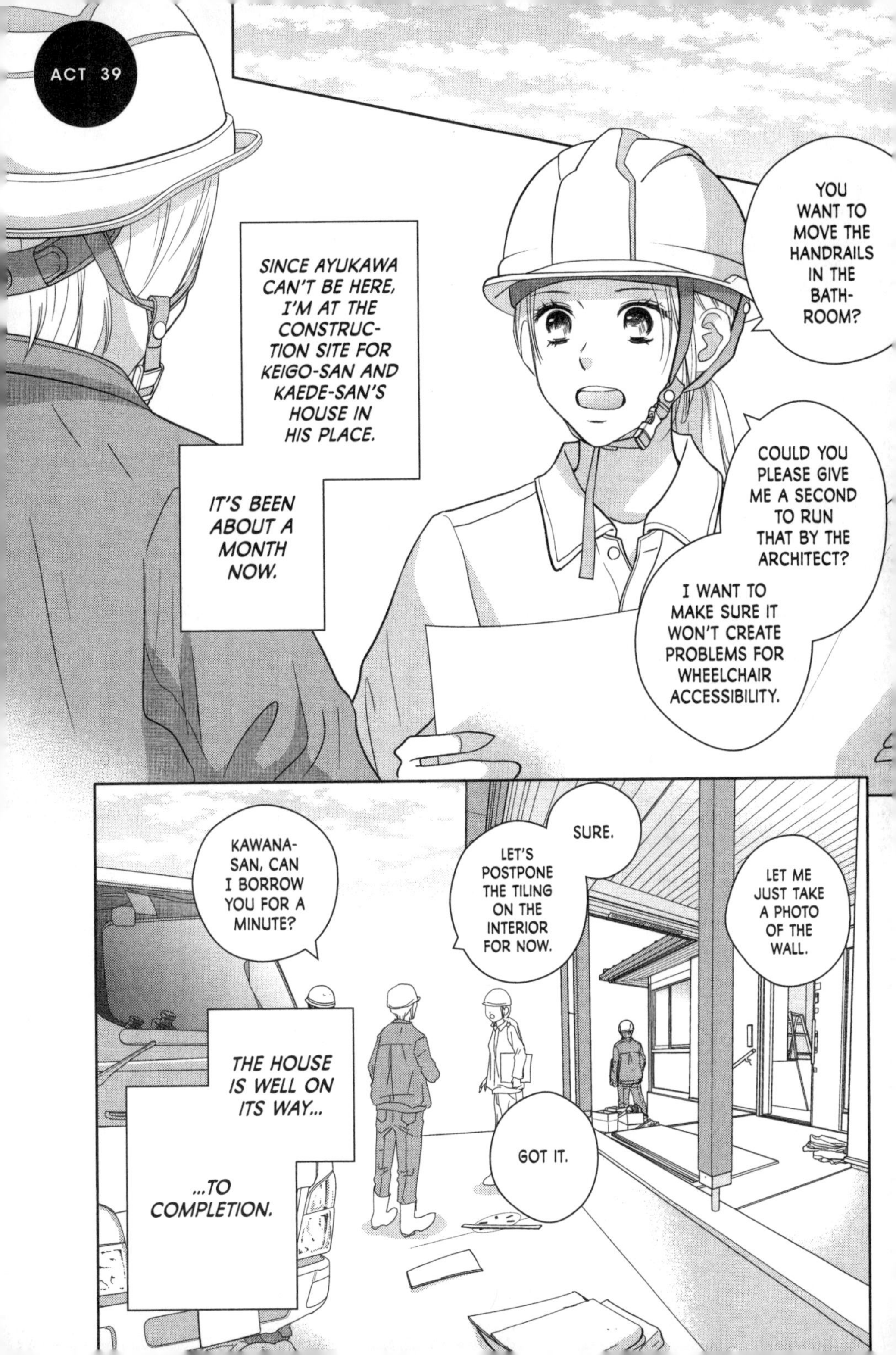
ACT 39
YOU WANT TO MOVE THE HANDRAILS IN THE BATH-ROOM?
COULD YOU PLEASE GIVE ME A SECOND TO RUN THAT BY THE ARCHITECT?
I WANT TO MAKE SURE IT WON'T CREATE PROBLEMS FOR WHEELCHAIR ACCESSIBILITY.
SINCE AYUKAWA CAN'T BE HERE, I'M AT THE CONSTRUC-TION SITE FOR KEIGO-SAN AND KAEDE-SAN'S HOUSE IN HIS PLACE.
IT'S BEEN ABOUT A MONTH NOW.
LET ME JUST TAKE A PHOTO OF THE WALL.
SURE.
LET'S POSTPONE THE TILING ON THE INTERIOR FOR NOW.
KAWANA-SAN, CAN I BORROW YOU FOR A MINUTE?
GOT IT.
THE HOUSE IS WELL ON ITS WAY...
...TO COMPLETION.

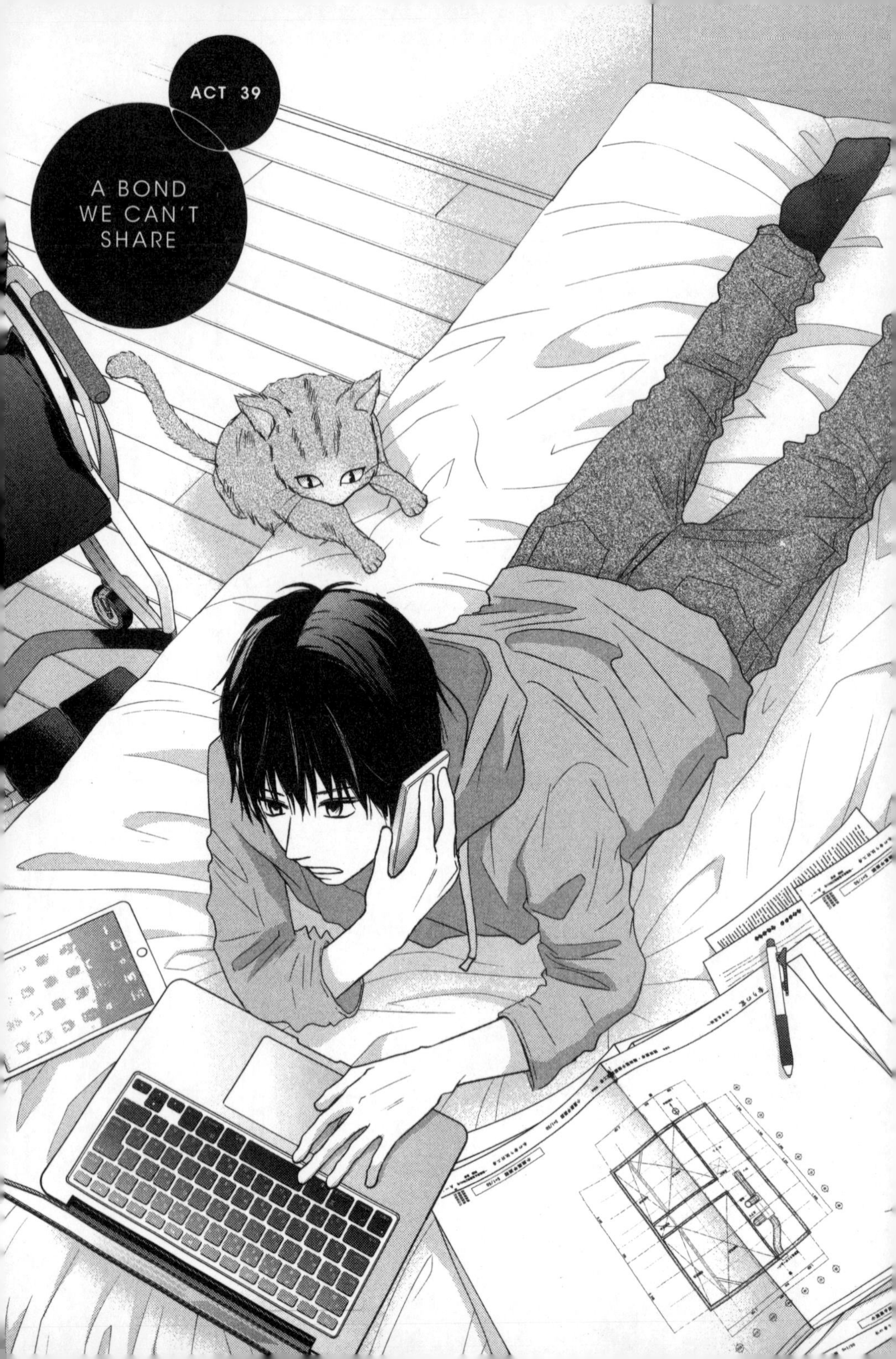
ACT 39
A BOND WE CAN'T SHARE

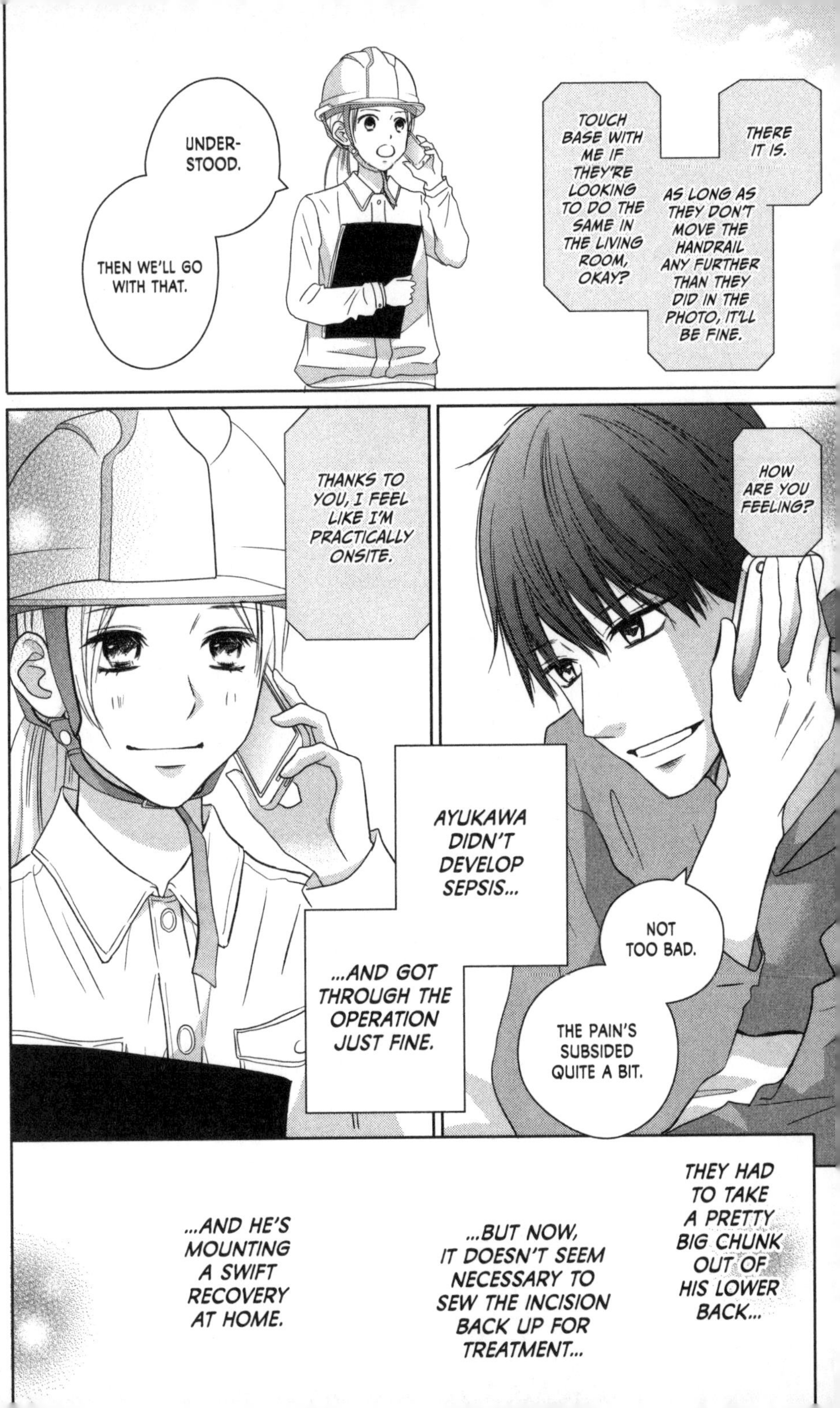
THERE IT IS.
AS LONG AS THEY DON'T MOVE THE HANDRAIL ANY FURTHER THAN THEY DID IN THE PHOTO, IT'LL BE FINE.
TOUCH BASE WITH ME IF THEY'RE LOOKING TO DO THE SAME IN THE LIVING ROOM, OKAY?
UNDER-STOOD.
THEN WE'LL GO WITH THAT.
HOW ARE YOU FEELING?
NOT TOO BAD.
THE PAIN'S SUBSIDED QUITE A BIT.
AYUKAWA DIDN'T DEVELOP SEPSIS...
...AND GOT THROUGH THE OPERATION JUST FINE.
THANKS TO YOU, I FEEL LIKE I'M PRACTICALLY ONSITE.
THEY HAD TO TAKE A PRETTY BIG CHUNK OUT OF HIS LOWER BACK...
...BUT NOW, IT DOESN'T SEEM NECESSARY TO SEW THE INCISION BACK UP FOR TREATMENT...
...AND HE'S MOUNTING A SWIFT RECOVERY AT HOME.

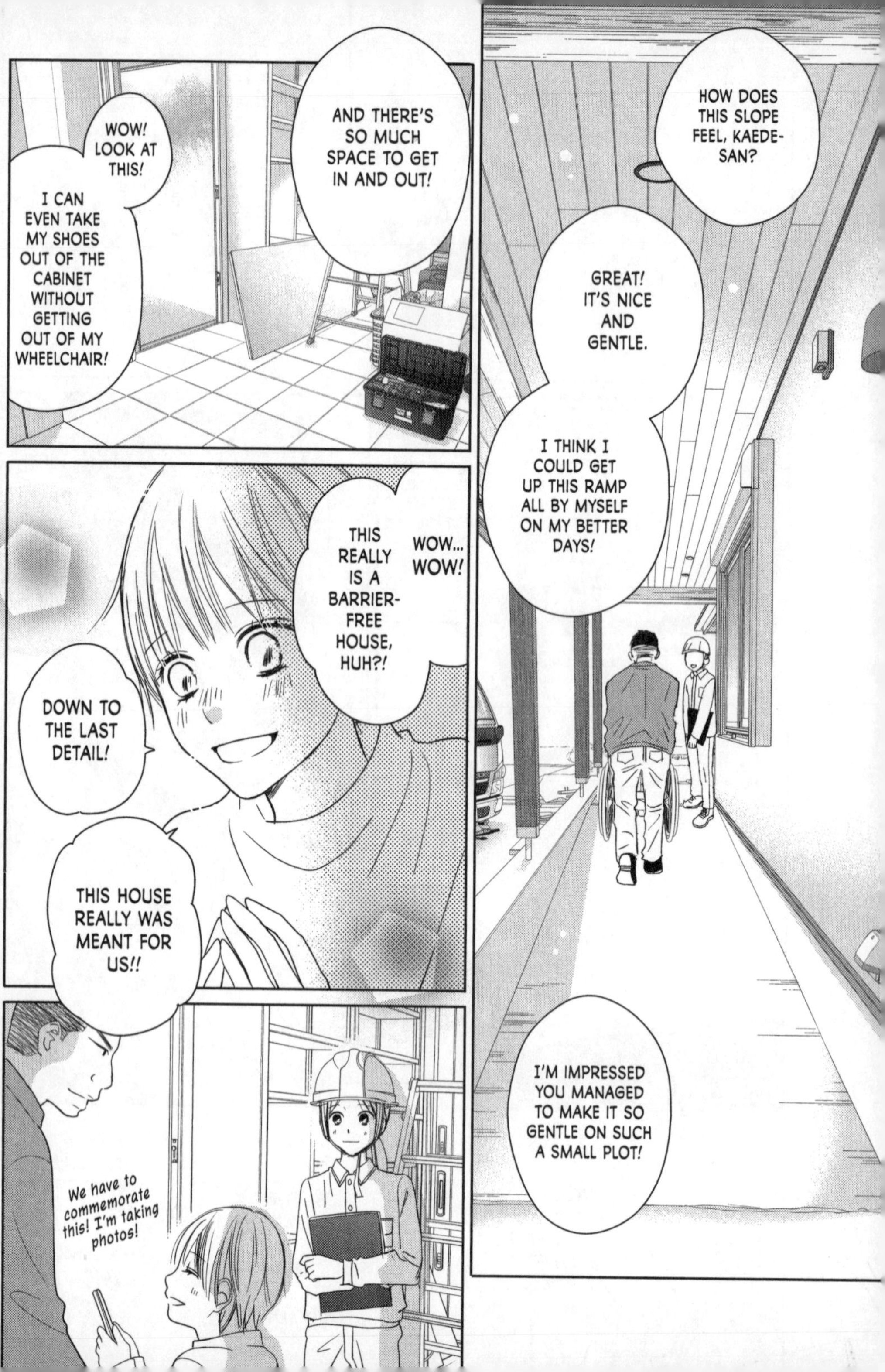
HOW DOES THIS SLOPE FEEL, KAEDE-SAN?
GREAT! IT'S NICE AND GENTLE.
I THINK I COULD GET UP THIS RAMP ALL BY MYSELF ON MY BETTER DAYS!
I'M IMPRESSED YOU MANAGED TO MAKE IT SO GENTLE ON SUCH A SMALL PLOT!
AND THERE'S SO MUCH SPACE TO GET IN AND OUT!
WOW! LOOK AT THIS!
I CAN EVEN TAKE MY SHOES OUT OF THE CABINET WITHOUT GETTING OUT OF MY WHEELCHAIR!
WOW... WOW!
THIS REALLY IS A BARRIER-FREE HOUSE, HUH?!
DOWN TO THE LAST DETAIL!
THIS HOUSE REALLY WAS MEANT FOR US!!
We have to commemorate this! I'm taking photos!

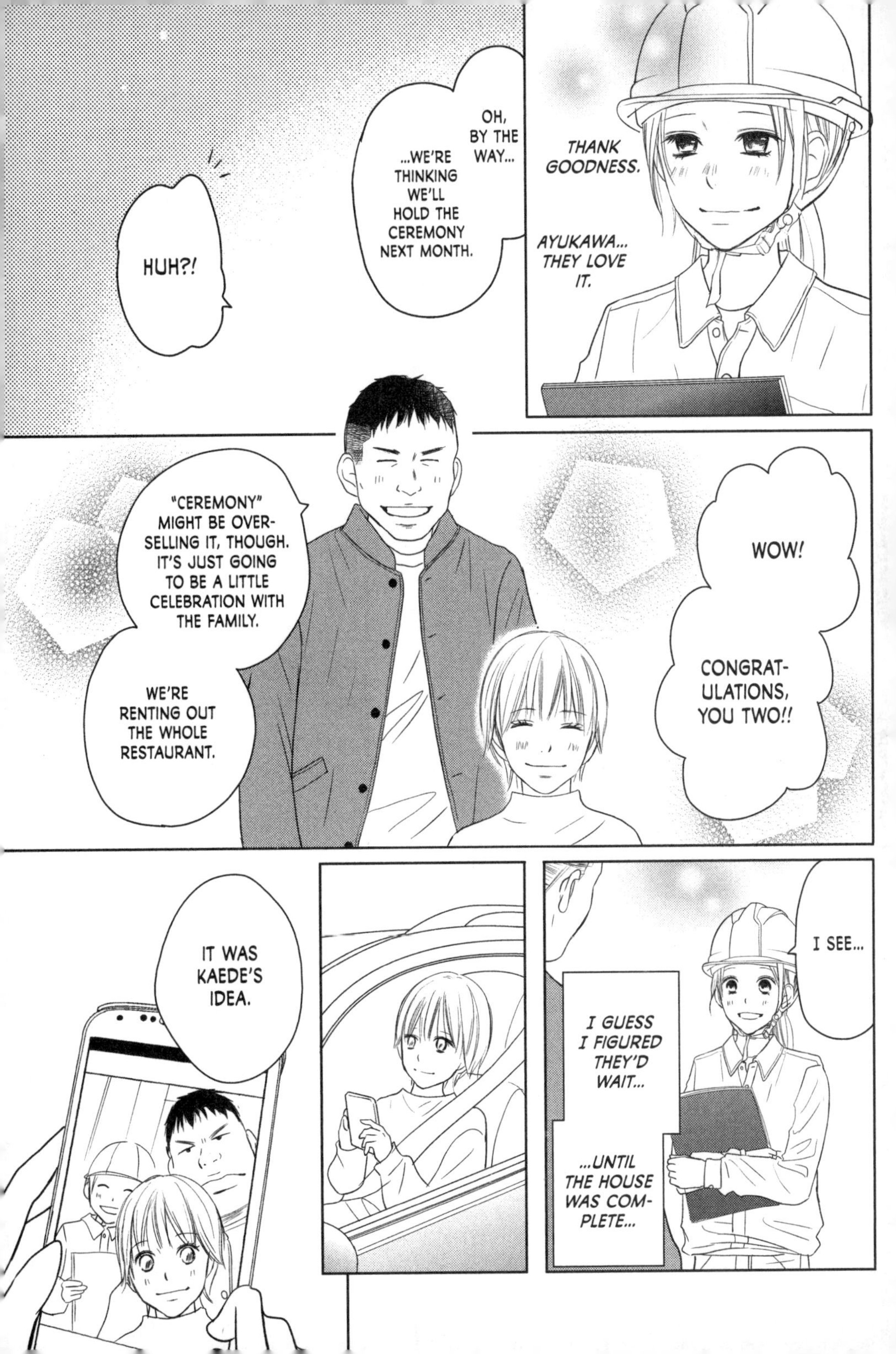
THANK GOODNESS.
AYUKAWA... THEY LOVE IT.
OH, BY THE WAY...
...WE'RE THINKING WE'LL HOLD THE CEREMONY NEXT MONTH.
HUH?!
WOW!
CONGRAT-ULATIONS, YOU TWO!!
"CEREMONY" MIGHT BE OVER-SELLING IT, THOUGH. IT'S JUST GOING TO BE A LITTLE CELEBRATION WITH THE FAMILY.
WE'RE RENTING OUT THE WHOLE RESTAURANT.
I SEE...
I GUESS I FIGURED THEY'D WAIT...
...UNTIL THE HOUSE WAS COM-PLETE...
IT WAS KAEDE'S IDEA.

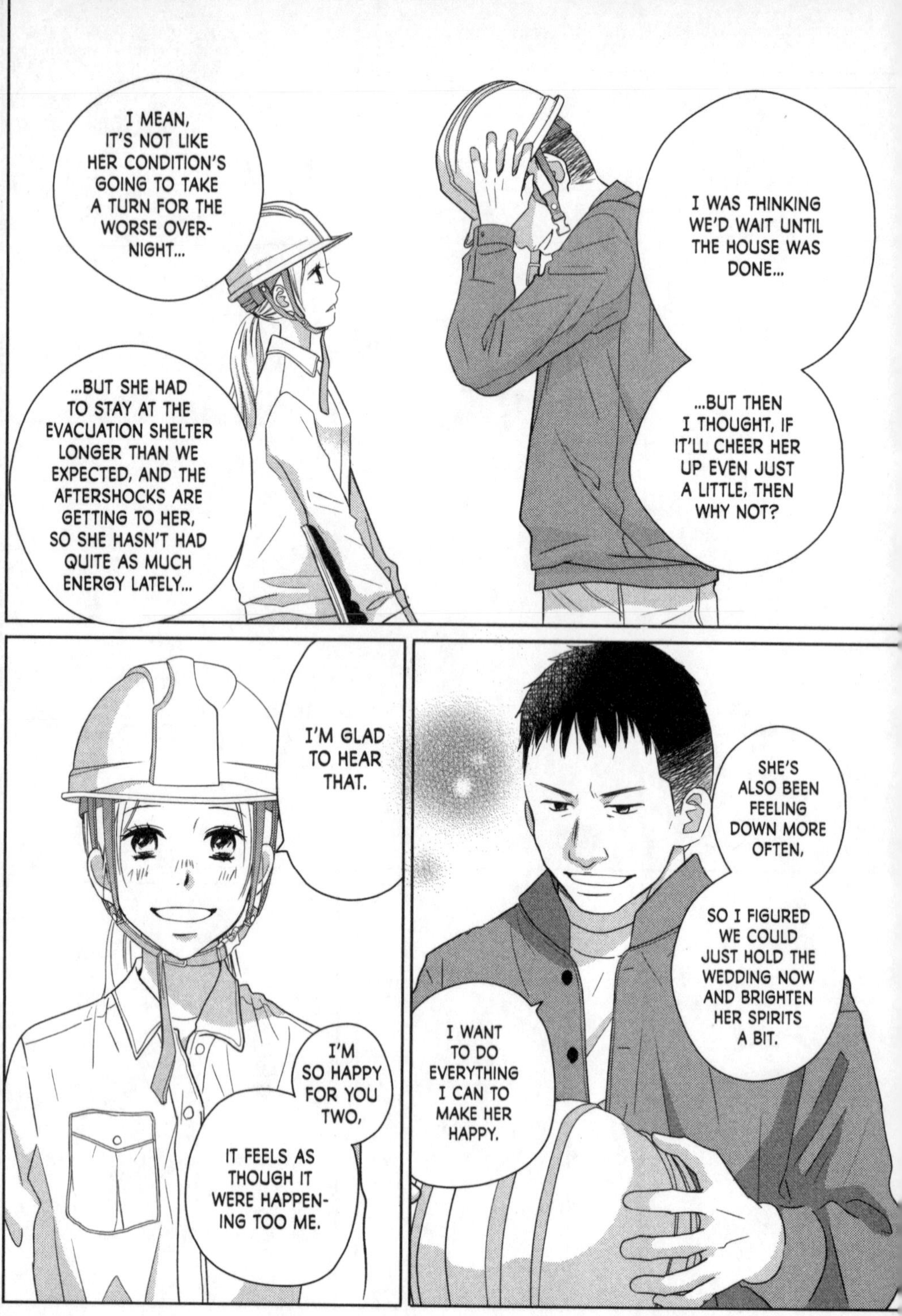
I WAS THINKING WE'D WAIT UNTIL THE HOUSE WAS DONE...
...BUT THEN I THOUGHT, IF IT'LL CHEER HER UP EVEN JUST A LITTLE, THEN WHY NOT?
I MEAN, IT'S NOT LIKE HER CONDITION'S GOING TO TAKE A TURN FOR THE WORSE OVER-NIGHT...
...BUT SHE HAD TO STAY AT THE EVACUATION SHELTER LONGER THAN WE EXPECTED, AND THE AFTERSHOCKS ARE GETTING TO HER, SO SHE HASN'T HAD QUITE AS MUCH ENERGY LATELY...
SHE'S ALSO BEEN FEELING DOWN MORE OFTEN,
SO I FIGURED WE COULD JUST HOLD THE WEDDING NOW AND BRIGHTEN HER SPIRITS A BIT.
I WANT TO DO EVERYTHING I CAN TO MAKE HER HAPPY.
I'M GLAD TO HEAR THAT.
I'M SO HAPPY FOR YOU TWO,
IT FEELS AS THOUGH IT WERE HAPPEN-ING TOO ME.

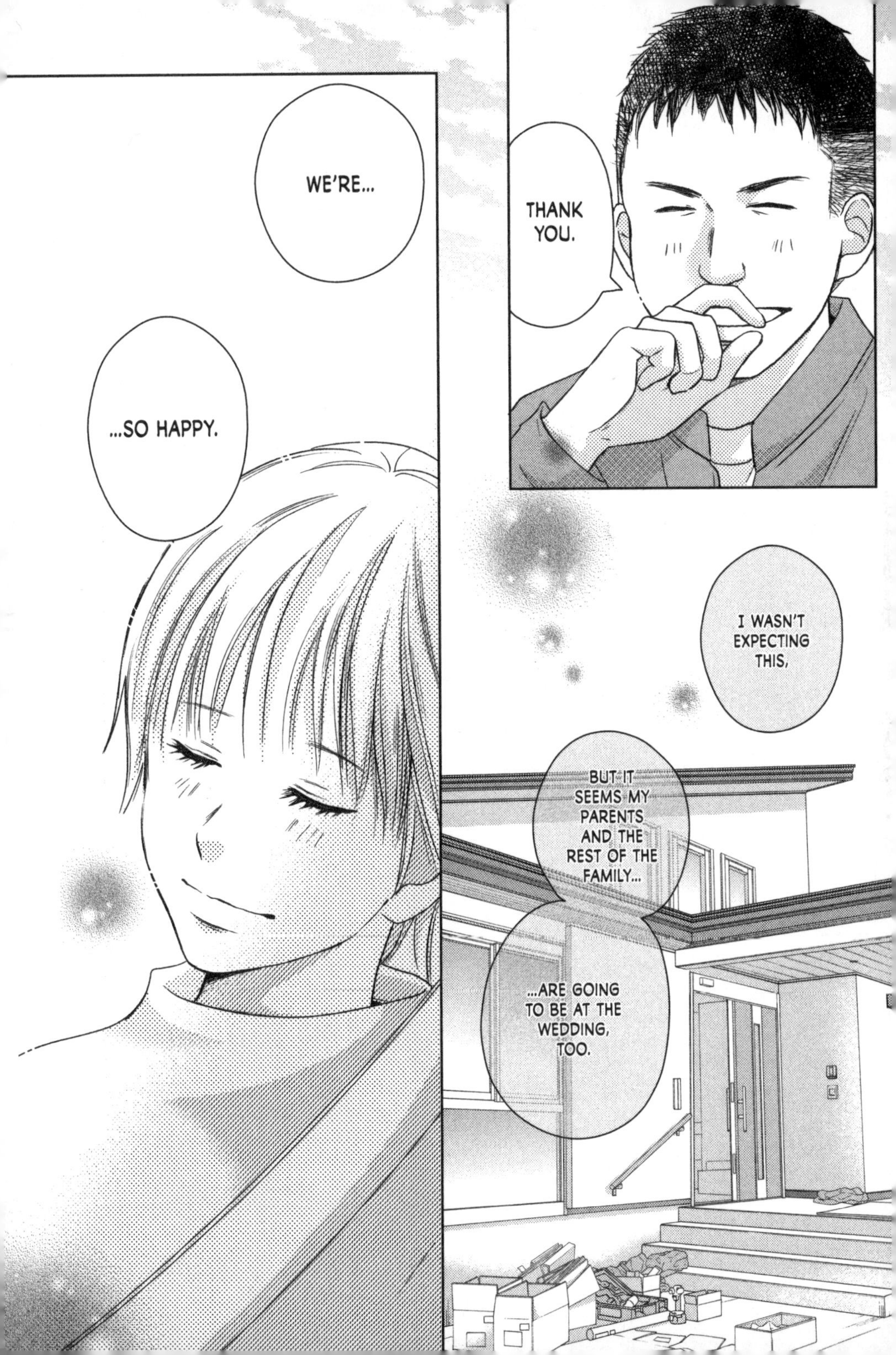
THANK YOU.
I WASN'T EXPECTING THIS,
BUT IT SEEMS MY PARENTS AND THE REST OF THE FAMILY...
...ARE GOING TO BE AT THE WEDDING, TOO.
WE'RE...
...SO HAPPY.

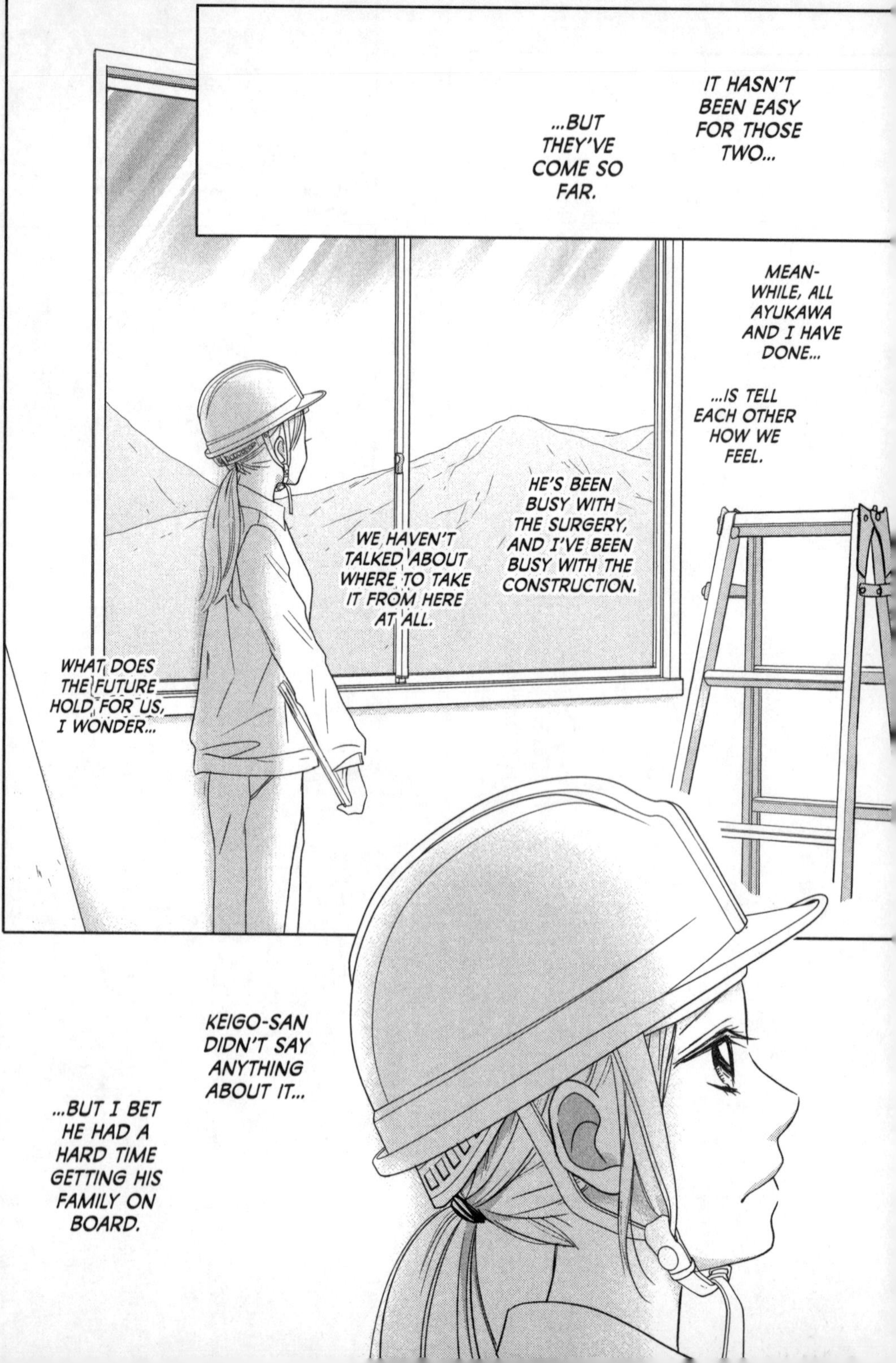
IT HASN'T BEEN EASY FOR THOSE TWO...
...BUT THEY'VE COME SO FAR.
MEAN-WHILE, ALL AYUKAWA AND I HAVE DONE...
...IS TELL EACH OTHER HOW WE FEEL.
HE'S BEEN BUSY WITH THE SURGERY, AND I'VE BEEN BUSY WITH THE CONSTRUCTION.
WE HAVEN'T TALKED ABOUT WHERE TO TAKE IT FROM HERE AT ALL.
WHAT DOES THE FUTURE HOLD FOR US, I WONDER...
KEIGO-SAN DIDN'T SAY ANYTHING ABOUT IT...
...BUT I BET HE HAD A HARD TIME GETTING HIS FAMILY ON BOARD.

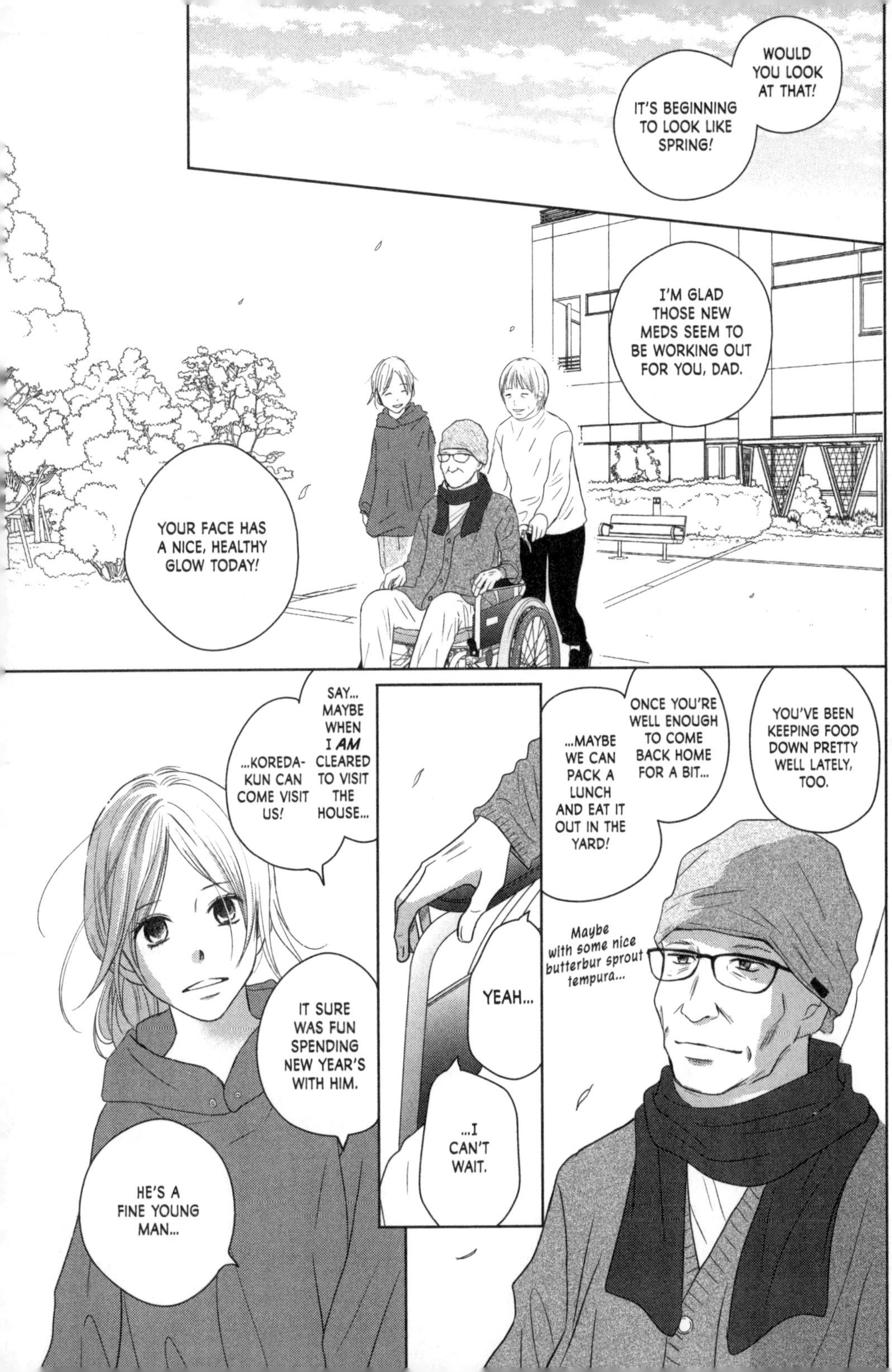
WOULD YOU LOOK AT THAT!
IT'S BEGINNING TO LOOK LIKE SPRING!
I'M GLAD THOSE NEW MEDS SEEM TO BE WORKING OUT FOR YOU, DAD.
YOUR FACE HAS A NICE, HEALTHY GLOW TODAY!
YOU'VE BEEN KEEPING FOOD DOWN PRETTY WELL LATELY, TOO.
ONCE YOU'RE WELL ENOUGH TO COME BACK HOME FOR A BIT...
...MAYBE WE CAN PACK A LUNCH AND EAT IT OUT IN THE YARD!
Maybe with some nice butterbur sprout tempura...
YEAH...
...I CAN'T WAIT.
SAY... MAYBE WHEN I ***AM*** CLEARED TO VISIT THE HOUSE...
...KOREDA-KUN CAN COME VISIT US!
IT SURE WAS FUN SPENDING NEW YEAR'S WITH HIM.
HE'S A FINE YOUNG MAN...

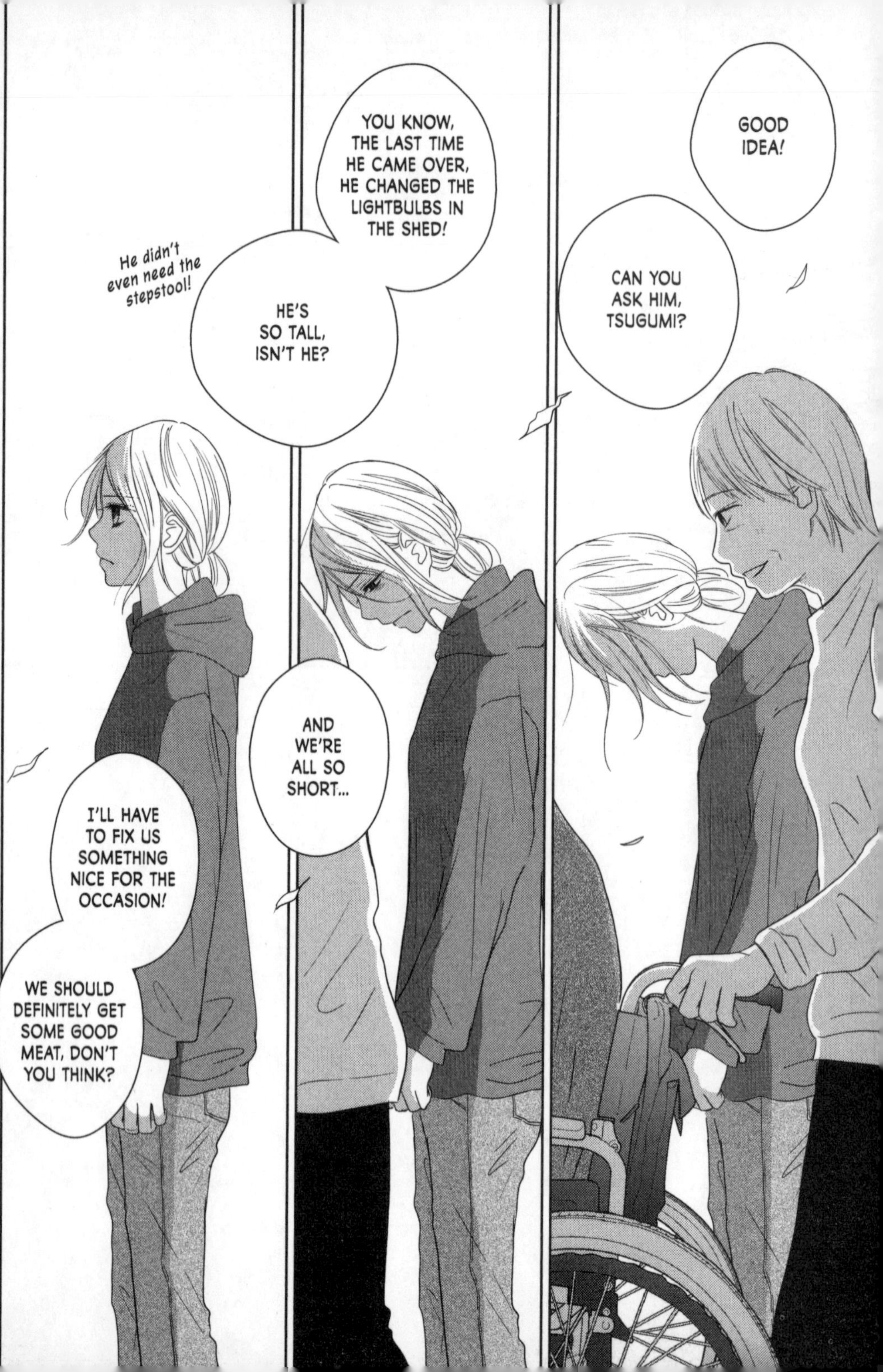
GOOD IDEA!
CAN YOU ASK HIM, TSUGUMI?
YOU KNOW, THE LAST TIME HE CAME OVER, HE CHANGED THE LIGHTBULBS IN THE SHED!
HE'S SO TALL, ISN'T HE?
He didn't even need the stepstool!
AND WE'RE ALL SO SHORT...
I'LL HAVE TO FIX US SOMETHING NICE FOR THE OCCASION!
WE SHOULD DEFINITELY GET SOME GOOD MEAT, DON'T YOU THINK?

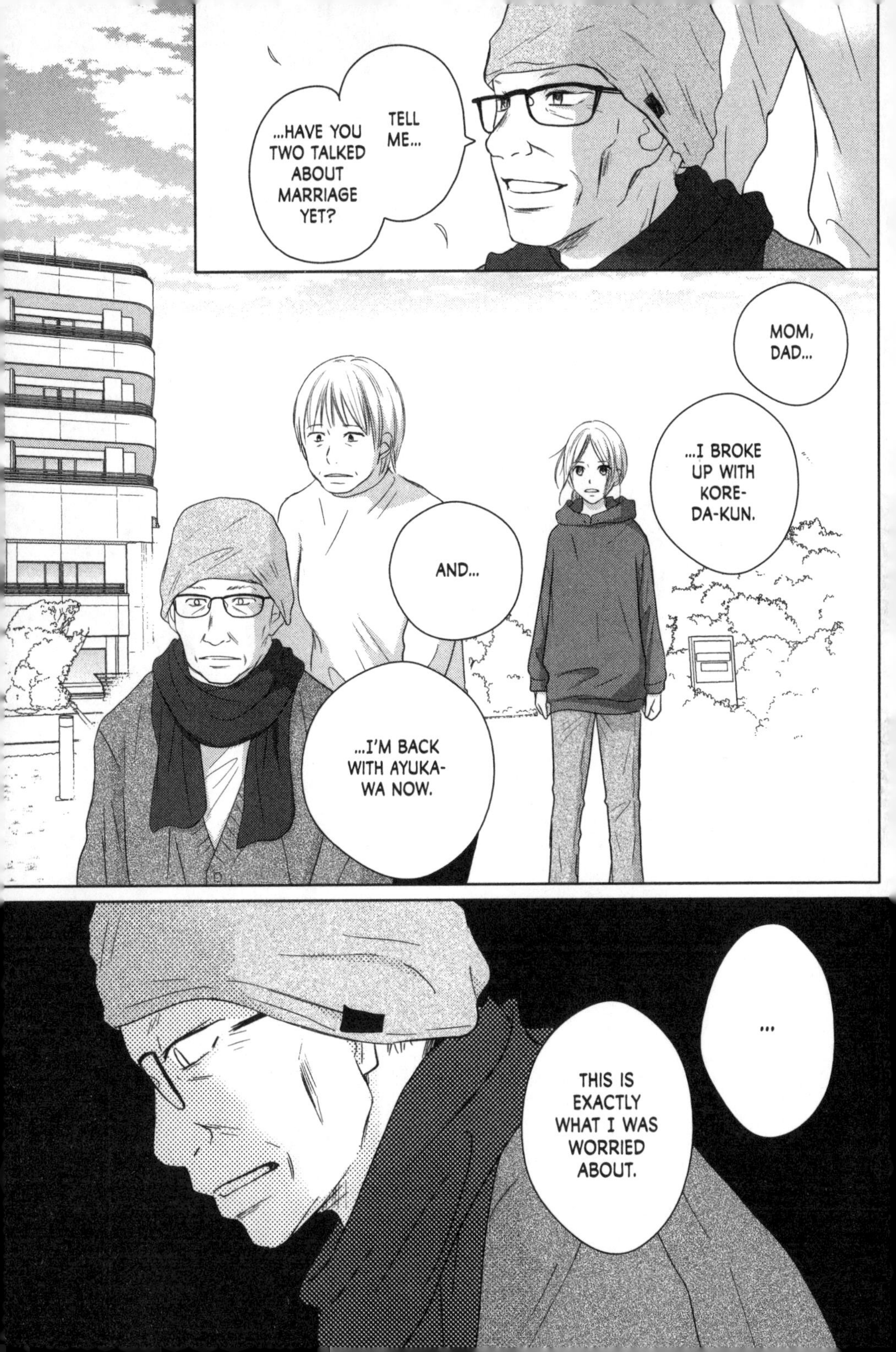
TELL ME... ...HAVE YOU TWO TALKED ABOUT MARRIAGE YET?
MOM, DAD...
...I BROKE UP WITH KORE-DA-KUN.
AND...
...I'M BACK WITH AYUKA-WA NOW.
...
THIS IS EXACTLY WHAT I WAS WORRIED ABOUT.

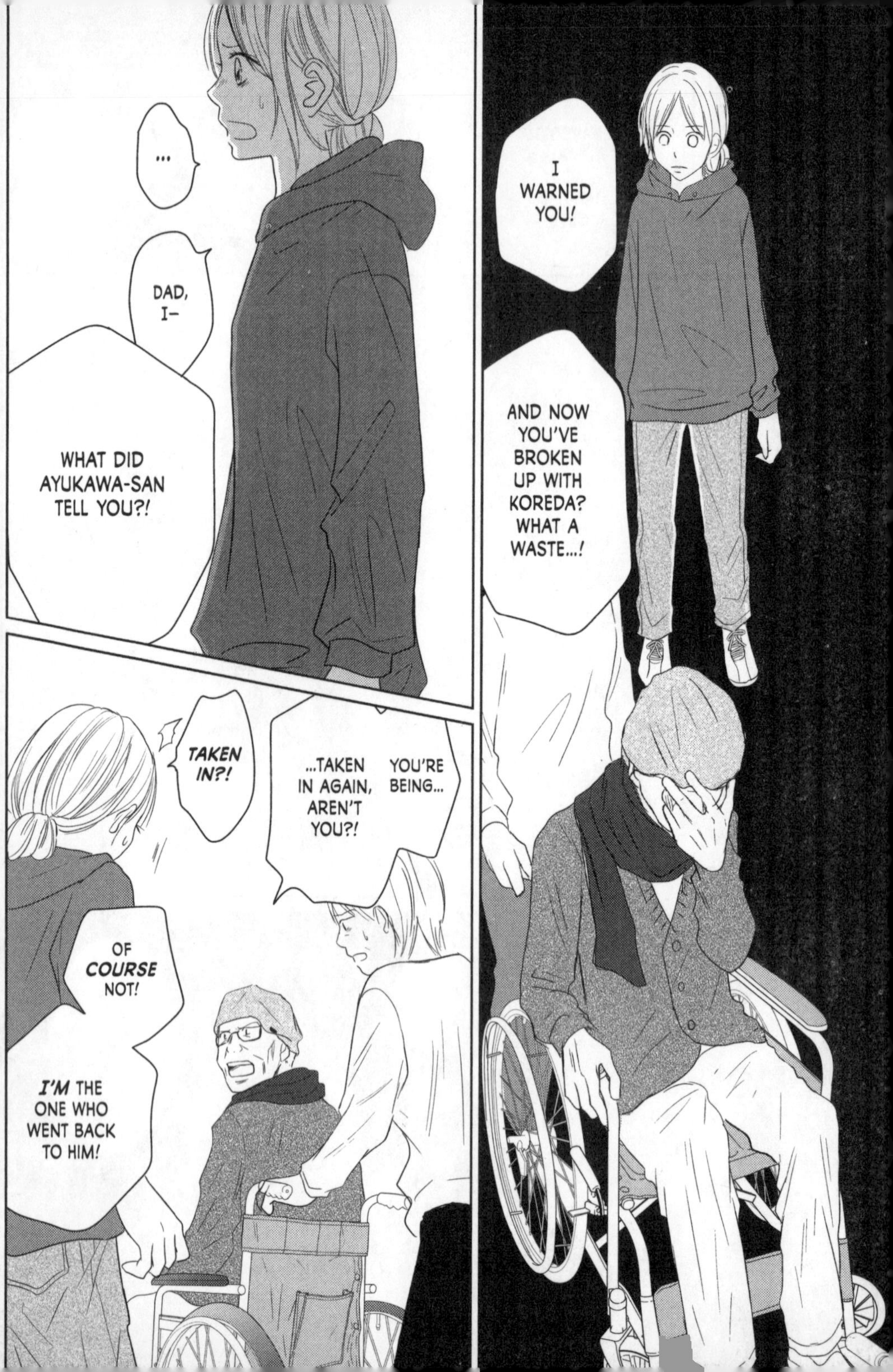
I WARNED YOU!
AND NOW YOU'VE BROKEN UP WITH KOREDA? WHAT A WASTE...!
...
DAD, I–
WHAT DID AYUKAWA-SAN TELL YOU?!
YOU'RE BEING...
...TAKEN IN AGAIN, AREN'T YOU?!
TAKEN IN?!
OF *COURSE* NOT!
I'M THE ONE WHO WENT BACK TO HIM!

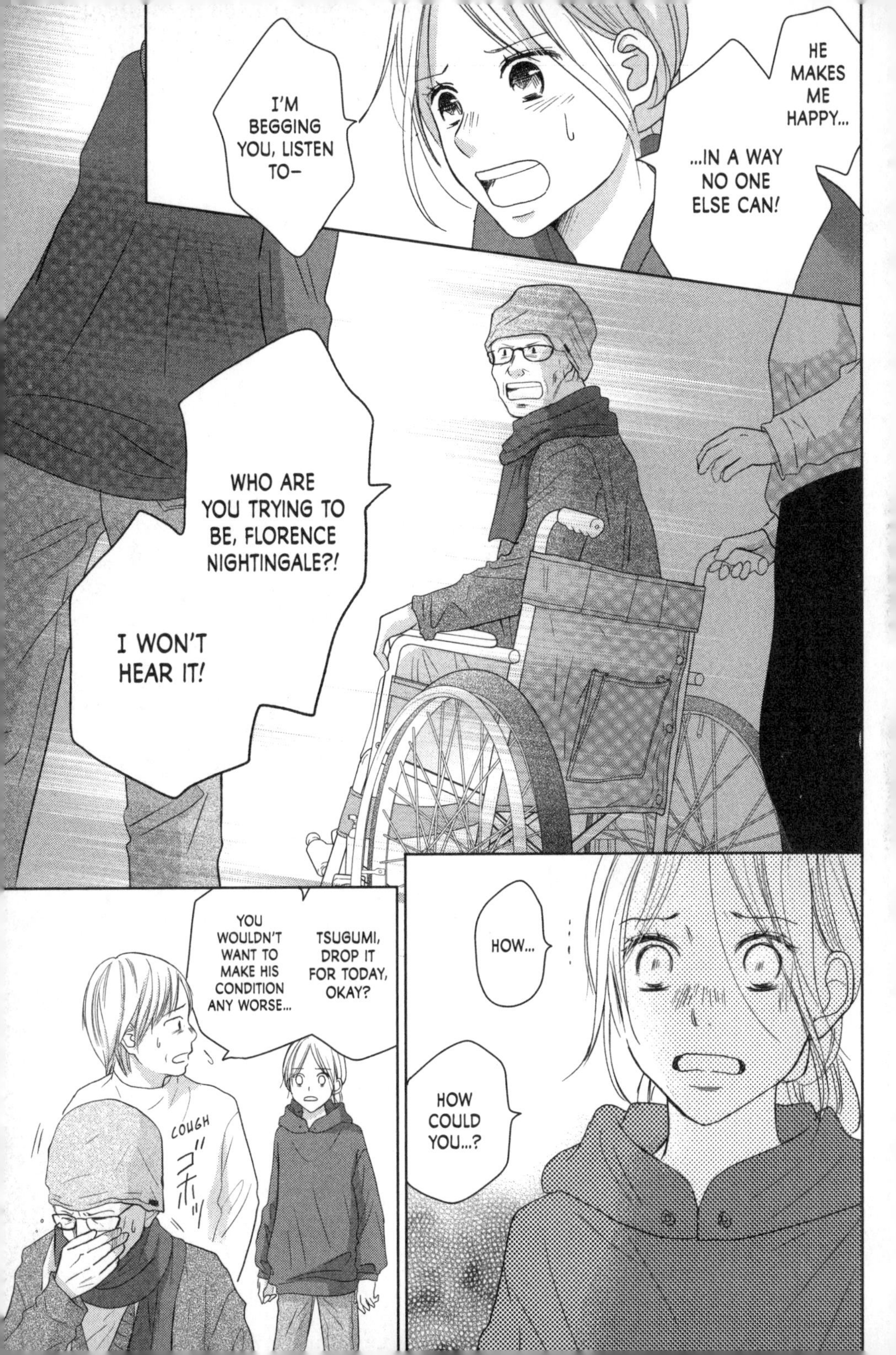
HE MAKES ME HAPPY...
...IN A WAY NO ONE ELSE CAN!
I'M BEGGING YOU, LISTEN TO–
WHO ARE YOU TRYING TO BE, FLORENCE NIGHTINGALE?!
I WON'T HEAR IT!
HOW...
HOW COULD YOU...?
TSUGUMI, DROP IT FOR TODAY, OKAY?
YOU WOULDN'T WANT TO MAKE HIS CONDITION ANY WORSE...
COUGH
ゴホッ

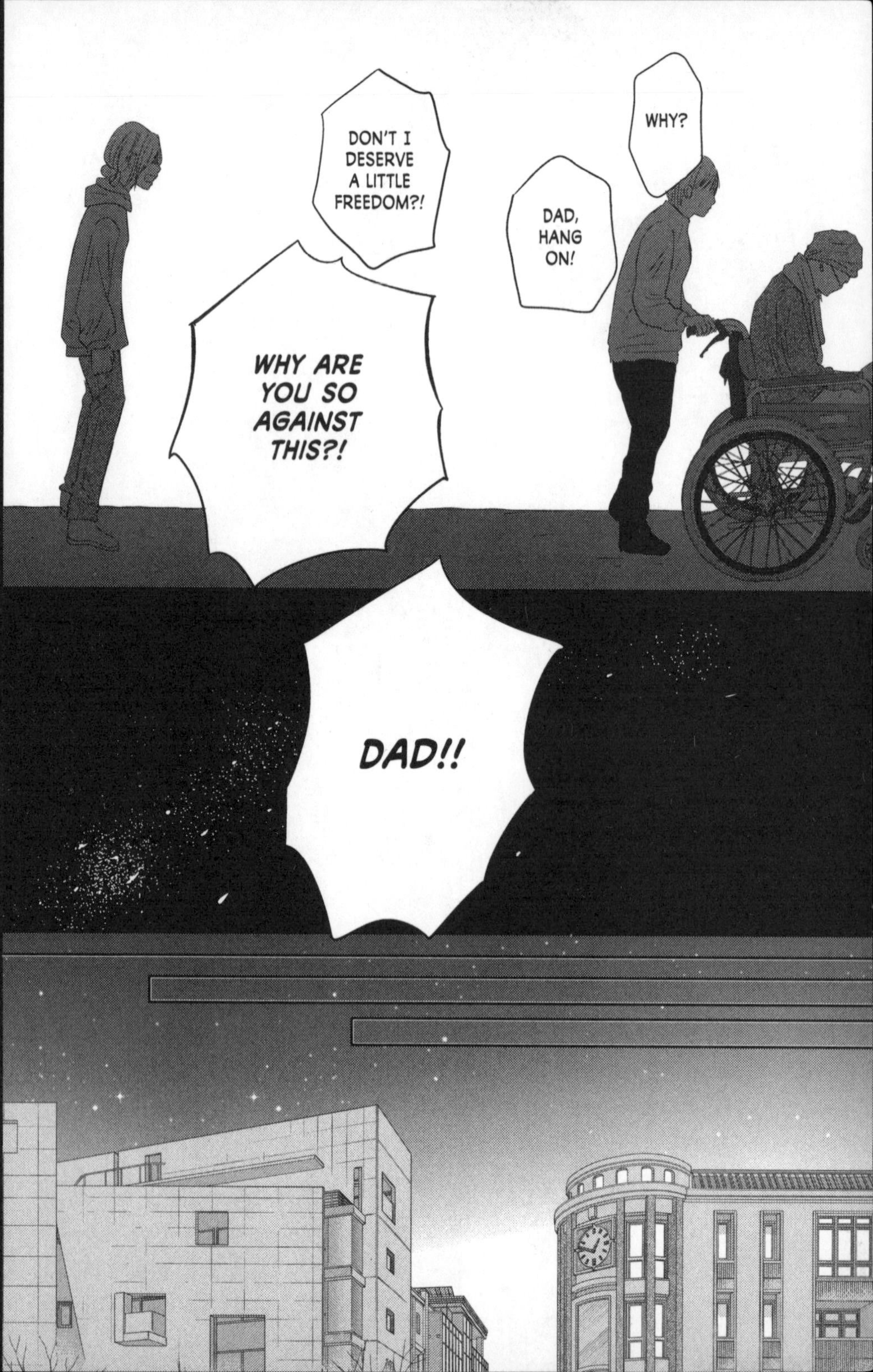
WHY?
DAD, HANG ON!
DON'T I DESERVE A LITTLE FREEDOM?!
WHY ARE YOU SO AGAINST THIS?!
DAD!!

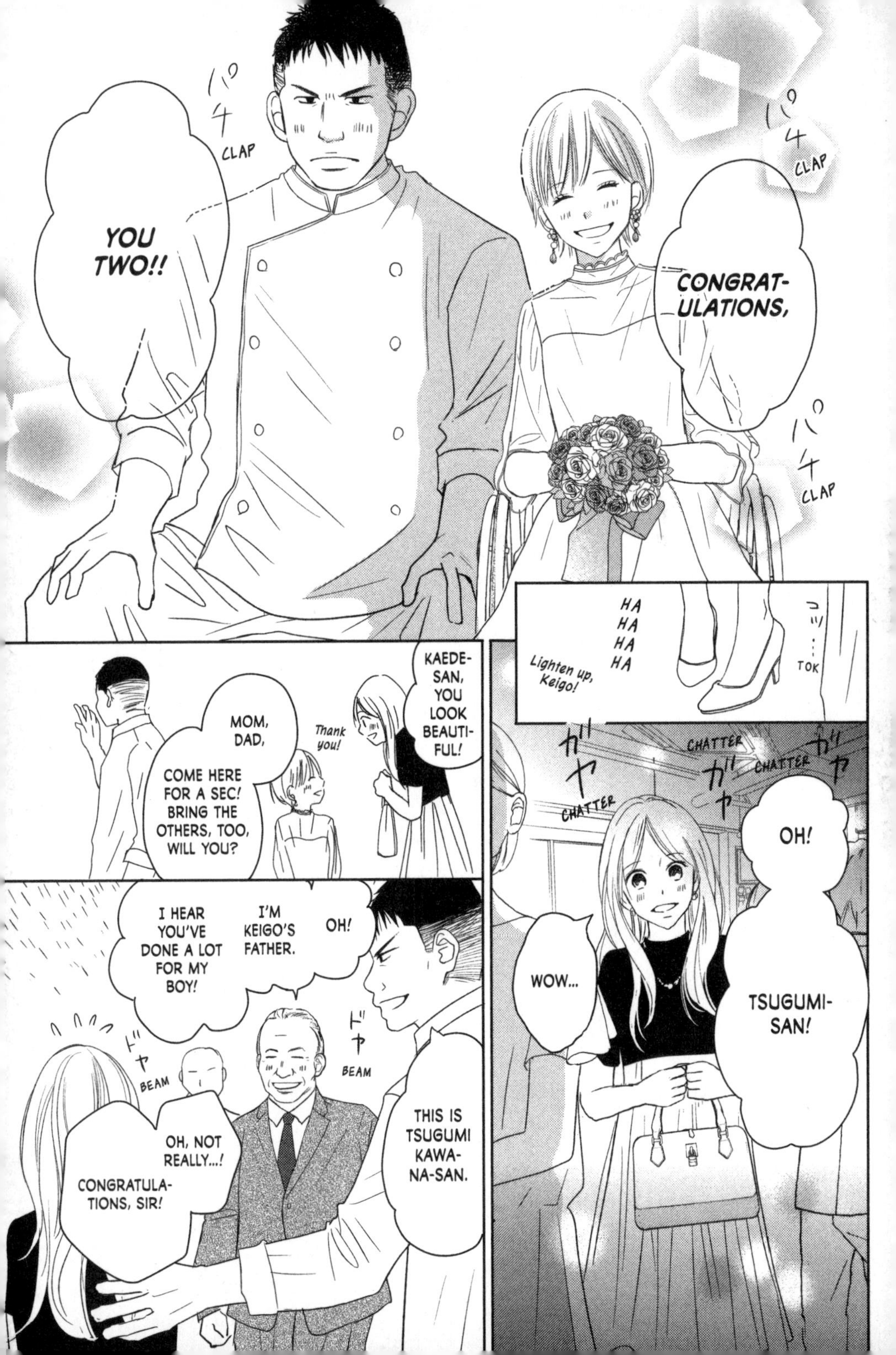
パチ CLAP
CONGRAT-ULATIONS,
パチ CLAP
YOU TWO!!
パチ CLAP
HA HA HA HA
Lighten up, Keigo!
コツ… TOK
ガヤ CHATTER
ガヤ CHATTER
ガヤ CHATTER
OH!
TSUGUMI-SAN!
WOW...
KAEDE-SAN, YOU LOOK BEAUTIFUL!
Thank you!
MOM, DAD,
COME HERE FOR A SEC! BRING THE OTHERS, TOO, WILL YOU?
OH!
I'M KEIGO'S FATHER.
I HEAR YOU'VE DONE A LOT FOR MY BOY!
ドヤ BEAM
THIS IS TSUGUMI KAWANA-SAN.
ドヤ BEAM
OH, NOT REALLY...!
CONGRATULA-TIONS, SIR!

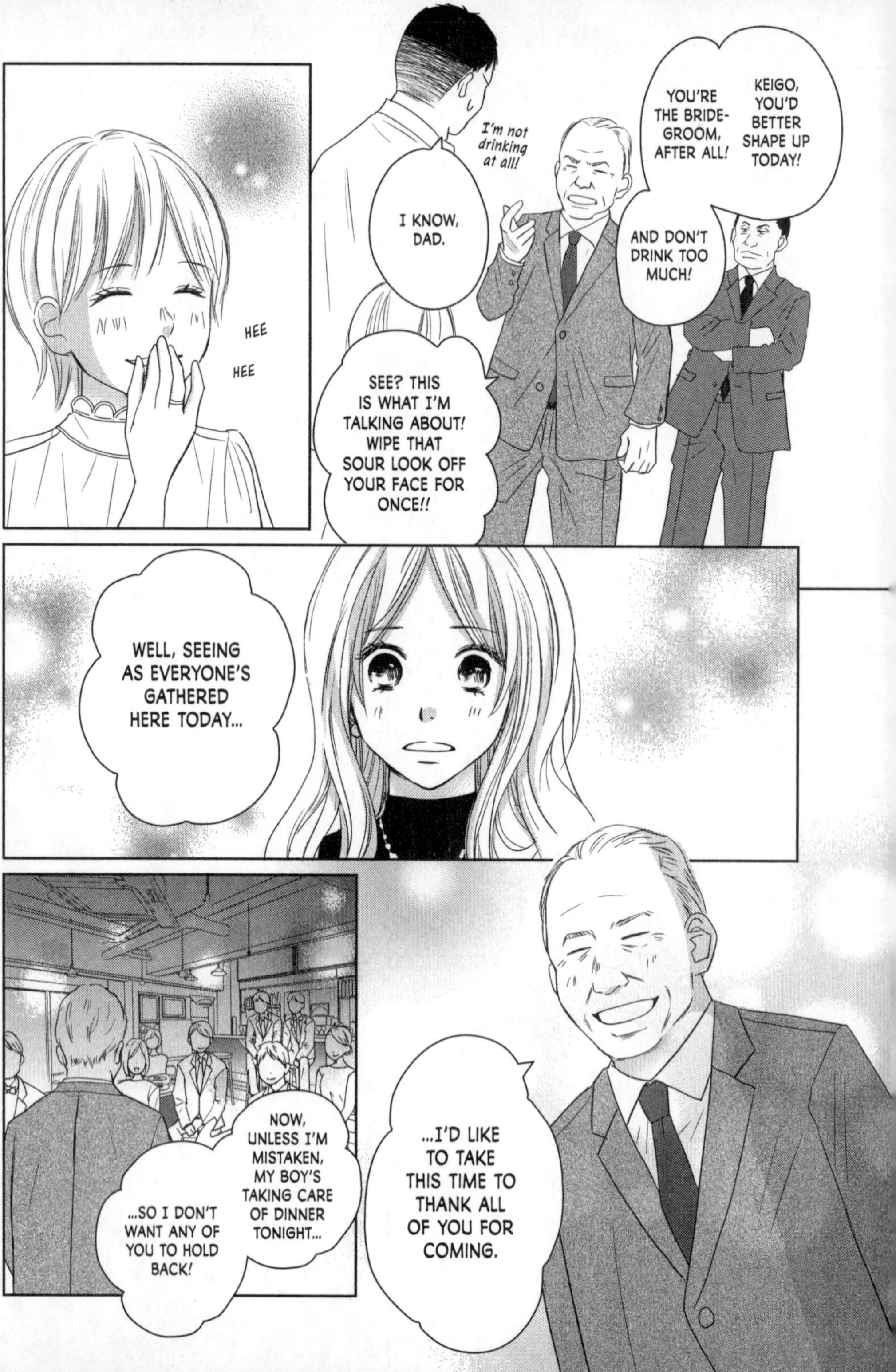
KEIGO, YOU'D BETTER SHAPE UP TODAY!
YOU'RE THE BRIDE-GROOM, AFTER ALL!
AND DON'T DRINK TOO MUCH!
I'm not drinking at all!
I KNOW, DAD.
SEE? THIS IS WHAT I'M TALKING ABOUT! WIPE THAT SOUR LOOK OFF YOUR FACE FOR ONCE!!
HEE
HEE
WELL, SEEING AS EVERYONE'S GATHERED HERE TODAY...
...I'D LIKE TO TAKE THIS TIME TO THANK ALL OF YOU FOR COMING.
NOW, UNLESS I'M MISTAKEN, MY BOY'S TAKING CARE OF DINNER TONIGHT...
...SO I DON'T WANT ANY OF YOU TO HOLD BACK!

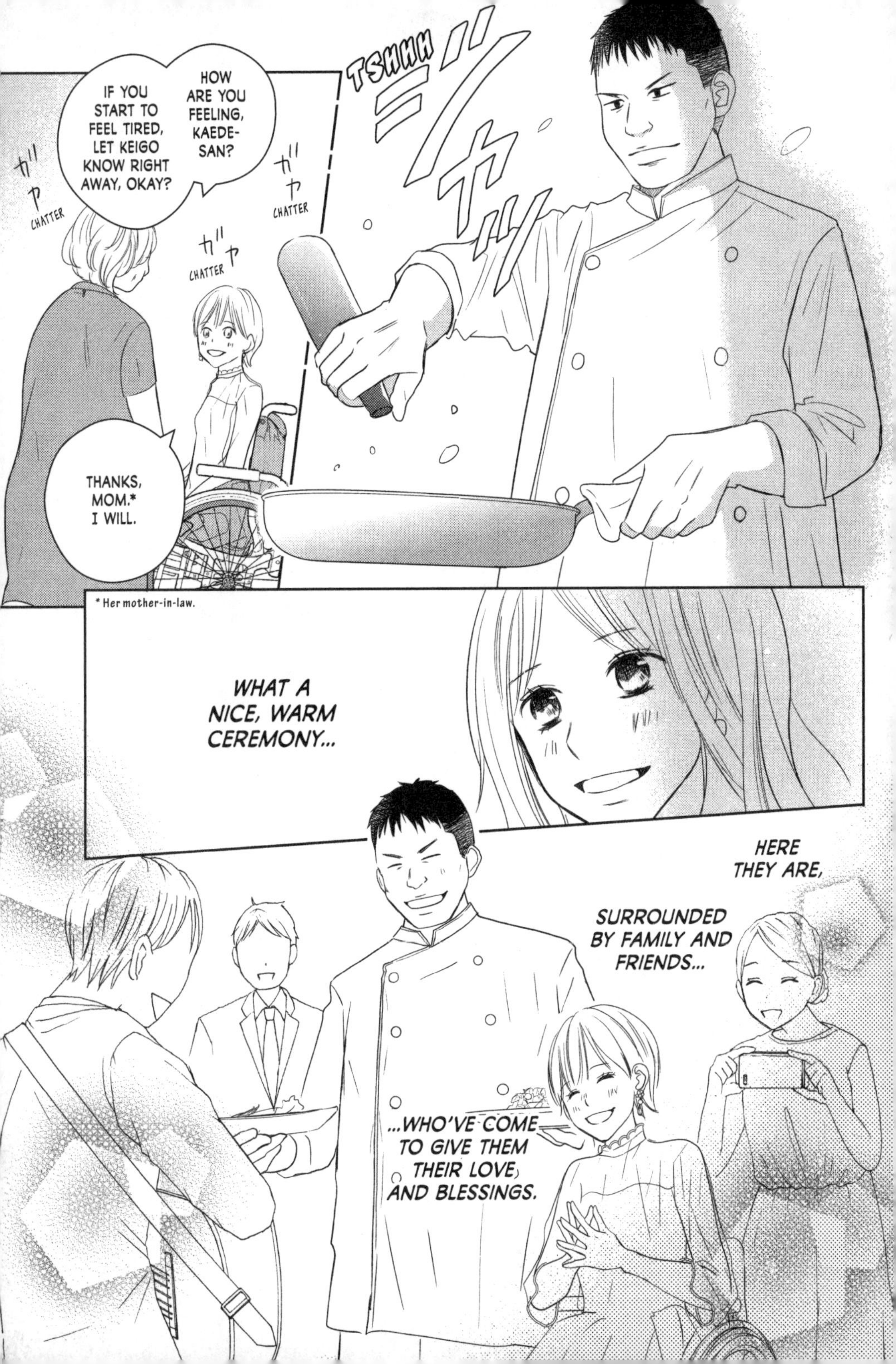
TSHHH
HOW ARE YOU FEELING, KAEDE-SAN?
IF YOU START TO FEEL TIRED, LET KEIGO KNOW RIGHT AWAY, OKAY?
CHATTER
CHATTER
CHATTER
THANKS, MOM.* I WILL.
* Her mother-in-law.
WHAT A NICE, WARM CEREMONY...
HERE THEY ARE,
SURROUNDED BY FAMILY AND FRIENDS...
...WHO'VE COME TO GIVE THEM THEIR LOVE AND BLESSINGS.

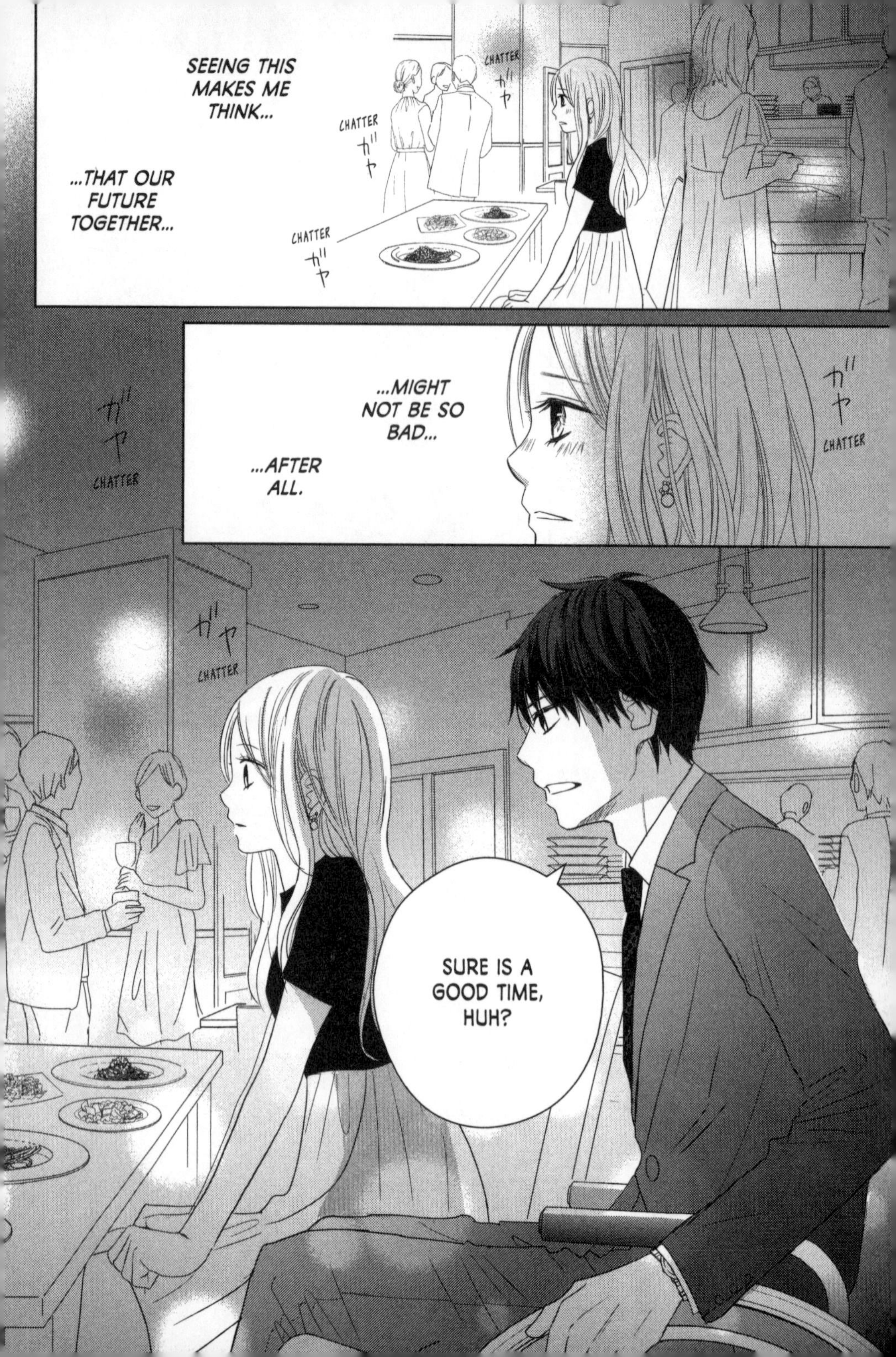
CHATTER ガヤ
SEEING THIS MAKES ME THINK...
CHATTER ガヤ
...THAT OUR FUTURE TOGETHER...
CHATTER ガヤ
ガヤ CHATTER
...MIGHT NOT BE SO BAD...
...AFTER ALL.
ガヤ CHATTER
ガヤ CHATTER
SURE IS A GOOD TIME, HUH?

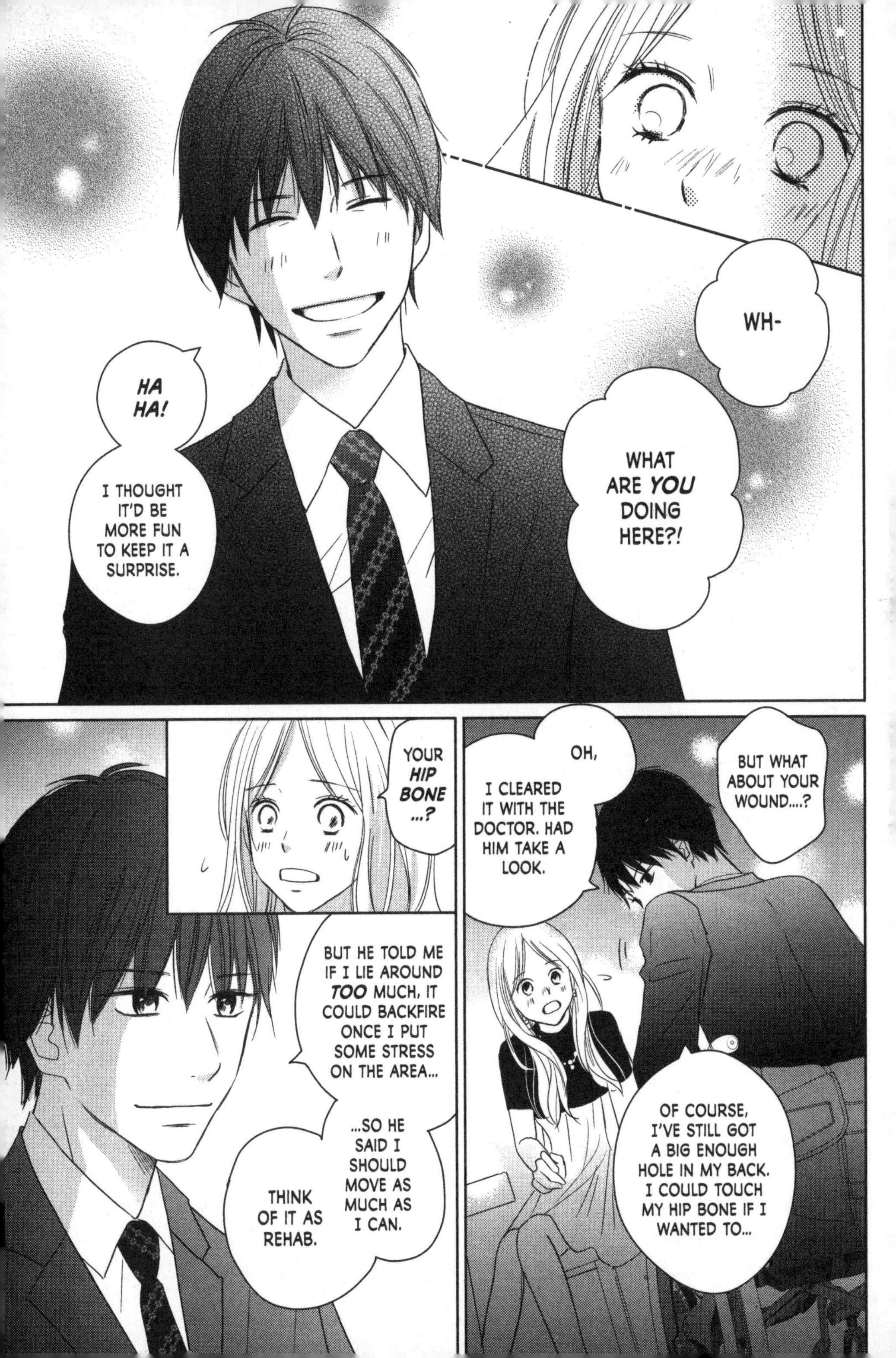
WH-
WHAT ARE *YOU* DOING HERE?!
HA HA!
I THOUGHT IT'D BE MORE FUN TO KEEP IT A SURPRISE.
BUT WHAT ABOUT YOUR WOUND....?
OH,
I CLEARED IT WITH THE DOCTOR. HAD HIM TAKE A LOOK.
OF COURSE, I'VE STILL GOT A BIG ENOUGH HOLE IN MY BACK. I COULD TOUCH MY HIP BONE IF I WANTED TO...
YOUR *HIP BONE* ...?
BUT HE TOLD ME IF I LIE AROUND *TOO* MUCH, IT COULD BACKFIRE ONCE I PUT SOME STRESS ON THE AREA...
...SO HE SAID I SHOULD MOVE AS MUCH AS I CAN.
THINK OF IT AS REHAB.

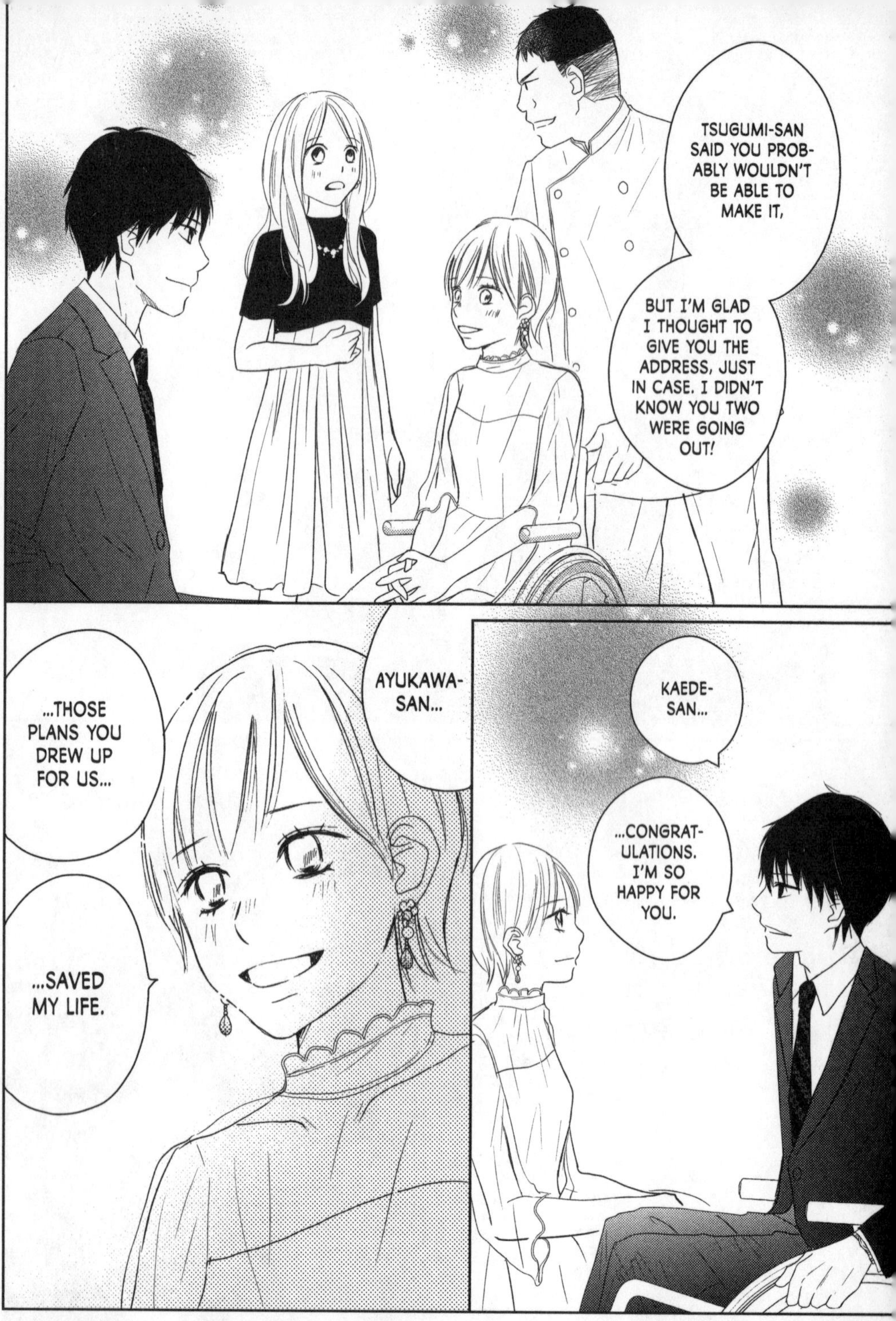
TSUGUMI-SAN SAID YOU PROBABLY WOULDN'T BE ABLE TO MAKE IT,
BUT I'M GLAD I THOUGHT TO GIVE YOU THE ADDRESS, JUST IN CASE. I DIDN'T KNOW YOU TWO WERE GOING OUT!
KAEDE-SAN...
...CONGRATULATIONS. I'M SO HAPPY FOR YOU.
AYUKAWA-SAN...
...THOSE PLANS YOU DREW UP FOR US...
...SAVED MY LIFE.

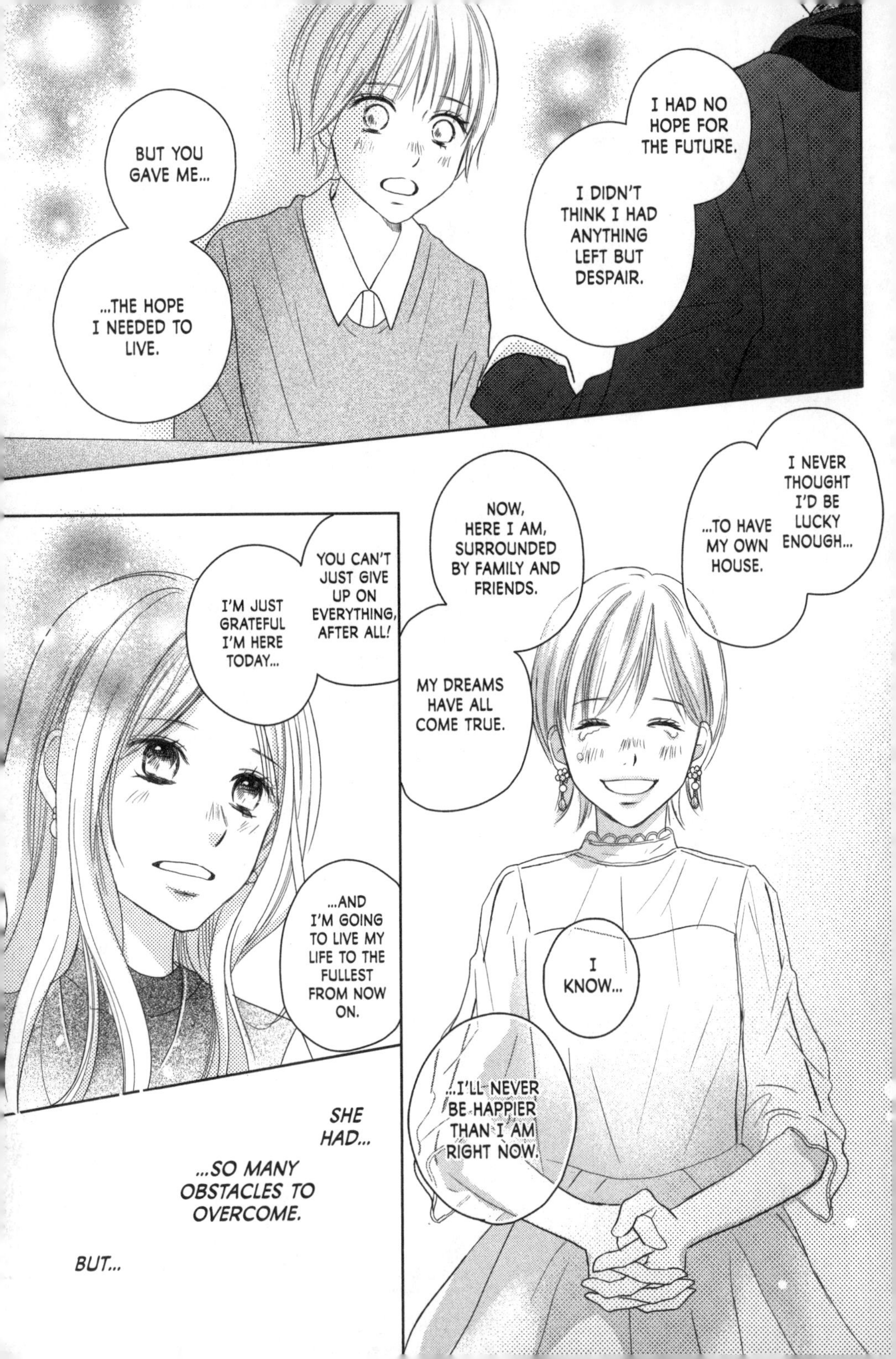
I HAD NO HOPE FOR THE FUTURE.
I DIDN'T THINK I HAD ANYTHING LEFT BUT DESPAIR.
BUT YOU GAVE ME...
...THE HOPE I NEEDED TO LIVE.
I NEVER THOUGHT I'D BE LUCKY ENOUGH...
...TO HAVE MY OWN HOUSE.
NOW, HERE I AM, SURROUNDED BY FAMILY AND FRIENDS.
MY DREAMS HAVE ALL COME TRUE.
I KNOW...
...I'LL NEVER BE HAPPIER THAN I AM RIGHT NOW.
YOU CAN'T JUST GIVE UP ON EVERYTHING, AFTER ALL!
I'M JUST GRATEFUL I'M HERE TODAY...
...AND I'M GOING TO LIVE MY LIFE TO THE FULLEST FROM NOW ON.
SHE HAD...
...SO MANY OBSTACLES TO OVERCOME.
BUT...

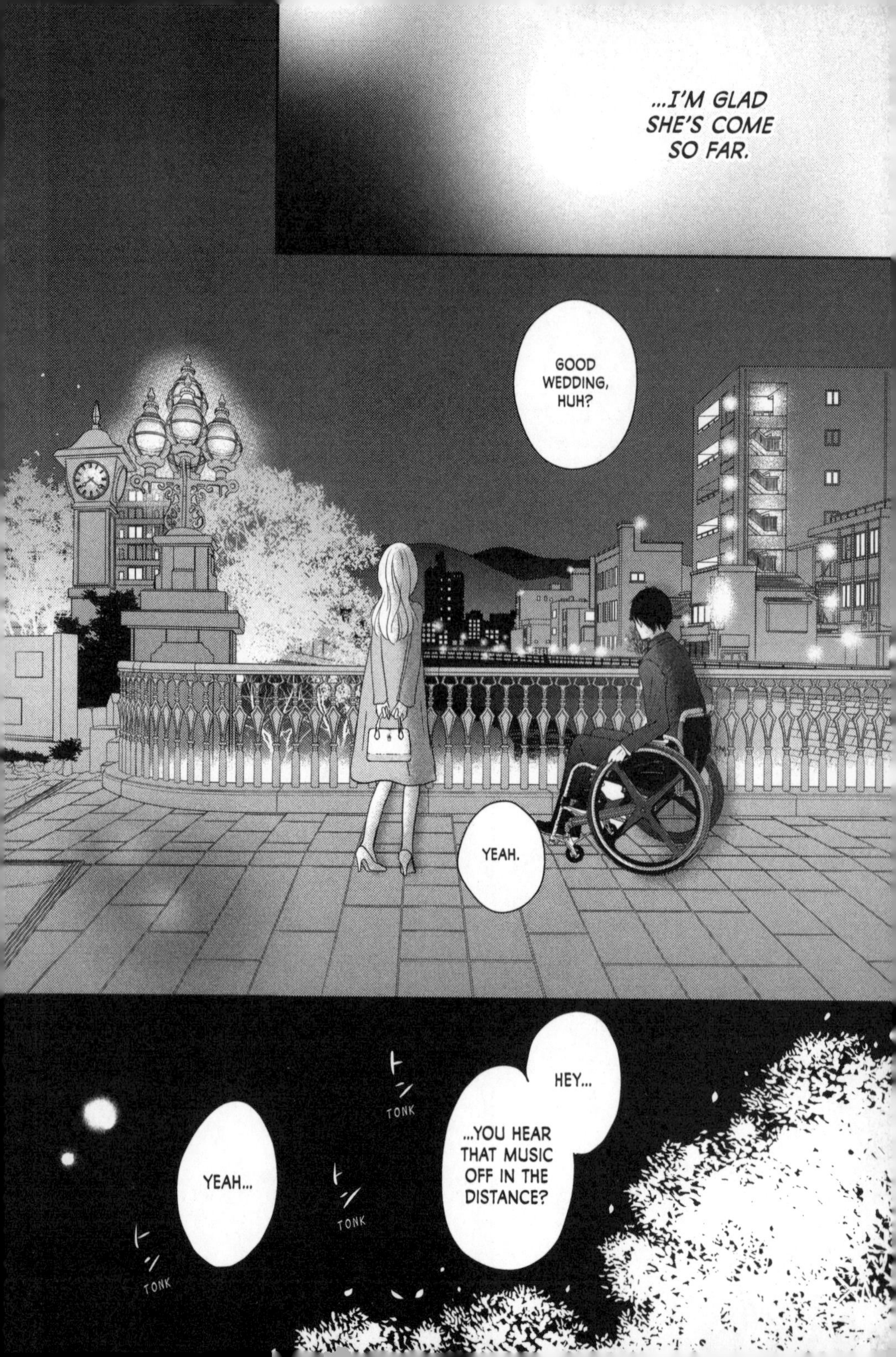
...I'M GLAD SHE'S COME SO FAR.
GOOD WEDDING, HUH?
YEAH.
HEY...
...YOU HEAR THAT MUSIC OFF IN THE DISTANCE?
TONK
TONK
YEAH...
TONK

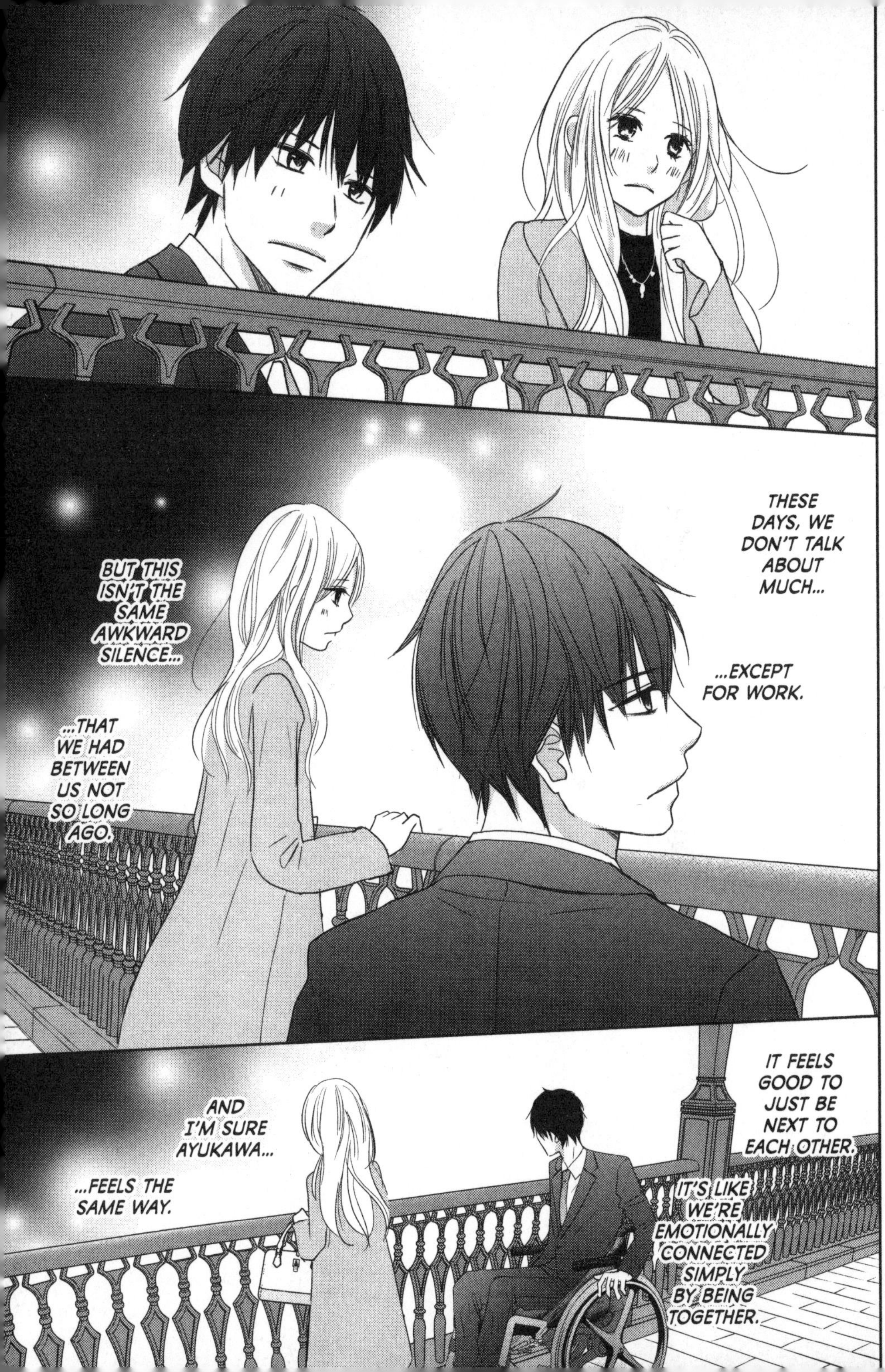
THESE DAYS, WE DON'T TALK ABOUT MUCH...
...EXCEPT FOR WORK.
BUT THIS ISN'T THE SAME AWKWARD SILENCE...
...THAT WE HAD BETWEEN US NOT SO LONG AGO.
IT FEELS GOOD TO JUST BE NEXT TO EACH OTHER.
IT'S LIKE WE'RE EMOTIONALLY CONNECTED SIMPLY BY BEING TOGETHER.
AND I'M SURE AYUKAWA...
...FEELS THE SAME WAY.

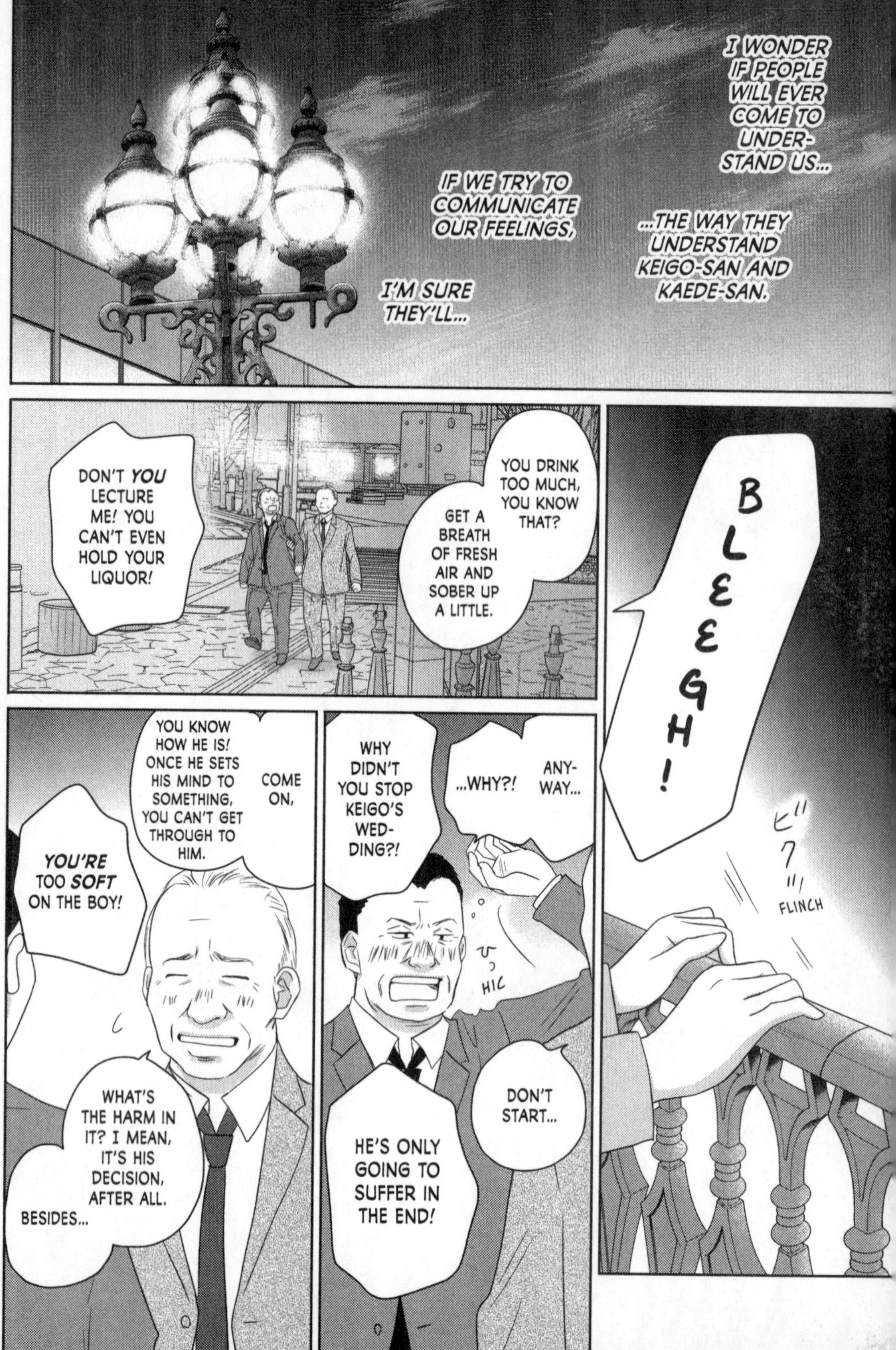
I WONDER IF PEOPLE WILL EVER COME TO UNDER-STAND US...
...THE WAY THEY UNDERSTAND KEIGO-SAN AND KAEDE-SAN.
IF WE TRY TO COMMUNICATE OUR FEELINGS,
I'M SURE THEY'LL...
BLEEGH!
ビクッ
FLINCH
YOU DRINK TOO MUCH, YOU KNOW THAT?
GET A BREATH OF FRESH AIR AND SOBER UP A LITTLE.
DON'T YOU LECTURE ME! YOU CAN'T EVEN HOLD YOUR LIQUOR!
ANY-WAY...
...WHY?!
WHY DIDN'T YOU STOP KEIGO'S WED-DING?!
ひっ
HIC
DON'T START...
HE'S ONLY GOING TO SUFFER IN THE END!
COME ON,
YOU KNOW HOW HE IS! ONCE HE SETS HIS MIND TO SOMETHING, YOU CAN'T GET THROUGH TO HIM.
YOU'RE TOO SOFT ON THE BOY!
WHAT'S THE HARM IN IT? I MEAN, IT'S HIS DECISION, AFTER ALL.
BESIDES...

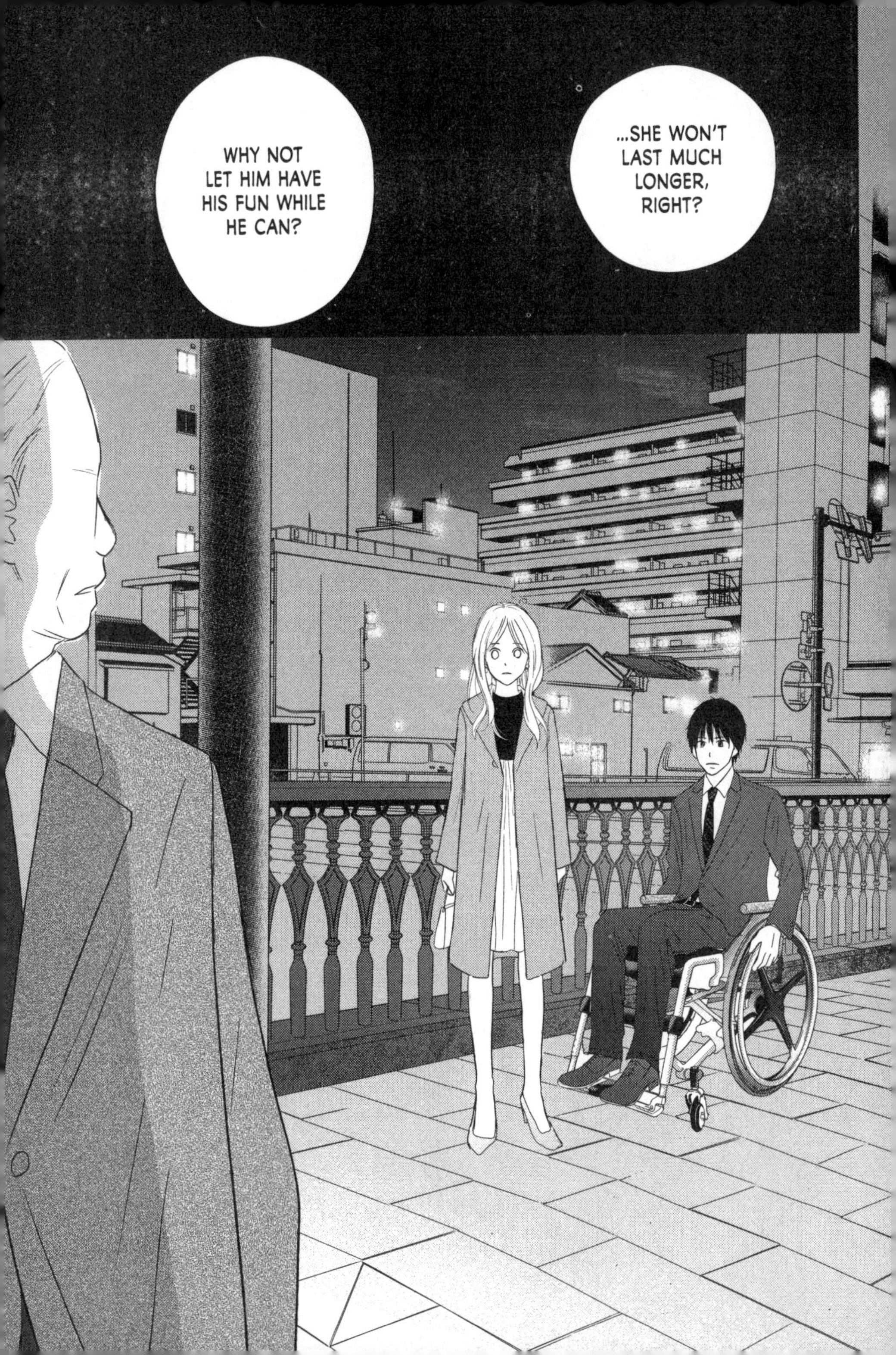
...SHE WON'T LAST MUCH LONGER, RIGHT?
WHY NOT LET HIM HAVE HIS FUN WHILE HE CAN?

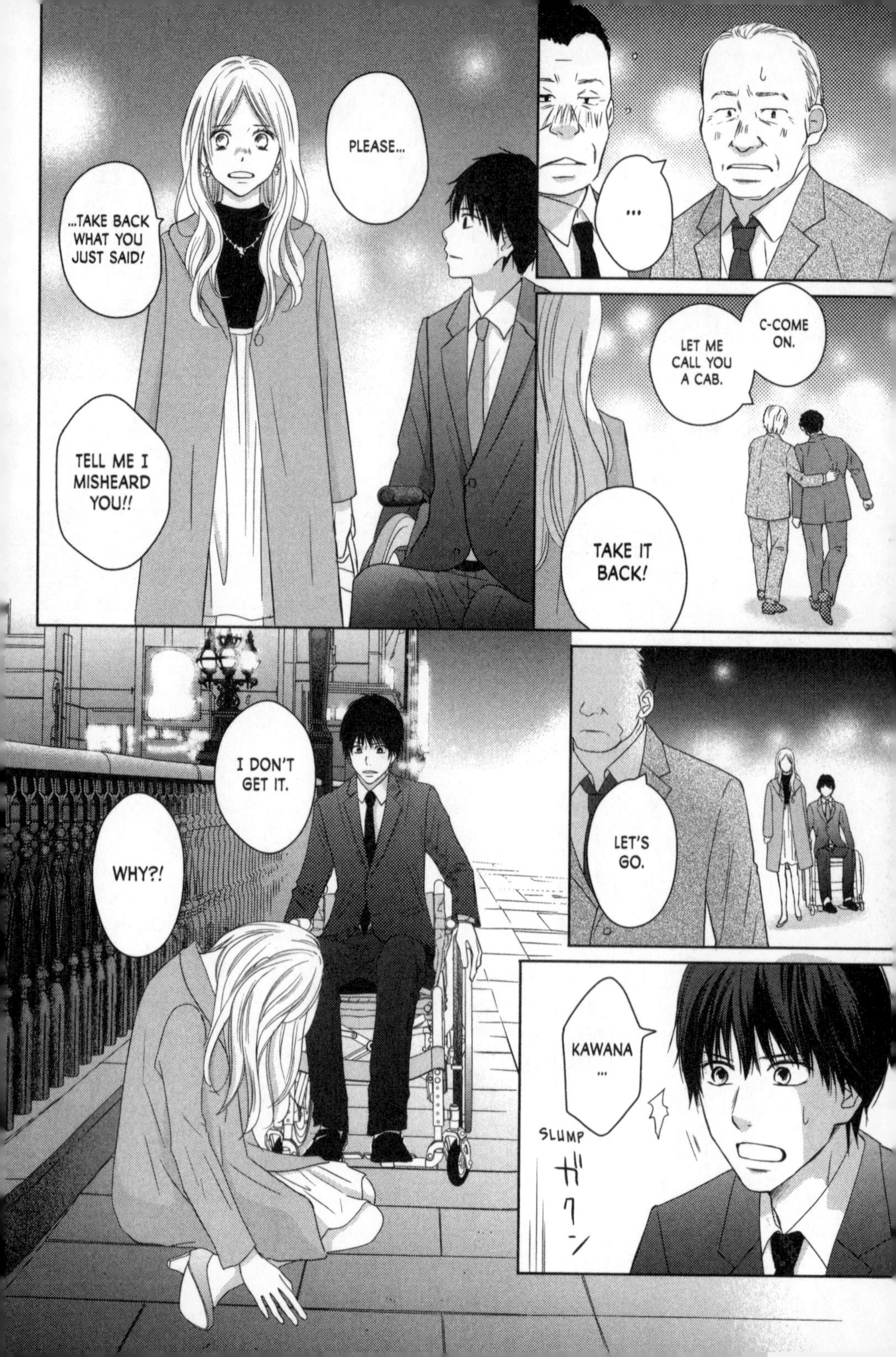
...
C-COME ON.
LET ME CALL YOU A CAB.
TAKE IT BACK!
PLEASE...
...TAKE BACK WHAT YOU JUST SAID!
TELL ME I MISHEARD YOU!!
LET'S GO.
KAWANA ...
SLUMP
ガクン
I DON'T GET IT.
WHY?!

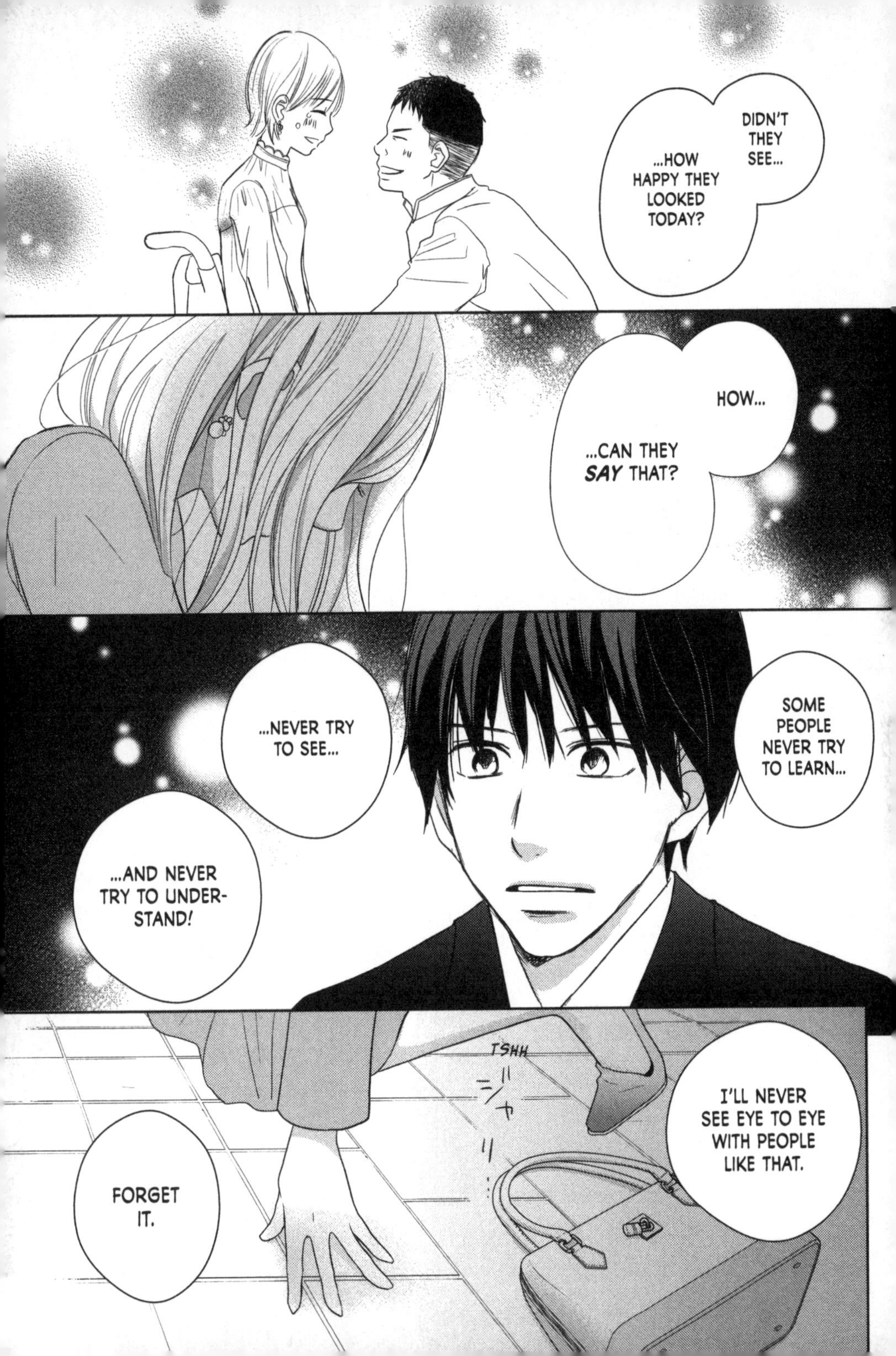
DIDN'T THEY SEE...
...HOW HAPPY THEY LOOKED TODAY?
HOW...
...CAN THEY *SAY* THAT?
SOME PEOPLE NEVER TRY TO LEARN...
...NEVER TRY TO SEE...
...AND NEVER TRY TO UNDER-STAND!
I'LL NEVER SEE EYE TO EYE WITH PEOPLE LIKE THAT.
TSHH
FORGET IT.

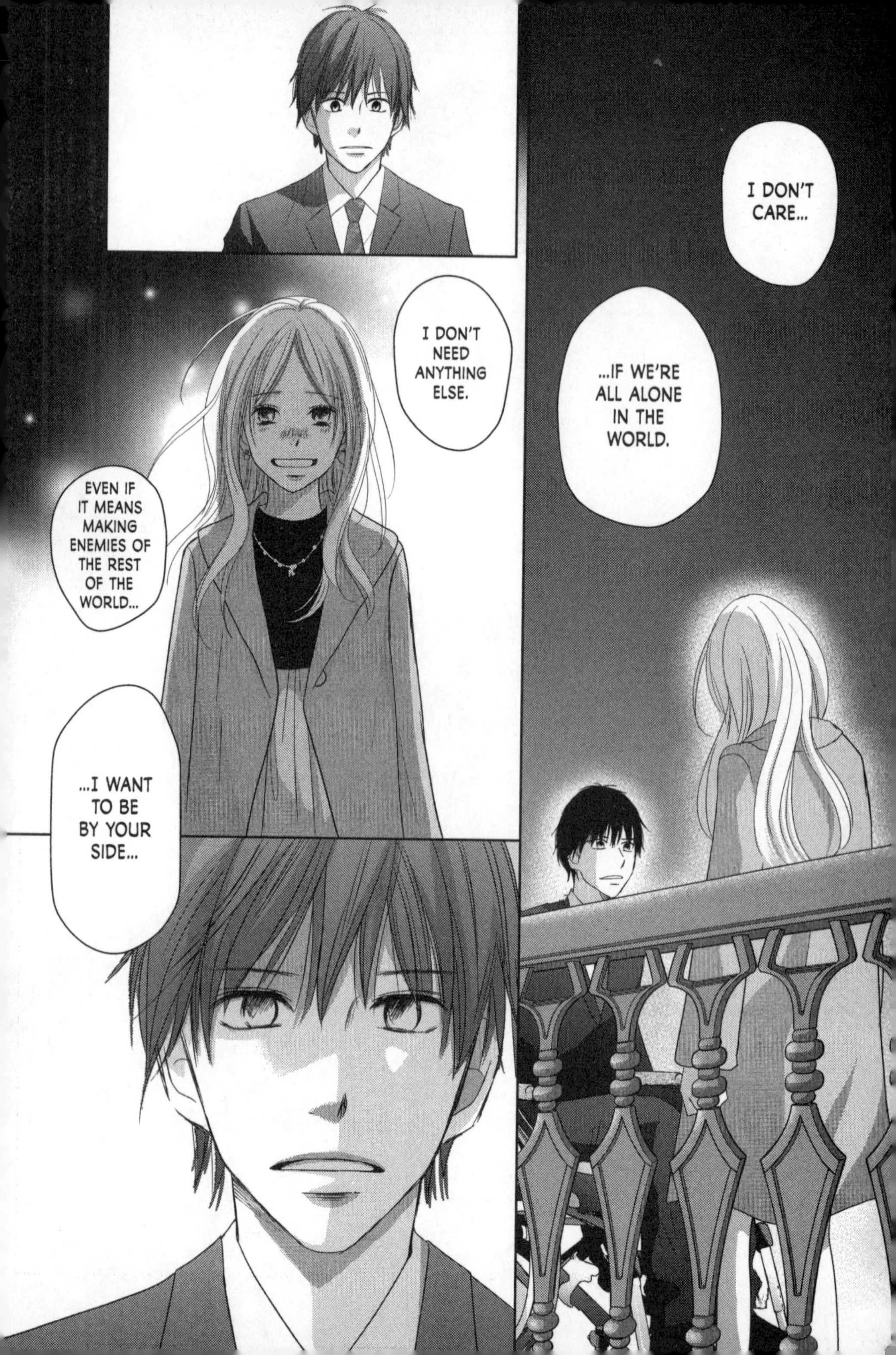
I DON'T CARE...
...IF WE'RE ALL ALONE IN THE WORLD.
I DON'T NEED ANYTHING ELSE.
EVEN IF IT MEANS MAKING ENEMIES OF THE REST OF THE WORLD...
...I WANT TO BE BY YOUR SIDE...

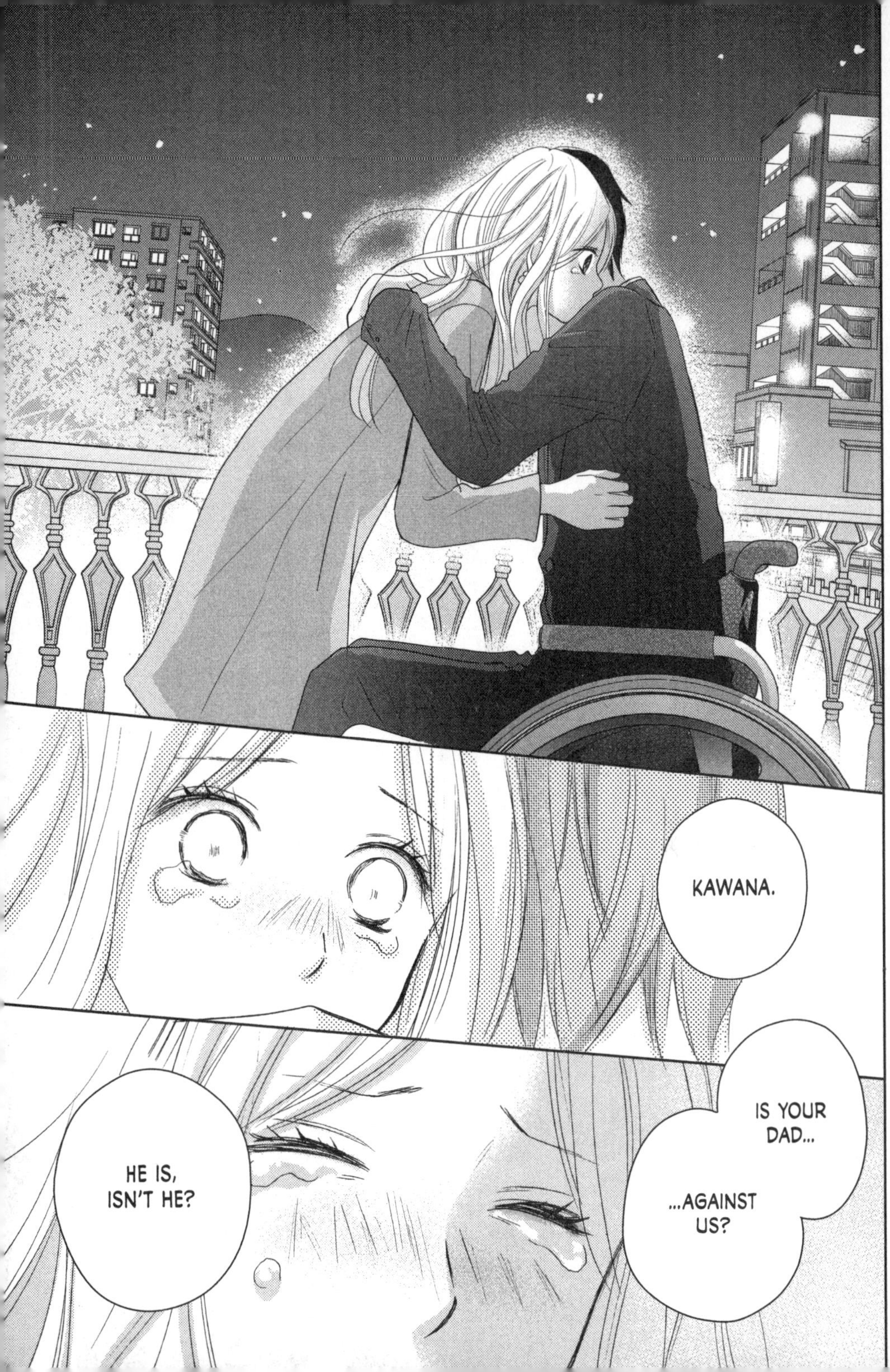
KAWANA.
IS YOUR DAD...
...AGAINST US?
HE IS, ISN'T HE?

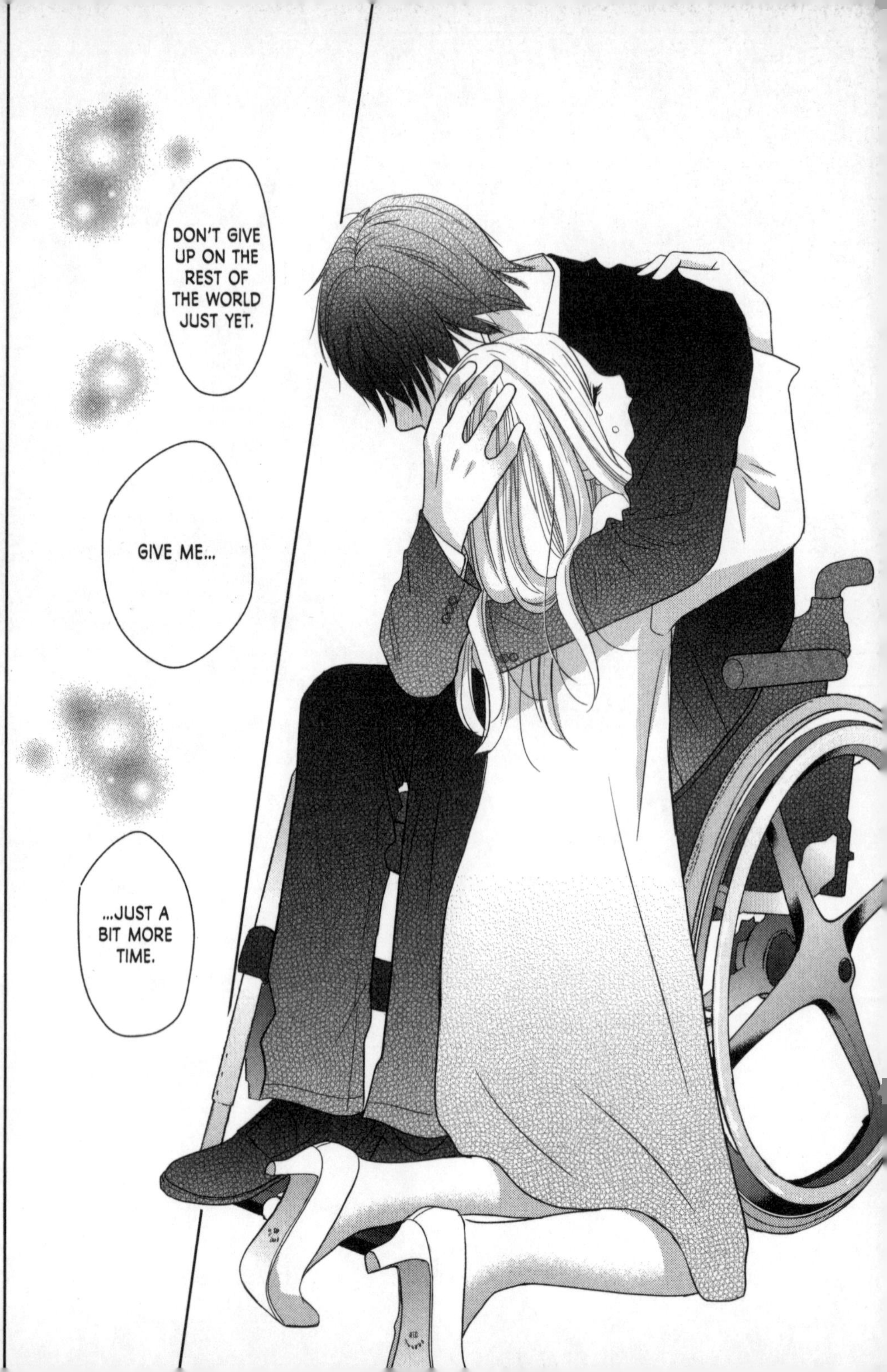
DON'T GIVE UP ON THE REST OF THE WORLD JUST YET.
GIVE ME...
...JUST A BIT MORE TIME.

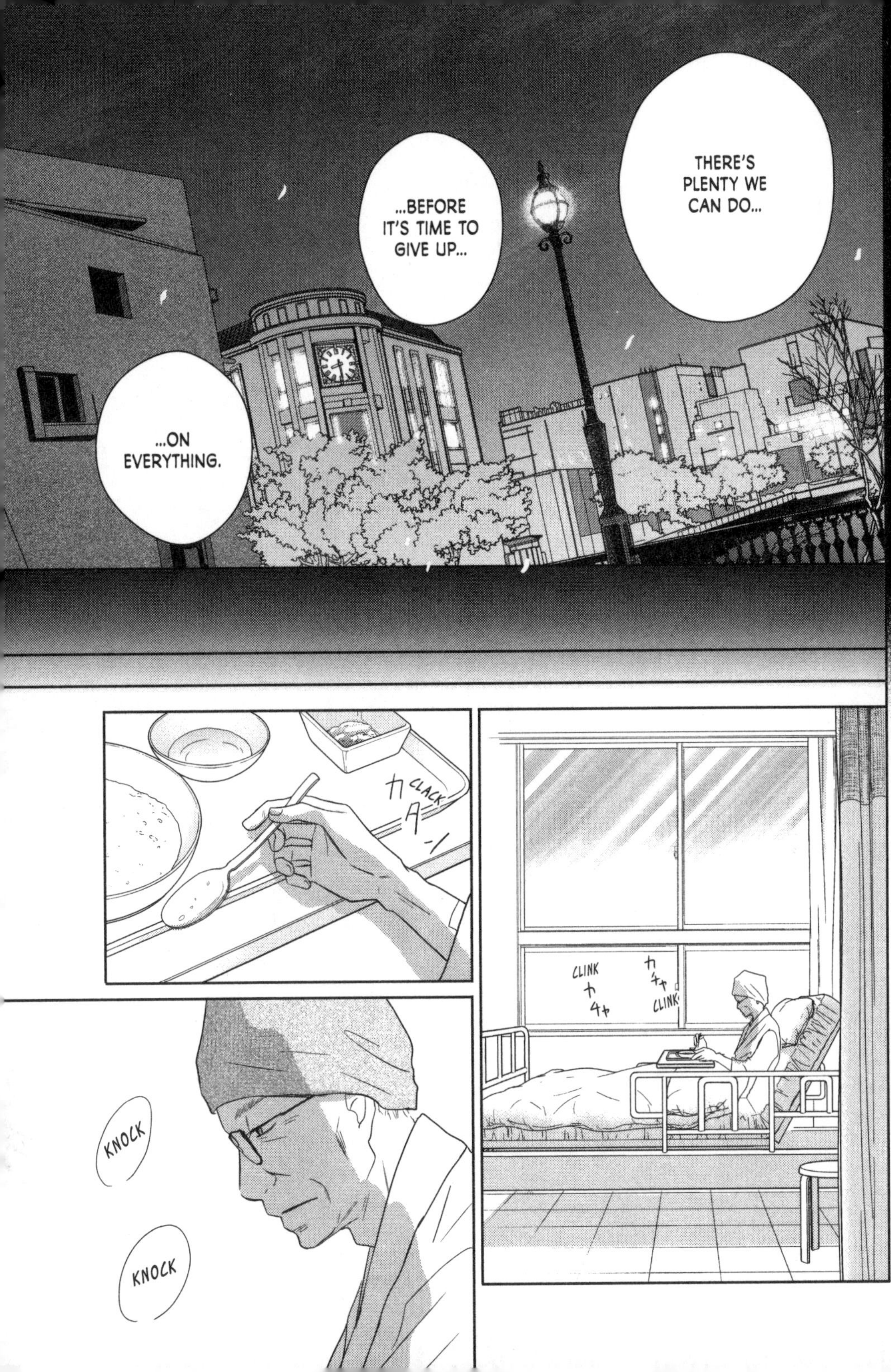
THERE'S PLENTY WE CAN DO...
...BEFORE IT'S TIME TO GIVE UP...
...ON EVERYTHING.
CLINK
CLINK
CLACK
KNOCK
KNOCK

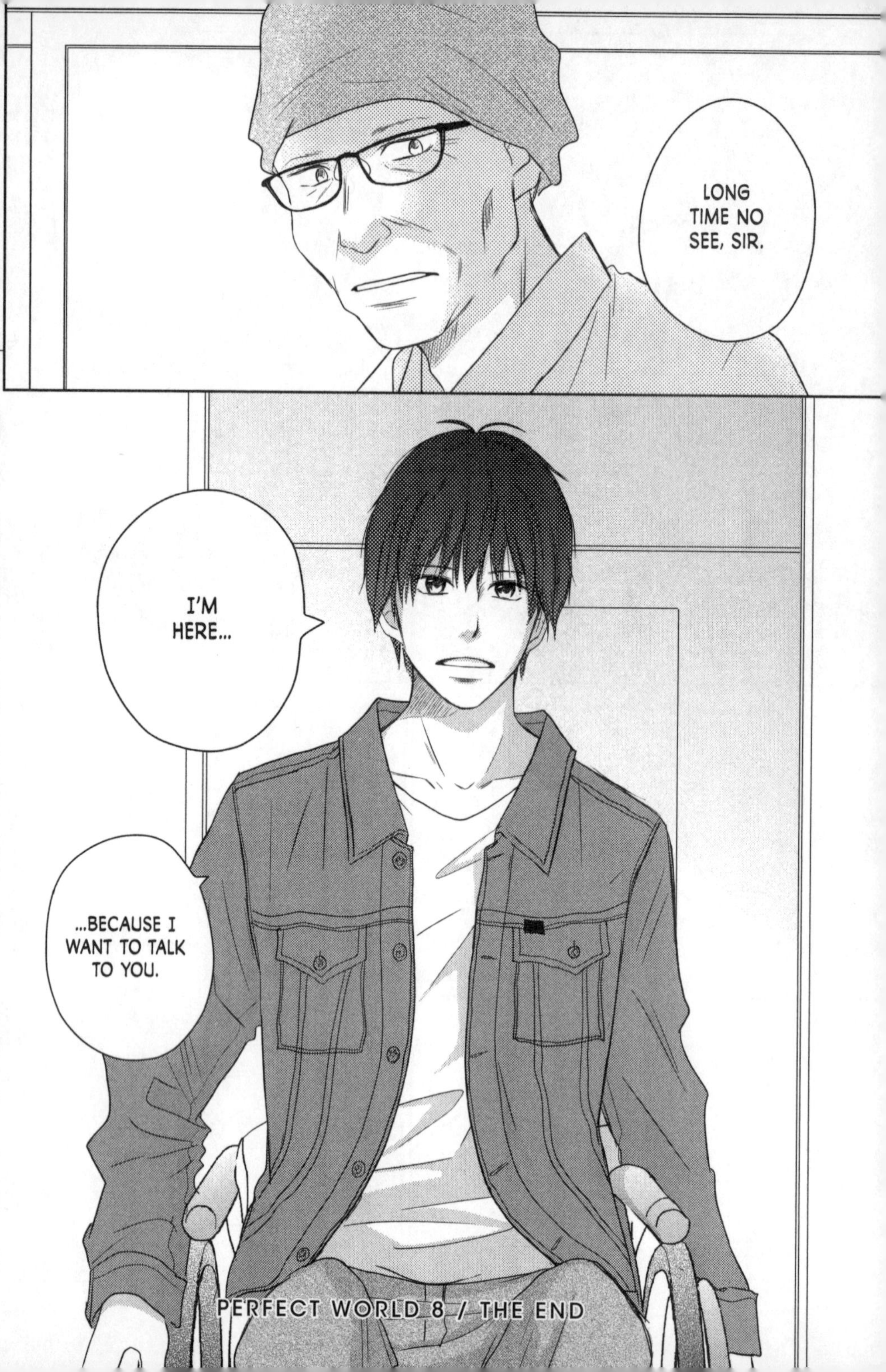
LONG TIME NO SEE, SIR.
I'M HERE...
...BECAUSE I WANT TO TALK TO YOU.
PERFECT WORLD 8 / THE END

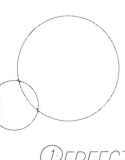
PERFECT WORLD

— Thank you so much for reading *Perfect World* volume eight! —

As always, I'd like to express my gratitude to the readers who have been with me every step of the way.

Now that volume eight is out, I have some big news.
The *Perfect World* movie is coming out in theaters!

Abe-san and I have been telling each other that when we first met, we never dreamed this day would come!
I want to thank everyone else on the staff for their faithful support, too.

Now, I suspect some of you are going to have a tough time getting used to live action.
Not to worry. I'm a manga artist by trade, and I'll do everything I can to tell this story!

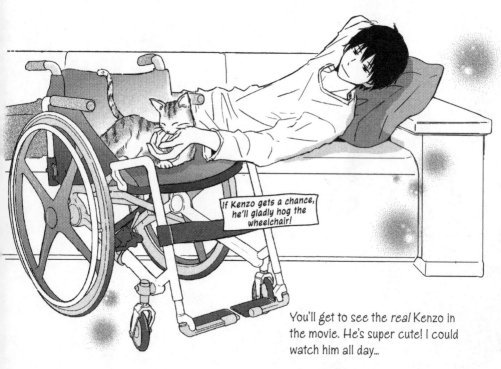

If Kenzo gets a chance, he'll gladly hog the wheelchair!

You'll get to see the *real* Kenzo in the movie. He's super cute! I could watch him all day...

By the way, about the name "Kenzo"... I haven't been able to touch on this before, but it doesn't come from nowhere! Itsuki picked Kenzo up in Volume One. He went back and forth on what to name him, but finally decided on naming him after Kenzo Tange, the master architect who put Japan on the map!

I hope you can be just as wonderful an architect someday, Itsuki!

— From the bottom of my heart, thank you to all of those who helped me. —

* Kazuo Abe-sama from Abe Kensetsu Inc.
* Ouchi-sama * Yamada-sama
* The staff at the Kanagawa Prefecture Convalescent Rehabilitation Ward
* Those at the Vivit Minami Funabashi branch of OX Kanto

* My editor, Ito-sama * Everyone from editorial at *Kiss*
* The designer, Kusume-sama and Agata-sama
* My assistants, T-sama, K-sama, and TN-sama
* Everyone involved in getting this sold
* My family, friends, and also my readers

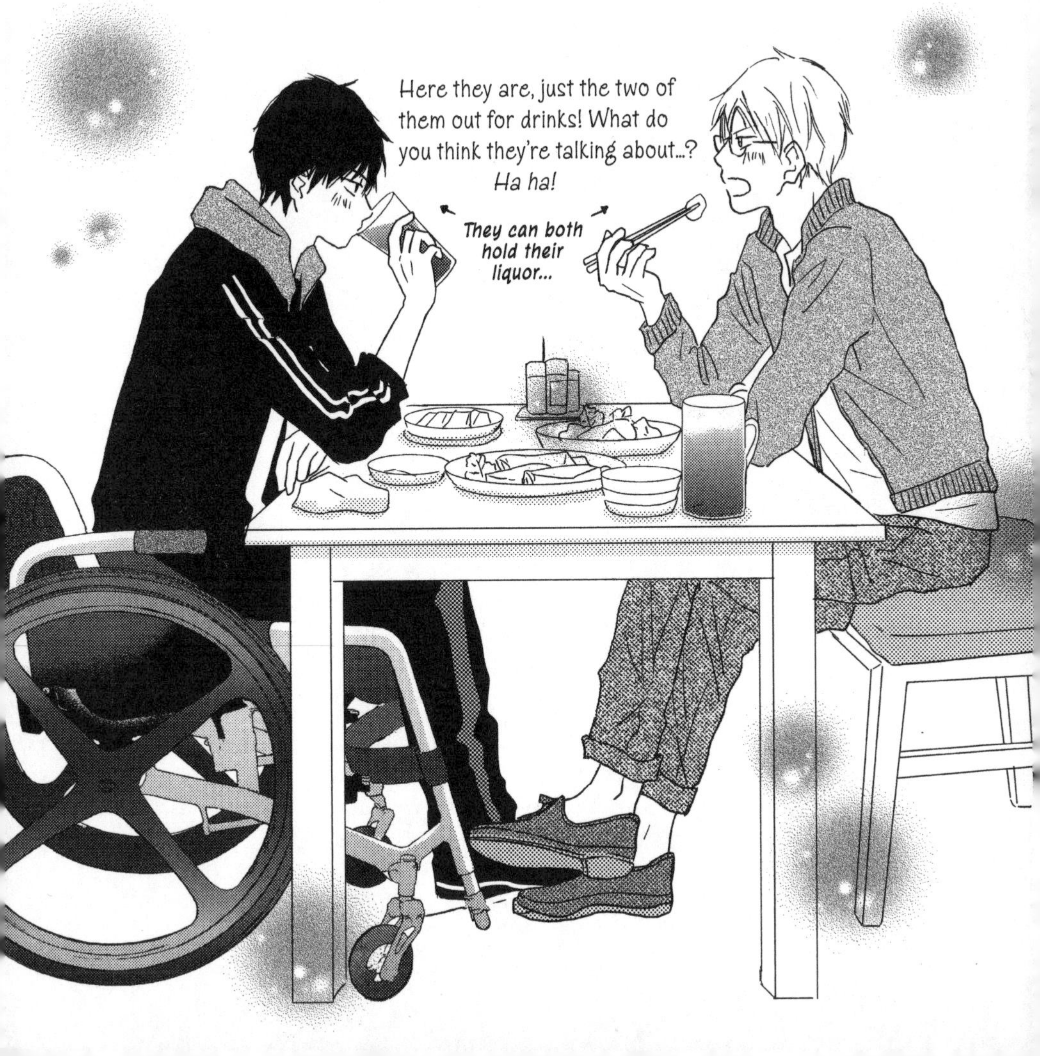
Here they are, just the two of them out for drinks! What do you think they're talking about...? *Ha ha!*
They can both hold their liquor...

a Silent Voice

The New York Times bestselling manga and Eisner Award nominee—now available in a complete box set!

Now a feature-length animation from Kyoto Animation!

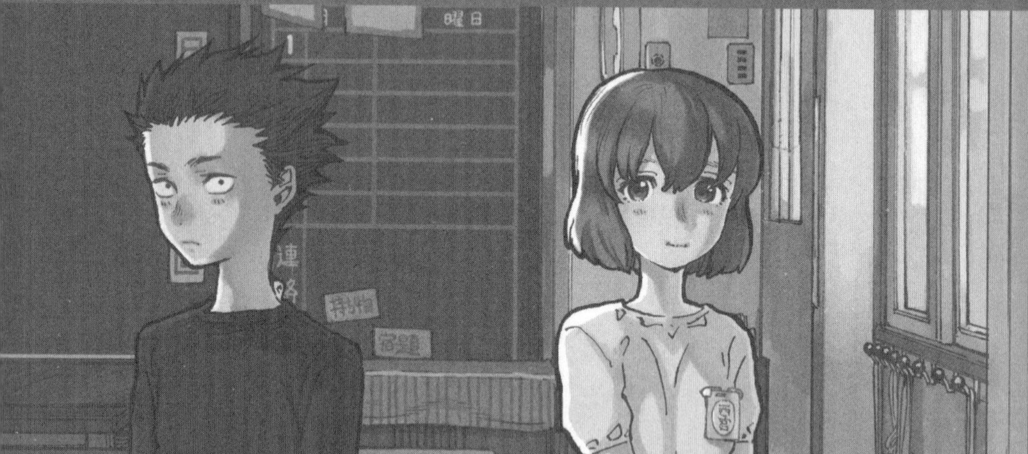

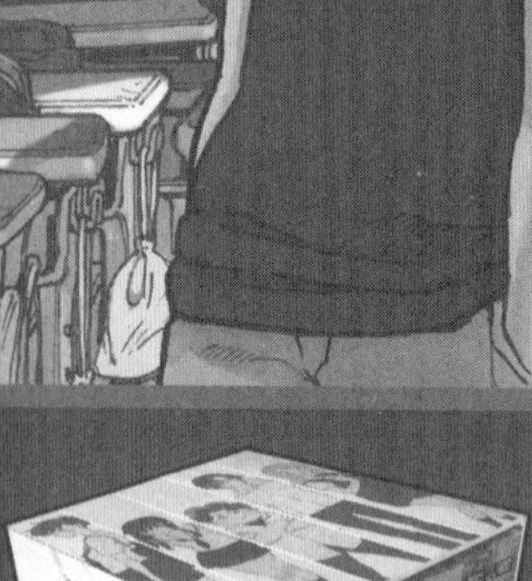

•Exclusive 2-sided poster
•Replica of Shoko's notebook
•Preview of Yoshitoki Oima's new series, To Your Eternity

Shoya is a bully. When Shoko, a girl who can't hear, enters his elementary school class, she becomes their favorite target, and Shoya and his friends goad each other into devising new tortures for her. But the children's cruelty goes too far. Shoko is forced to leave the school, and Shoya ends up shouldering all the blame. Six years later, the two meet again. Can Shoya make up for his past mistakes, or is it too late?

Young characters and steampunk setting, like *Howl's Moving Castle* and *Battle Angel Alita*

Beyond the Clouds © 2018 Nicke / Ki-oon

A boy with a talent for machines and a mysterious girl whose wings he's fixed will take you beyond the clouds! In the tradition of the high-flying, resonant adventure stories of Studio Ghibli comes a gorgeous tale about the longing of young hearts for adventure and friendship!

One of CLAMP's biggest hits returns
in this definitive, premium, hardcover
20th anniversary collector's edition!

CLAMP

1 Chobits

20TH ANNIVERSARY EDITION

Chobits © CLAMP·ShigatsuTsuitachi CO.,LTD./Kodansha Ltd.

Poor college student Hideki is down on his luck. All he wants is a
good job, a girlfriend, and his very own "persocom"—the latest
and greatest in humanoid computer technology. Hideki's luck
changes one night when he finds Chi—a persocom thrown out in
a pile of trash. But Hideki soon discovers that there's much more
to his cute new persocom than meets the eye.

KC
KODANSHA
COMICS

A SMART, NEW ROMANTIC COMEDY FOR FANS OF *SHORTCAKE CAKE* AND *TERRACE HOUSE!*

A romance manga starring high school girl Meeko, who learns to live on her own in a boarding house whose living room is home to the odd (but handsome) Matsunaga-san. She begins to adjust to her new life away from her parents, but Meeko soon learns that no matter how far away from home she is, she's still a young girl at heart — especially when she finds herself falling for Matsunaga-san.

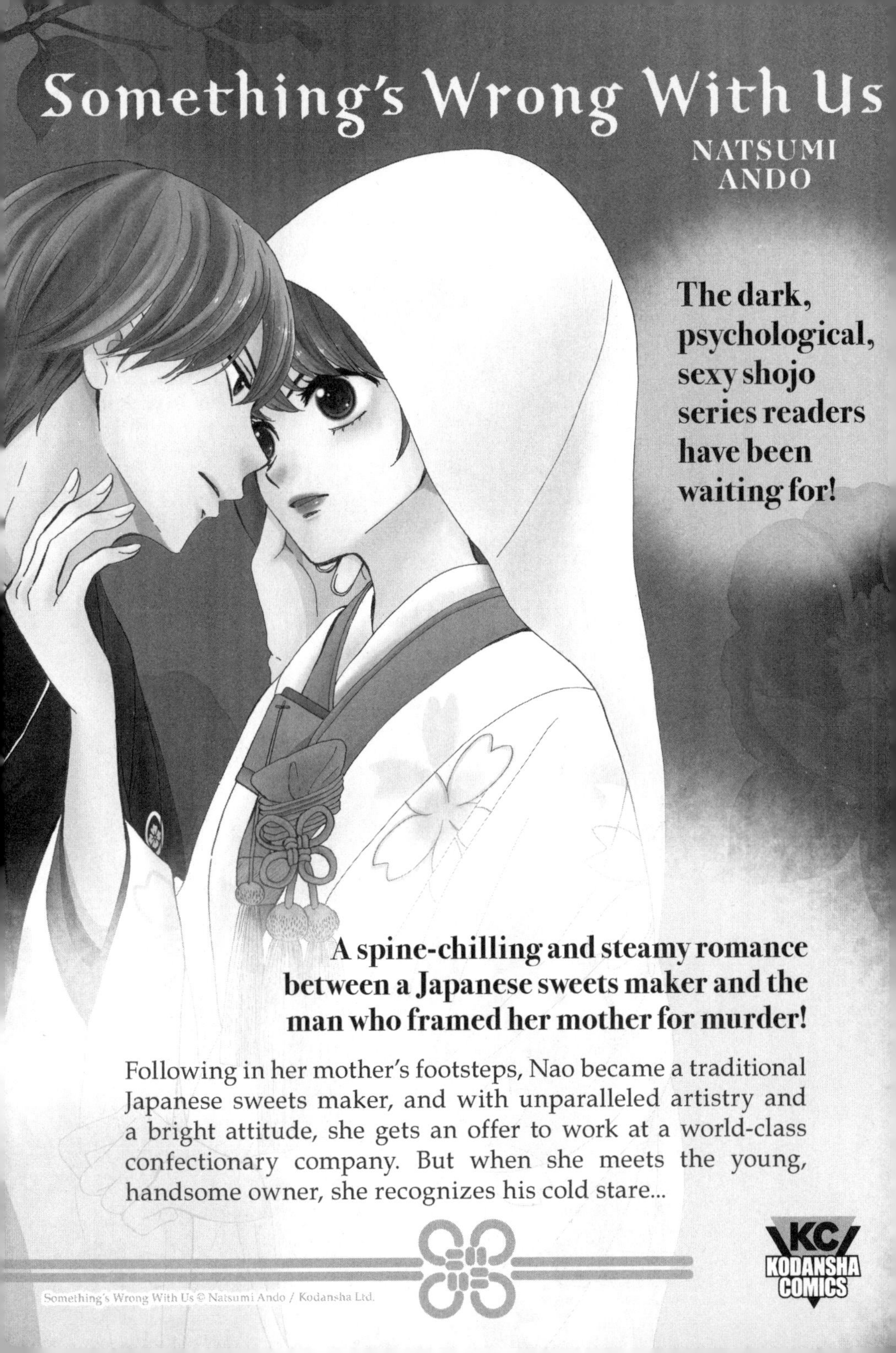
Something's Wrong With Us
NATSUMI ANDO
The dark, psychological, sexy shojo series readers have been waiting for!
A spine-chilling and steamy romance between a Japanese sweets maker and the man who framed her mother for murder!
Following in her mother's footsteps, Nao became a traditional Japanese sweets maker, and with unparalleled artistry and a bright attitude, she gets an offer to work at a world-class confectionary company. But when she meets the young, handsome owner, she recognizes his cold stare...
KC KODANSHA COMICS
Something's Wrong With Us © Natsumi Ando / Kodansha Ltd.

The adorable new odd-couple cat comedy manga from the creator of the beloved *Chi's Sweet Home*, in full color!

Praise for *Chi's Sweet Home*

"Nearly impossible to turn away... a true all-ages title that anyone, young or old, cat lover or not, will enjoy. The stories will bring a smile to your face and warm your heart."

~School Library Journal

Sue & Tai-chan

Konami Kanata

Sue is an aging housecat who's looking forward to living out her life in peace... but her plans change when the mischievous black tomcat Tai-chan enters the picture! Hey! Sue never signed up to be a catsitter! *Sue & Tai-chan* is the latest from the reigning meow-narch of cute kitty comics, Konami Kanata.

KC KODANSHA COMICS

THE SWEET SCENT OF LOVE IS IN THE AIR! FOR FANS OF OFFBEAT ROMANCES LIKE *WOTAKOI*

Sweat and Soap © Kintetsu Yamada / Kodansha Ltd.

In an office romance, there's a fine line between sexy and awkward... and that line is where Asako — a woman who sweats copiously — meets Koutarou — a perfume developer who can't get enough of Asako's, er, scent. Don't miss a romcom manga like no other!

A Kodansha Comics Trade Paperback Original
Perfect World 8 copyright © 2018 Rie Aruga
English translation copyright © 2021 Rie Aruga

All rights reserved.

Published in the United States by Kodansha Comics, an imprint of Kodansha USA Publishing, LLC, New York.

Publication rights for this English edition arranged through Kodansha Ltd., Tokyo.

First published in Japan in 2018 by Kodansha Ltd., Tokyo as *Perfect World*, volume 8.

ISBN 978-1-64651-108-2

Original cover design by Tomohiro Kusume and Maiko Mori (arcoinc)

Printed in the United States of America.

www.kodansha.us

1st Printing
Translation: Erin Procter
Lettering: Thea Willis
Additional lettering: Sara Linsley
Editing: Megan Ling, Jesika Brooks
Kodansha Comics edition cover design by Phil Balsman

Publisher: Kiichiro Sugawara

Director of publishing services: Ben Applegate
Associate director of operations: Stephen Pakula
Publishing services managing editors: Madison Salters, Alanna Ruse
Production managers: Emi Lotto, Angela Zurlo